Rainbow Flowers by Zandra

"Be thou the rainbow in the sto
that smiles the clouds away, an˻
prophetic ray." - Lord Byron

"Try to be a rainbow in someone's cloud." - Maya Angelou

Abstract

A series of vignettes depicting people whose lives yoga has touched and how it has been useful. In the cases of those for whom yoga was not an option, it is explained how yoga could have benefitted them. Primarily the self study of one person, these stories also explore people who impacted her life, as well as total strangers.

Trigger Warning

The content in this book contains some material written on sensitive topics which could potentially trigger memories for audiences with similar experiences. This sensitive material is not suitable for very young audiences, and readers are expected to read at their own risk.

Disclaimer

Should this book inspire anyone to study or practise yoga, further research is suggested. Opening the mind to the study of yoga allows for the brain to begin working differently, prompting lifestyle changes. One person's account of what yoga is is not enough to grasp a true understanding of the concept.

Table of Contents

Introduction

Yooso

The Basics of Yoga
1. What is Yoga
2. The Bhagavad Gita
3. Dharma Talk
4. Types of Yoga Mentioned in the Gita
5. The Yoga Sutras of Patanjali
6. Patanjali's Eight Limbs of Yoga
7. Why Yoga
8. Types of Yoga
9. Energy/Chi/Kundalini
10. Energy Centres (Chakras)

Theories of Learning and Play as they Relate to Child Development
Lexicon of Yogic Terms
Chakra Case Study Introduction

Jaime's Story (the Jaime Alexander Chronicles)
Days of the Old
Relational Aggression
Middle School Recess and How it Stunted Jaime's Growth
How Jaime's Friends Mirrored Findings in Odd Girl Out
Why Girls Travel in Packs
Benefits of Solitude
Types of Alternative Aggressions Girls Engage In
Ways to Help Young Girls Communicate Effectively
Selective Memory Blocking as it Relates to the Brow Chakra
The Brain on PTSD
Jaime's Journal Entry About What Happened in November
Jaime's Journal Entry About Coming Out
Bisexual Movies

Part of Why I'm Gay
#Saybisexual
The Bend it Like Beck Effect
Jaime's Gender Confusion
Jaime and Non-Pagan Religion
Jaime's Discernment
Ore Wa/Manga
The Story of Jaime Before Syd
Benji the Biphobic
Serviceman Todd
Jaime Teaching Todd to Like Poetry
Experience
Who Knows
Todd Tidbits
Jaime and Tinder Springs (2,800)
B-Boy Feori
Feori Backstory
Edit
Two Hypersexual
Vital Energy
Soul Food
Friendship Set on Fire
Sun Showers
Weekend at Feori's
Gods and Monsters
Teaching Feori
One of the Guys
Jaime's Spark
Same Name James
Learning from Rosie
Jaime and Life After Sports
Jaime's Journal Entry on Body Awareness
Being Responsible
Jaime and Syd's First Rock Ballad
Jaime and Julio
Chicago Bikram
Enter Logan
April and Marcie
Ticks

Tongue Piercing
Opposites Attract
Compass Rose
The Ballad of Syd and Jaime
I Bleed Pink, Purple, and Blue Parts 1-4
A Few Words about Jaime and Syd's Demise
Little Conversations
Telling Rick Batch
Smile, Hug, Repeat – Jaime's Midnight Patronus
Choosing Teams
Little Things About Jaime
Necessary Vacation
Pride in the Park
Glitterboii's Advice for Pride
Jaime's First Pride Parade
Jaime's Sciatica
Jaime's New Life
Punk Boi
Mind the Gap
Mature, Well Spoken, and Sensible
Two
The Queerness of Jaime's Flatmates
Cigarettes and Fidgets
Perianth Things*
One Petal Flower
New Territory
Mandie and Lizzi
Skylar and Emerson
Jaime's Jealousy
Love, Sex, and Fancy Things
The Spaces Between Us
Safe Space

Sean's Story
Half Red, Half Blue
Rad Warriors Union
Hardest Story for Me to Write
Prove Them Wrong
Bishi Bestie

Slay/Stay
What It's Like Parts 1-2
Sound Therapy
TLC
Gender Dominance in Flow Communities
Friends are Music
Music and Child Development
Sensory Experiences
Sean and Scientific Inquiry
Bits and Pieces
Break Stuff
Crystal Children
Natural Remedies

Energetic Emissions
Absorption of Egocentrism
Sean and Guided Sleep Meditation
Sleepovers
When
Gravity Found You Here
Bowling
Tight
The Seven Layer Haunting

Jaime and Le Feu
Not Afraid to Touch
Male Partners
Masculinity in Making the Moves
Liam
Jaime and Le Feu Against Toxic Monogamy Culture
Burn This Letter
Online Dating
Letters to Benji
Boys Against Gender Norms
Masculine Décor
Unspoken Argument
Ruling the Throat Chakra
Skinny Love
Just a Title

Le Feu's Label
Wristcutter Game
How Jaime's Boys Differed
Jaime and Le Feu's Past
Honto Ni?!

Root Chakra
Ana
Black and Blue Tapestries
Before I was Theirs
Boy Sawyer
Those Three Boys
To Her Apartment
Visiting Sister
Root Chakra Connections: Ahimsa, Aprigraha, Asana, Astya, Bandhas, Bathing, Body Breath, Body Isolation and Awareness, Body Poetry, Erikson's Trust vs Mistrust, Mudras, Physiological Needs and Safety, the Physical Realm, Physical Touch, Pratyahara, Receiving Gifts, Unveiling

Sacral Chakra
VHS Tape
Girls Make Boys Cry
Friends?
Boys Too
Posh Town Boys
Dates with Posh Boy
Conversations with Rick Batch
She Said Please
November
The Face in the Mirror
Artwork by Aryn Taylor
Sacral Chakra Connections: Agender Yoga, Bramhacharya, Bi Positivity, Ritual Dress, Virginity Myth

Solar Plexus Chakra
Sakura Pazina
Jeiken

Moonage Daydream
Brian Molko Wouldn't Break My Heart
Dancing With Molly
Suicide Note
Revenge
Wrong Room
One With the Mat
How to Kill Yourself
How to Live
The Story of Dawn the Destroyer
Youth Groups
Convicts and Crazies
Ace of Magical Girl Swords
Positive
Solar Plexus Connections: Ambition, Energy, Erikson's Autonomy vs Shame and Doubt, Industry vs Inferiority, Initiative vs Guilty, Maslow's Esteem, Self Defense, Swadyaya, Tapas

Heart Chakra
Japanese Love Letters
Bright Yellow
Losing Manny
Aprigraha and Polyamory
Erika and Manny Listening Club
Your Little Pastry
Poetry for Bookish Bounty
Same Name as my Surfboard
Dancefloor Sweetheart
Dream Girl
Silk Street
New Clothes for Simone
The Girl I Never Write About
Heart Chakra Connections: Erikson's Intimacy vs Isolation, Love and Relationships, Maslow's Love and Belonging, Perfect Love and Perfect Trust, Pranayama, Soul Mate Friendship, Yoga for Recovery

Throat Chakra
What Does God Look Like?
Anya
What They Never Tell You
Ash Supernova
Lavender Lights
Erika's Song
We Thought We'd Never See The Sun
There is Only Prey
Rated R
Sweet Songs Were Wrote for You
25 to Life
Maybe We Had More Than We Thought
Nefertiti
I Could Make a List of Why Mechanics Is Not For Me
Throat Chakra Connections: Communication and Social Interaction Theories, Feminism and Yoga, How to Tame a Wild Tongue, Intentional Language, Mantras/Aum, Satya, Words of Affirmation

Brow Chakra
Sunshine Soul
How To
Boys Don't Cry
Children of the Internet
What's the Difference?
Always a Center Kid
Election
Try Not to Mention It
Becoming Glitterboii
Teaching Lil Lars and Twister
Eyes on Our Kids
Jaime's First Lesbian
Akiko's First Girlfriend
Brow Chakra Connections: Anarcha-Feminist Yoga Empowerment, Carpe Diem, Covens and Wise Ones, Created Queer Culture, Decolonising Yoga, Detachment, Dharana, Dhyana, Dreams, Identity vs Role Confusion, Gaydar, Healing Mandalas and Colour Healing, Why

Humans Have an Innate Desire to Get High, Inclusive Community, the Last LGBT History Lesson, the Medical Marijuana Dilemma, Santosha, Shaucha, Swadyaya, Why Jaime Taught

Crown Chakra
Sequined Jacket
Sleepover
How Do You Become a Wise One?
Sky Bound
Some People Make Love to the Sky
The Ones I Never Fell For
Artists and Colour Schemes
Living Seeing
Base of the Pyramid
Crown Chakra Connections: Acts of Service, Alignment, Bloom's Taxonomy of Higher Order Thinking, Celtic Magick, Crystal Healing, Erikson's Generativity vs Stagnation, Intergrity vs Despair, Identity?, Ishvapranidhana, Jean Piaget and the Atman, Maslow's Self Actualisation, Quality Time, Stopping Time, Stopping for a Breath, Yoga for Recovery

List of Deities Who Will Accept You For Whoever You Are

Epilogue

References and Acknowledgement

Introduction

Jaime stood at the door of her new job, the new business that she'd started. Jaime looked after children, and she also taught yoga. In a way, she'd meshed the two. As she always said, "why not both?"

There were two dedication plaques outside the studio. One in honour of Erika and Manny. The other in honour of the "children of September" as well as the victims of the Pulse shooting.

Her brand was called Rainbow Flowers. Rainbow Flowers Childcare and Spiritual Wellness Centre. Jaime breathed a sigh of relief as she opened the door. She was not scheduled to open for two weeks yet. Upstairs was the wellness centre with studio rooms for yoga classes, as well as occasional self defense classes taught by her older brother Dex. There was the cafe, and the shop stocked with books, crystals, essential oils, incense, candles, windchimes, body scrubs, bath bombs and gels, lotions, dreamcatchers, blankets, statues, herbs, yoga props, workout clothes, and the like.

"Well, everybody, this is it. What do you think?" Jaime asked an empty room. "I couldn't be here without all of you." She smiled tearfully, thinking of all the stories which led her to this business venture. She had finally made it here.

Years before, Jaime had fallen for two of her best friends. That's where it had all begun.

But first, why yoga? Jaime had gotten mono for her sixteenth birthday, and her brother showed her yoga as gentle physical activity she could do while her spleen was enlarged. She ended up getting her 200-hour yoga teaching certification on her twentieth birthday.

To truly understand, one must understand yoga.

To be willing to understand yoga, one must recognise the body as the vessel for the soul. The body must be treated with respect, when its strength and ability is realised. The body is filled with sacred consciousness and intelligence.

You may not understand until or unless you've meditated in the morning because you didn't want to get out of bed, or you've turned your thinking around from "that was a disappointing sunset" to "every sunset is amazing because life is a gift," but maybe you will want to understand. Most people don't appreciate how beautiful it is that we all want change but none of us want the same change. Just because there is so much hate in the world, do not doubt the love which surrounds us.
Find it. Be grateful for it. Cultivate an abundance of it.

Jaime fell into yoga like she fell into being gay. Slowly, hesitantly, and then it became a huge and important part of her life. Things she'd never thought were possible [happened]. Her life became a quilt – pieced together, a bit taken from here, a bit taken from there. She started to know herself. She became more authentic. She had read that yoga was a form of bonding with the self and with the world.

She realised anyone has the power to be the master of the vessel housing their soul during this life experience, controlling the body, emotions, nourishment, thoughts, and brain. She realised that there is beautiful science of how the body can move. What a beautifully amazing magical gift it is the way the body works. To be able to understand yoga, one had to be willing to heal. Jaime was willing to heal. Jaime was interested in healing. She was struck by two quotes, feeling like they summed up what she was learning through yoga.

"Every day, in every way, I am getting better and better." - Emile Coue
"Continuous effort – not strength or intelligence – is the key to unlocking our full potential" – Liane Cordes

Jaime's journal entries and conversations with

therapists contained words like,

"You start to wonder if it even mattered when you remember your first kiss, or the person whose first kiss you were, or your ex-girlfriend or best friend, because they never seem to think of you."

"I'm sure my professors knew I smoked pot. When I think back on it, it's bold, but you talk to a kid like me when they're crying and trying to drop out of school and you sort of understand why they smoke pot."

"I'm the kind of person who knows my healthy bloat weight, the last time I got tested for STDs, the directions around Disney World in French, but not how to keep a bedroom clean."

"Despite the fact that my mother took away my electronics after a certain time of night, I still struggled with sleeping. I recall being tired and cranky every day, becoming anti school because of it even though I've always been pro-learning. I recall incessant worry about my dad's health, then worry he'd truly have another heart attack if I came out to him like mom said he would."

"I remember when he had his stroke and I never got picked up from Courtney's trailer and then when I got home spending every day on my front stoop with Liam wanting to blow up."

"Sometimes some of my new friends catch me worrying about my dad and they don't know what my deal is when I stop them from talking to listen for if his machine is working, if he's breathing."

Jaime had developed a steady interest in yoga for a combination of reasons after Dex had introduced her to it while she had mono. She had an interest in breathwork and health benefits of it due to cardiovascular problems in her genes, and due to her dad's history of health events she sometimes took a nivrtti approach to yoga and used it to focus her mind away from worrying about those things. She was interested in sticking her inversions (handstands and forearm stands) to gain a stronger core and stronger arm muscles for surfing. This was how she transitioned into becoming a practitioner of yoga. As she grew older and yoga became more integrated in her life, she used it to help treat her PTSD. Jaime felt compelled to share her wisdom with friends, and taught Ana, among other people, about yoga.

Jaime decided to become friends with her body, and her body whispered to her that it had been waiting its whole life for that. Through this process she aimed to ease tension headaches, grinding her teeth, clenching her jaw, sacrum pain, insomnia, anxiety stomachaches and chest pains, backaches, fatigue, and panic attacks (which sometimes included fainting). These were physical manifestations of Jaime's anxiety as well as reactions to disease – chronic fatigue syndrome, a byproduct of mono, and reaction to trauma – sacral problems. Befriending her body meant kicking the physical manifestation of a suicidal intention, one symptom of which was smoking cigarettes for Jaime.

Jaime noticed an inner desire to hurt herself. It was part of her reason for her fear of heights. In high places, she was almost overcome by an inexplicable desire to jump. She wondered if this secret desire to hurt herself was what made her keep toxic people in her life. She sometimes engaged in risky behaviour, but never as risky as Dex, who wondered what life was without risk and saw himself as invincible. She didn't know how far into a manic episode an ego check would make a difference for her brother.

Jaime's older brother Dex had manic depression, or bipolar disorder. Dex frightened Jaime when she was younger both while he was on and off his meds. She became both anti-medication and straight edge for some time because of her brother. He described his actions as a result of his early discernment of the truth of the world being an unkind place. Dex thought it was a perfectly normal response at age thirteen to get involved with sex, drinking, and drugs, and make their parents fully aware of it. Professionals have described this behaviour as not normal for a thirteen year old, but it was all Jaime knew. Jaime wondered if she shared her brother's mood disorder, but didn't want to know. She didn't know her family's entire mental history, which worried her (in the Dance of Anger, it is mentioned that when we understand our family's patterns of anger, we can understand those which we have inherited). Whenever anyone said anything to Dex about his mood disorder, he would say, "I think everyone is bipolar, like the planet, because of our inner magnetics." Jaime knew that she could absorb Dex's energy and feel like she was getting secondhand manic. Sometimes, she felt crazy, but it wasn't her crazy, she would be feeling Dex's feelings.

A "mood disorder" was characterised by altering states of high highs and low lows. Bipolar 1 disorder was characterised by alternating manic and depressive episodes, while Bipolar 2 disorder was characterised by alternating hypomanic and depressive episodes. Hypomania refers to a mild state of mania. The manic state is when one feels up, up, up, whereas hypomania is just the feeling of up. Mixed states refer to feeling up and down at the same time, and rapid cycling is when one experiences four or more episodes within twelve months. Euthymia is a balanced state, where dysthymia is a chronically low state. Mild depression refers to feeling low, and depression is when one feels the lowest. Everyone's natural baseline varies depending on their body chemistry. Everyone experiences daily highs and lows like tides, and well as monthly highs and lows like the moon phases, which relates to the inner chemical production levels changing throughout the month (like serotonin, dopamine, hormones, endorphins, etc.) and were also based off of inner body levels such as blood pressure and blood sugar.

Jaime recognised that one some level, certain chemicals helped balance the brains of some people. She also worried that Big Pharma doctors had tendencies to put kids on medication for anything (i.e. Benji in fifth grade at age nine) without targeting or pursuing root causes behind problems.

When Jaime was with Julio she met two girls - Mini (Minerva) and Andie, who were both bisexual and interested in yoga. Andie was Julio's best friend and later dated SLB Benji, introducing Julio and Jaime to Benji. Mini was the girlfriend of Julio's other best friend, Keys. When Jaime asked Mini what she wanted to do, she said she wanted to go to college in Colorado to become a yoga teacher. Jaime had attended a few yoga classes with Andie at the gym she belonged to. Jaime had already been practising, just not at a studio, and was interested in what moved Mini to wanting to teach yoga. Ultimately, Jaime thought she would like Andie better than Mini, and was closer to her at first, but ended up liking Mini better than Andie and chose not to stay friends with Andie even during her relationship with Julio once Andie and Benji broke up.

As a girl who respected other girls, Jaime did not think that Andie deserved any kind of unfair treatment, trauma, or harassment, and she wished her well, despite not personally enjoying her company. It was through disliking Andie and her friend Stella that Jaime truly began to learn that it was possible to respect those she disliked. Here Jaime expressed true feminism, not believing that Stella and Andie were undeserving of their rights, though she believed they were undeserving of her personal generosity, time, and attention. She would never have wished anything bad upon Andie or Stella. Stella was also bisexual and much later developed an interest in yoga, but it did not bring them closer after their friendship had ended. Jaime recognised that not everybody was meant to help her grow.

Mini, however, Jaime regarded as an important business contact. At first glance, Jaime had disregarded Mini as someone who had been irresponsible because she'd witnessed her doing certain drugs, but as she got to know her she developed a deeper respect for her. It was a unique situation for Jaime to have had such profound respect for all three bisexual women she met through Julio. It was her first attempt at making female friends since Darcy, Rosie, Dawn, and Karoline, except for the Honduran girl Xyla who had helped her through her breakup with Syd. Jaime was fiercely protective of other girls by nature, feeling that none of them deserved abuse, rape, cheating, lying, sexism, lower wages, harassment, trauma, double standards, oversexualisation, rights taken away, or bodies policed by males. She had inherently always been a feminist. Stella, Mini, and Andie were the kind of girls who also felt that way. Jaime felt naturally inclined to feel deeper respect for women who understood their worth and the worth of other women, and was more inclined to not think terribly of Stella and Andie when deciding that their friendship was not going to work out because they were understanding of their own worth as well as the worth of other women. Jaime was less inclined to talk trash about them as they parted ways as well.

Yooso (the first studio at which Jaime worked)

Jaime was in touch with the elements and intimate with the sun, moon, stars, and planets. The moon helped her remember it was okay to change. Jaime had been called many names, including psycho, slut, stalker, spaz, and stoner. She had also been called a flower child, a clone of her brother, a squirrel face, and a dork. She knew she was a moon child, someone who was deeply in tune with the phases of the moon. She was born under a full moon. Her moon sign was the same sign as her brother's sun sign. Being into the moon, she was into the water. She was even a water sign. Jaime was watery in nature, both soft and strong. She tended to go with the flow, she was relatively even tempered and non confrontational, or even conflict avoidant. It took a lot for her to resist the current, but like water she could erode that which had stood forever. Her chaos was that of the water, the chaos of storms and the chaos of ocean's waves. She was the wave that smoothened the rock as well as the wave that knocked houses off of stilts. Being ruled by water, she was also ruled by the emotional element. Her emotions ran deep like the ocean, and her experience with them could be choppy like the waves. She appreciated storms, because she recognised that she had one inside her.

Jaime had discovered Yooso all on her own, and that was important to her. In fact, she was quite proud of that fact. It made itself a part of her all on its own, and that was important to her, too. Organic growth.

It started with the children's museum. The children's museum helped reshape Jaime's brain. The museum won her over at the interview by talking about how they were all about continuous improvement. She had had a job lined up to sell her soul to the dream of being a princess in the corporate world of fast food and was meant to embark on a potentially life changing adventure starting that job just a month after the interview with the museum. For many reasons, she chose to work for the non profit, eco conscious, educational facility. When she started there, the museum had a yoga teacher who taught the children based on different themes. This fascinated Jaime, a young budding practitioner of yoga at the time. Such forward thinking at the museum required Jaime's thinking to adapt, and inspired her to want to include yoga in her future classroom.

Jaime did research on how to obtain a certification to teach yoga and once she localised her research it led her to Yooso. She had never stepped foot in the studio before the informational meeting about their teacher training. Immediately she fell in love, thanks to kindred spirit Misty, who had been taught by Christine Christie, both of whom would later be Jaime's teachers and colleagues. From age nineteen until after her twenty first birthday, she was a part of the Yooso Kula. She had never felt more welcomed in a studio or more connected in a taught class. When she completed her training, Jaime was blessed to be given a job and classes to teach there. Before the studio closed, Jaime packed it up really small and stuck it in her suitcase heart, in hopes of cultivating the feeling she got from Yooso in a new place that she'd one day create.

The elements were generally recognised as earth, water, air, fire, and sometimes there were options for metal or ether (akasha). Water was known to be grounding. Air was known to be uplifting. Fire was energetic, and earth was stable. In the world of witchcraft and tarot, the elements were represented by the suits of the cards.

Water correlates with the house of Cups, representing the Emotional realm.
Fire correlates with the house of Wands, representing the Spiritual realm.
Earth correlates with the house of Pentacles, representing the Physical realm.
Air correlates with the house of Swords, representing the Mental realm.

    Jaime dabbled in tarot cards and worked to understand the meanings in her readings. When she found multiple cards of certain suits coming into her readings, she understood that it gave her clues about what her reading referred to. She also understood that when all the elements were mastered, she would also be the master of herself by being in balance with the world. That made it amusing to her that the first yoga studio she was employed by had a name that translated to mean elements.

    Jaime felt that to be a witch is to be a healer, teacher, seeker, giver, and protector of all things. If this is your path, may you walk it with honour, light, and integrity. You are a magic maker. You weave words and intentions into ways of manifesting your visions. You adorn yourself with crystals and metals, skin decorations, and with those things that make you feel like your sacred self. You throw down cards and whisper into burning herbs your wishes, letting the smoke swirl around you and carry them into the night. Her soul was a kaleidoscope, busting with every shade and hue, but with a slightly shifted gaze she's something entirely new.

    Jaime observed and collected ways to experience the self. They included the cycle of emotions, one's habits, rituals (nudity, food, etc.), languages (of learning, of love, spoken), stages of development, collectivity of selves (the learned and taught selves), viewing the self as a divine light and representation of the universe , viewing the self as a tool (for fixing the world), viewing the self as a representation of ancestors and genes, and sensory experiences; which for adults included things like laundry (sorting, folding, and hanging clothes), doing dishes or putting them away (chores), music, movement – yoga or stretching (physical practise), sports, dance, sex and drugs (unconventional and less common ways to achieve higher states of consciousness), breath work , meditation and lucid dreaming, herbals, smells (candles, incense, bath products, food), art, pets, cooking and eating (which relates to our nutritional health), theatre and drama, being in touch with the elements (fires, bubbles, baths, pools of water, sandcastles, fans), and learning (through books, films, and countless other resources.) People are natural born learners, but some people become anti-school for reasons outlined in the Bully Society, which affect the Solar Plexus. Jaime felt it was important for those anti-school people to understand the importance of learning, even if not in a school situation. Her aim was to bring to life a more holistic way of learning which encompassed many ways of experiencing the self.

The Basics of Yoga

What is Yoga?

Yoga was first introduced in print in the Bhavagad Gita.

The Bhagavad Gita

The Bhagavad Gita is a sacred ancient Indian text which relates to Hindu religion. The Bhagavad Gita is an epic poem about Lord Krishna, which was the first written mention of yoga. The Gita discussed yoga as the skill of union with the ultimate reality, which was Krishna. The Gita was intended for the masses, not individual consumption. The story is based around a conversation Arjuna is having with Lord Krishna about whether he should finish the war, though everyone in the war was his family. The poem includes a lot of circular points about accepting Krishna as the universal truth. Sri Krishna was the master of all yogis, and his ultimate power manifested by yoga was to appear in a multifaceted form, his universal form in which all could be seen.

The Gita explains how Krishna is where everything begins. Uniting with his Prakriti, he birthed the cosmos. "Thus I gave birth to first begetters of all Earth's children. Who truly knows me, in manifold Being everywhere present and all prevailing, dwells in my yoga that shall not be shaken of this be certain. I am where all things began, the issuing forth of the creatures, known to the wise in their love when they worship with hearts overflowing. Mind and sense are absorbed, I alone am the theme of their discourse, thus delighting each other, they live in bliss and contentment."

Krishna explains that "when the heart is made pure by yoga, when the body is obedient, when the senses are mastered, when man knows that his Atman is the Atman in all creatures, let him act, untainted by action. Understanding that the physical body may be doing things but you, the soul, the Atman, does nothing but be – the body is the instrument, knowledge of the essence of self, other than the instrument makes the heart grow pure. In the battle for authenticity, life and death of the soul, the struggle against greed, hatred, ignorance, ingrained selfishness which covers our natural luminosity, the slightest clarity or opening of the heart is a major triumph."

In the Gita, we learn that no mortal could become immortal like him, but they could get off the wheel of life and join the immortals in Enlightenment and spiritual pleasures. We also learn that Krishna will accept worship to any deity if the worshipper accepts Krishna, and then gives such deity the power to grant what the mortal is deserving of. It is taught that Krishna is within all, all are created in Krishna's image, therefore all are perfect as long as they do no harm. One must not hate as well. By this logic, Jaime discerned that queer folk are perfect, should not be hated, ad need not hate themselves when they have Krishna's love. If you accept Krishna, Krishna will come visit you in mediation in any manifestation you're comfortable with – Indra and Shiva are listed in the Gita, who are other queer positive deities. Krishna says, "a leaf, a flower: I will accept it. That gift is love, his heart's dedication. Whatever your action, food or worship, whatever the gift that you give to another, whatever you vow to the work of the spirit."

Krishna said to Arjuna, "I give you divine sight. Behold – this my yoga power." Yoga gave Krishna the power to become his multifaceted form. "Arjuna was beholding the whole universe within Krishna in his multifaceted divine form of multitudinous diversity." This is Krishna's primeval form, the form of fire, the worldwide and supreme form, which is manifested by yoga power. Sri Krishna is master of all yogis, and shows this form to Arjuna out of love. (all magic must come from love.)

When describing Krishna's universal form, Arjuna says "Universal form, I see you without limit, infinite of arms, eyes, mouths, and bellies – see, and find no end, midst, or beginning... when I see you, Vishnu, omnipresent, shouldering the sky, in hues of rainbow." He also says, "many are the forms of the living, many the wombs that bear them."

Prakriti is the principle of consciousness in all beings, and source of life in all, sustaining the universe. It contains earth, fire, water, air, ether (akasha), mind, intellect, and ego. It is the womb of all wombs and Krishna is the seed giving father. "Know this my Prakriti united with me, the womb of all beings – I am the birth of this cosmos, its dissolution also."

From Prakriti comes the creative energy of Brahman, which is immutable and independent of any cause but itself. Brahman causes all existence to come into being, and lodged within an individual being it is called Atman. Realising Atman is entirely satisfying, they know infinite happiness can be realised by purified heart but is beyond grasp of senses and stand firm in this realisation, never again wandering from the inmost truth of their being. Faith is so certain they shall never be shaken by heaviest sorrow.

We learn that the purpose of life is fulfilled when Krishna is recognized as Supreme Reality for then all is known which can be known and Krishna is adored wholeheartedly. By taking delight in Krishna we may turn from the joyless world. In the strength of this yoga, faithfully followed, the mind is firm and the heart so full, it hardly holds its love.

Krishna teaches us that we all act according to tendencies of our own nature. It is better to do your own duty, however imperfectly, than to assume the duties of another, however successfully – your own nature will drive you to the act, for you yourself have created karma which binds you. "A man's own natural duty, even if it seems imperfectly done, is better than work not naturally his own, even if well performed – when a man acts according to law of his nature, he cannot be sinning. Ergo, no one should give up their natural work. "Acts of sacrifice, almsgiving, and austerity should not be given up (performance is necessary) sill they must be performed without attachment of regard for their fruits.

"The man of discrimination I see as my very Self. For he alone loves me because I am myself, the last and only goal of his devoted heart."

In the Gita, discrimination is used to describe the ability to discern between right and wrong.

"Through yoga we act without desire, with doubts torn to shreds."

Krishna describes both divine and demonic tendencies. Demonic tendencies – hypocrisy, arrogance, conceit, cruelty, anger, ignorance, lack of truth/purity/right conduct, lustful, vain, drunk with pride, gratification of senses, anxiety, ceaselessly busy, addicts of sensual pleasure, restless, delusional, haughty, show off, fake religious, godless, intoxicated by wealth, egotism, excessive body mortification, foolishness. He said that, "pious men eat what gods leave over (sinless) – cooking good food for greed of stomachs sin as they eat it, sacrifice speaks through ritual, without it living is evil, joy is in lusting, life is for nothing. "Hungry still for the food of the senses, drawn by desire to endless returning."

Krishna teaches us about meditation by saying, "shutting off sense from what is outward, facing the gaze at the root of the eyebrows (the 3rd Eye chakra)"

Krishna also teaches us about the Gunas. The Gunas come from Prakriti, and are the doers of all action. One transcends the gunas when the light of sattwa, activity of rajas, or delusion of tamas while these prevail is not hated; and yet does not long for them after they have ceased, by resting in the inner calm of the Atman, regarding happiness and suffering as one. Faith is characterised by gunas according to dominant tendencies. Food being agreeable to different people is a matter of the gunas.

Rajas is the action of the passionate, those thirsty for pleasure and possession. Rajas binds you to hunger for action, enslaves doers, who are seized by it when it prevails. Rajas is green, eager enterprise, restlessness, sacrifice for show in hope of reward. When one dies in it they are reborn to those whose bondage is action, pain, and this world, who worship power and wealth. Rajasic foods are bitter, sour, salty, hot, pungent, acid, and burning, cause ill health and distemper.

Tamas is the action of those who disregard instructions, the ignorant, and bewildered. Tamas binds with bonds of delusion, sluggishness, stupor, enslaves the deluded, darkens judgement. When it prevails one yields to it, and when one dies in it they become reborn to the womb of a dullard, darkness. Tamas is the action of the underworld, and those who worship the dead. Tamasic foods are stale, tasteless, rotten, impure, and they eat the leavings of others.

Sattwa is the action of the shining, it can show the Atman, and pure light. It binds you to search for happiness, longing for knowledge, and enslaves the happy. When it prevails it is felt, and there is understanding. When one dies in it they are reborn to a sinless home, experiencing the purest joy, higher realms, sacrifice, inner duty, threefold austerity, and the worship of a god, Sattwic foods add to pleasure and increase vital force, energy, strength, health, juicy, soothing, fresh, agreeable.

From Krishna we also learn about dharma.

Dharma Talk

Dharma means what is right. Dharma means behaviours in accord with rta (the order which makes life and the universe possible). In Hinduism, dharma is the principle of cosmic order – virtue, righteousness, and duty. In Buddhism, dharma was the teaching and religion of Buddha, as well as one of the fundamental elements of which the world is composed. It contained rituals and rites of passage, yoga, personal behaviours, virtues, law and justice, sannyasa and stages of life, and duties. In Jainism, dharma was the teachings of Tirthankara (Jina) and body of doctrine pertaining to the purification and moral transformation of human beings. For Sikhs dharma was the path of righteousness and proper religious practise. Dharma is mentioned in the Vedic religion, but for them dharma was an unreal concept.

    The accepted definition of dharma is that which all existing beings must accept and respect to sustain harmony and order in the world. Neither art nor result, natural laws that guide the ace and create the result to prevent chaos in the world. Innate characteristic which makes the being what it is – pursuit of one's nature and true calling (playing one's role). In Patanjali Yoga, elements of Hindu dharma are attributes, qualities, and aspects of yoga, including the yamas (restraints) and niyamas (observances), two of the eight limbs of Patanjali's yoga, and applied in action, speech, and mind.

    Jaime's chosen acceptable methods of worship were allowing the mind and senses to wander, seeing Brahman within all sense-objects, pranayama, and practise of Raja Yoga (Patanjali's Eight Limbs). Other methods accepted by Krishna included worshipping the devas, meditating on the identity of Atman with Brahman, withdrawing senses from contact with sense-objects (self discipline), renouncing all actions of sense and functions of vital force (self control), renouncing sense objects and material possessions, setting austerities and disciplines for the self, self control through mortification and fasting, and monk/priesthood (strict vows and worship)."All of these and others prescribed in scriptures involve the doing of some kind of action, the reward for which is Enlightenment."

Krishna outlines for us the various types of yoga which get us to Enlightenment. Further research must be done to understand these types of yoga more deeply, because this is only an inkling of background knowledge.

Types of Yoga Mentioned in the Gita

Aksara-brahma yoga – The "religion by devotion," in which Krishna describes differences between the material and spiritual worlds, the light and dark paths the soul takes after death, and the importance of one's last thought before death.

Bhakti yoga – The "religion of faith," or the process of devotional service.

Daivasura Sampad Vibhagaa yoga – The yoga of separating the divine from the undivine, involving giving up lust, anger, and greed, and discerning between right and wrong action.

Dhyan yoga – The "religion by self restraint," through which there is an introduction of Ashtanga and the mastery of the mind.

Gunatraya Vibhaga yoga – Yoga which involves the separation from three qualities – goodness, passion, nescience (ignorance).

Gyaana-Karma-Sanyasa yoga – The "religion of knowledge," in which one learns that Krishna always teaches yoga for the protection of the pious and destruction of impious, and the importance of accepting a guru.

Gyaana-Vigyana yoga – The yoga of "absolute reality and illusory energy."

Karma yoga – The yoga of finding virtue in work, or virtue of actions. "Inaction in action and action in inaction" (Yoga Sutras 4.18) This involves doing the actions necessary to life and avoiding those based on desire or self-gratification. Karma yoga contains the outer action (seva) and inner action (puja), which involves various forms of rituals.

Karma-Sanyasa yoga – The "religion by renouncing the fruits of works."

Ksetra Krestana Vibhaga yoga – Yoga revolving around the separation of matter and spirit, understanding and recognising the difference between the body and soul.

Laya yoga – The yoga of inner sound and light.

Moksha Sanyasa yoga – The yoga of deliverance and renunciation, involving abandoning all forms of dharma and surrendering.

Purusottama yoga – The yoga of attaining supreme divinity.

Raja yoga – Refers to the goal of yoga, but also refers to the eight limbs of Patanjali's yoga.

Raja Vidya Raja Guyha yoga – The yoga of knowledge and mystery, in which one discovers how Krishna's energy pervades, creates, preserves, and destroys the entire universe.

Sankhya yoga – A book of doctrines, one of 6 orthodox schools of Hindu philosophy, which discusses the two bodies, the one which dies and is made of matter, and the one which is subtle and lives on in spirit through all lives.

Sraddhatraya Vibhaga yoga – The threefold kind of faith which includes thoughts, deeds, eating habits, and are influenced by the gunas.

Vibhuti Vistara yoga – The yoga of recognising Krishna as the cause of all existence.

Visrarupadarsena yoga – Krishna's universal form of facing

every way and emitting radiance of a thousand suns, containing all other beings and material in existence

"If a woman sits with folded hands in her lap for a few minutes every day, and feels she is a container so vast that she contains the whole universe, she will never feel weak or have any problems. There is nothing beyond woman except god." - Yogi Bhajan

The Yoga Sutras of Patanjali

"When an individual has achieved complete understanding of their true self, they will no longer be disturbed by the distracting influences within and around them."

"Yoga is the journey of the self, through the self, to the self."

"Evenness of mind is called yoga" (2.47-8)

It is said that Sage Patanjali brought yoga to humans and we used it as a way to help ourselves get off the wheel of life.

Patanjali said that mastery combines a balance of science and art. Knowledge of science is like the colours on an artist's palette – the greater the knowledge, the more colours available. The body is the canvas and the asana are the art we create.

Yoga means to yoke, which is like the holding of a powerful force. Some people's goal of yoga is to yoke the self to the its purest form. Some people's goal of yoga is to unify the self and the universe. In the Bhagavad Gita, it says "yogakshema" which translates to "yoga cooks." With yoga, people can cook their lives into something meaningful to them. Yoga as participation helps get more out of life and allows greater opportunity to savour the short time we are given on this planet. Yoga is seen as a vision that excludes nothing from its practise. It invites us into complexity, allowing us to realise that there is no one true self to get back to, helping us see our collectivity of selves, and allowing us to experience the self in as many ways as possible.

The First Four Yoga Sutras of Patanjali

Samadhi Pada, which is about Enlightenment.
Sadhana Pada, which is about practise.
Vibhuti Pada, which is about results.
Kaivalya Pada, which is about liberation.

The Yoga Sutras say among many other aphorisms

"When you are in a state of yoga, all misconceptions that can exist in the mutable aspect of human beings disappear."

"If practise is aligned with a goal [samadhi], obstacles on the spiritual path will disappear and a goal will ultimately be reached."

There is no right kind of yoga except what is right for the individual.

"True yoga is not about the shape of your body but the shape of your life. Yoga doesn't care about what you have been, yoga cares about the person you are becoming." Aadil Palkhivala

"Yoga allows you to rediscover a sense of wholeness in your life, where you do not feel like you are constantly trying to fit broken pieces together." B.K.S. Iyengar

"Yoga does not transform the way we see things. It transforms the person who sees." Unknown

The goal of yoga is to remove the veil of false perception and ignorance (avidya) and see the truth.

"Self–discipline, self–study, and devotion are yoga in the form of action" (Yoga Sutras Ch. 11 v. 1)

"Unified am I, quite undivided, unified my soul. Unified my sight, unified my hearing, unified my breathing, both in and out, unified is my continuous breath. Unified, quite undivided am I. The whole of me" Atharva Veda

Thus, we must ask ourselves, energetically who are we? Emotion means energy in motion, and it should flow through us. Jaime used yoga as a way to get better at living.

Patanjali's Eight Limbs of Yoga

Yamas deal with ethical standards and integrity. The yamas are discussed individually further as they relate to the chakras. The five yamas are as follows:

Ahimsa involves non harming. This includes no physical harm, verbal harm, shaming, clear boundaries, and reaches the physical and emotional levels, affecting the root and throat chakras most predominantly.

Satya involves truthfulness. Truthfulness involves being real, personal expression, the sharing of experiences, and shown self, and is primarily seen in our lives through the throat chakra.

Astya is the concept of non stealing, and also involves giving credit where due. Astya typically affects the root chakra most since it is mainly in the physical realm.

Bramhacharya is the concept of appropriate sexual behaviour. The original intended meaning was chastity and abstinence, but being in the 21st century appropriate sexual behaviour is looked at with an anarcha-feminist approach.

Aprigraha refers to the concept of non hoarding or greed, as well as the concept of non attachment. Primarily, aprigraha affects the root chakra, mainly being in the physical realm. Aprigraha involves not attaching success to material items.

The niyamas are about self discipline and spiritual observation. The niyamas are also discussed further as they relate to the chakras. The five niyamas are as follows:

Shaucha is about purity, honesty, ego, and self reflection, affecting the brow chakra.

Santosha is the concept of contentment, affecting the brow chakra.

Tapas is the skill of self discipline, the energy for which is found in the solar plexus.

Swadyaya is the skill of self study, and putting teachings into the self and taking them along in life. The energy for swadyaya is found in the solar plexus and the brow chakra.

Ishvarapranidhana is the concept of devotion spiritually and the emulation of one's own light. This concept resonates with the crown chakra and is different to each person.

The third limb of Patanjali's yoga is asana, which means a physical posture, and the physical practise of yoga. Any yoga class is directly engaging the third limb of Patanjali's yoga.

The fourth limb of Patanjali's yoga is pranayama, breath work. Affecting the heart chakra, pranayama involves deliberately interfering with breath, hacking the system, and participating in the dance of breath. Breath helps to recognise if stress is real or imagined. Breath is a gift, reminding us we got lucky. The best way to breathe is the way that supports the activity you are doing. Breathing stimulates all of the body to work better. If stress occurs for too long and with too little time in between to recover, we can forget how to relax. The momentary becomes permanent state of being, a habit, and we become hyperalert regardless of circumstance, which is exhausting. We can use the breath as a counter to sense, locate, and define our experience. Allowing ourselves to breathe gives us moments in which we are allowed to reconcile what we feel and do, able to match words and actions to values and beliefs, and figure out how to communicate with precision when we know what our own feelings, needs, and desires are.

The fifth limb of Patanjali's yoga is pratyahara, which is the internalisation of the perceptive senses.

The sixth limb of Patanjali's yoga is dharana, concentration, affecting the brow chakra.

The seventh limb of Patanjali's yoga is dhyana, meditation, which resonates with both the brow and crown chakras.

The eighth and final limb of Patanjali's yoga is samadhi, which resonates with the crown chakra as self realisation through saprajnata samadhi (the conscious) and asamprajanata samadhi (supraconscious).

Why Yoga?

There are many health benefits to yoga. Yoga lowers blood pressure, reduces stress, increases flexibility, and increases muscle strength and tone which offer protection from injury, among many other benefits to physical and mental health.

The five components of fitness are
1. cardiovascular – the ability of the heart and lungs to sustain effort over a long time
2. muscle strength – the ability of the muscles to work against resistance
3. muscle endurance – the ability of the muscles to sustain an effort for a long time
4. flexibility – the ability to bend the joints without injury
5. body composition – the proportion of lean tissue compared with fat tissue

Yoga targets all five components of fitness. Yoga includes a balance of strength and flexibility. Pranayama targets the cardiovascular system, and holding postured for long periods of time works on muscle endurance. Pracitising yoga for a length of time may have an impact on body composition as well.

What are the components of health? Health is defined as not being ill or constantly ill, free from disease and negative states, being able to sleep, being able to exercise, and includes a range of states – physical, mental, and social. wellness is defined as maximum well being at the top of the range of health states, and being able to realise one's full physical, mental, and social potential.

Things that affect health are heredity, environment, and available health care. Sophrosyne is define as a healthy state of mind characterised by self control, moderation, and deep awareness of one's true self and resulting in true happiness. It is said that, "if you practise yoga once a week you'll change your mind, if you practise twice a week you'll change your body, if you practise every day you'll change your life." It also said that the body takes the path of least resistance, and what comes easiest is the smartest. The body is the natural teacher. Yoga promotes living less out of habit and more out of intent.

It is also said in the Yoga Sutras that, "supernatural powers (siddhis) arise from birth, drugs, mantras, austerity (life of plainness and simpleness), or yoga (samadhi)."

"The ego is not master in its own house." Sigmund Freud

Yoga is often connected with Ayurveda. Ayurveda is a mind-body health system based on the principles of the mind and body being connected, and that the mind can heal and transform the body. Ayurveda involves understanding your specific mind-body type (dosha) and its needs. Ayurveda also revolves around eating a diet which contains the six tastes – sweet, salty, sour, pungent, bitter, astringent. Ayurveda also includes the Sattyic Diet (the diet of truth), which contains many fruits.

Ayurveda suggests creating a lifestyle based on one's dosha or mind body type. Each dosha represents prakruti, or body constitution. The belief is that all body constitutions must be improved, and none are favourable, but that a lifestyle can be modified to fit one's dosha which would include altering diet, herbal supplements, and physical asana practise.

The three main doshas are
Vata, the constitution of kinetic energy, with cold, dry, and irregular tendencies.
Pitta, the constitution of balancing energy, with hot, oily, and irritable tendencies.
Kapha, the constitution of potential energy, with cold, wet, and stable tendencies.

Most people have constitutions which are a combination of two doshas, and can further explore Ayurveda if they choose to investigate altering their lifestyles based on their dosha. Jaime had a Vata-Pitta constitution. Working with your dosha is similar to realising that everything you engage in is a spell, making everything you put into your body essentially a spell or potion which will either nourish or poison it. Sexual experiences contain the energy of spells. Things you put into your body may affect your doshas, for example, pungent food increases Jaime's pitta and vata constitutions, sometimes making her a smelly person.

Yoga should be used as a healing practise with a spiritual and physical benefit, as opposed to yoga as a workout with a goal or an extreme physical activity that is fun, challenging, and risky. Asana aims to strengthen the body, but when yoga is used as a workout method, it needs a balance of other fitness activities used in collaboration. Yoga is meant to be used as a union of the body and the spirit. True yoga is about spiritual bypassing, allowing recognition of feelings, learning how to offer self compassion, treating the self with love. True yoga helps to embrace emotions while figuring out our place in space. We discover aspects of ourselves where we feel more or less comfortable, and some ways of experiencing aspects of ourselves are universal while others are individual The practise comes off the mat through compassion, kindness, and an open heart.

Physically, yoga is about creating sense of ease in the body. The body has shaped by the way the life has been lived. Everything the body does is to fix everything it's done (continuous improvement). Yoga can be used as a daily, self reflective practise for witnessing habit patterns, feelings, and sensations. It gives you no choice but to be body aware – the body doesn't lie. Natural patterns can be changed or exacerbated, finding the path of least resistance through the body. Aristotle said, "you are what you do repeatedly. Excellence isn't a quality, but a habit."

The body requires a balanced diet of motion in all planes, movement is also nutrition for the body. The constantly growing body also requires daily movement snacks. Yoga helps see more choices that nurture the body.

What has been done to the body cannot be undone, but new choices can be made about where the body will go from there.

Always ask in life – is this adding value? Assisting in the yoga practise involves asking "how does that feel?" Answers are based on a scale of better, worse, or the same. Those lessons can be applied to real life situations off the mat.

An amazing thing about the human body is muscle memory. Muscle memory is a result of embodied learning. Once the body knows how to do something, it can do it automatically. The more you do vinyasas, the more prepared your body will be to do more, and the more naturally it will come.

Jaime had taken a lot of jobs that required a lot of standing around, but she wasn't allowed to lean against anything. She had taken to filling her standing time (specifically when she worked at the children's museum) with standing yoga postures. She originally did this so that she would stop standing in unhealthy ways, like with her hip jutted out tweaking her sacrum, or with one knee hyperextended. This became so natural to Jaime that she ended up taking it with her to other jobs. When she was a life model, she was drawn, painted, or sculpted in yoga poses ninety percent of the time. At her restaurant she could be seen practising while waiting for guests to arrive for her to seat. When working out became that natural, she could do it at any time. Some days, she had to motivate herself for her workouts by remembering what an inspiration Bethany Hamilton was, but most days her body guided her. This coincided with her knowledge of child development, because she'd learned that children naturally seek out the movement their bodies need.

Through the first level of thinking in Bloom's taxonomy, remembering, and one of the most basic needs in Maslow's hierarchy, safety, we can figure out where we were wounded. When we figure out where we were wounded we can begin to decipher what is truly meaningful and what things are worth to us. This means in both our bodies and our lives. When we are injured, we remember the injury and our body creates a new way to live around the injury. Our bodies decide for us what we are capable of after the injury and during the healing. The same applies to injuries of the mind and soul.

      Yoga teachers when teaching a pose will discuss the "optimal expression" of the pose, which involves having and maintaining good stability, good freedom, and balance of action. This optimal expression also refers to our lives. Good yoga is something which will offer us consistency, modifications, and an approach which is not static.

Types of Yoga

Acro/Partner – Yoga which involves multiple people, often achieving postures involving lifting others, acro yoga has many therapeutic benefits, and helps to build trust and community.

Aerial – Yoga which uses silks, hammocks, or other apparatuses to remain elevated from the ground while in postures. Many aerial classes use restorative postures.

Anusara – Yoga which is about looking inward for light. This practise is upbeat, uplifting, a celebration of heart, and builds community.

Ashtanga – A lifestyle changing type of yoga, which is very physically demanding. It is based around six sequences, and focuses on building strength.

Bhakti - The yoga of devotion, sweet yoga. This yoga is about tapping into the universal love, developing sense of trust that the universe provides, whatever strikes the heart with beauty, and inspires one to feel the love. This yoga includes blessings and individual feelings of divinity vary.

Children's – Yoga specifically designed for growing bodies, typically taught by people who are already professionals in early childhood or in education.

Hatha – This refers to any physical practise of yoga, which may typically be slow or gentle. It focuses on building strength in the body and the mind, as well as conscious awareness of the combination of movement, breath, and awareness.

Hoop – Yoga mixed with hoop dance, in which the hoop is used to typically deepen postures or make them more accessible, similarly to how a yoga strap would be used.

Hot – Yoga done in any environment that is purposely heated for the stimulation of sweat. Bikram is a type of hot yoga practised in 105-degree Fahrenheit rooms with 40% humidity, and is a sequence of 26 poses repeated twice.

Iyengar – A type of yoga which integrates the eight limbs, props, alignment, and sequences, developed by B.K.S. Iyengar.

Jivamukti – Yoga which is a combination of vinyasa flow, chanting, and a vegetarian lifestyle.

Jnana - Yoga which is the path of wisdom.

Karma - Yoga which is the path of action.

Kripalu – A type of yoga which is about letting the body be the teacher, and which is meditation based.

Kriya - Yoga which is a mix of pranayama, mantra, mudra, and mentally directing kundalini to revolve upwards and downwards around six spinal centres to speed spiritual evolvement. Kriya yoga is a rigorous and vigilant practise with no attachment to the outcome.

Kundalini – A type of yoga which involves a lot of chanting, and focuses on the awakening of the primal energy.

Men's – Yoga designed for the male body and ailments which may affect males more predominantly, typically taught by men and intended to help build community between men.

Nude – Yoga performed without clothes on.

Power – Yoga which is fast, used as more of a workout.

Prenatal -Yoga for pregnant women, which focuses on easing

the pains of pregnancy and making space for the baby, additionally focusing on maintaining strength through pregnancy.

Restorative/Gentle – A slower yoga practise, designed to be more relaxing, and often uses a plethora of props.

Sahaja – Sahaja yoga is a movement and a philosophy, created by Nirmala Srivastava. Sahaja is the name of the movement as well as the meditation technique and state of awareness believed to be achieved by the technique. This meditation brings a state of self realisation produced by kundalini awakening and is accompanied by mental silence. Sahaja also includes elements from other religious, spiritual, mystical, and even scientific frameworks.

Senior – Yoga specifically designed for senior bodies and their medical concerns.

Sivananda – A type of yoga which only involves twelve poses, the sun salutations.

Special Needs – Yoga specifically designed for people with special needs, with many modifications, and often taught by someone who has been professionally trained in working with people with special needs.

SUP (Stand Up Paddleboard) – Yoga performed on water, on a stand up paddleboard.

Tantra - The yoga of desire, which builds strength, clarity, and bliss in every day life through the five forces of Shakti. Those forces are 1. asana 2. mantra (words of power) 3. mudra (symbolic/ritual gesture) 4. bandha (energy lock) 5. chakra (energy centre). Tantra seeks to help people move through the world with more confidence and contentment.

Viniyoga – Adaptable yoga.

Vinyasa/Flow - Fast paced yoga, in classes of which one will go through a lot of postures.

Women's – Yoga designed specifically for the bodies of women and their needs, often taught by women, and intended to form communities for women.

Yin/Taoist - Quiet, meditative yoga with therapeutic value.

Yoga Hybrids – Any yoga which is a mix of several types of yoga.

Yoga for Recovery – Yoga used as a type of therapy alongside other methods with intentions of helping people recover from addiction, trauma, disease, or disorder.

Yoga Therapy – Yoga as therapy from illness, injury, or mental illness, often taught by someone clinically trained in the world of medicine, and used alongside other measures.

*These are mentioned in the Gita.

    Jaime was a practitioner and teacher of Hatha and Tantric yoga, in general. She also had experience teaching children's classes, restorative classes, and vinyasa classes. Through Jaime's teacher training, she was also trained in Rajanaka. To practise rajanaka means to be sovereign in one's life to the degree which we are able, to look at what we came with and figure out what to do with it, and to balance our nature with our culture. Rajanaka asks you, "what will you cook out of your life's ingredients?" Rajanaka encourage us to figure out what the ingredients we've been given (our gifts) can help us cook. Rajanaka yoga teaches us how figuring out how uncomfortable emotions can become assets, skillfully cycling through emotions. Your nature is your prakriti, the way you came out. Humans all share some universal experiences and the full spectrum of emotions. When figuring out your gifts, it is important to ask yourself where do you stand the best chance of success? Working very hard on what comes easiest is smartest. How much do you care, and how much are you willing to devote? (time, energy, money, etc.) Rajanaka is about practising making yourself powerful. If you want to be a force of good you better damn well be strong. Rajanaka allows us a recognition of the collectivity of ourselves. Rajanaka recognizes that life is a science experiment, made with uncertainty, and pinches of things – a sensory experience. Because yoga cooks, we can use the ingredients we were given to make a meal out of our lives. Rajanaka is about maintaining the creative wisdom we were given as children and the awareness of the infinite joy we create with each breath.

"The unity of every country is the family and the strength of the country is based on the smiles of the children and songs of the adults" - Yogi Bhajan

Energy, Chi, or Kundalini

All energy vibrates at different vibrations. There are energy emanations of the physical body – light and colour, sounds, thermal energies, magnetics, electricity, and heat.

Many who believe in metaphysics understand the way that energy can be felt. These same people also tend to understand subtle energy stimuli – vibrational remedies which revive the proper flow of energy. Some of these subtle energy stimuli include sounds, aromas, flower and gem essences, crystals, thoughts, and colours which interact with the body to stabilise life conditions.

Kundalini yoga uses a lot of chanting. Kundalini is a type of energy, and kundalini yoga uses a metaphor of climbing up the ladders of the self to get to enlightenment transcendence. Stored in our spines, kundalini is referred to as a serpent coiled and we must wake it up. Often in the yogic world, the human experience is described as looking at a lake, with a mountain behind it. The mountain represents the self, ripples in the lake are emotions, making us unable to see the reflection with clarity. With a calm mind, we catch glimpses of truth. Yoga aids the calming of the mind through karmic healing.

It is important to manage the body's energy and maintain balanced chakras, because energy gets stuck or blocked when we don't speak truth or hold things back or in.

Energy Centres (Chakras)

Chakras are translated to mean spinning wheels of energy. These seven wheels each reside in particular places in the spine. Each chakra represents a different kind of energy, and balancing the chakras helps us to harness the energy in all of them. Imbalances in the chakras affect us differently and will be explored more deeply in the case studies.

The Sushumna Nadi is the main axis of energy in yogic thought, and it runs upwards from the pelvis to the top of the head. According to Astrology Weekly, a chakra natal chart can be designed with the first six chakras projected onto different levels of the Sushumna Nadi. Planets in the projection area of the chakras will influence them according to the nature of the planets and which side of Sushumna Nadi they fall on in the chart when someone is born. The left side represents energy received, our receptive side. The right side represents controlled energy, our emissive energy. The energy received from the root chakra is physical, material energy. The energy received from the sacral chakra is sociability, and sexual potential. The energy received from the solar plexus is what gives you self confidence. The energy received from the heart chakra is what you like, and the love received. The energy received from the throat chakra is passive intuition. The energy received from the brow chakra is memory, interest, mental, analysis. The energy received from the crown chakra is transcendence, the link to the spiritual world. The energy emitted from the root chakra is stability, controlled energy. The energy emitted from the sacral chakra is seduction, and sexual energy control. The energy emitted from the solar plexus is willpower, perseverance, and charisma. The energy emitted from the heart chakra is the love emitted. The energy emitted from the throat chakra is active intuition and contact with other worlds. The energy emitted from the brow chakra is logic, mental, creativity, and synthesis. The energy emitted from the crown chakra is transcendence, the link to the spiritual world.

When chakras have imbalances to the right the energy is masculine, of leadership, logic, aggression, and future. When chakras have imbalances to the left the energy is feminine, of emotion, intuition, and is receptive. When most imbalances of the chakras are in the lower body there are physical and mental concerns. When most imbalances of the chakras are in the upper body there are mental and spiritual imbalances. (Gay Witchcraft) The base chakra involves physical urges, basic principles of pleasure and pain, and those we trust for immediate survival. The Belly chakra involves ability to relate, physical contact, and trust. The Solar plexus chakra involves the relationship of trust and power. The Heart chakra involves empathy, love, compassion, and balance. The Throat chakra involves communication and expression. The Brow chakra involves perception, visulisation, manifestation, and reception of information. The Crown chakra involves the connection to the divine.

In the archetypical chakra natal chart presented by Astrology Weekly, we are presented with ideal planetary influences on the chakras, creating signs which rule over the chakras. The Root chakra is ruled by Gemini and Cancer, the Sacral chakra is ruled by Taurus and Leo, the Solar Plexus is ruled by Aries and Virgo, the Heart chakra is ruled by Pisces and Libra, the Throat chakra is ruled by Aquarius and Scorpio, and the Brow chakra is ruled by Capricorn and Sagittarius.

Theories of Learning and Play as they Relate to Child Development

"Truly I tell you, unless you change and become like little children, you will never enter the kingdom of heaven." - Matthew 18:3

All learning styles are mimetic in nature. Many learning styles intersect with Gardner's theory of multiple intelligences. Gardner's types of intelligences are verbal/linguistic, logical/mathematical, visual/spatial, bodily/kinesthetic, naturalist, intrapersonal, interpersonal, existential. People are thought to contain all of these types of intelligences, but be particularly strong in a few of them. Mimetic learning styles include solitary learning, social learning, visual (spatial) learning, logical learning, verbal (linguistic) learning, physical (kinesthetic) learning, aural (auditory and musical) learning.
It has been proved that children learn through play, and that they naturally seek out the movements their bodies need. Play is defined by each theorist of child development differently. Knowing all of these things, we can figure out our own learning styles and intelligences and learn to utilise them as adults and help ourselves learn and grow. We can take our lead from children and seek out the movement which our bodies need more often.

Jean Piaget said that children are little scientists, naturally curious and eager to make discoveries. This is the creative wisdom children possess which we hope to hold onto as adults. Some aspects of our practise allow us to cultivate and nurture such creative wisdom. All theorists of child development have different opinions on play. Froebel saw play as a natural part of growth and development. Piaget believed play was influenced by the intellectual stage of development the child was in at the time. Erikson viewed play as the opposite of work. Vygotsky viewed imaginative play as the key to development. Elkind saw play as how children deal with stress, while Bruner saw play as learning without risks. Dewey said that doing gives activities value.

Piaget viewed children as natural scientists, and Jaime felt that correlated to how children naturally seek out the movement their body needs (as pointed out in <u>Balanced and Barefoot</u>). Through play, children attend to their movement needs and sensory integration. "Children with healthy neurological systems naturally seek out the sensory input they need on their own. They determine how much, how fast, and how high works for them at any given time. They do this without even thinking about it." (Hanscom, A. 2016) Hanscom describes how because children are naturally curious, they experiment with their surroundings, take risks, make mistakes, and learn, seeking out every opportunity to make sense of the world.

    As adults, we don't often take opportunities to receive sensory input, and engage less frequently in play. We can take some advice from children and listen to our bodies, and by discovering how we learn best we can figure out how to adapt our practise to our learning needs. Even as adults, without giving our bodies the movement and sensory input they need, we negatively impact our senses, most notably our vestibular senses. We must model continuous improvement in order to help create a better world, and by attending to our sensory needs through play and activity the same way children do, we will be improving ourselves. Yoga helps us to learn ourselves more intimately, and it is with this knowledge that we may begin to understand why we behave and feel as we do. Approaching yoga playfully helps us to maintain the curiosity and creative wisdom we have as children, and thinking of it as a way for us to play with our bodies can help us to pay better attention to our sensory and movement needs.

    In order to better understand some yogic terms, a dictionary has been included. There are many more terms in the world of yoga, but these are a few worth mentioning.

Lexicon of Assorted Terms in the Yogic World

Adhikara – qualifications
Amrita – ambrosia in brain
Apana – outgoing breath
Apanavayu - "down and out" energy, downward flow – essential for menstruation, childbirth, elimination, digestion
Apeshka – your proclivities, preferences, things you're drawn to
Asana – pose
Atman – Prakriti within one being
Aum (ohm) – totality of existence
Brahman -
Drishti – focus point
Ha – right breath
Kala – nature, left side
Kula – community, family
Nadi – channel of energy
Nivritti – turning away from the world – viewing emotions as a problem, calming them, and making them go away
Pavritti – turning toward the world – recognition of emotions that might not go away
Prakriti – all that which moves in the universe
Prana – incoming breath
Sadhana – means of accomplishing something, ego transcending spiritual practise
Samadhi – intense concentration through meditation
Savasana – corpse pose, final relaxation at the end of a practise
Siddhis – supernatural powers
Sidha – accomplishment
Sri – culture, right side, refining of nature
Sushumna – central breath
Tamasic – slower
Tha - left breath
Ujani – turn view upside down
Ujayi – uprising breath
Upasana – ideas and principles of why we do what we do
Yoga seva – service – essential to path of the yogi

Chakra Case Studies

To further understand the chakras, case studies have been provided. Each case study represents an aspect of a particular chakra. Perhaps a character displays an imbalance of excess or a deficiency of energy flow through the chakra. Contrarily, the character may be an example of having balanced energy flow through the chakra. Some of these case studies depict the lives of Jaime and her friends.

These case studies come with a warning – a trigger warning. Many sensitive topics are touched on in the following case studies, including but not limited to: sexual abuse, suicide, mental illness, eating disorders, substance abuse, and violence.

The case studies are typically told about the characters from an omniscient point of view, though some are written in the form of journal entries, mostly Jaime's. Jaime's story is the story within the whole story. Many of the other stories were based around friends or acquaintances she'd known.

Research Methods

Many of the characters presented in the case studies are based off of real life people with whom interviews were conducted. To preserve the identities of everyone and keep it anonymous, all names have been changed, except for Erika and Manny. Their names have been kept true to honour them and their stories. Interviews were conducted with consent, follow up interviews were occasionally held, and many of the people got an input on what aspects of their story they would like to be told and how they would like their character to be portrayed. The interviews were done as an attempt to represent people from all walks of life and to get more quantitative data about the experiences of LGBT+ people in society. Most interviews were done in person, but some were conducted over the internet or over the phone. There are also a few pieces which have been submitted, artwork for which permission was requested, and plentiful research was done online with the aim of providing the most holistic as possible representation of the ever-growing queer community.

Chronology

First, Jaime's story will be presented. It is important to learn about Jaime first to understand why she became who she became, and then the seven separate chakras will be laid out and described, with evidence provided showing how the chakras are represented in daily life. The purpose of these case studies is to provide examples of how and why yoga has value in the lives of many different kinds of people. Jaime has given herself nicknames in some of her stories because she thinks of her stories as representing parts of herself that don't exist outside of that period of time. Her story starts at the beginning, but doesn't explain how she got her studio, it only explains how she realised what an effect yoga had on her life. Some things ought to be left to the imagination.

Jaime's Story

The Jaime Alexander Chronicles

The Jaime Alexander Chronicles depict Jaime's story, beginning when she discovered her queerness and ending when her life was consumed in the best possible way by yoga. Jaime discovered many benefits of yoga, and truly did not know where she would be without it. Her story represents the constance of the chakras within daily life, and she travels through all of them, experiencing different blockages and balances. Yoga found Jaime because she needed it. By sharing her story with others, Jaime hoped to help others who needed yoga become found by it. All Jaime wanted was to be for someone who she had needed in her youth. She followed her soul path to become a teacher, and brought yoga into her classroom. She regarded her formative years as lessons which were necessary to her discovering truth through yoga and the truth about herself. Jaime's story is the main case study for the seven chakras, but there are many other examples provided.

Days of the Old

They were friends during the awkward years. The years between age ten and age fifteen, sixteen for some. During the middle school years, and only just into high school.

That's how Jaime thought of her old group of friends. They were friends during the awkward time where nothing really important in life happened but also at a time where everything important in life happened. At least, for Jaime's life, because she will never know for them.

They were Jaime's friends after her dad's first illness but by the time of his most recent they were not anymore. That was more than five years ago now. Everything that happened in her life when they knew her revolved around her, actually, which was strange when she considered that most of her important life events involve other people. The effect that people have on others is insane.

The two events were that Jaime got suspended from middle school, and came out as bisexual.

It seems strange to break an entire five years and friend group down into those two events, but by the time the next big event happened, all but two of them were gone.

Some of them had come with their company from elementary school, the kids they had grown up with. That's how it all worked; everyone came in with whoever they knew, met some new people, and everyone formed cliques and most people stayed there all the way through high school in this terrible tiny town (those lucky bastards that got to stay together, Jaime thought.)

Darcy she'd met in a class, and had also met her on a soccer team, and she came with Dawn. Jaime came in with Karoline, and she had organically met Darcy through a class. Their personalities matched. Jaime knew Rosie, who was a year older than most of them and her and Darcy got on when she joined Jaime and Rosie's girl scout troop. Rosie and Dawn became inseparable at a point, though. Dawn was two years her junior. Dawn was the last girl Jaime was in love with. She may have destroyed her for girls.

When Jaime first met Dawn, she was a ballerina in the fifth grade. Jaime never dreamed that she would fall in love with her. Jaime was a sixth grader with a frizzy ponytail down past her back who had for the first time been told she had a "fat ass" when she met her.

The slumber party is where it all started. Jaime blamed this first party entirely for everything that followed. When she was eleven she got invited to a birthday party slumber party and the girl who threw the party (Darcy) had a hot tub, a pool, and a trampoline at her house.

The girl who complimented Jaime's backside after she changed into her bikini was called Jeannie and she was a black girl that Jaime had known from elementary school who took orchestra with Darcy. The only reason Jaime remembered of the color of her skin was because she had always been hyperaware of how the black girls in her classes had always developed so beautifully before everyone else and it was simply the strangest thing for Jaime to have ever heard. The term she had used was, "fatty," which was a term that she had heard boys use about girls like her.

To this day she didn't know how it happened. She didn't know who started it or why. But as they were in the hot tub together they all touched, and took off their swimsuits. This went on for years at Darcy's. None of them ever kissed.

Until eighth grade. When they were thirteen, Karoline kissed Jaime first on the couch in Jaime's basement when it was turned the other way and they were watching a VHS tape on a snowy afternoon. Neither of their middle school boyfriends ever found out.

Karoline was the first girl Jaime was ever in love with. She was the reason Jaime came out.

Jaime was the first person out in her grade. She came out on New Year's Day, after the night before when her thirteen year old boyfriend had tried to con her into sex with him by making up a long winded story about cheating on her.

Karoline's immediate response had been, "have you

ever kissed a girl before?"

When Jaime was thirteen, people (boys and girls) had told her that the curves of her body were perfectly proportioned, that her jeans made her ass look good, and access to those jeans had not only been requested, but demanded.

Karoline and Jaime had known each other since they were seven, and after that seventh grade trip became inseparable. They got into the habit of holding hands. They rode bikes together. They talked about everything. They spent the day together from noon till night in the summer; mosquito-bitten, bruised and scraped, sweaty, and smiling into the ether. Jaime thought that if Karoline were a sound, she would be the essence of the purest summertime laugh, on a songbird's sticky night in the midst of a slight ripple of a swimming pool, out of smiling sunrise lips.

They were children of the internet and as they grew older their curiosity grew stronger. At a sleepover, late into the night, Karoline and Jaime investigated porn- straight, lesbian, and gay male. Sometimes, at Darcy's, they would all watch porn together, too.

In seventh grade, Jaime knew her first lesbian. She was a year older than Jaime. Jaime was afraid to be alone with her.

In eighth grade, Jaime met her first gay boy. He was the older brother of a boy new to the school who she had gotten friendly with. He had met Rosie in high school. His name was Jacob, and he was interesting. A little friendly, a little scary, a little funny. Seemed nice, and smart, and he and Jaime had common interests. Jacob and Rosie took Jaime to my first youth group, at which she began to acknowledge the questions and the feelings.

Ever since Karoline kissed her, Jaime couldn't get enough of her. Everything Jaime did was wrong. She knew that now. She did not know that then. Karoline would stare longingly at the models in Jaime's mother's Victoria's Secret catalogues and Jaime would touch her body and beg her to decide whether or not she liked girls.

For two weeks after eighth grade they dated, and

even kissed in front of others. When she broke up with Jaime, she said she was straight.

She never held against Jaime what she did, perhaps because she loved Jaime too.

In their later teens, she would drunkenly proposition Jaime. At that point, Jaime knew better.

Dawn was Jaime's best friend when Karoline wasn't for a little while. When Darcy, Karoline, and Jaime went into high school, Dawn went into depression.

Dawn used to light up the room. She had a way about her where she could just keep everyone's eyes on her all the time. And then she tried to disappear.

Nobody warns you about these kinds of things or tells you how contagious it can be. It wasn't until people like Rosie cut shapes into her arms because her two best friends who she crushingly adored did it that they even knew what they were doing. She could only explain it after.

Dawn began to consume Jaime's life. Jaime spent time with her trying to keep her happy. She had always been so much fun. All of those girls, Dawn, Darcy, Karoline, and Rosie had been – they had been some of the first people to make Jaime laugh so hard her ribs ached before drugs broke their innocence. Jaime was in love with the fun.

Dawn was mean to Jaime. Dawn did not appreciate Jaime's efforts. She made fun of Jaime and called her names. Dawn hated Jaime because she and Dawn's mom shared concern for her life. She would not accept Jaime's love.

Jaime watched Dawn take a hair straightener to her wrist and as Jaime tried to keep her from hurting herself she resisted, and later degraded Jaime to where she wanted to feel the pain Dawn had inflicted on herself.

Love had left Jaime at rock bottom.

Relational Aggression

Jaime could never quite riddle out why her old friends were so mean to each other. There were times, of course, where they were kind to each other, and that's how it becomes confusing. Pulling away the veil and discerning that the truth of her old friends was that they were mean to each other took Jaime a very long time, because her vision was clouded by emotionally missing the people she had an attachment to.

Darcy and Dawn were a stick together pair and so were Glitterboii and Rosie. Though there were others in the group, those two pairs and Jaime were the pillars of their social circle. Darcy had been bullied all her life for being overweight and having bad acne. She was a practitioner of "fat talk" (Odd Girl Out) in which she would either point out her own body's flaws, or bash her other friends for being "soo skinny." Dawn sought the spotlight. Dawn's Muslim father valued her older brothers over her. Rosie didn't get enough attention from her parents as the oldest of four, she had even taken up cigarette smoking so that her mom would find out and yell at her about it, but it went unnoticed. The girls acted "wild" for attention, being overtly silly and affectionate. They joked about things that weren't funny, because they'd been desensitized due to the media. Some slut shaming went around the group, particularly aimed at Jaime, who had had many boyfriends in a short period of time.

Rosie and Dawn discussed self-harm in unhealthy ways. Rosie's two best friends were going through a lot and self-harming, and Rosie openly talked about how she cut herself because both of her best friends did. Rosie and Dawn both took approaches in which they would essentially say "here is my harm" instead of taking approaches in which they explained their pain and asked for help. Dawn harmed herself in front of other people, and became manipulative, threatening to people that she would harm herself or kill herself if they didn't do certain things for her.

Perhaps the most curious (or to some, perhaps the most obvious) function of the group being mean to each other involved the fact that they had all shared experiences at Darcy's skinny-dipping/experimenting in the hot tub. Their mean behaviour was likely reactions fueled by fear of feelings stirred up during experiments (and the danger of knowing each other's secrets). If the girls were mean and manipulative, they felt that they could control each other, and when they felt like they had control over each other they felt as though they had control over their secrets. Though the girls were openly overtly affectionate with each other in public, there were things that they had done that they had pressured each other into never telling anyone about.

Why was it that Jaime thought she was happy laughing and acting dumb with people who were mean to each other? Because she had people to be with, even if they were mean, because they could be nice sometimes, nice enough to invite her places and make her laugh, because the other members of her friend group were also very needy people, they were very affectionate, hanging all over each other and having no physical boundaries.

There was a relationship between the mean girls Jaime hung out with and a fear that anger would lead to loss of friendship. This tended to be why the girls engaged in relational aggression toward each other. The girls never wanted to have certain conversations for fear of them leading to fights. Fearing that fights would lead to friendships ending, the girls left many of their concerns up in the air. They never talked about the things that happened at Darcy's slumber parties, they just left them suspended between them, like telephone wires keeping them connecting. This bottling of emotion and blockage of throat chakras causes a lot of misplaced anger in the girls. This misplaced anger was likely the reason behind the girls being mean to each other.

Middle School Recess and How it Stunted Jaime's Growth

The popular kids always got the sports courts and all the balls, so Jaime and her friends were left with the rock on the field. They did not move their bodies, and they did not breathe the fresh air deeply. Jaime remembered that they were not allowed to explore the woods through which she walked home after school. She and her friends lingered around the edge of the woods. Jaime and her friends were all creative people, but they did not create any scenarios during recess that would have led to play. They wasted their time not building their strength or helping their brains, and instead helped build a culture of bullying, cruelty, and gossip.

As an adult, Jaime wondered how this could be changed in schools, how could recess be of better use to tweens? She wondered what their movement and sensory needs were, what stimulation they needed, and how to provide them with freedom and opportunities to connect with nature, themselves, and others as well as the values adults hope for them to develop such as compassion and respect. She became committed to learning how to keep outdoor free time from turning into a negative experience full of bullying, gossip, screen time, lack of movement, and a lack of fun.

Recess is an integral part of the school day. "Up until the late 1980s, it was not uncommon to have a full hour recess session and another one or two shorter recess sessions" (Nussbaum 2006). "However, in the 1990s improving achievement scores became a critical issues for schools and legislators, and it seemed logical that increasing time in instruction would improve success with these tests. With limited hours during the day, recess became the most rational activity to reduce, despite a growing body of research that demonstrated the importance of recess for child development and school achievement" (Pellegrini and Bohn-Gettler 2013). Allowing children to move for hours supports attention and healthy sensory integration. Recess combats obesity, improves behaviour, develops social skills, gets the brain working, and reduces stress (Hanscom, A 2016).

Angela J. Hanscom, author of the book <u>Balanced and Barefoot</u>, proposes ways to make recess a play experience, which include extending the time, reducing the rules, offering children loose parts, and giving them the freedom to get dirty. Hanscom explains that "there are only two rules at TimberNook: (1) children have to be able to see an adult at all times, and (2) children need to show respect to the other children and adults...kids can climb trees, yell, run, jump, go barefoot, use tools, get dirty, create their own societies, and build with whatever they find out in the woods. When we allow children adequate time to play without adult interference [at TimberNook] we observe significant changes in the way children play over a short period of time" - it goes from simplistic, to explorative, the creative and independent. We find that with fewer rules there is less testing of boundaries." She also found that "girls who avoid risks have poorer self esteem than girls who can and do face challenges" (PBS Parents, n.d.) Therefore, in order to help deter the rise in social-emotional issues we are witnessing in children today, we would be wise to provide thrilling play experiences for children." (Hanscom, A. 2016) The Journal of Outdoor Adventure Education has many resources available for teachers interested in this approach, which Jaime made use of.

How Jaime's Friends Mirror Findings in Odd Girl Out

In her book Odd Girl Out, Rachel Simmons discusses her findings on the hidden culture of aggression in girls. She discusses the way that girls are portrayed as disloyal, untrustworthy, sneaky, fake, unforgiving, crafty, jealous, underhanded, prone to betrayal, disobedient, secretive, and using intimacy to manipulate and overpower others. She brings up the model of the "good girl" that many girls are pressured into adhering to - the girl who have no bad thoughts or feelings, and who was quiet, calm, kind. Everyone wants to be with that "good girl." The "good girl" is in contrast to the girl who is "all that," the girl who other girls don't want to be friends with. The "all that" girl is assertive, confident, resists self sacrifice and restraint, has appetite and desire, and uses manipulation or sexual manipulation as her path to power. She "works it," appearing sweet with sin under the surface. Sexuality is seen as breaking the rules because the girl is entertaining and pleasuring herself. The "slut" is seen as disconnected from her partner(s) and other girls. This culture idealises girls as caring and "nice" - not aggressive, not angry, not in conflict. Assertive or aggressive attitudes are seen as unfeminine, the hallmark of masculinity. This presents a double standard, allowing boys to get angry and preventing girls from being anything but "sweet." One girl interviewed in Simmons' book articulated that "girls have more of a nervous system, boys don't care if they get in trouble but girls don't want anyone to know."

There are cultural rules against overt aggression that girls learn through the "hallway curriculum," and attitudes toward aggression crystallise sex roles. There are negative attitudes toward selfishness in girls, and those who are competitive are seen as "not nice." Girls are even told that telling truth about anger can lead to being "not nice." There are unspoken rules against truth telling. Therefore, girls end up engaging in a denial of anger. They absorb the anger instead of voicing it, and even when they are jealous, they feel wrong for feeling jealous, and feel like it must be sequestered. Insecurity breeds a fear of jealousy ending things. A fear of being at fault leads to panicking and impulsive decision making, like not finishing fights. Girls lack the tools to deal with (daily) anger, hurt, betrayal, and jealousy. They grow to mistrust their feelings through the sequestering of anger.

This culture is demanding perfect relationships of girls, and this leads girls to feel that they would rather not hurt others at the expense of themselves. There is a pressure to deny the authenticity of themselves, and a pressure for a nonexpression of feelings. This culture of indirection leaves girls with an inability to communicate and a loss of the ability to assert feelings of hurt and anger toward another personality. It also leads to a loss of self esteem in girls as they battle with what they know to be true versus what they must pretend to feel. There are findings of girls not trusting other girls, with their fears, secrets, or anything. Because girls are often the bully in the mirror and prone to self dissection, they tend to have a desire for acceptance and connection.

Why Girls Travel in Packs

Because of stereotypes that females mature into caregivers, and people believing that girls should reserve their true emotions for boys or children and that anything else is practise, girls are expected to easily maintain relationships with other girls. While men view aggression as means to control their environment and integrity, women believed it would terminate or endanger relationships. Girls fear that conflict equals loss, even everyday acts of conflict, and are therefore unprepared to negotiate conflict. Boys are encouraged to separate from mothers, adopt the masculine posture of emotional restraint, and describe danger as a fear of entrapment or smothering.

Differently to boys, there is a noticeable centrality of relationship in girls' lives. Relationships play unusually important role in girls' social development, and danger is perceived as isolation or abandonment. Women's development involves human attachment, stressing continuity of relationships. This indirect culture ignores the closeness of girlfriends, yet it is with best friends joys of intimacy and human connection are first discovered.

Fear of isolation or abandonment comes from a fear of solitude. In social situations, there is also the idea that one is imperfect for not having friends. A fear of exclusion drives people to cling to their friends. In stressful situations females often seek company, drawing power and security from close relationships in life. People often draw self esteem and strength from friends. Due to Maslow's need for love and belonging, we often tend to cling to groups to cling to our sanity, and feelings of powerlessness often lead us to seek support. Making friends is seen as alliance building, but on the flipside when you lose support you're seen as the bad one. The isolation that girls sometimes experience is often a self imposed isolation coming from the bottling of feelings. Strong, positive female friendships leave each feeling grateful for the other, and in some cases give girls the strength to trust again.

"The circles of women around us weave invisible nets of love that carry us when we're weak, and sing with us when we are strong." -Sark

The Benefits of Solitude

In isolation we can be more in touch with our thoughts and feelings. Solitude offers us a new perspective and self awareness. Isolation helps us develop respect for ourselves, which makes us demand respect in relationships, being able to discern whether or not they are healthy. Solitude creates a lack of relying on others and helps us to live without fear of abandonment. Through solitude we may confront culture's discomfort with female strength, voice, and aggression, and we may be inspired to defend ourselves publicly, provide for our families, speak our hearts and minds, and disrupt the social and sexual order of society.

Types of Alternative Aggressions that Girls Engage In

Nonphysical aggression is described as an unconventional, alternative aggression. "When aggression cannot, for one reason or another, be directed (physically or verbally) at its target, the aggressor has to find other channels." (Simmons, R. 2011)

Relational aggression starts in preschool when children notice the first signs of sex differences. It begins as soon as children become capable of meaningful relationships. The lifeblood of relational aggression is the use of relationship as weapons. Relational aggression is intended to escape detection and punishment when a social universe refuses girls' open conflict. Social aggression is intended to damage self esteem or social status, and targets are victimised, portrayed as having a social skills deficit. Manipulation is one form of alternative aggression. Indirect aggression avoids confrontation by using tactics like covert behaviour and rumours.

Relational aggression involves acts that harm others through damage or threat to relationships or feelings of acceptance, friendship, or group inclusion, such as ignoring, exclusion, negative body language, or facial expressions, sabotage, friendship manipulation.

    Silence is used as a path around conflict, but deepens the conflict's intensity. Silence tells conflicts it's not worth someone's time, and not getting to find out why someone is mad leads to the other believing they are at fault. Silence means that you can't get a rebuttal, and therefore, you win. Girls recognise the power in body language and silence.

    Since it is the digital age, relational aggression also manifests through cyberbullying. All forms of alternative aggressions are damaging to the self esteem of young girls and to their abilities to communicate feelings and negotiate conflict.

Ways to Help Young Girls Communicate Effectively

    As an educator, Jaime wanted to help girls honour the truths of their peers while trusting their own truths. She wanted girls to share a desire for confidence in other girls, and to develop concepts of body positivity. She wanted to help girls understand that there were more female powers in the world other than sex. She wanted to foster a more girl positive school experience, and an atmosphere of less competition. She knew that in order to do this, other women recognising their own capacity to injure was important, admitting that they do not perpetuate the nonaggressive stereotype set upon girls. She knew that women must also offer positive vocabulary for girls to tell each other their truths.

    Girls combat alternative aggressions when they summon the strength to confront their aggressors and are no longer besieged by doubt, and no longer believe the conflict was their fault. Girls also combat alternative aggressions by not letting others determine who they will become. Fostering confidence and celebrating differences will help to breed girls who are more able to combat alternative aggressions and will be less likely to be as negatively influenced by conflict in relationships as Jaime was by the conflict in her relationships with the mean girls that she was close with in her youth.

Selective Memory Blocking as it Relates to the Brow Chakra

Jaime noticed that she had a fuzzy memory. She had a good memory of elementary school events, but her brain seemed to block out most of age eleven because of how traumatic life became at ten and a half when she watched her dad have his first heart attack. Ten and a half eclipsed eleven for Jaime, and it was never addressed. She recalled a few key things, like her crush at the time, being bullied and the lack of surfing in her life. She recalled that it was the first year that it felt like she had to make it through, like it didn't come easily, and it never got any easier. Jaime recalled that she found herself through loneliness and dove into books, art, and writing. She knew that she had gone into middle school with two close friends and established a friend group toward the end of the school year. She remembered the first slumber party over at Darcy's, her interest in manga, and her introduction to the queer community. Jaime vividly remembered laughing with her friends and being silly, which she learned had been a coping mechanism. Jaime remembered becoming anti-school, and sometimes forgot to remember that it had to do with getting up early and her lack of sleep which wasn't being addressed. Not sleeping gave Jaime a cranky attitude. It took a long time for Jaime to remember her irritability in middle school, she always idealised the times she'd had with her friends. She hardly recalled middle school besides her friends and getting suspended. Her memory blocking skills had made Jaime remember in blocks. "We don't remember the days, we remember the moments." - Cesare Pavese

It takes a long time to discern the truth of blocked memories behind the many layers of fuzz. Jaime noticed that as her brain grew, it learned to subconsciously block itself from wasting memory on insignificant daily details and events, and to focus more on saving the overall emotion and some specific, important memories. Jaime experienced some lapses in her memory, which could be explained by a lack of sleep and hypervigilance. Medical marijuana for people with PTSD aimed to ease hypervigilance and aid sleep. Jaime noticed that there were blocked memories which were inaccessible and there were those which could be retrieved. The ones which could be retrieved felt like they came out of boxes when Jaime revisited them. She kept her old friends in those boxes, blocked so she didn't waste time thinking about them or waste space in her brain – they'd been "unnecessary facts" removed by the inversion of Contentment. If she ever wanted them or needed them, though, she could open the box and remember all the details

The Brain on PTSD

Exhale to Inhale was a program which made yoga available to survivors of sexual assault. Researchers for this program found that post-traumatic stress disorder immediately affects 94% of all survivors of sexual assault. Exhale to Inhale outlined the ways in which PTSD affects the brain. Because of PTSD affecting the brain stem, people could experience changes in their breathing, difficulty swallowing, nausea, and balance problems (meaning the vestibular sense was affected.) The prefrontal cortex, which is responsible for emotional regulation, shows decreased levels of grey and white matter in brain scans of people with PTSD. This can cause changes in social behaviour, and explains why bad memories are often relived. The prefrontal cortex is involved in stress response. The hippocampus is the part of the brain responsible for distinguishing past from present memories, and is smaller in the brains of people suffering from PTSD. The thalamus is a part of the Limbic System, and helps relay sensory activity. The thalamus in people with PTSD shows decreased blood flow. The amygdala is the emotional memory centre, which becomes hyperactive, and can cause insomnia. The cerebellum receives an increase in adrenaline, cause anxiety disorders. 30% of survivors sustain symptoms on some level of severity.

Jaime's Journal About What Happened in November

Jaime wrote in her journal about "the separation of the experience, memory, and lesson from the person involved." She wrote, "why is the same person who would take me on nighttime walks and teach me awareness by asking if I'd noticed whether certain cars were on or had people in them the same person who would later traumatise me? He taught me a skill I'd carry forever. Why is he the one who told me to hit guys when they tried to go too far, but then he still went too far? Contradictions and lacking the awareness to notice them until it was too late, why? Emotion? Youth? Mistrust?
I got advice from my therapist to integrate the trauma overtime and give it new meaning. For me this means having the awareness, learning self-defense, and being able to be protected – being able to have those skills without thinking of him, being able to think about it without crying, and being able to pass on those learned skills. It is important to recognise the time that it takes to pull away the veils of pain and emotion covering the truth of how to heal from the experience and move on – self-discovery through self-care. You learn over time to give trauma new meaning and integrate the experience so it no longer defines who you are, she said.

His lessons on awareness relate to how I don't like doing drugs in uncontrollable environments, I feel the need to keep my wits about me and constantly check in with myself to make sure my awareness is functioning. I know the senses can distract from awareness, including sensory indulgences, or overstimulation, which relates to pratyahara."

From within detachment from such a memory, she could still find togetherness, oneness, and wholeness from her lessons learned and strength gained. To Jaime, it related to the concept of Tikkun Olam, whereby people found togetherness through acts of kindness while putting the pieces of the world back together.

Jaime's Journal Entry About Coming Out

"Coming out – get out of your shell and make the best of yourself" -Akiha Hara, Hana-Kimi

Eight years ago, two months into my first year of teenage life, I came out as bisexual. Eight years ago today, New Year's Day. Last New Year's spent at twenty in a hotel with friends. Eight years ago, New Year's was spent at the house of a friend's family having a slumber party while two thirteen year old boys tried to convince me to sleep with the one I was dating by having him threaten to cheat on me.

I dumped him. Twelve or so hours later, he was one of the first people that I came out to. I came out over instant message. I had a computer to hide behind even though I knew the way that things could spread like wildfire on the internet.

I was the first person out in my grade. It was hard to start saying it out loud. I had to tell the girls at the slumber party out loud. They all said they knew.

I came out because it made things rational in my head when I realised that I was attracted to both genders. I felt enlightened about a truth and I felt the need to share my truth with my loved ones and my world. I didn't even think about the way that some thirteen year olds could come out of the closet and get kicked out of their homes. The world is a scary place for the youth. My parents didn't believe me. I guess that was lucky. Eight years have passed and they still don't.

Most other people thought already that I was into girls. My older siblings both could tell, so they told me when I came out to them. Apparently, I used to play "lesbian dollies" as my brother called it.

I remember being younger than thirteen and watching Matthew Lush's videos on YouTube about coming out. He had different kinds – coming out to your family, coming out to your friends...

58

Knowing yourself is the most important step to successful relationships. I know myself quite well. For example, I know I get sad around every Samhain season. September is hard for me. October is hard for me. Halloween is my favourite holiday, but October is hard for me.

In October 2010, my grandfather passed after a battle with pancreatic cancer. I was recently single, but since the boy and I were on good terms, he's the one who really consoled me during that time. My friends had proved to be fairly insincere, ditching me at Homecoming after our gay youth group meeting and train ride back to town.

My grandfather was the only grandfather I had known, and I had only known him fourteen years of my life. Living less than twenty minutes away, I was used to seeing his warm smile, hearing his hearty laugh, smelling the bread he made, and sharing meals together. At my age I hadn't been able to make the most of our time together. I did always remember his kindness, his warmth, and how he never spoke badly about anyone. I had the deepest, most inexplicable desire to come out to my grandfather when he was in the hospital during his last few weeks of life. At fourteen, though out to my peers, I was still sworn to secrecy when it came to my Roman Catholic Italian grandparents. Though I always felt my grandfather would be accepting, I never got the chance to tell him because his room was always occupied – I couldn't make anyone leave for fear of the question why.

I never got to come out to him out loud, though I have at his grave.

When he passed, I threw myself into my youth group. In the time of the suicides, the group was organising a vigil. I launched myself full force at my community, and even came out publicly.

I use "when I was straight" as both a qualifier and a time frame. I dated four boys when I was straight before I even considered liking girls. I didn't know I liked them until someone asked me if I did. I was never inherently homophobic when I was straight. Karoline and I used to pretend to date when I was straight. I met my first lesbian when I was straight, back when she was bi and also a she.

I'll admit that the first time we hung out along I was a little nervous, but realised quickly she wasn't going to hit on me. I was the first person in my grade to come out. I recall the three month questioning period easily, the progression through a year of my relationship with Karoline, who was the first girl I kissed. I recall my mom's opinion and my first relationship with a girl. I also remember receiving a rainbow scarf as a belated Christmas present with the comment, "I hope you don't think I think you're gay" and laughing in her face telling her, "I am!" For years it has been, "yeah, I swing that way. And this way. And whichever way the mood strikes." It was tougher, but now that I'm over eighteen it feels different. Easier. Not a problem. Not my problem. Just my heartbeat.

Of course I remember my first official girl crush, my first girlfriend, but what of the crushes I may not have realised were crushes? The fourth grade teacher whose birthday I would always remember, the elementary school art teacher, the girl whose grandparents owned the campground, my idols Gwen Stefani and Shirley Manson, countless ex-girlfriends of my brothers, and the beautiful Greek girl who came to my seventh grade birthday party. Possibly even girls on the soccer team. I used to want to be the girls I thought were hot, including the ones from the manga I read. By high school, I was already out. I remember getting turned on by my own body in younger years.

Sometimes I considered myself a combination of the best and the worst, as a genderfluid bisexual swinger. Hot whatever gender, perpetually horny, with a thing for queer boys. Like a dolphin, mating for pleasure. Sometimes I have a strong desire to be femme as fuck and other times I want to be bro as fuck and there's no in between. But it's better to know what you like. What you're like.

"Bisexual Movies"

Bisexual movies. As soon as I read the phrase in the book [Bi Any Other Name] I knew exactly what kind of movies this meant. Though my list was not the same as the author's, it still meant the same thing.

It meant the movies I grew up with like the Rocky Horror Picture Show and Billy Elliot. I first saw Rocky Horror around age ten, Billy Elliot I feel like I've known forever. By the time I was thirteen I'd already seen Rocky Horror live and Billy Elliot on Broadway. I had always felt an intense connection to these films.

It meant the kinds of films we watched at Darcy's slumber parties. Why were we twelve and dying to see nipples? It was always movies with topless girls, like American Pie, European Vacation, and Good Luck Chuck.

It meant Rent, which never failed to make me cry, as well as Repo which helped me realise feelings I had for girls. It took a long time to figure out what all of these were for me.

I didn't understand why I liked some of them so much or why I grouped them together in my head.

"Part of Why I'm Gay"

Even at my scariest
I will still get catcalled
not just catcalled
but also honked at

my name is not baby
but even on my ugliest
I will still get groped
by pricks with pricks

#SayBisexual

There was an angry bisexual in Jaime who wondered why it was so hard for people to just say bisexual. Representation mattered to Jaime. She knew that bisexual people made up the majority of the LGBT+ community (52%).

Why, then, did even queer media fail to say the word bisexual? One of Jaime's favourite films was Kaboom, directed by Gregg Arakki. Kaboom's main character was a boy who engaged in sex scenes with people of either gender. He stops in the middle of his own fantasy to clarify that he is not gay but, "undeclared." Shortly after, his best friend dismissed his bisexuality by saying he needed to monitor his drinking. When describing his orientation to his roommate, he said that he "gets with guys sometimes...sexually." When he meets his female lover in the film, he gets offended when she addresses him as "gay dude," but answers, "not exactly" when she asks if he is bi. She later gives him a number rating on the Kinsey scale but never in the film is he referred to as bisexual.

Jaime used to love the film for being a queer film. Now, the angry bisexual in her wanted to hear the word bisexual. She wanted to hear the words pansexual and polysexual. She wanted representation. Everyone did. It made them feel like they weren't alone.

In recent times, out of 66 regular or recurring LGBT characters on scripted cable TV there were 35 gay men, but only 4 bisexual males. Out of 102 LGBT inclusive films released in 2013 there was only one bi male character. Less than 6% of LGBT representation on TV was of bi men, and less than 1% of films in 2013. The lack of representation contributes to systematic bi erasure. The mainstream media was constantly depicting bisexuality as fun, voluntary experimentation, or myth. Many people were beginning to join the school of thought that historically, labels have been used to define the differences between us and that no labels should be the new thing. This combats community unity and identity in a way. Jaime still wanted her representation.

The Bend It Like Beck Effect

As both an English person and a soccer player, Jaime was a proud owner of the film Bend It Like Beckham.

Jaime was passionate about soccer for ten years. It was in her blood. She remembered being terribly upset when she got too old for playing co ed. She loved playing with the boys. She ended up having wonderful experiences on girls' teams, some years with the same team and coaches.

Bend It Like Beckham opened Jaime's eyes. It also gave Jaime some unrealistic expectations.

First of all, one of the characters is played by the beautiful Kiera Knightley. In the movie, she's got short hair, a lean figure, and usually is shown in sporty clothes like track suit bottoms. Talk about drool. Back when Jaime was into the "dykey" type. Plus, her character – she plays a passionate and ambitious sports star.

Second of all, there is a plethora of scenes in which the girls on the team are practising in their sports bras, gorgeous fit bodies glistening with sweat. Can a movie make you gay? This one might have turned Jaime. She wanted soccer to be like that.

Real life girls' soccer was not like that. True, the girls on her team were still attractive in general. They were too young to practise without shirts on (she stopped playing when she was fourteen). Shame for Jaime that none of the girls on her team ended up being queer. They actually gave Jaime a bit of grief when I turned out to be.

The movie also presents a queer male character, who comes out to the main protagonist. She tells him, "it's okay with me."

The movie is also full of interesting stereotypes and drama. The mother of Kiera Knightley's character mistakenly assumes the two main girls are having a lesbian love affair, just because her daughter is the sporty type. The classic line was, "mother, just because I play sport and wear trackies does not make me a lesbian."

The movie offers various reactions by people thinking the girls are lesbians. The movie in itself offered Jaime a perspective that opened her eyes. It's as much a part of Jaime as her passion for the sport is.

Jaime's Gender Confusion

"Bisexuals sometimes do not feel or define themselves as wholly male or female – in earnest desire to dissolve gender roles, we may pretend to achieve androgyny, as if male and female's liberation can be accomplished without arduous and powerful work of unravelling effects of this oppression and realising liberation for all females and males." - Bi Any Other Name

Jaime recognised her body as a girl body, but viewed her soul as genderless, a fluid shapeshifter containing both boy and girl in the same way that she contained both light and dark (and much like she had fingernails that were half mom's half dad's). She recalled one time when Nef said Jaime had no gender, because Jaime used the language of a boy with phrases like, "suck my dick," "I wanna get laid," or with the way that she expressed her thoughts about sexual encounters and people as conquests. Nef also noticed the way Jaime allowed herself switch roles in sexual encounters with either gender – she enjoyed being both dominant and submissive, sometimes for the same person. The last reason that Nef said Jaime had no gender was because Jaime's style of dress was so fluid. One day she could wear a dress or skintight clothing, the next day a baggy shirt and joggers, or she'd even mix collared shirts and skirts.

What creates a "gay relationship"? Two gay people who love each other, correct? For Jaime, any relationship she was in was a gay relationship as she was both genderfluid and bisexual. She called this "Schrödinger's gay," as it also tended to make whoever she was seeing at the time thereby also gay, depending on which gender she felt.

Jaime and Non-Pagan Religion

Jaime recalled visiting with her Catholic grandmother once, and her grandmother brought up Jaime's lesbian cousin's upcoming wedding. Jaime also had a closeted gay male cousin on the same side of the family, a thespian. Her grandma had asked what she thought of the wedding, and "do you think those people have a choice? Do you think they're born like that?"

Jaime had been taken aback, and had to take a moment to construct her answer so as not to give herself away. "Well, Nan, I believe in love and happiness." Her grandmother answered, "if they're happy, they're happy, and they're not hurting anyone." Her grandmother subscribed to Christian kindness and forgiveness, not Catholic fear-based hate. Still, Jaime struggled between what she felt was the honest answer versus the "right" answer. Especially after her grandmother went on to talk about how she thinks that feminists spoiled it for themselves and don't get treated like ladies. Jaime felt a lot of pressure to appear to her grandmother as the sweet, beautiful, good girl that she wanted her to be. She also felt a lot of pressure to be her truth, and spent a lot of time silent, contemplating who she wanted to be outward, knowing who she would always be inward.

Music Education

It was Jaime's dad who was the fan of R.E.M., and why Jaime grew to like the band. She felt their music was soothing, and felt a connection because Brian Molko had been a fan of R.E.M., and had done a song with Michael Stipe, the lead singer. Jaime's mother, however, hated R.E.M., and always made a point to mention the "ugly, gay singer." Jaime never understood why her mother felt she had to vocalise that, especially when she loved David Bowie, who was gay enough, and the Rocky Horror Picture Show.

Jaime grew to feel particularly close to the song

Losing My Religion. She felt that this song expressed feelings of being rejected by personal form of spiritual devotion because of sexuality. Jaime particularly liked the lyric "choosing my confession" because she thought of it as coming out. She deciphered the lyric about being "in the corner losing my religion" as meaning engaging in the physical act of homosexual love. This song made her wonder how people cope with spiritual rejection, and made her think of why queer youth might be at higher risk for substance abuse, among other reasons. Jaime knew that people had an innate desire to get high. She could see that drugs simulated religious experiences, providing shortcuts to spirituality. When people experienced spiritual rejection, it made sense why they might turn to something which simulated spiritual experiences.

Jaime also knew it was important to know your rights and the laws protecting you. These laws were protecting you from becoming a statistic product of society. It made Jaime's faith grow stronger to know that even if she was rejected by religion for who she was attracted to, she was protected for her right to be attracted to them, by some part of the government, at least.

Jaime's Discernment

Jaime often wondered how she was able to discern her polyamorous truth by age fourteen when she was with Todd. Was it the great influence of the Rocky Horror Picture Show or her manga characters in Hana-Kimi? Or was it simply because Todd had been such a no pressure person? Never at any point did Todd force Jaime to be exclusively committed to him, and he never got jealous. He not only had no problem with her bisexuality, but had no comment to make about it. He just let it be a part of her, allowing her to let that part grow larger and healthier, until she reflected her true self. She thought it was a very young age for her to realise that her ideal partner would let her have one partner of each typical gender.

Ore Wa/Manga

Jaime liked manga, Japanese comics. She discovered manga around the age of ten, wandering through a bookstore she frequented with her dad, picking up a magazine to look at while he fingered through a magazine about model trains, the one she happened to pick up was a magazine full of manga, and she was hooked enough to buy it. The manga type the magazine showed was predominantly shoujo manga, which is aimed towards girls. The next time she visited the bookstore, she discovered the manga section, with full books of manga, printed like the Japanese would have, reading from right to left. Along with shoujo, she quickly developed an interest in both yaoi and yuri manga, meaning "boy love" and "girl love," respectively.

Jaime's favourite manga was called "Hana-Kimi: for you in full blossom," which comprised 24 books and starred a crossdressing female character who went to an all boys' school to meet her idol, a jump star. It was probably the first exposure to crossdressing Jaime had, besides perhaps David Bowie. This manga also had a doctor in it who was gay, and a friend of the doctor's who was a bisexual male. Jaime regarded this character as having had quite an influence on her, especially since now she is an out bisexual person.

Because of manga, Jaime took an interest in Japanese language and culture. She studied Japanese for seven years from ages ten to seventeen. She eventually outgrew manga as she grew into her pursuit of the language. She had wanted to cosplay when she was young, but her parents had denied her the ability to go to conventions. Even though she stopped actively reading manga as she grew, she still held it dear in her heart. Because she studied Japanese language, she ended up travelling to Japan through her high school.

In her high school Japanese class, due to anime and manga, Jaime used the self addressment of "Ore" instead of "watashi" one day. Her teacher had asked her not to use it, saying that it was for boys. Typically, boys used the self addressment "boku" while girls used "watashi." Jaime argued the point that she had read in manga and watched in anime instances in which girls used "ore" as well as boys. Her teacher ended up compromising and telling Jaime, "you can use it in Japan and in conversation with friends but not in my classroom." Jaime understood that her teacher had her own thoughts about the self addressment, and for the sake of group harmony, opted to using "Watashi."

The Story of Jaime Before Syd

Jaime grew up many times. First when she was ten. The years from ten to twelve are difficult to explain. By twelve and a half she grew into a questioning individual. At thirteen she began to grow up bisexual.

Growing up a girl was tough enough. Growing up a girl with a sick dad was tough enough. Growing up a bisexual girl was a different story. At thirteen she experienced discrimination, thanks to Benji the Biphobic. At thirteen she experienced her first real heartbreak thanks to Karoline. At fourteen, she was spoiled with a boyfriend who was open minded, though she experienced turmoil in her friend group when Karoline's new, older boyfriend found out about their previous relationship. At fifteen she experienced violence at school, getting assaulted and called a dyke by a girl from her French class who followed her to her locker. At sixteen and seventeen she experienced more discrimination from another boyfriend.

At fifteen, she grew up genderqueer. At fourteen, abandoned by her closest female friends, she grew up as one of the guys. One of the guys in the elementary school parking lot with a skateboard. One of the guys who'd greet Le Feu's parents as they bounded up the stairs to his bedroom. Even Mr. and Mrs. Le Feu, Le Feu's parents, recognised Jaime as one of the guys even though when they met her she was very clearly a girl in her tank top and shorts with her long hair. Liam's parents as well, though they had known Jaime since she was a baby, recognised her as one of the guys, simply because there was something different about her from the kinds of girls that their boys tried to date. Nobody could quite place it, but something about her stuck out.

Benji the Biphobic

Benji Rod is the first Benji Jaime knew, not the fun one she writes letters to. Benji Rod was her third Latino boyfriend. Benji Rod is the first person she came out to on New Year's Day. He said, no way. It was just after they broke up, but they "dated" again. Benji Rod was her first biphobic boyfriend. She couldn't believe she tolerated a second. "You're going to cheat on me with a girl," he argued. Karoline, he thought. Benji Rod had divorced parents. He and Alberto, though friends, had anger issues and controlling natures, possessive tendencies, and a desire for acceptance.

Benji's biphobia came out in several ways. When he couldn't go on a field trip with Jaime, he asked Alberto to watch over her. He wanted Alberto not only to watch over Jaime but to stick close to her, to try and keep her apart from Karoline. Benji never expressed a reason for his lack of trust. A second field trip, he still wanted someone keeping an eye on her. Again, he was asking for her to be kept away from Karoline. It made Jaime nothing but angry.

Benji requested she stop keeping company with her queer friends, like Glitterboii. He called her queer friends extraterrestrials. In an act of absolute mania, he outed her to her mother with intentions of getting her kicked out of her home. Benji the Biphobic was a ball of destruction for Jaime, though after she left him, she went straight to Karoline. She recognised his reason to worry. Still she resented him for his biphobia and its lasting effects on her.

Serviceman Todd

Serviceman Todd is relevant to mention because of Jaime's amazing communication skills at age fourteen. When she was thirteen and fourteen, he was fifteen. He was in the ROTC program at their high school.

Jaime met Todd through Akiko. When they started dating, Jaime discussed her bisexuality with him.

Their first fight was on National Coming Out Day. The GSA at the high school which Jaime was a part of was giving out black bracelets with a pink bead on them to people who wanted to identify themselves as safe listeners. Todd and a friend had made fun of the cause.

At Jaime's first queer convention, she kissed several girls and successfully told Todd about it immediately after. She also successful admitted to him that she wasn't ready to have sex yet. As an open minded fourteen year old, knowing her boyfriend was older, Jaime offered Todd the option to sleep with other girls if he "needed to" while she wasn't ready to sleep with him.

Jaime and Todd parted on good terms after their relationship ended, not really going anywhere. When Todd got older he went into the army. He discussed with her the concept of being "infantry gay" and how some boys in his platoon were afraid of him because he wasn't afraid to kiss another guy.

Todd lost a leg in the army, and spent a lot of his serving time on online dating sites and talking to Jaime about his feelings about his own bisexuality. She often felt like someone from the old days who wrote letters to soldiers, even though they were merely text messaging.

Todd's Poetic Education

"Experience"

Eyes like unakite jasper
stone of protection and perseverance
years ago he had to have her
this time their encounters came by chance

how can it feel so easy?
They just seem to get along
finally someone who isn't sleazy
who doesn't convince her who she is is wrong

what a treat it is to be treated nice
and how fun to still have firsts
though she's sure he can see every vice
considering he's seen her at her worst.

"Who Knows" a Haiku Suite

I said don't fall in
love with me again, I meant
right now but who knows

who knows what this does
who knows how our lives will change
if we'll feel the same

I don't know how to
harness these feelings inside
I'll just let them rock

what does history
and feelings make I don't know
or why I feel deep.

"Maroon Shirt, Coin Skirt"

She thinks herself a mermaid
yet he can separate her legs
she worries about her siren songs
mind full of brainwashing about her wrongs

she's a crystal witch
full of blessings only,
though often called a bitch
she turns his power back on him

intensity helps her to create
she only gives him her good energy
the same she only takes

many protective spells she makes

he thinks she's sweet
she wonders how,
when she must taste of so many others
his kindness for not minding can't be beat.

Todd Tidbits

      Something had always stuck out to Jaime when she had read <u>Balzac and the Little Chinese Seamstress</u> in World Literature class. It was a passage about how two characters had made love standing up, "like horses." She never understood why it stuck with her until she was taken by a fantasy involving Todd, in which her hindquarters invoked the horse spirit and she became a mare as she imagined him mounting and riding her. He let her be as wild and free as a Dartmoor pony. Perhaps that was why that passage stuck out.

      Jaime felt bad when she started watching gay military porn and thinking of Todd, but she couldn't help it. He asked her how she felt about his uniform, which she had never given any thought. He told her some girls had fantasies about military uniforms, so she decided to look up some military porn. Having mostly grown out of porn, anything hetero bored her. Of course, she could still get off to two boys getting off together. She was sort of surprised that Todd hadn't already had a gay experience in the army. He told her that everyone he worked with was gross, and she understood how he felt that way after being with the same people every day for years.

Jaime and Tinder Springs

Candy was Courtney's nickname for Jaime. This is the story of Courtney, Jaime's long distance long time best friend, one of her few female friends.

2,800

Small town, tiny state. Two girls from different states had families who had permanent trailers in an RV resort. It was a popular vacation state because of semi-famous beaches.

They met between seventh and eighth grades. The group of girls out of the campground kids was rather small, and they were introduced by other girls completely by accident. One day Vicki's sister Ashley was with Elyshia and the two of them were intrigued to see another girl around the campground. They discovered her name was Courtney, and took her along. The girls had plans to meet up with one of the only other girls at the campground, as she was arriving that day. Thus, Courtney from California met Candy from Connecticut. The girls naturally exchanged phone numbers after the first meeting during which many laughs were shared.

That's how it was at the campground. The kids flocked to each other. At first, the campground had a big field with a playground, a basketball court, some picnic tables, and a small hut in it across from the pool. As it evolved, a big building was added to the field. The youth of the campground would linger on the field and everything on it. Everyone knew everyone, most people had each other's phone numbers, Myspaces, Facebooks, and video chat accounts. There were friends, there were cliques, there were crushes, and there were enemies. Courtney and Candy became friends.

There was a group of boys who weren't too fond of Candy. Candy had once told another girl, Celeste, that a boy called Ray was cute and everyone ended up thinking that she had a crush on him. His friends didn't think she was very cool because of things she said about her beliefs when she was eleven. Naturally, when the boys met Courtney they were astonished that she was from California since it was so far away from the state Tinder Springs was in. Courtney didn't really mind the boys, and wanted to hang out with them. Candy was reluctant, because of questions that they had asked her before, but agreed. It may have been when Courtney told off Lou S'Bara (back then called Fat Lou as there were two boys called Louis at the campground) for grabbing Candy's boobs out of her tube top without permission that they truly became friends for real.

  For the first year of their friendship they mostly texted and sometimes talked on the phone. It was the year Candy came out but she didn't bother to tell Courtney (she had told Elyshia and the response wasn't pleasant). One day that summer, they met up at a mall. Candy sent Courtney a postcard from her family vacation that summer.

  During their freshman years, Candy got a boyfriend called Todd, while Courtney obsessed over a boy called Johnson. They talked over the phone, over text, and video chat. Candy started going to her school's straight and gay alliance. Courtney made friends with two girls, Stella South and Kylie Morgan, and partied with them. Candy cheated on Todd and kissed girls she met at an event she had gone to with her school's straight and gay alliance on the bus on the way home during a game of truth or dare. Courtney told Candy one day, "I think I'm bi-curious."

  Candy was pleased, and told Courtney about how she was actually bisexual and hadn't come out to her. The girls were fairly close. Courtney called Candy when she got her first kiss (from a boy) at fourteen. Courtney also told Candy about the girls she had started experimenting with, including her friends Kylie and Stella. Candy recalled to Courtney her first girl experience with her ex-best-friends slash ex-girlfriend and the experiences she had had with the straight and gay alliance event girls on the bus. Somewhere in the mix of planning when they would see each other next at the

RV resort, they also planned to experiment with each other. The girls had worked it out with Todd (who wouldn't have been there to stop it anyway).

      Candy's family had sold their trailer, but it had been arranged that she would stay at Courtney's family's trailer and also at her grandparents' house, from where her mother would pick her up. The first day she got to Tinder Springs, Courtney told Candy she wanted to hang out at Ray's friend' Jose Verriagos' family's trailer. Candy was apprehensive about hanging out with the boys because of how mean and rude they could be, but Courtney insisted, so Candy reluctantly agreed. When they got to Jose's trailer, he was laying in his bed with a few of his and Ray's other friends watching ESPN on his park model loft TV. He was quite literally tucked into bed, under the covers in the middle of the summer with Alex Denning, Kyle Tuthe, and Jake Bratt. Jose Verriagos was famously hailed as "The tree" due to his tall and lanky stature. Jose Verriagos was between a year and two years older than Candy and Courtney. At a campground where so many people lied about their ages, it was hard to remember and keep track of how old everyone really was, the youth just assumed they were all somewhere in the same age range. Courtney was freshly fifteen at the time, and Candy, whose birthday was in November, was still just fourteen caught between freshman and sophomore year. The girls had been let in by Jose's dad, who brought him McDonald's and apple flavored baby cigars and then promptly left. The only thing more interesting than sports and smoking to Mr. Jose Verriagos "the tree" of Tinder Springs was seeing Courtney and Candy kiss because he had heard from Courtney about her bi curiosity and about Candy's bisexuality, and how they planned to hook up and experiment with each other.

      For this unique day, Candy was not entirely an uncool, creepy loser. Candy, with her bleach blond curls, tight blue t-shirt, short boardshorts, and perky B-cups could actually have been considered hot by these boys. If, of course, she kissed Courtney (which she was all for, especially considering the way Courtney looked in her tiny green shorts), and if she kissed her in front of them. Candy and Courtney both knew that they looked good enough to be called "hot" by both boys and girls, to be grabbed at and catcalled and to be asked to do things or to date. Courtney felt a little like she had something to prove to these boys, and she said to Candy on the walk to Jose's trailer, "you'll see. They won't be so mean anymore. They'll see. I grew boobs and I grew an ass and they'll think we're hot." Candy recalled previous summers, and during one of the early times of knowing Courtney, Murphy Stephens had said to her, "you're from California? Aren't girls from California supposed to be hot?"

  Jose Verriagos was a stoner, and Candy was a stoner in the making. He let her smoke one of his apple flavored baby cigars, out of uncharacteristic act of kindness. Jose Verriagos' family's trailer was different from the trailers that Courtney and Candy's families had at their sites at the campground. His trailer was what's called a park model, which essentially means that it stays parked in one place as opposed to some of the trailers at the campground which were drivable or towable. His trailer – park model – looked like a small house. It was painted yellow on the outside, and when you walked in the first room was like a sunroom or a porch. Through a sliding door was the rest of the trailer – to the right a small bathroom, kitchen, and living room area with a door to a master bedroom, and straight ahead, stairs to the loft, which was Jose's room on one side and storage space on the other. Jose's "room" was only about six stairs up carpeted steps, and contained a mattress on the floor (which the boys were laying on), blankets (which the boys were laying under), a camp TV, cable box, an Xbox with controllers and games, and one of those soft, circular fold up chairs. Candy planted herself at the top of the stairs, with her back against the wall, on guard against the boys and the closest to the exit. Courtney sat beside her, also with her back against the wall, but closer to the boys in the room. Eventually, someone said what they were all thinking.

  "So, are you gonna kiss her?"

  Candy smirked. She said, "yeah," and leaned over

and planted a kiss on Courtney's lips. Candy always thought one thing about kissing girls – they were softer than boys. The boys applauded and Candy leaned back, satisfied. This time, Courtney leaned in to kiss Candy, and Candy's head hit the bumpy walls of Jose's trailer as Courtney slipped her the tongue.

"Damn," rang a voice that was distinctively belonging to Alex Denning. "They're getting into it!"

Candy grinned into Courtney's lips. When she was eleven, Jose Verriagos and his friend Riley Jackson, also known as Dusty, had asked her if she knew what a dyke was.

The girls spent most of the afternoon attached at the lips. The boys didn't do much talking, but when they did, they made jokes or talked about girls or sports. Jake Bratt took a video of Candy and Courtney kissing at one point.

"Send that to me!" Candy demanded, but he did not ever send her the video of her kissing her friend.

Jake Bratt peed in a water bottle one of the days that Courtney and Candy hung out at Jose Verriagos' family's trailer, and he threw it across the loft (closed, luckily for the girls) while the girls were kissing at one point. The first day the girls were at Jose Verriagos' family's trailer, Alex Denning nearly killed them all trying to make s'mores in the microwave and setting off the smoke alarm.

Courtney and Candy had some times with the boys at Jose Verriagos' family's trailer, but none could forget when Courtney and Jose Verriagos shared a kiss in the loft of his family's trailer. A few of Jose Verriagos' friends witnessed the kiss, including Alex Denning. Candy, of course also witnessed the kiss between the boy and the girl.

That summer, Courtney and Candy got kicked out of a pharmacy for causing shenanigans and kissing in the aisles. The girls planned a Christmas visit, since Courtney would be on that side of the United States at that time of the year to visit her family. Candy and Todd broke up.

The beginning of sophomore year was trying for the girls. The girls were now always on the phone with each other.

In December, before she came out to the east coast,

while she was on the phone long distance to Connecticut, Courtney said, "you're my girlfriend."

Candy continued with her typical homework on the phone routine with Courtney, wrote down more notes, and agreed into the phone.

"Okay?! Okay," Courtney said, and then continued with her Candy phone routine as well.

The girls could've been on the phone or video chat with each other for up to fourteen hours at that time. They would do a lot of their tasks while on the phone like homework or eating.

Courtney told people at her school about her girlfriend who lived across the country, but she still kissed people where she lived. She would just tell Candy about it, and Candy would agree into the phone by saying, "okay."

Candy was excited. She told all the boys that she hung out with about her hot girlfriend who lived across the country. She told people in her classes at school about her girlfriend who lived across the country. That month, Candy spoke aloud in front of the teacher and students in French class about her girlfriend and a girl in her French class followed her to her locker between classes and as Candy bent down to switch some of her textbooks, her classmate kicked her in the back and called her a dyke.

Courtney came to visit at Candy's house when there was nearly six feet of snow on the ground. She met an interesting cross section of Candy's friends. Courtney and Candy had never hung out with together with anyone from outside of the campground before, so Candy had been excited to introduce Courtney to her friends, and Courtney had been excited to meet the people Candy always told stories about. The people Candy spent time with were interested to meet Courtney, as some of them had talked to Courtney on the phone, or heard stories of Courtney. Courtney had a unique personality.

Candy introduced Courtney to her typical female companion at the time, Rochelle, and the three girls walked around the town Candy lived in visiting her guy friends. Rochelle and Courtney got along fine. Candy didn't have the best timing with her friends, and her, Courtney, and Rochelle accidentally woke up her friend Keith, and Candy could only introduce her friend Le Feu to Courtney for a few seconds. Courtney did get to spend a good amount of time with Candy's close friend Liam. Liam came to Candy's house to hang out with her and Courtney, and the girls went over to Liam's house with Rochelle to hang out with some other people. Courtney met Candy's friend J.Emballer in Liam's basement. Keith and Le Feu were there too, Keith was with his girlfriend Tina. Liam was with his girlfriend Carmela, doing something under a blanket on the couch. Somehow that night Courtney and Rochelle made out.

Courtney came to breakfast with Candy's family during the sleepover. Neither of the girls were out to their families or told their families about their relationship. Snuggled in Candy's tiny twin bed, Courtney requested access to Candy's panties. Candy denied it, but Courtney went ahead anyway. She could be unstoppable.

Courtney was the kind of a girl who would wear booty shorts and a crop top with snow on the group that was as tall as she was. She went back home to the Golden State of California, and the girls continued their long distance relationship. They wrote letters, mailed packages, and even started a shared journal which they mailed back and forth. Candy loved having a girlfriend, especially one who didn't care if she sometimes kissed other people, which she did. Candy loved showing Courtney off when she had come to visit and she loved spoiling her. When Courtney left that winter, she hooked up with another girl, too.

Their relationship continued until the summer. Candy went back to visit Courtney at her family's trailer at Tinder Springs for a few days. That summer, Courtney had brought her friend Kylie Morgan along to visit the East Coast and see the sights and Courtney's family, and, of course, meet Candy. Courtney assumed Candy and Kylie would get along – they were both bisexual stoners. Kylie was one of the friends with whom Courtney had experimented back in freshman year. Candy and Kylie got along well enough for Kylie to become the personal photographer for their relationship, coining the quote that later became famous to Candy and Courtney's friendship, "smile, you stupid lesbian."

That was the summer Candy and Courtney met Veronica LaSallio. They had only ever read Veronica LaSallio's name online as mentioned by the boys who frequented Tinder Springs RV Resort. They met Veronica LaSallio at the basketball court picnic tables, where the youth of the campground convened. Candy found her to be strikingly beautiful, even in gym shorts and a hoodie, because Veronica had a stunning facial structure and was quite slim with a dark, curly ponytail. However, Candy knew well enough from the internet that Veronica LaSallio was dating Jose Verriagos. When Candy got up to talk to one of the boys, Veronica and Courtney got to talking. Before Candy knew what was going on, Alex Denning and a few of the other boys had flocked over to Courtney and Veronica were screaming, "no, no, she's lying, and that never happened Veronica don't worry."

Courtney ran over to Candy with Kylie, grabbed her hand, and started pulling her away.

"Candy, let's go. I think Veronica wants to fight me."

The girls started off in the direction of Courtney's family's trailer.

"Uh, Court, why exactly does Veronica LaSallio want to fight you?"

Courtney started laughing nervously.

"Court...what did you say to her??"

"Uhhh... I kind of told her about how I kissed Jose Verriagos last summer.. and apparently they were dating back then."

"Oh, good God Court you couldn't keep your mouth shut? Now I'm Going to have to fight her if she tries to fight you."

Candy tensed up. She knew how to fight, and she had brought the small weapons her older brother had made for her after that girl in her French class assaulted her at school.

Courtney was scared. Veronica had seemed very upset with her, and Courtney was too scared to leave her trailer.

"If I go outside, Veronica will beat me up," Courtney had said to Candy.

Kylie Morgan was annoyed at her friend.

"This trip sucks!" she whined. "I just want to go outside and see people and do something!"

Kylie Morgan was more unreasonable than Courtney was. Courtney was prettier, nicer, and more thoughtful, but Kylie was mean and push (which is why their friendship did not work out). Kylie demanded that they go outside. Courtney refused to leave her family's trailer. Kylie decided to walk out of Courtney's family's trailer and Candy had to follow her because she could not let Kylie go out to those people because Kylie did not know how they could be. Courtney was furious but did not dare to leave the safety of her family's trailer.

Outside of Courtney's family's trailer and deeper into the campground, Candy and Kylie naturally ran into the rest of the campground's youth. Veronica was still in tears, and to Candy's pleasure, Jose Verriagos was nowhere to be found. Veronica was with Alex Denning and Jake Bratt, both of whom had witnessed Courtney and Jose Verriagos kissing the same day Candy had at Jose's family's trailer the previous summer. The boys, however, had been insisting to Veronica that Courtney was lying because she just had a crush on Jose or something.

"Candy!" Veronica called, wanting to get her attention and talk to her. They stepped away from Kylie and the boys, and Veronica said, "girl to girl, what's going on here?"

Candy was an honest girl, and looked Veronica right in the eyes when she told her the truth.

"Last summer at Jose's trailer, I saw him and Courtney kiss." Candy explained. "But Courtney didn't know that you and Jose were dating at the time I mean he didn't say anything and neither did any of his friends and he kind of initiated it, "Candy nervously rushed, but Veronica looked ready to listen.

"Listen, I would say you've got a jerk of a boyfriend

to deal with but it's been a year, hasn't it? Does it really even matter? I'll keep my girl in like, and she won't talk to Jose," Candy reasoned.

"She better not!" Veronica grumbled.

"Don't threaten me, Veronica." Candy stood her ground.

Veronica looked Candy up and down. "Okay," she crossed her arms. "But I have to threaten her so that she knows that if she ever touches my man again I will beat her up." Veronica tried to seem tough.

Candy chuckled, acknowledging her own jealous side and said, "fair enough."

Veronica told Kylie and the boys her new feelings while Candy called Courtney.

"Court, Veronica is NOT going to hit you, but will you come out and talk to her?"

"Noo, Candy, she's gonna hit me!"

"Courtney, I promise you she is not going to hit you. She just wants to tell you to stay away from Jose."

Eventually Candy got Courtney to agree, and walked over to Courtney's family's trailer with Veronica, Kylie, and the boys. She watched very closely as Veronica and Courtney talked. Alex Denning and Jake Bratt watched Veronica threaten Courtney if she was going to talk to Jose. It was all very dramatic. Apparently, Jose and Ray had been hiding out that night anyway.

Courtney, Kylie, and Candy spent a few days together. Kylie got mad because one night on th other side of the divider Candy and Courtney hooked up. Candy had been annoyed with Courtney most of the trip because of the Veronica drama, because Courtney had been being rude to her mom and grandparents, and because Courtney had been on her period and Candy didn't get a chance to do anything to Courtney when they hooked up. Candy didn't like being out of control, and she also liked taking the typical "boy role" in their relationship. But because Courtney was her girlfriend, Candy let her do what she wanted. She figured that was what you were supposed to do. The next day, Courtney told some of the campground boys that her and

Candy had had sex, so Candy counted it as her first time with a girl, even though she didn't really think it could count. Candy got picked up a few days later than she was supposed to due to a family problem.

Later that summer, Candy and Courtney called it quits, but decided to remain friends. It was a mutual break up. Courtney and Candy had never really fallen in love with each other, they had just sort of tried it out. They had both liked the feelings of being in a relationship but they both felt like they didn't really do it right.

In the autumn, the girls both got boyfriends. Candy visited the West Coast and stayed at Courtney's house that winter. Candy fell in love with California. Later in life candy was around for when Courtney's parents got divorced. The next time they saw each other they had both lost their boyfriends. That year Candy took Courtney to her job and also introduced her to other friends. Courtney smoked with Candy and her friends. Every time they parted they would say that they were only a phone call away. At the end of their senior year, Courtney got a boyfriend, Candy had a short term girlfriend, and before Candy started college she got a boyfriend as well.

While Courtney dated Tiberius, she said some things to Candy that made Candy feel sad and hurt even though the girls had admitter how their relationship was never real. Courtney had told Candy that she would never be attracted to a girl again and that sex with girls didn't count as sex. Although Candy's boyfriend Julio didn't count hooking up with girls as cheating, Candy counted sex with girls as sex. That winter, Candy went out West to visit Courtney and met Tiberius, who was rude to the both of them. Tiberius made fun of Candy for never going down on Courtney when they dated. Candy made out with Tiberius' friend Juliette in Courtney's bed one day and booked her trip home early, but the girls remained friends. During their friendship, they ended up with their tongues pierced. Candy rid herself of her boyfriend Julio and finally had a somewhat more real experience with a girl. Courtney continued to date Tiberius and came to visit Candy at the end of the summer. That

Halloween she was done with Tiberius.

Courtney came to visit Candy that winter and met Candy's short-lived ex-girlfriend Sammie under bizarre circumstances. Courtney met a girl on the internet and started dating her. The girl lived on the same coast as Candy, but in a different state. Courtney started telling Candy that she was a lesbian and that she would never be into guys again. Most of the time, Candy would roll her eyes. Courtney flew out to meet the girl, and flew out a second time just to see her. The second time, Courtney and the girl, Christina, broke up, and Courtney took a train up a few states to Candy's while she figured out how she was going to get home. Candy took Courtney to party at April's house, which is where Courtney met the two strung out girls Candy had sort of been with, April and Logan. April and Candy had cheated on each other with boys they ended up dating. They had been too young without cars to make a relationship across town lines work when they wanted to see each other. Logan had been at the time on again off again dating a boy and while she was off with him, and Candy was single, they got off with each other briefly. It was a time Candy felt insecure about. Courtney was friendly with April and Logan though she knew their stories. While Courtney stayed with Candy, she started talking to a girl online who lived in Courtney's area and who was also a lesbian. Her name was Rain.

Courtney and Rain became extremely close friends in the months to follow. Courtney worked hard and visited Rain often. Then, her mother planned a move for them to the same state as Candy lived, an hour away from Candy's house and in the same area as Courtney's mom's family.

Courtney and Candy were excited to finally live close enough to each other to regularly hang out. Courtney was also really sad to leave her new friend Rain back home, and made plans to move back and stay with Rain as friends.

2,800 miles had not been enough to come between Candy and Courtney's friendship for some reason, and neither wanted to lose the other. Though they never had romantic feelings toward each other, they planned their lives together and hoped to become successful people who had had good experiences in their youth. Candy and Courtney always tried to be supportive of each other.

B-Boy Feori

Jaime met Feori when she first started dating Todd, when he busted out a backflip on the beach. He was a dancer and a wushu artist. He danced ballet and classical styles as well as hip-hop. Jaime thought he was beyond cute but he had a reputation for being a bit of a boyslut. This scared Jaime, because she knew he wasn't a virgin. She feared that if she fell for his charm he would want to have sex with her. She loved his campy, somewhat questionable personality as well as his looks but tried to keep her distance, knowing their shared tendency to flirts. (Plus, Jaime had Todd, who she really enjoyed being with.)

But one day, Jaime invited Feori over, and he ended up kissing her. She made him tell Todd, because she felt it was wrong even though she liked it. She told Todd about every time she kissed someone else (and, therefore, cheated on him). She felt better that way. Guilt ate at her.

Feori Backstory

At thirteen, Glitterboii had invited Jaime and the rest of their friends to a party on the beach for Center Kids. It was Jaime's first event out with Todd as a couple, and the first time she had ever met Feori. There's a photo of Jaime scowling because someone had mentioned how small she was. In typical Jaime fashion at the time, she had run around the party taking photos of all these strangers, who would later become her school friends. Besides Glitterboii and their group, the only one Jaime knew was Oliver, back when he was still going by Akiko. It was Jaime's first time meeting Akiko's girlfriend, Dromi.

Jaime wasn't sure why she was so into Feori when she was thirteen and met him. She vividly remembered the day she met him, at that party at the beach, where he busted out a backflip. She was starstruck, having never seen anyone do a backflip before. He threw it like it was nothing, kicking up sand. She noticed his puppy dog face, his sunshine hair, but not the way she noticed those acrobatic skills.

While Jaime was dating Todd, she harboured a crush on Feori the whole time. Being scared by his reputation, she didn't have enough of a crush to leave Todd. They hung out sometimes in school, but not much because Feori was a few years older than Jaime. They were text message friends, selfie sending friends, Center Kid friends. As she got older, Jaime couldn't quite remember the substance of their conversations. She knew that they talked about sex, and that was about all she could remember.

Jaime had always been fascinated by Feori. He would throw backflips anywhere, and if he stood for too long or there was music around, he would start moving and dancing. He was classically trained in ballet, which also fascinated Jaime. When she thought of boys doing ballet, she thought of Billy Elliot. He consistently fascinated Jaime for years after he stopped going to the Center.

After Jaime and Todd broke up, Feori visited the Center to give a wushu performance. Stoked to see him again, Jaime waited up after the performance, and they shared a kiss in the hallway. Jaime remembered Rosie making fun of how happy she was when she went down to lunch. Courtney also loved Feori, texting him from California after seeing his photo on Jaime's phone.

Slowly, Jaime and Feori rifted out of each other's lives. Feori changed schools and subsequently went away to college. He stayed in the place he'd gone to school, liking the atmosphere and opportunity. Jaime pursued her ambitions and got trained to be two different types of teacher. They didn't even chat, for Jaime feared that she would annoy him while he was off chasing his dreams, and she felt that most conversation was useless since they couldn't hang out. They had scarce, brief conversations about how great his sets looked or when he was returning to the state in which Jaime lived.

When Jaime was dating Sydney, and working at Yooso, she and Feori were meant to meet up. They had been planning to practise at her studio. Sydney, however, was not having any of that. He said flat out to Jaime, "I don't want you to do yoga with some guy who you think is good looking, especially not acro where he'll be touching you."

Jaime was unfazed.

"You could always come, Sydney. Then you'd see for yourself that nothing would happen."

"Why would I want to watch you do yoga with some guy you think looks good while he'd be touching you?!" Syd scoffed.

Jaime sighed. "I just can't win with you, Sydney."

She was right, of course, because bad men were not prizes. Yet she still catered to Sydney's insecurity. Thus, Feori and Jaime did not meet up that winter.

"Edit"

He fascinated her
with his body isolation
his pure concentration
and understanding of himself

She submit to him
almost completely
to see what he could teach her
learning that somehow she'd struck him

the way she is struck by
the sky and its contents-
the moon, stars, sun, and colours
such a sweet dance they shared.

"High School Crush"
She loved the way the waves
crashed into the sand
were she the water when they crashed into each other?
She had to grab his hand

he used it to help her turn

to face them through the mirror's glass
sparks overdue to burn
each obsessed with the other's ass

watching her own face
listening to his words
all pleasure, little grace
they flew high as birds

he said she laughed during sex
she blushed, forgetting
he didn't know she was
like a teapot

she steamed until she screamed
and then she overflowed
the times that she brewed happy tea
were the only ones she wanted him to see

he'd said she was a ball of energy
just like when they were in school
she saw him a ball of passion's light
following his gifts to dance all night
she made him know that while his body was hot
she liked most that part of his soul which was cool.

"Two Hypersexual"

He recognised her as the goddess she was
so she felt through the respect he treated her with
even when the loving was rough and dirty
it was strong and steady
built on mutual admiration
steeped in concentration
lovemaking as moving meditation
accepting and connecting
worthy they were for this worship
meeting for a moment in a place between time and space
meeting, pausing, breathing to create.

"Vital Energy"

It wasn't just teaching
they were moving together
[together] they were breathing

later, after their energy swap
with her hand on his anahata
she could feel the force of his prana

we are not breathing,
we are breathed
moved by his prana to move with ease.

"Soul Food"

Polyamory often gets a bad rep
with swingers described as
people who can't commit
or are afraid to try
yet what a lie
for dancer boy and yoga girl are living proof
breathing their truth
with pure dedication to their craft
to claim they can't commit would be daft
their earnest commitment is to the self.

"Friendship Set on Fire"

It was just my luck
that my camera decided to stop
recording what would have been
the most valuable shots
of us comparing and contrasting,
learning and teaching,
living and breathing
I was uncharacteristically in the moment
fully present, no eyes behind a lens

enjoying the vibe, enjoying the zen
at least my luck held out to see him
at least his lips set fire to my skin
so I can't be sad
I can only be glad
and ever so grateful
for the moments we shared
the special times we had
so meaningful to my growth
to practise with someone who knows
how moving works, how bodies create
finally understanding why
our friendship was started by fate.

"Sun Showers"

A secret, savoury moment
for her memory box
scrapbooking the sand from his back
as he sprayed her chest
pausing for a kiss
full of laughter
sharing a breath
their first washing shared
with comfort and ease that she'd miss.

      One day, Jaime was pleasantly surprised to find out that she had her chance to flow with Feori because he was visiting his home state. They practised on the beach together, she did yoga while he practised tricking – handstands, forearm stands, flips, handsprings, and power moves. Jaime had a beautiful time practising with him between the sand and sky, watching the waves go by. There they were, secrets shared and bi with bi, enjoying presence as Jaime uncharacteristically took no pictures to remember it by. She even got him to help her fly.

Weekend at Feori's

Jaime drove to Feori's house after a double dose of Camp Prom at the community centre, and arrived in her orange dress. She took a few minutes sitting on his couch to focus on breathing after being at work all day, and he stared at her. When they started talking, she was cheerful.

"I'm in awe," Feori started. "You're a ball of energy, just like you were in high school."

Jaime knew it was no coincidence that Ponytail Ash had also recently referred to her light, but a synchronistic reflection of her ability to connect with others.

Jaime had been direct with Feori before going over about her willingness to sleep with him but he did not mention it when she arrived. The moment struck them and suddenly they were kissing. He whispered questions of consent into her ear and automatically knew what to do with her. He made a point of asking what she liked, too, and when he said something he wanted to do with her, he added, "I hope it's something you'd consent to." Their sexual chemistry was undeniable, and Feori was thrilled with Jaime's performance. Jaime was thrilled to have such a positive encounter.

Jaime knew that Feori knew she had always had a crush on him. She made sure he knew that she didn't objectify him, that she wasn't just lusting after him. She told him how attractive it was that he had been passionate at such a young age when she'd met him, and had been chasing his passion ever since.

Feori ordered them diner and they cuddled and caught up. As they caught up, Feori casually came out to Jaime, weaving into conversation when something came up about her bisexuality.

"Funny story," he'd said. "I'm bi."

"I figured," she said, then blushed. "That's hot," she giggled.

She told him about seeing Todd recently, and he told

her he thought Todd was pretty. He also told her that he was always a top, and that he was very dominant.

Jaime had a tendency to learn the people she spent time with like she learned her students. She stored all the information she learned about them and used it when necessary. She'd noticed that many of her close friends were both touch and movement based, like Liam, Le Feu, Sean, and Feori. They all had inclinations to move and had trouble sitting or standing still. Jaime had given Sean a twiddle cube for this reason. She noticed that Feori was one of those kinds of people when they were cuddling on the couch and he was unintentionally jittering his leg. She knew that for most of her friends, the fidgeting was a symptom of anxiety, so she asked, "What's on your mind, Feori?" When he answered, "music," she smiled, glad that he wasn't anxious about being alone with her. She knew she could be intense, even when the intensity manifested positively, like with her extreme excitement.

Feori's physical inclinations made Jaime wonder how he would do with flow arts and she asked if he had ever heard of poi. He told her that some poi skills were similar to the wushu chain he'd used before, and that he could show her some moves with a staff as well.

He told her, "the most romantic thing than anyone could do for me is to dance with me."

Jaime could tell that movement was that important to Feori.

Feori was the kind of boy who wanted poetry written about him. He knew he deserved the poetry. To some, Feori seemed cocky, arrogant, vain, and conceited. He was also stubborn with strong opinions, and a feisty attitude. To Jaime, she felt like he had opened himself to her when he showed her poetry that one of his lovers wrote about him, she didn't think it was narcissistic. When Jaime complimented his appearance, he told her that he put a lot of work into maintaining it. She laughed because that was the answer she gave people often. Having always thought she had been blessed with good looks until she realised that she had been an athlete during her formative years. She imagined Feori felt similarly, as a dancer, the difference being that what he practised was his passion. Both of them became bashful when complimented by the other. They both were also the type to track their athletic progress through photos and videos.

Before they went to bed, Jaime said to Feori, "I wonder what it's like to really know you, to be close to you."

She wondered if she one day might get to know. Uncharacteristically, Jaime fell asleep with ease next to Feori. She felt she was lucky that she didn't have nightmares. She was glad to learn his light energy kept them away.

Feori had told Jaime about how one of his lovers painted him as he slept. They discussed how he had the figure to be painted, so Jaime could understand why Feori's lover would want him as a subject. He replied, "I'd be totally cool with being painted if it was something I had consented to." Then he told Jaime how this particular girl took photos of him while he was sleeping, and then used them as reference for later painting. It made Jaime angry. As a former life model, she knew Feori would be great at being a life model, but his consent was the most important thing. She was overwhelmed by the instinct of the bear within her to protect this twenty-four year old man from the people who wanted his body without asking his permission.

Jaime woke up early and admired Feori while he slept. Jaime respected Feori so much, that when she decided she wanted morning sex, she stopped in the middle of kissing him.

"What is it?" he asked.

"I just want to make sure you're awake enough to want this," she whispered.

"Really?" he was surprised to be asked for his consent.

"Yeah, really, I want to make sure that I'm not taking advantage of you."

Feori smiled. "I want this," he whispered, and Jaime went back to kissing him and smiled into his lips.

After a few rounds, they headed downstairs to the kitchen, where Feori decided to make them some scrambled eggs and broccoli. He started telling Jaime about how he was working on getting off of eating meat because it was not environmentally sustainable. They sat on the couch in his living room, eating and talking. Jaime let Feori nap in her lap until she eventually got up to take a shower and start their day.

Over breakfast they had talked about their bisexual polyamory and how it was actually hard to be promiscuous.

"You have to be okay with a totally casual experience," Jaime pointed out.

"Yes, exactly," Feori agreed. "And you have to be able to have open conversations about safety, sexuality, and boundaries. Otherwise it's not healthy, and you have to be able to have healthy adult sexual relationships or else there's no point cause it's not good for you."

Jaime told him that she had found that it was much easier to have such necessary conversations with people that she was maintaining ongoing sexual relationships with, because people involved in one night stands were usually more likely to only care about themselves.

As they were getting ready, Feori asked why she was smiling so much.

"I just can't believe that I finally got to hook up with the hottest guy I've ever met."

Feori was in disbelief, and Jaime had to explain that he was the only person who had consistently remained attractive to her, and that his personality made him just as hot as his looks did.

On the way to the beach, they had amusing conversations. Feori started talking about boys.

"My problem is that men are disgusting," Feori said.

"Yeah, mine, too!" Jaime laughed.

"It's kind of bad, but it's kind of a dominance thing for me with boys," Feori started.

"No way!" Jaime exclaimed.

"Yeah, I really like to get with guys who are bigger than me." Feori started laughing. "I once avoided a fight by yelling at the dude, 'I fuck guys bigger than you, so you want some of this? Cause you're just turning me on!' Straight guys are so scared of guys who do guys because they don't want to get treated the way they treat women."

On the beach, Jaime rolled out her mat. They each went to practise their own things. Jaime gave herself a full, heart opening yoga class type flow. Feori worked on drilling skills. Jaime liked the way he just went into movement mode and wasn't staring at what Jaime was doing. She didn't like to be watched in that way when she was practising, so she admired his professionalism. She was surprised to notice how much she didn't notice Feori practising while she was. She knew he was throwing tricks, she could hear it, see it through her peripherals, and she caught a few tricks when she happened to be facing him in an upward position. When she was younger, she was too in awe of the way that he could throw tricks, she could not move before him. In the sun on that beach, she moved with him and felt the energy from it. Out loud he took a moment to point out that she could do things he couldn't.

Later in the day at a friend's, they got to practising acroyoga. Somehow the practise turned into comparing skills, asking each other excitedly, "can you do this?" "is this something you do?" They ended up teaching each other some skills. Jaime liked learning what some poses were called in the dance world. It made it like learning a language.

Jaime noticed that children could be fearless, and that age made us more afraid to do things, even things we've done many times before. Jaime's most relevant example was forming relationships with people, but she noticed that this concept applied to things like taking physical risks and speaking one's mind. This concept showed to Jaime when she noticed her fear of annoying Feori by trying to build more of a relationship with him by talking to him more after they had finally seen each other. Jaime had formed tons of relationships in her past, yet at twenty-one it seemed nearly impossible to her.

Gods and Monsters

"One of my favourite games to play with Phillip is one that we call Gods and Monsters," Glitterboii began. Jaime had been buzzing to him, overflowing with information from experiential learning regarding both Feori and Todd, and emotions about it all.

"How can we compare our sexual experiences with people when we know everyone is different, yet still feel as though we'd prefer someone over someone else?"

Glitterboii went on to explain the game.

"Comparing people to gods and monsters, trying to find ways to compare people and places today to ancient mythology helps to break away from comparing all of these real things to other real things. Constantly comparing, we run the risk of dehumanising people if we spend too much time breaking apart their personality, but when you take somebody as a whole, it's harder to compare them, so we also look at pieces of them. Comparing can become like trying to fuse two puzzles together."

"Okay," Jaime agreed. "Then Feori is like Adonis – good looking, and he is also like Xochilpilli – full of passion and dance. From Mercury, he found music and gymnastics. Though, I could see him getting mercurial, he is rather intense. Todd is like Macha and Freyja, because of the battle in his life, yet also like Freyr and Avalokiteshvara – peaceful and listens."

As she compared mythology, Jaime had revelations. The reason she didn't get why Feori had stayed so attractive to her after all those years was because he wasn't just Adonis to her. What similarities he had to Xochilpilli and Mercury heightened his beauty in her eyes. She knew, though, that she also liked and wanted those peaceful and listening qualities of Freyr and Quan Yin. She wondered if anyone had all the divine similarities she felt she needed, and wondered if she was a polyamorist because of the many combinations of divine similarities that she might find. Sometimes she tried to seek these answers when she slept with ancient deities during crystal ritual.

Jaime noticed that Feori and Todd shared what she considered to be a fault. She also knew that what we don't like about others was a map of what we don't like about ourselves, and with that in mind she knew that, as a millennial, she was guilty of this fault, too – spending too much time on their phones. She knew that there were similarities between Feori and Todd, including both of them being bi, into comic books and video games, having anxiety, and being genuinely nice to women. Their similarities and how truly difficult it was to compare them made it just as hard for Jaime to "decide" between them as it was to choose only boys or girls. She felt lucky not having to decide between them, as all three of them were polyamorists, and she stopped thinking about comparing them altogether. Since discovering Glitterboii's game, Jaime preferred to compare herself to deities as well, seeing a myriad of them in the mosaic of her being. She knew that flowers did not compare themselves to the ones blooming next to them. Jaime was a shapeshifter, knowing that like Krishna she contained multitudes. When recognising her inner divinity, she was recognising that she had been created in the image of the divine, and that everything she would do would be returned into the world, with the purpose of creating more divine light. Nothing would stay, not even her one day.

Teaching Feori

Feori had asked Jaime about access to the studio she'd worked at, and when she told him that it had gone out of business, she had offered to find out if she could teach him in the studio room at the community centre where she was currently working. Jaime had gotten very lucky, and the director had given her the okay. Jaime was slightly in disbelief that Feori thought he could learn from her. She was both flattered and inspired by it, and tried to write him a class that was challenging and gave him what he asked for in his body.

When she taught him, she could tell that the class was both accessible and challenging. She could tell it had relaxed him, she felt the shift in his energy. She was fascinated by what it was like to teach someone who was so body aware, and who was familiar with vigorous training. Every so often Feori would say something. "Oh, I do this differently, look, this is how." "I need to practise this more." "I'm gonna use this one." Jaime was amazed at the way she could see him learning from her and taking what he learned to make it his own.

After class, Feori told Jaime that she was skillful at teaching, and that he knew she was serious about her craft. He also talked about how he was born to break (dance) and Jaime was happy to hear about his passion. Then he talked to Jaime about how he pushed himself and was often hard on himself if he felt he didn't perform well. Feori told Jaime about how his mother used to make him sit in his splits for long periods of time. It sparked conversation about their work getting invalidated by people who thought that they were naturally thin, flexible, and could do certain tricks. These people neglected the fact that Jaime and Feori had been athletes all their lives and made active effort most days to get their bodies to be able to do the things they could do, such as maintain flexibility, body weight, muscle, throw tricks or pose, or (in their opinions) exist at all. Jaime mentioned how inspiring it was that he set physical goals for himself, committed to practising with people, and was committed to himself. Feori mentioned how he was rather selective about the people with whom he would practise, and Jaime felt honoured that he allowed her access to that part of his life. She also felt honoured when he showed her videos or told her things about his world, in the same way that she felt when Liam showed her drum core or Le Feu showed her scootering.

On their last day together, Jaime bought Feori dinner, because, in her mind, that was what a feminist did. He jokingly said to her, "you're treating me so well, you could definitely get into my pants after this date." Jaime noticed that he was nice enough to kiss her in public, or that he possibly couldn't stop himself from it due to their chemical connection, and she liked that. She laughed in her head about how if anyone saw them kissing, nobody knew anything about the nature of their relationship.

Though Jaime had made a point to notice flaws in Feori so that she did not idolise him and put him on a pedestal as some perfect person, and though she made sure she was understanding of his other obligations while he was in the state, she had had a lot of anxiety about Feori bailing on her on the day of the class. She did not want him to think that she thought he was the type of person who would bail, because she thought of him as a professional, and knew that it was her anxiety replaying experiences she'd had with bad people, so she tried to hide it. Still, he told her that he felt it before he got on the train. Jaime apologised for her anxiety, and Feori told her that apologising so much was a symptom of anxiety. He understood, letting her in on how he used to dress to intimidate people, trying to look weird and creepy, so that he could avoid talking to people, which was a symptom of anxiety. Later in conversation, Feori recognised Jaime's relationship with Syd as an abusive one even though Jaime didn't feel like she had said many details about the extent of dating him. She never intentionally talked about him, things just always seemed to come up that related to that time in her life.

When Jaime found herself surrounded by the kind of high frequency Feori vibrated by pursuing his passion, she got extremely excited. This excitement spilled over the days they'd spent together and into trying to make more plans with him. Jaime felt the need to apologise for this excitement, it was just the magic she saw in the world. Jaime had always fallen a little in love with her friends. Feori saw the magic himself, seeing that she truly was a witch, and also apologised to Jaime for his distance when it came to making plans at the end of his visit. He told her that she was a very supportive friend and that he enjoyed what she brought into his life.

After Feori had gone, she knew she would miss having someone to talk movement with, who watched feminist videos with her, and who recognised and reminded her that she was capable of things he wasn't, even if he was capable of things she wasn't. She felt satisfied by interacting with him, feeling like he didn't see right through her, but instead saw all of her. Feori's two weeks home were valuable to his personal growth, necessary, and pleasurable, and Jaime felt the same way about her time with him. Feori treated Jaime with the utmost respect and she found that he was easy to be with. Ultimately, however, she was glad he was going, for fear of getting too attached and that he would become a distraction from her soul path. Jaime also knew that Feori's stubbornness and strong opinions could easily become faults that clashed with her own, and that just because she thought he was wonderful did not mean he was the perfect partner for her. She was completely content with releasing him back into his world, holding a welcome place for him in hers. He helped her feel better about being home, knowing she had still grown. She also felt complete understanding about why her attraction to Feori had always been so strong, because she saw him as light energy – the light of passion of a flame ignited at a young age.

These days, Feori has become a professional dancer. He could do headstands and other yoga poses. He cared about things like how women were treated and current issues. Jaime couldn't tell if he'd grown up or always been so nice, but she wanted to try acroyoga with him and see how he flowed with a prop

One of the Guys

They let her hang around because she could keep quiet and she liked girls too, so when they were talking about girls, she could join in. somehow, they respected her for that each in their own way. Of course, they all grew accustomed to hearing girls who liked girls talk about girls, but Jaime was known to be very blunt and open. Sometimes she said things that shocked people.

They let her hang around when she was a crying, anxious mess. She had just lost two female loves along with their mutual friends all while having a boyfriend she didn't actually care about. She went out to venture on her own – with few real friends and single. When she found them, she would accompany them as they smoked cigarettes and sometimes she would watch them all have fun and listen to them talk, sometimes she would talk, and sometimes she would sit there and cry. They took her places and showed her the world.

Their world. The world of sidewalks and parking lots, convenience stores and playgrounds, skateparks, and changing seasons. A walking world, a world for learning the place you grow to know best, with your eyes closed, like the back of your hand, no matter how old you get.

She was the girl of the group. Other girls came and went. Girls mingled with her boys and they'd call the boys their best friends. Girlfriends hung out with the group until they stopped dating. She always tried to be nice and friendly to the girlfriends, but they were never the same. Some of them tried to make her like they were, but she just wasn't.

The boys saw many sides of her. Mostly, they saw her messy side. They saw her cry, shake, and scream about a wealth of things everywhere from grades to friends to lovers to death and sickness. Sometimes her messy side was when she was covered in acne, wearing her glasses, or her hair was a mess. Other times her messy side was when she looked like a boy. These were times when she dressed down, with hoodies and joggers, a beanie on her head. Jaime had an androgynous face. Sometimes the boys practically forgot she was a girl. They didn't always consider her to be one. They would apologize whenever this came up in conversation, but she would just smile and brush it off.

"Don't worry about it," she'd say. "I don't always consider myself a girl either."

Other times she was pretty. Jaime was actually quite a good looking girl, especially when she tried. She never wore makeup, but sometimes she threw parties in her backyard, where she would greet the boys in her bikini, and they would be reminded of how very much of a girl she actually was.

They saw her cheerful side, her excited side. They saw her with boyfriends, they saw her with girlfriends. They saw her ambitious side, her proud side. They saw her clever side, her unique side. They saw her scared side.

They'd probably say that the best side of Jaime that they had ever seen would be her, "I-don't-want-to-kill-myself-anymore" side. She would say they saved her life.

She reached out to them. Sometimes, they reached out to her. She grew up as one of the guys, and since found it increasingly difficult to maintain friendships with females. Five years after the boys so graciously welcomed her, she could finally say she was trying to have friends who were girls. But no one could compare to the guys who changed her.

It was interesting for Jaime to be best friends with someone who didn't have an anxiety problem (Liam) as well as someone who did (Sean). Jaime recalled Liam describe feelings of anxiety in his stomach when he had to have a serious talk with Le Feu once. Jaime had to tell him, that's what anxiety feels like. Liam felt bad that Jaime had experienced that feeling so intensely that she wanted to start smoking, and that she regularly experienced that feeling. Yet,

Sean, he sometimes shook, despite his desire to be unbreakable and to have all of his pieces together at all times. Sean knew about peaky stomachs and feeling short of breath and well as nervous hands and feet. Jaime not thinking of Liam as someone who suffered from anxiety until he started expressing his anxieties to her in their college years. Then she realised that he just didn't suffer from anxiety the same way she did. Jaime was close with many people who suffered from anxiety, and they all experienced it differently.

Jaime's Spark

There was a spark within Jaime, which fueled the fire of a child. This child was full of laughter, one who used to create elaborate fantasy play scenarios for her dolls, including making them her students at some points, and lesbian strippers at others. Jaime felt that she had always lived within two extremes, or mixed states – crying or giggling.

Jaime's boys had seen glimpses of her spark, especially whenever she brought her friends around, like Rosie, Glitterboii, or Sean. Le Feu would see her spark return when he hung out with her after she'd gone to yoga class. Her boys had seen Dawn, the energy vampire, used her powers for evil and suck the colours out of Jaime. Seeing Jaime's spark was rare but pleasant. Dawn suffered her karma for putting out Jaime's spark.

Jaime's inner child was flexible, she threw herself around every which way, bending and stretching, flipping, and flopping. Jaime had been called hypermobile, "too flexible." She also ran the risk of being too flexible with people.

Forming a new kula was important for Jaime, it protected her and helped her to grow. Eventually Jaime realised that if she couldn't stop complaining every day, she could neutralise any negative energy she put out. Her kula helped her find reasons not to complain. Being part of a community meant something to her.

As Jaime pulled away the veil of ignorance, she started being able to discern the truth of which people can be trusted in her life. It was like being a child in a big family, confused about who was related to you and here to help. She had always heard that "the blood of the covenant is thicker than the water of the womb," meaning that chosen relationships were the most powerful.

Though she grew up flaunting her athletic body, her boys helped shape her genderqueer mindset. Since fifteen, she grew up afraid to tell boys who were interested in her, if anything at all. She grew up learning to be selectively open. Only certain people could know she was out since she grew up in fear of being outed to her dad and kicked out.

Jaime was relatively out about her genderqueerness, though she identified with her female side. She knew that biologically she was a girl, but sometimes she felt in between. She felt particularly constrained by gender roles imposed on females. But she had no preferred pronouns, she was fine with "she," and had no real boy name for when she felt like a boy. She felt that gender, just like sexuality was more fluid than black and white. In the same day, she could feel both boyish and girly.

Same Name James

James was an important friend to mention, because he was one of the only ones in Jaime's guy group with whom she had never been involved. Because Jaime tended to fall in love with her friends, she had been temporarily interested in Liam and Le Feu before coming to her senses. She had also hooked up with Keith and Rocco, both in the same way. Her friendship with James was untainted and pure. He was a great listener, a kind and caring friend, and full of understanding. He was very mathematically and logically intelligent, and followed a sensible path to become a data analyst. By hobby, he was a gifted musician with several instruments.

Jaime recalled being seventeen and hearing James admit to having anxiety. She felt closer to him knowing this, and got a deeper understanding of why he put up with her anxiety. Jaime had known James since they were ten, and been close friends since they were fourteen. He had been around when Jaime had to give up on Dawn, around for her crying panic attacks, and for when she would get drunk off a bottle of wine and cry all night. James never passed judgement on Jaime. They used to ride the bus together, and when James got his license he would drive Jaime to school some mornings. They lived within walking distance of each other and had lots of lovely memories.

James made sure to visit Jaime before she moved to England. He happened to visit her with a friend from university. Before seeing her, he had been visiting with Le Feu and Keith at Keith's house. Jaime knew she was growing because for the first time in her life she didn't get jealous that her friends hung out without her, but instead she was over the moon that they got to have that time with each other since it was so rare in their twenties. As James told his friend about the places he and Jaime had been together and how far back they went, she melted. She was so proud to see him pursuing his ambitions and being successful. His energy was pure light, and Jaime felt blessed with the gift of his friendship.

Learning from Rosie

Jaime credited most of her knowledge of sex to Rosie. It was thanks to open and honest conversations with Rosie that Jaime was able to learn so much.

Rosie, despite her faults, had been a seeker of information at a point. She had also had two years' worth of experience on Jaime to discuss where Jaime had none. It was through Rosie (and Jaime's first gay boyfriend, Parnav) that Jaime learned about the acidity of her girlhood. Rosie also taught Jaime about kink culture a bit, and opened pathways for her brain to explore.

It was from Rosie and Glitterboii that Jaime started learning the hallway curriculum. The hallway curriculum was how Jaime learned to talk about gay sexual acts, relationships, and safe sex. The hallway curriculum was also where Jaime learned about intentional sexual using. The hallway curriculum is a type of informal learning which is accidental – unintended by the learner, and unbeknownst to them at the time.

Jaime sometimes used to call Rosie "Radio Rosie" when they were friends. This meant what Jaime had once described to Erika. "She sometimes tells other people's secrets without even realising it." Because of her own very open throat chakra (as a ruling sign of it), Jaime had to be very careful herself not to turn into a radio. Her biggest problem was when people neglected to mention that something they said or did was meant to be a secret. Jaime noticed her tendency to repeat information she learned, regardless of how she'd learnt it. It took many years of swadyaya to become so self-aware that she wanted to change her habits.

Jaime and Life After Sports

After being a sports player for ten years, Jaime didn't know what to do with herself when she stopped. Sports had given her a place to put her aggression. Jaime had loved running laps and she had loved being a defended, applying pressure, and body checking opponents without using her hands. Kicking the ball really helped her let off steam. Quitting sports cold turkey was incredibly hard for Jaime. She knew it was even harder because she had a tendency to eat her feelings, and she didn't want to suffer from it. Her body craved movement, so she took up swing dance.

Life after sports was Dex teaching Jaime how to fight. It was coming home from school and shooting the bow to let off steam. It was not knowing what to do with her feelings because she wasn't going somewhere multiple times a week to deal with them. It was finally learning how to skateboard but not learning tricks, and it was missing running.

    Jaime wondered what to do with the aggression she had in her body. She wasn't a fighter like Dex was. Being a touch based person, she got too turned on from combat, even though it wasn't sexual. She still wanted to be aggressive, and felt like her level of activity was inadequate. The only time she got to truly let out her aggression was when she was surfing. That was the kind of full body workout she knew she needed forever. Jaime found that her aggression made its way into her personality, making her edgy. She also noticed that she used her aggression to be an activist, having anger at the oppressors. Lastly, her aggression turned her into a bit of a hunter, seeking to satisfy her libido, and it was aggression that powered her inappropriate impulses to speak her mind to the objects of her interest.

Jaime's Journal Entry on Body Awareness

At what age did I begin to pay attention to what was going on in my body? I ask myself as I'm sat outside of my workplace at age twenty waiting for my charge. My workplace was Christian, which I chose to ignore for the greater good it offered. I'm sat outside, focusing on my breathing. Doing my yoga, for half an hour, without doing any asana. There was once a time when I didn't' do that, though I can hardly remember that time. Just like how there was once a time when I didn't find myself in asana, or paying attention to any injuries, how they've occurred, or how they can be fixed.

Was it when I started getting chest crushing panic attacks that I started paying attention to my body? Even though I didn't even know what these panic attacks were for quite some time. And even though I'd been an athlete for ten years prior to my anxiety disorder rearing its ugly head.

There was this baton of my older sister's that used to incessantly twirl around in my backyard, I can recall countless hours spent passing the time dancing to nature's music.

These are experiences children generally don't get anymore – hours of unregulated, creative, outdoor play. The world is different now.

I think experiences like this helped contribute to the discovery of my flow prop. Despite the fact that I did not grow up with a background in dance, dance resonated with me. There was a brief period during which I took swing dance lessons but I always felt troubled by choreography. Funny to think of how dance became such a huge part of my daily life practise.

Being Responsible

Jaime was often the "mom friend," because she was a teacher, because her name made her the helper and protector of humankind, because of the bear in her. She always had snacks, was often prepared, liked to drive everyone around, was often making sure friends don't forget things and encouraging friends to be healthier, and she cared about their growth – which could make her a nag (i.e. to Syd, Le Feu, or Sean when they' weren't doing as well as they could for themselves). Like a mom, she was always tired, cleaned up after people, and was-watching out for people, being observant. It was no coincidence that she worked with children.

Jaime and Syd's First Rock Ballad

When Sydney broke her heart, Jaime decided a few things. She never wanted to date someone who was biphobic again. She never wanted to be with someone she had to fight again. Having fights was one thing, but having to fight someone to talk to her, or give her time and attention, or do the right thing for themselves was not anything Jaime wanted to be a part of.

Breaking up with Sydney was one of the hardest things that Jaime ever did. It was also one of the greatest acts of self-care that she allowed herself. She felt the same way about when she had to break up (terminate her friendship) with Dawn.

Jaime had absorbed negative energy from Sydney's biphobia, and as a result she had developed a lot of self-criticism, particularly about her bisexuality and her actions. Similarly to when Jaime had absorbed enough negative comments from her old friends like Dawn, Darcy, and Rosie about how her singing was tone deaf, it required a powerful ongoing spell to pull the negative energy out of her and return her to her normal and true self. Jaime had believed she was tone deaf and didn't sing openly until she had a car to sing in. Jaime didn't recover from Syd's negative energy until after leaving Julio.

Jaime and Julio

Julio started as a rebound from Syd when Jaime was still in high school. Jaime met him at a party at her old manager's house. A girl Jaime had met previously, Stella, was there. Stella knew Julio and got him and Jaime to hang out more after that party.

Jaime dated April before she dated Julio, but had already been seeing him. Eventually April left Jaime for Posh Boy. Benji was there when Julio asked Jaime to be his girlfriend.

Julio didn't know Jaime was bi until after they started dating. He said that she cold kiss girls, and made comments about being excited to watch. Initially he'd claimed to be down for threesomes, but after some time passed he admitted to Jaime that he didn't think he could focus on two people at once. They stopped looking for threesome partners. He let her kiss girls for the whole duration of their relationship, and in this respect Jaime felt spoiled.

Through dating Julio, Jaime formed a close though brief friendship with Benji. Benji occasionally flirted with Julio and his older brother, to Jaime's amusement. The other boys of course denied any reciprocated flirting.

Jaime never truly fell for Julio, which was ultimately why they broke up.

Jaime learned from dating Julio, who liked action movies, that there were several bisexual superheroes. Deadpool, Harley Quinn, Poison Ivy, and Wonder Woman. These heroes helped Jaime remember when she felt big and bloated that Wonder Woman was a bisexual Amazon who everyone wanted and that she was still a goddess and worthy of love when she felt as big as an Amazon. Jaime felt it was quite important for girls to have the Athena-esque warrior woman who can hold her own that Wonder Woman portrayed. She was career girl, but it was important not to be portrayed as anti-family. She's not too independent to not care for others, she is still compassionate, but she is physically, emotionally, mentally, and spiritually strong, and holds the power to overcome. She portrays equality ad challenges gender roles. She was a beacon for body positivity, bi positivity, and strong woman positivity.

Body positivity begins with education, education on how our bodies work, how to take care of them, and why they look the way they do – especially bodies with uteri. Consent and body ownership was necessary. Teaching children of any gender body ownership and consent was simple – they don't have to hug or kiss family members, teaching them to ask permission to touch anyone. People must ask permission of children to touch their bodies – anything like, "may I help you with that?" to "may I pick you up?" or "can I have a hug?" Body ownership encourages children to develop their own concept of how their body should look and feel – not letting their body become owned by society's beauty standards – living for themselves. Body ownership breeds body positivity. It helps teach respect for differences. Understanding of human anatomy and what healthy expectations are for the self and others were necessary. There also needed to be education to cultivate understanding that one can be body positive while maintaining preferences for a particular body type.

Shaucha breeds body positivity. Keeping the body clean we are honouring it. The purity of shaucha shows us our ego versus comfort, and teaches us that we must learn to love and honour the comfortable self. Clothing can have many purposes, from showing off to expressing the self or being comfortable. Often, people use clothes to wear to take lots of "smile for the ego" photos. Though loving ourselves is radical in our culture of hate, shaucha involves finding a balance.

Jaime was used to hearing comments about her young and healthy body. She wondered, though, how her body could feel the way it sometimes did if it was supposed to be young and healthy. Her sacrum ached, sometimes sending shooting pains up and down her spine. She felt wracked with fatigue at times.

Dex challenged Jaime when she talked about being afraid to walk by herself.

"How well can you fight, and how fast can you run?" He'd asked.

Some days Jaime felt like even if she had been classically trained in self-defense it would make no difference because her body felt too weak, like there was no power in it.

Jaime was sick of hearing about her small body. People made it seem like life was easier for her because her build was petite and athletic. She gave up trying to talk to people about her form in asana because too often she heard, "it's easy for you because you're tiny." It wasn't because she was "tiny" that Jaime could backbend, forearm stand, or split. It was because she diligently stretched and practised.

Most of this size talk came from other girls. In a culture that prized girls with slim waists and accentuated curves, girls who didn't fit that ideal bashed those who did. Girls had the short end of the stick, it seemed, with overweight girls both being shamed for their bodies and told to love their sizes, yet naturally thin girls got shamed for their bones. Jaime had been lucky enough to have been comfortable in her body for most of her life. She felt bad for people who didn't feel at home in their skin, but it was usually bigger, taller girls who complained about having too much body who were the ones who told Jaime of her smallness. In truth, it bothered Jaime because she did not feel small, she felt like an Amazon goddess, she felt like a vast container.

The other thing that bothered Jaime was that people acted like she had some unreasonable luck to look the way she did. Whether or not Jaime had a genetic predisposition for being small and slim, she had been an intensive athlete into her high school years. At seventeen Jaime decided to alter her diet and stop eating the fast food she had been brought up on. When people talked about Jaime's size, they neglected to mention all the work that went into maintaining it. Jaime put a lot of effort into herself, working out for strength, flexibility, and mental clarity. She may have been naturally driven to do this, having been brought up sporty, but her body was not mere luck. People also often acted as though she couldn't feel pain because she was young, but she suffered sacrum trauma and chronic fatigue syndrome.

Jaime noticed her size fluctuate daily. She noticed what made her feel small, and when she felt large. She noticed the way clothes felt throughout the day.

Chicago Bikram

While visiting her sister in Chicago, Jaime ventured into the city on her own for the first time. She came across a hot yoga studio and decided to try it.

The whole studio room was mirrored, and the room was above 100 degrees with 40% humidity. This meant that the students were barely clothed during class.

Jaime could watch herself practise from multiple angles for the first time. She noticed the others in the room, enjoying their practises. Distracted by what was going on in her own body, she couldn't judge any of theirs.

Inherently, Jaime had always practised body positive yoga, though she had not always been kind to her body. She felt that yoga was Krishna's gift to all. She had always accepted students of all sizes, shapes, abilities, and colours. She made sure not to overestimate her strength when assisting (especially with inversions) and had a co teacher when necessary.

Students of all sizes, shapes, colours, and abilities were welcome in Jaime's wellness centre. If classes didn't give students what they needed, Jaime and her colleagues were willing to work one on one, developing a curriculum adapted to their unique needs.

Jaime's fundamental principle when it came to body positive yoga was that the body should be loved and taken care of, as it is the house for the soul, in which many miracles happen daily. Jaime knew firsthand about miracles, having almost not made it past birth, failing at taking her first breath of life, and ending up in an incubator with oxygen pumps as a newborn infant. She believed the body should be the teacher, and guide the learning by doing the movements the body is craving. She also believed in listening to the body and stopping when it hurt or one became tired.

Julio unintentionally helped Jaime make friends with girls, something that didn't come easily to her since she was fourteen. Though these friendships were brief, they had value for that time. They were with girls who empowered other girls despite their shortcomings and weirdness.

Enter Logan

Logan was April's friend, who at first Jaime got along well with (like with all of April's friends, really). Logan was vocal about injustice, especially with local lady killer Party Boy Jacques when he was being rude.

Logan dated a friend of Julio's for a period of time while Jaime and Julio were together. She and Jaime ended up spending a lot of time together. Julio and Logan's boyfriend were okay with Logan and Jaime making out, and, in fact, sometimes encouraged it. Logan was the first girl that Jaime had ever gone down on. Sometimes, Jaime got insecure with girls because she remembered the time that Logan asked her to stop.

Jaime had really wanted Logan to participate in

physical activities with her, like yoga or hula hooping, but Logan was usually reluctant. She sometimes was willing to go to parks, but she wasn't always willing to go for walks. Jaime didn't like having to push people to do things.

Eventually, Logan faded out of Jaime's life. They never developed problems. Jaime stopped speaking to Logan when Logan began dating a friend of Julio's who had pressured Jaime into sleeping with him at a party when she was seventeen, but never said anything to Logan about why she stopped talking to her.

April and Marcie

Jaime met April and Marcie through Julio and Rigby Wilton. Much younger than her, April and Marcie were already into hard drugs. They shared Jaime's mixed sexuality, and were also into yoga, so Jaime could tolerate their company. At first, she thought that they would become good friends because they were all feminists, but Marcie proved to be unfulfilling company to Jaime, and April didn't make the effort for other people anymore.

April and Marcie both recovered from their opiate addictions before age 21. they both followed a vegan diet. April studied at community college and got certified in nursing and subsequently got a job at the local hospital. Marcie worked at a vegan restaurant and juice company. Though they had never properly gotten close to Jaime and therefore drifted from her, the two maintained the friendship they had already had with each other and helped each other stay clean by meeting up to practise together, eat vegan food, and create.

Marcie, however, was still dating Freddie Pasto. Freddie sent Marcie into several relapses, and when Freddie was in jail, Marcie tried to get clean. She got distracted by her lust for a different boy, who was also not off drugs. Though she took great care when it came to what food she put into her body, Marcie remained helplessly chained to her addiction, and Jaime decided that she was unfit company to keep.

The thing about making friends was, for Jaime, that she became too easily frustrated with having to explain herself. People who knew her for a long time knew and understood – Jaime didn't like chicken, soda, bubblegum, ketchup, or spicy food, she rarely used condiments, her mom never let her watch SpongeBob, she had two passports, her dad was sick, and she was absolutely petrified of tow trucks, red trucks, loud trucks, white trucks, car problems, and mechanics.

People like Sean knew her deal and catered to it. He occasionally tried to show Jaime that eating spicy foods or using condiments could be fun. People like Liam and Le Feu didn't even think twice about the way that they could be out with Jaime and she would snap her head around upon hearing a loud truck, or the way she'd shudder and shake if she saw a red truck pass by. Sean and Le Feu thought nothing of her nervous hands and knew that the best way to get her to stop shaking was to hold them. Her boys all knew when they were at her parents' house that she would check to make sure her dad was breathing.

The thought of making new friends made Jaime very nervous. She didn't want to have to explain to a new person why she would get up from her nighttime cup of tea and shush them, why she had to obsessively check her sleeping father for breathing. She didn't want to explain her problem with mechanics. In this way, she was a lot like Sean, who didn't like to repeat himself (since they had learned how to talk with their minds, they sometimes did not use their mouths for conversations). She sought people with whom she could cultivate silence, though she enjoyed talking (as a ruling sign of the throat chakra). She had mastered that with her boys, but with some people, silence was deafening. Most people didn't make it past the silence test. Cultivating silence was part of having misophonia, getting frustrated by certain sounds. Jaime and Sean had occasional misophonia. In her mind's eye, Jaime thought of people she could cultivate silence with as "kiku" people because to her they could listen. Kiku is the Japanese word for "to listen," and Jaime valued most deeply those friends of hers who knew how to listen to her silence.

Sean noticed when something was on Jaime's mind. He put on ocean music to soothe her nerves and coaxed out of her the words. He knew her well enough to know what would calm her down and make talking easier. That's how Jaime knew that Sean really knew her. Because of this, she knew he was one of her kiku people. She could calmly discuss serious topics with Sean to ocean sounds.

Jaime had also noticed that she had an easier time making friends with boys than with girls. She found that she was much more likely to see what she was getting with boys, even though Glitterboii had pointed out that boys sometimes lied about the personality they put forth while girls who might have lacked confidence would be manipulative. As a feminist, she hated to stereotype women, but she had noticed them acting significantly meaner and more manipulative than boys, and found it hard to trust girls. Jaime herself, however, sometimes gave an impression of trusting girls, because she could talk about things like her sex life. In general, she found girls more competitive, and boys more cooperative. Jaime had to unlearn this internalised sexism, which had overpowered her for a long time, preventing her from forming meaningful relationships with other women.

When Jaime wasn't trying to cultivate silence, she was looking for people with whom she could converse as her and Rosie did – freely and openly about sex as well and current events, educationally based with vulgarity and sass as well as humour. She didn't know where talking with Rosie had started like that, but most of the time that was all she remembered about being Rosie's friend.

If Jaime wasn't talking, Sean knew something was wrong. Jaime was like a teapot. She boiled until she steamed, and then she screamed. When she screamed, she shrieked, and she also spouted water.

Jaime had a tendency to buzz when she was overstimulated. Sean would be the kind of friend who asked if she had practised today, and he would tell her, "I don't want to talk to you until you've practised, go practise right now."

Learning to Drive with Benji

Benji helped Jaime learn how to drive. She never forgot how he told her that when you went into a turn you had to both brake and accelerate. She often felt this applied to life. When change was happening, there were many reasons to slow down and also to speed up. She related this to the aphorism "one step forward, two steps back." Balancing conflicting energies such as these could easily become overwhelming. It was something to return to many times, in many ways.

Ticks

Jaime thought her biggest vice was her nail biting. Her parents tried to get her to stop for a terribly long time. It was her earliest anxiety tick. She didn't even notice that she would start doing it.

At fourteen, Jaime began her attempt at stopping biting her nails because she enjoyed holding hands with Todd and she noticed how often she'd drop his hand to bite her nails. When Dawn was pushing Jaime to the edge, Jaime began clenching her jaw and grinding her teeth because she tried to eat all of the words that she could not say to dawn and all of her friends. Everyone would invalidate Jaime's feelings and blame Dawn's depression. Not wanting to fight and lose all of her friends, Jaime chose not to speak, and her mouth suffered for it. A habit formed at fourteen, it would follow Jaime into adulthood.

The trouble with being born into a cigarette smoking family was that I was the only impression Jaime was given about how people deal with stress. When she started clenching her jaw and grinding her teeth, and when she started getting panic attacks, Jaime also started smoking cigarettes. She decided to befriend her body, however, and choose life over cigarettes.

When Jaime would panic, her hands would shake. At seventeen, Julio gave her hakky saks to squeeze. It worked so well she began to carry them in her handbags. At eighteen her tongue piercing helped distract her mouth from reverting to its habit.

Tongue Piercing

When children asked Jaime about her piercing, she told them that she had it because she thought it was pretty. If other adults asked Jaime why her tongue was pierced and she was in a safe environment, she usually would say, "so girls know I like them." However, her tongue piercing served other purposes. For one, she used it as a fidget for her anxiety, to offset the grinding of her teeth. SLB Benji taught her different ways she could play with it, because his tongue was also pierced. She also used it as a bit of self-punishment or when she wanted to remember feeling alive – if she pulled on it the wrong way, she could easily feel pain.

At twenty and twenty one Jaime finally got into gum (which she had never grown up chewing) as a way to stop her tick. She clenched her jaw so much that she'd moved the position of some of her teeth which she could feel when cutting her tongue or through tension headaches. At twenty one Jaime took note that without smoking weed or practising physical asana, it took her mouth an hour and a half to relax from a panic attack. Jaime did other experiments with her body like this, which is how she learned she needed at least an hour and twenty minutes of exercise to get out of a bad mood and how she learned that without glasses she could only see clearly to her wrist.

She recalled Le Feu once saying, "you need a fidget" to Jaime one day when noticing her nervous hands, and recognising that he once was a child who needed a fidget in school. She replied, "I have one in my mouth."

"Opposites Attract"

she was a rock 'n roll girl
made up of swirls
he was a death metal guy
because he wanted to die

perfect relationship
opposites,
but both of them bi

her bi boyfriend teaches her
how to play the electric bass
every Friday night
and she teaches him
how to move his body
so he's never sore anymore.

"Compass Rose"

I kiss you
and I cling to
the feeling of
everything being alright

I miss you
and I need you
but you don't trust me

and I can't trust myself
and I don't even try to hurt you
I guess it's just my personality
you say you wouldn't rather love anyone else

on a good day
we're the perfect couple
I'm half and half
and you're eighty twenty
we still have the world to explore.

"The Ballad of Syd and Jaime"

it was date night
and she
wanted to go bowling
but he wasn't down

even though it was the
only alley in town
and it was brand new
tricked out

he was too worried about
someone working behind the bar
she'd only met him at the park
and never heard what happened from the start

Jaime had to let this boy know
regardless of how long it was ago
what he did was not at all right
she longed to make him know with all her might

so Jaime took herself down to the lanes
met her friends for several games
naturally, she walked up to the bar
spotting him from afar

"I hope you know how bad you are,"
Jaime isn't trying to be mean with what she says
"we've all been there
we've all had those days

but I don't know if anyone's ever told you
and you're way too old not to know
what you did is what you can't do
an intoxicated friend is not a sign for green means go"

Syd is displeased with Jaime's words to the boy
but as it turns out

she never let him know Syd wasn't a toy
the boy was never even about

he's fucked right off right out of town
they'd never see him hanging around
rejoice, for now they could go on dates to the lanes
and for Syd and Jaime no more hard pains.

"I Bleed Pink, Purple, and Blue"

each person
filled with fluidity
the line between is not where it's done
everybody falls on both sides of the line
we are all flexible acrobats
people need to learn that it's fine
it is certainly about of times

I've always called myself flexual
because to the line I am blind
it is not completely sexual
and preference I don't mind

drag your nail across my back
doesn't matter as long as it's you
sure you wouldn't be okay
I'd be happy to work it through

my tummy flares and my heart races
my voice shakes when I talk to you
your appearance is aces
these nerves just won't do

but what would people say
if I hold your hand in the hall
or if I ask you out one day
or push you against a wall

why do I care anyway?
Judgment I can bear any day
but I guess when you get kicked in the back
called a dyke at school

understandable to have a panic attack
when you want to play it cool

I see no difference between curves and lines
both are pleasing to the eye
there's nothing here but what here's mine
and I'm not naturally shy

we are conditioned to walk a line
and fluidity you will find
but given time
and people who don't mind

screw the generic expected rules
and screw all of the lying
emotionally it takes such tolls
just leads to crying

I wanna tell you to open a door
but I know why you won't
just because I don't need to hide anymore
doesn't mean you don't

sometimes we're both a girl and boy
sometimes we're neither
sometimes everyone is a toy
and sometimes they're neither

I am not a church kid
but I know that god made me bi
I trust that more than a choice did
so I don't bother asking why

I've wished that it would go away
tried to walk a straight line
but I've realised I have no say
this is something that is mine

curves and lines are a part of me
and I am not the only one
if you love me let it be

[if you want] it can even be fun

it once was a struggle in my head
but it's not a problem anymore
I wouldn't kick stars out of my bed
beautiful souls are a score

my parents can think what they want to
I'll always be on the fence to them
to myself I'd rather be true
even though they asked, "since when?"

it has been too long and
far too much mind
hiding because you said
I was wrong
and you no longer want to bother trying

think before you speak
but go ahead make fun of me
go ahead I dare you to call me a freak
and wouldn't you love to see

thankfully words don't cut me anymore
I bleed just like you
but staying on one side of the fence is a bore
and I bleed pink, purple, and blue

"I Bleed Pink, Purple, and Blue parts II-IV"

{Part II}

my love rides on sunshine's rays
both of us here wishing for better days
days to laugh and days to play
they seem so far away

right now we two must make such strife
work so hard, it brings us tears
to make a life
but this love fears

that my eye will fade
because I see no great divide
no preference by whom to get laid
girls and boys I pick no side

yes I see no difference
this much is true
here's when we always end up screaming
that what I want is you

how can that be true
when waking there's the two of you
something you said you'd never do
I always knew you bled pink, purple, and blue too

{Part III}

something always stuck out
and I know why they hit on you
something I always knew about

he was talented
a musician - tight pants, nice hair
the kind I was always drawn to,

heart, soul, and brain a breath of fresh air

I knew him when he painted his nails black
I have almost always been able to tell my people
before they even know it sometimes
couldn't even believe he took me back

after all, he always used to be the scared one
because my eyes wander in both directions
we are not all promiscuous
although people like me are the reason we get a bad rep

I have always been so crazy
so jealous, so needy,
he amazed me
I would have really hurt those girls

that was years ago,
and so much has changed
different friends and different people
our entire lives got rearranged

I thought I called that guy my friend
but he is crazier, and to what end?
now thanks to him, my trust is left here to mend
we've turned our car down a new and different bend

I knew we'd end up here one day
and love feels awful, he wanted to be true
it's okay and I'm okay and we're okay yet still he can't just say
to anyone, not even me, "I just can't help it when my blood runs pink, purple, and blue"

{part IV}
closet case,
it's no race
I'm not telling you to come out
that's not what I'm talking about

he thought I didn't know what it was like
but just because it's been seven years doesn't mean it's been bliss
after all, I've been assaulted and called a dyke
thank everything for the youth groups I never wanted to miss

I'm just saying, we know and you're safe
you're too loved for anyone to tell
but since you won't we'll all wait
it sure showed us an act of fate

you told the best girl in the world your secret
even though she can barely keep it
it's just that she will always understand
sticking by you in every land

the trouble is the ones who don't
the ones who think that we made an active choice
the ones who make you want to do what you won't
the ones who made sure there was one less voice

one less voice to tell how this is right
normal, in fact, and that you can sleep another night
one less voice to tell you not to cry
just another star shining in our sky

like the one I lost to overdose
so many of our sisters and brothers gone ghost
it is you who I am working for
when I consider the help I must send from my core

though this is your own battle to fight
know you always have me, keeping your fire burning bright
it is you who makes me reach for those in need
those destroyed for their alleged greed

we are not greedy or on the fence
and no it's not a phase

all who say that are entirely dense
it's how we were made

we must rejoice in what we are
others cannot do the same
they reject the way our bodily reactions and their ideas sit apart so far
trying to make us feel shame

A Few Words About How Jaime and Syd Broke Up For Good

It started before it finished, in November, which was always one of the worst months for Jaime, despite it being her birth month.

Jaime witnessed everything that happened with Sydney and Phillip on her twentieth birthday, yet she had no idea what she'd witnessed. Syd refused to say whether or not he had been taken advantage of, but also refused to say he wanted it. She'd thought he'd been coherent enough to stop whatever he didn't want, and had been immobilised.

Jaime knew nothing about what happened between Sydney and Phillip the second time. Just hearing about it was enough to make her nearly crash her car pulling into the breakdown lane on the parkway, enough to make her incapable of driving, going from eighty to zero real fast.

Sydney repeatedly lied to Jaime. The company he kept made her uncomfortable and she became unable to sit by and watch his actions. Sydney and Jaime burned out. The light that was once there grew into darkness as it consumed them. The two were both guilty of partner abuse, and had a great deal of repair work to do on themselves and their lives. Jaime loved Syd. Syd loved Jaime. But their love did not save them. They would have to save themselves. Of course, they were both stronger than the storm. They just didn't make it out together.

And Syd had the audacity to tell Jaime that orientation didn't mean anything. The same Syd who cried trying to tell her about the first time he had sex with another boy, the same Syd who asked her if he could kiss Phillip while they were drunk. The same Syd who got her into a two male queer threesome on her birthday and subsequently cried and self harmed about it, provoking the one and only time Jaime had ever self harmed. The same Syd who was terrified that his family might find out he only liked girls eighty percent of the time and disown him. Jaime wish him well. He was not on her level.

Jaime didn't think that Syd realised he was telling his girlfriend that orientation didn't mean anything when at fifteen she had been repeatedly sexually abused by a man while she had a girlfriend, as he told her that her girlfriend would never be as good as he was, and when at nineteen she was raped by the same man while dressing (as she thought) like a boy in a hoodie and sweatpants. Jaime couldn't expect Syd to understand all of that. He was as supportive as he could be expected from someone who couldn't recognise his own sexual abuse. The boy he told her about having sex with had taken advantage of him while he was intoxicated. That's why it was so hard for Jaime to get the whole story out of Syd. There was also speculation that Phillip had also taken advantage of Syd on Jaime's birthday and the subsequent time. Jaime did not take it personally.

Tried as she might Jaime couldn't help Syd. He practised with her sometimes, but only in private. He liked the studio she worked at, but refused to take classes with her. Syd was shy. His yoga included playing his guitar. But Syd didn't like to listen to his body and he didn't take care of himself. He had alcohol abuse issues due to repressed feeling about his sexuality. Syd and Jaime did not make it because he refused her help. Jaime and Syd had a deep and passionate relationship, and Jaime was overjoyed to find out that she had a bisexual partner – it was all she ever wanted. She was thrilled with the way that Syd let her reverse the gender roles. She knew he didn't like her crossdressing but he still let her be the boy sometimes. He let her pay for dates and he would cook for her and they both really thought that they would be together forever.

Jaime knew when they broke up for the third and final time that Syd would not love again. Jaime knew that even though Syd was incredibly emotionally abusive, he truly loved her. Jaime knew Syd would never be able to love unless he loved himself. She simply wished him well.

Little Conversations

Glitterboii asked Jaime about her love life one day, wondering why he hadn't heard anything lately, because for as long as he'd known her, Jaime had caught people's eye.

"You know, I think that I am serving karma for outing people," Jaime said to Glitterboii. "Of all people, I know it's not okay to out anyone, yet I still have many malicious intent, but it's still not okay. I have no excuse. I still feel guilty about it, too. I think sometimes that my throat chakra is too open, I just talk and I don't think. You know, in all my life, I've only ever successfully kept a secret for one person.:

As an Aquarius (the ruling sign of the throat chakra opposite Jaime's Scorpio), Glitterboii could talk like there was no tomorrow. He chose to listen and let her work this out on her own. Though he hadn't always had the language, he'd always known Jaime's throat chakra was too open. She was the type of person who had no filter between her mind and her mouth – the words just fell out. Back in the day, their old friends used to accuse her of starting drama because of this quality.

"Are you saying that you would like me more if I were bisexual?" Que Foi asked Jaime.
Jaime laughed and thought of the checklist she'd made with Benji. Bisexuality was indeed a top quality on her checklist for both boys and girls.

"I mean, yes, I am most attracted to bisexual men out of all men, but it doesn't really matter. I am most attracted to bisexual people in general but like... you've got your things it doesn't kill you to live without." Jaime kept her eyes on the road as she spoke, hands at ten and two. She laughed as she thought of which qualities on the checklist that Que Foi's friend Syd, her ex, had possessed. She felt herself grow red in the face as she thought of which qualities on her checklist Que Foi himself possessed, and she made sure she stopped talking for a little while.

Telling Rick Batch (Further Conversations with Rick Batch)

When Jaime talked to Rick Batch about how she had been seeing Todd while he was home on leave, Rick felt it necessary to offer her advice.

He had asked her about what was new as they caught up over salad pizza (and for the second time, no sex) and had asked her for advice. She thought he must have felt that if he received advice he should give some, too.

Jaime explained to Rick how she knew Todd, and how their young dating history made it feel crazier. She told Rick about all the feelings she and Todd were experiencing.

Rick told Jaime she shouldn't be scared to get into a relationship just because she might go away to school or he's in the army or whatever reason. Jaime wasn't sure where Rick was getting the idea that she wanted to be in a relationship, and started thinking that maybe she shouldn't be scared to go away to school because of what she would miss.

When Jaime told Rick about the seemingly bi boy she'd found in England, she thought about the irony of when Que Foi had asked her if she only slept with bisexual boys. Almost all the boys she had been with in the past year had been bisexual. Bisexual boys were a decently sized chunk of her total number, with bisexual people being about half of her total. That pleased her.

Smile, Hug, Repeat – Jaime's Midnight Patronus

Jaime awoke from a nightmare panting, having a full-fledged anxiety attack. Her PTSD nightmares could wake her up into complete consciousness and her body would not let her go back to sleep, suffering physical reactions to anxiety, her mind terrified of more nightmares.

She spotted the troll Sean had gotten her for Valentine's Day, which held a banner reading, "Smile, Hug, Repeat."

Pranayama and a Patronus, she thought to herself. That was what she needed. She brought her hand to her nose to begin nadi shodhana, alternate nostril breathing. Like a mantra, the banner's slogan repeated in her head, "Smile. Hug. Repeat."

She began trying to imagine and count hugs she'd received from Sean. His eighteenth birthday in her backyard. One. When she was crying in her car. Two. When she left his house the other night. Three. Her twentieth birthday party at Syd's. Four. At the nightclub. Five. Her breathing started returning to normal, her chest didn't feel crushed.

Thinking about Sean was usually Jaime's strongest Patronus. Inspired by Harry Potter, a series that Jaime loved, a Patronus was a happy thought that acted as a shield from negativity. In Jaime's favourite book, Peter Pan, happy thoughts could make you fly. For Jaime, summoning a Patronus could sometimes stop her anxiety in its tracks.

In the series from which it originates, a Patronus can take the shape of an animal. Jaime had several animals which she considered her Patronus, including a badger, a bear, and a dolphin. Each animal had its own wisdom and lessons to teach people. The stone Irai Jasper brings out deeper connections with wisdom from animals. A Patronus is not a spirit animal, which is a sacred Native American tradition, but instead a shield of protection and a muse. Only natives can have spirit animals (Anishinaabe and other tribes), but anyone can use a Patronus.

One of Jaime's Patronuses was singing in the car with Le Feu. Le Feu didn't like to admit it, but he would sing along to Fall Out Boy with Jaime any day. There were plenty of other artists he would sing along with her to as well. Singing in her car was quite therapeutic for Jaime. It gave her a time to open her throat chakra in a positive, constructive way. For some reason, enjoying singing was socially considered feminine. Le Feu would not sing along around other boys, typically.

Choosing Teams

   Jaime leaned into a new boy, whose phone rang.
   "Anything cool?" She'd asked.
   "The Rangers just scored." He answered.
   "Oh cool, they're playing tonight? You like hockey?" she inquired.
   "Yeah, I do, do you?"
   Jaime nodded eagerly.
   "Who do you like?" the boy wondered aloud.
   "Well, at my house, we like the Penguins, the Rangers, and the Devils."
   "Can't you pick a team?" the boy chuckled.
   The bisexual in Jaime was who answered.
   "I am so sick of hearing that." Then, looking at his face, she quickly added, "because I'm bi and that's what people say about that, not because of this." Jaime, being herself, began to speak her thoughts. "Although, come to think of it, I am a bit anti-competition. I've got several English footie teams I support, not exactly one in particular. And I would never compete in my favourite sport."
   It excited Jaime when the boy asked which sport was her favourite, and as they launched into a discussion about surfing, she explained how she practised yoga for the purpose of being an accompaniment to surfing, to help her with strength and balance. After ten years of a competitive sport, Jaime became a person who did not believe in competition. She preferred cooperation.
   "I don't want to be the best," she started. "I just want to be myself. And just get naked." She finished quoting a

Borgore song, which references getting high, getting wasted, and ends with "let's be ourselves and just get naked."

Being high, wasted, and having sex were ways of becoming naked, ways of experiencing the self.

Little Things About Jaime

Jaime's closet was colour coded. The colour she had the most of was blue. (bested by black, but that which is not a colour and instead the absence of light, clothes of which represented Jaime's inner darkness) Blue was a "boy colour." Jaime found a lot of comfort in blue, though it was deemed a colour which represented sadness because one could "feel blue." The sky and the water were blue, two things which Jaime loved. Whether her attraction to the colour had to do with her being a water sign and a ruler of the throat chakra or her genderfluidity was up for speculation. Purple, often deemed her favourite colour as the colour of spirit and royalty, was the second most popular in her closet, followed by green, which was another "boy colour." Common colour combinations found in Jaime's life were pink, purple, and blue (her bi pride flag), as well as purple and green.

Jaime knew that because cleaning her room was a math experience, it was hard for her, even though she liked doing it. She noticed that she thought of everything in terms of child development since getting her degree. Cleaning her room involved a lot of sorting, and sorting was a math experience. Sorting could be therapeutic for some, Jaime especially when she was sorting by colour. Sorting by other categories and characteristics was more difficult for her, like sorting by size, importance, or purpose. She took pride in her room when it was clean, for then it could be her altar and her sacred space.

Peter Pan floated outside her window.
"Why do you call yourself a grown up?" he asked.
"By age, I am," she replied, and sighed.
"I don't think you are really a grown up, though," he remarked, peering at her.

"Good," she replied. "Then maybe you'll still let me into Neverland."

"We need someone like you to teach us things..." he muttered.

"How do you become a grown up?" he asked.

Jaime pondered the answer. Get a job? Pay bills? Have sex? Set Goals. Smash them.

Jaime said to herself, "your dreams are as hungry as your demons – make sure you're feeding the right ones."

Necessary Vacation

Jaime knew that she was naturally very European, but it didn't dawn on her how European she was until she went to England by herself at age twenty one. While visiting the seaside with her cousin, she noticed people casually stripping and changing to or from swimwear without using changing rooms, both males and females. Jaime thought of this as normal and did such changing herself back home, even though it was frowned upon and people at home were more uptight about nudity. She also noticed the nightclubs were equipped with poles all were welcome to dance on, and people were allowed to dance on the tables and bar. In America, you wouldn't find clubs like this, and if you did, they would be considered trashy. In England, it wasn't just girls dancing on the poles and tables, but boys as well. Jaime also noticed how much more willing boys were to dance with other boys, or even to wear colours like pink. Jaime ended up going home with a boy after she had seen him dirty dancing with another boy.

In the same day, Jaime was able to do more than she'd dreamed on her trip. Within minutes of meeting Jiya, the hula hooper, she had invited Jaime clubbing that night with her friends. Jaime decided that she'd only be twenty one in England all by herself once, and told Jiya she would meet them at the club. As Jaime continued her walk to the foreshore, she noticed four girls in her peer group practising yoga on the other side of Smeaton's Tower trying to photograph themselves. She went up to the girls and complimented their practise, and offered to photograph them. The girls got to talking, and the Greek one, Samini, happened to be a certified yoga teacher as well. In exchange for viewing Jaime's hoopdance moves, Samini was willing to teach Jaime an acroyoga posture, and then invited her to an acroyoga class with them the following night. Bringing her practise abroad helped Jaime feel strong. Samini was a bright light and helped Jaime take flight.

A moment happened at the nightclub which Jaime wished she could bottle. She was dancing on the boy she'd later go home with, and the hooper girl friend of his started to dance on Jaime. One of the boy's friends passed by this and said to him, "you dog!" The girls burst out laughing and Jiya said to Jaime and the boy, "I think she's the one who's the dog – she's got a lady and a man dancing with her!" They all laughed, and Jaime thought to herself that she could die happy in that moment.

Jaime left the nightclub with a male friend of Jiya's. When Jaime said to him, half joking half serious, "what, you're not even going to ask my permission if you can take my leggings off?" the boy stopped in his tracks and replied, "alright, can I take them off?" For the kind response to her wanting him to ask for consent, she granted him entry. She had a good time with him, but when she was done she was exhausted, and since he'd been drinking, he was having a hard time finishing. She was glad that he was okay with her wanting to stop, especially since he was bigger and stronger than she was. Positive experiences with boys like this were very important to Jaime so she did not consider her experience with Ray to have been junk sex. Later, she reflected on the fact that she was the one who had gone for a condom, she was always prepared with condoms in her tin with spare contacts and tongue rings which she kept in any handbag, just in case. She thought that carrying condoms had saved her from many possible experiences of being forced into unprotected sex.

Jaime had made friends in England the most recent time she had been there before her trip alone. It happened that they were able to meet up, and spent the evening at the foreshore. Due to missing the last bus back to the neighbourhood in which she was staying, Jaime and her friends ended up walking home. For Jaime, it was about a three and a half mile walk. She and her friends parted somewhere around halfway home. She found her way in the dark without directions, and nothing happened to her. She just made it home safely. That was very important to Jaime, and it fascinated her to begin a mental map in another country. Jaime was grateful to be geographically minded. She was proud to have given herself such a necessary adventure. Such experiences aided Jaime in deeper healing from the trauma of being sexually abused. Knowing she could go walking in the dark by herself in an unfamiliar place without getting attacked, or knowing she could go out to a nightclub and get respected made her feel less afraid to go out. Jaime knew that terrorists and abusers wanted to make people afraid. When her cousins and her new friends she'd met asked if she was afraid to travel alone, she told them that she was choosing to become less afraid.

Pride in the Park

When Jaime was with Julio and decided to get back into the queer community, the Triangle Community Centre was in the midst of planning a pride event in her city. Of course she jumped right in, got the day off for the event, and volunteered for it. It was early in her hoop days, and she was taught how to chest roll by a professional hooper at the event. Julio had accompanied her, being supportive. Many of Jaime's coworkers from the children's museum attended the event.
  The next year Jaime went after work with coworkers from the museum. She was PROUD to be with them, proud to know them. Proud to be one with her own kind. She didn't stay long that year, but loved it all the same. It was her first year with a gay guardian angel.
  Last year it piss poured like a monsoon and Syd was pissed at Jaime for going, and for bringing a male friend.

The friend was a cute, Latino coworker at Jaime's new party job, who had basically just turned eighteen and come out and wanted to learn the community. Jaime was proud even in the pouring rain.

This year, Jaime was on her own, even though she brought friends. First, she went, with Dylen, because other hoopers would be there hosting a hoop zone, and as Dylen's car approached the event, Jaime messaged Glitterboii.

"Why do I feel like I'm about to cry upon just seeing the event?"

Glitterboii replied, "Joy, fear, wonder. Pride." Jaime felt the tears well up in her eyes and Glitterboii sent another message. "This is what we always talk about. Today you see it in action. We may not always partake, but it happens every day. Today, you just all do it together."

When Dylen had to leave, she took Jaime home and Jaime went back with Sawyer. Both Sawyer and Dylen had bisexual tendencies that they were aware and accepting of, but identified as mostly straight. She invited her friends to share in her joy, but none of them were as joyous as she was. They didn't understand why it melted Jaime to be there. Jaime saw all the babyqueers with sparkles in their eyes and pride flags around their necks, like it was their first big Out event with their friends. She could feel it coming out of them so intensely. Jaime knew what to say to people at the booths, dressed with a purpose, and brought her pride hoops.

Every year Jaime expected to see Darcy and Dawn, she knew they were part of the community, and braced herself each time she went for the possibility of running into them. This year, sitting on the steps of the mansion, Jaime nudged Sawyer during the drag show. "Look," she subtly pointed. "It's those girls I used to be friends with." Sawyer replied, "Jaime, I'll take both of those girls if they wanna start a problem with you." One thing Jaime loved about Sawyer was that she was fiercely loyal, always ready, and not afraid to get down and dirty. Darcy and Dawn were leaning over the fence, talking to the lesbian facilitator from the youth group they all used to attend together, who was backstage. They noticed Jaime pointing them out to Sawyer.

The part in Jaime ruled by Mars and Pluto reacted first in her mind, encouraging her to wave at them when they noticed her and to wave them over to her and Sawyer, so that Jaime could give thoughtful introductions. "This is Dawn, who tried to manipulate her friends with suicide, this is Darcy, who introduced me to her, and this is Sawyer, who at least has the decency to be directly mean to me and doesn't bother doing it behind my back or in catty, manipulative ways." She had to quell that urge, and told Sawyer that they could leave, since Sawyer had somewhere else to be. She laughed, remembering that Dawn wouldn't even bother with them – she would disapprove, for they were not on the straight and narrow been through rehab path that Dawn was on. She smiled knowing she had better laughs anyway with Sawyer and Sean than she'd ever had with Darcy and Dawn. She knew it was the ego talking, but she felt she knew better people now. She knew Darcy and Dawn were getting better, but also knew they had much longer to go and that their versions of getting better were vastly different.

  Dylen expressed feelings of being judged for not being gay enough. She felt she didn't belong there as an ally. Like the joy was not hers to have. Jaime wanted to explain that the queer community felt that all the time, and that she had to learn to be comfortable with saying to folks, "hey, that's okay if it's not my joy to have, but I'm here, I'm a number for y'all, I may not know how to be the best ally, but I don't hate you, and I want to learn how to support you."

  Jaime knew Erika would have loved Pride in the Park, so she wore her angel earrings and brought her along. Afterwards, she had a hoop session in her backyard, crying and worshipping Erika's light, the only way she knew how to absorb it.

"Glitterboii's Advice for Pride" (c) GB
Fly solo and pick up a cutie
Bring a hoop and go get groovy
You don't need friends to have some fun
Just enjoy pride in the brilliant sun.

Jaime's First Pride Parade

When Jaime pulled up to Sean's apartment, she had him come out so they could handle the boring car stuff first. They were so broke that they used coins to fill her gas tank. But Ana celebrated her birthday at Pride every year and she wanted them to be there with her. Jaime had never been able to go to Pride before, and at twenty one the idea of attending her first Pride Parade in the City was tantalising to her.

In the morning at Sean's, Jaime got dressed in her crystal leggings, and wore the rainbow Pashmina that Rick Batch had given her as a shirt. She wore rainbow rave kandi, and made sure she wore her angel earrings in one of her piercings so that Erika and Manny could go to Pride with her, and so that they could protect her and all of Pride from harm. Sean wore some of their rave kandi, too, as they prepared for their big, all day party. When Jaime opened her phone, the very first thing that popped up was a tarot card reading with a card called, "the Tribe." The reading said that the card spoke to her people – not necessarily physical family, but the ones who get her, who she can count on, and who can depend on her. She thought that was some crazy irony. Jaime and Wes were a little afraid of Pride being a terror target, but Jaime knew that with her angels and with Tess' angel, they would be safe. Jaime brought Manny's smokey quartz to Pride and a kandi he'd traded her so that she could feel him there. Sean wore his red skinny jeans and the Superdry tank top Jaime had brought him from England. He looked at Jaime and asked, grinning, "you ready to go celebrate the sin?"

With that, they drove the couple of hours into the City, avoiding toll bridges. The thought of being on her way to her first Pride gave Jaime chills. When they got to Ana's, she was painting the chakras on her body with her watercolours. Ana showed them a painting she had made with Pride in mind and a poem she'd written. She wanted all of her friends to sign the painting. Jaime and Sean waited until after, when they were fully inspired. Jaime put glitter in her hair at Ana's, for Glitterboii.

As they walked to meet up with Tess and her squad, Sean kept hold of Jaime's speaker, blasting the music for them. In the car he had played a lot of music that made Jaime feel like they were going to an all day rave, and he played a lot of that kind of music while they walked. Jaime smiled thinking about how rave principles of peace, love, unity, and respect were core principles of Pride Day. She knew it was more than just a parade, but a big party. Once they saw Tess, she led them to where her group of friends was watching the parade. From there, Jaime could see the city stores all decked out for Pride, and upon first sight of the parade she cried. People were walking around wishing each other happy pride, and Jaime could feel the energy emanating off of the event. She had brought her rainbow flag that said peace on it, but didn't wave it. She was too moved and needed to hoop without music for the sake of hooping with her bi pride hoop in front of her first pride parade. She felt her heart melting and expanding. She was twenty one and living, breathing, proud. She was waving her bi pride flag by dancing with her hoop. She was enjoying everyone's presence, and let some pretty girls who asked use one of her bi pride hoops. Part of her wanted pride kisses, and part of her wanted Todd to be there celebrating, too, because he'd said he wished that he could be there with her.

  Their group took some time to wander around, in search of a liquor store. They stopped in Madison Square Park, where Jaime, Ana, and Morgan busted out handstands. Being upside down made them feel just as good as Pride did. They had to leave the parade to walk Tess and her crew to Grand Central, and ended up walking through and around the parade at different vantage points. From these points, Sean was lucky enough to be handed two souvenirs from different groups, a bracelet and a bandanna with the event and date on them. These groups were followed by the New York Area Bisexual Network, and seeing the bisexual contingency in the parade made Jaime cry again, especially seeing them carrying signs saying, "I march because bisexuals matter," and "Wonder Woman is bi." She also cried seeing a sign that said, "the first Pride was a RIOT!"

After dropping Tess and her girls off at Grand Central, the four remaining friends headed to Central Park for Ana and Jaime to do yoga. They did a quick, separate warm up, and got started on their acroyoga. In the place where pride and joy intersected, Jaime taught Ana the bird to throne acro sequence. Jaime brought up the discussion she'd been a part of at the Yoga Loft about how acro related to "real" yoga. She mentioned how acro helped teach trust, faith, strength, improved focus and breath work, helped balance masculine and feminine energies, and helped build communities. She also mentioned how some partner poses were meant to be therapeutic. Ana agreed with her on all the points she made. All the qualities of acroyoga related directly to Pride in Jaime's mind. By the end of their flow session, Jaime was quite proud of Ana for having been able to base for her.

They all had to take the subway to get back to Ana's apartment. At the subway station, Jaime saw a boy with two of the Pride bracelets Sean had been given. She asked if she could trade him kandi for it and he obliged, which made Jaime ecstatic.

However, Jaime was reminded of the people who had places to go home where they couldn't go with their pride gear. She knew some people couldn't go home with any souvenirs, and inkling that they had been there. Since Pride was at the end of Pride Month in her area, she was sad to know Pride Month was coming to an end. Even during Pride Month, she didn't feel the support of the whole human race, though she felt it from the natural universe. She knew that this was one of the reasons why Pride existed and why it was necessary. Everyone who went to Pride needed it to be something for them. An escape, a release, a celebration, an exploration, a place of worship, a place to belong, and so many other things.

Perhaps this was why Jaime questioned if she was doing Pride "right." She wondered if she'd been there with the right people, because she wasn't close with Tess and her friends. It also made her sad that Sean had been required to bring his boyfriend Alo, but had decided that he didn't want a boyfriend anymore. It had been Alo's first Pride, too, and naturally Sean felt pressure to "show their pride" because Alo wanted PDA and attention. Jaime had been frustrated at the amount of time they had spent not watching the parade when they were looking for a liquor store for Tess and worried that she had built up the idea of what Pride was supposed to look, feel, and be like, and that through doing that had made it into an ego problem for herself. She was frustrated at herself for feeling weird about Dylen going to Pride with her lesbian friends and trying to meet up with Jaime. Jaime was mad that Dylen had felt she didn't belong at a smaller scaled Pride event, but that she somehow felt she belonged at the larger scale one. Yet Jaime was also frustrated at herself for feeling like it wasn't Dylen's party to attend as a self-proclaimed Ally on a day that was supposed to all about peace, love, unity, and respect.

Because of all of these feelings, Jaime wondered for a minute if Pride had been worth it. They were hot, broke, tired, wandering around. Sean seemed over it and unhappy. Jaime had been stressed about driving there and leaving her car parked in the city. Ana got slightly egocentric at points, and it was a combination celebration for Ana's birthday and Tess' send off. Yet still, Jaime went home to Sean's that night feeling so glad to have gone and absorbed the energy from the event, despite being physically, mentally, and socially exhausted.

Jaime's Sciatica

One day after a vigorous yoga practise, Jaime went in her family's pool. The pool took all the pressure off of her sciatica, the constant reminder of the sexual abuse in Jaime's past. Truly grateful for and in need of the pool, Jaime found herself not only swimming and stretching, but playing as well. First she made freestyle laps, and noticed that she was twisting and turning in the water from freestyle to backstroke to accommodate her sciatica. Some days it was almost paralysingly painful.

Truly the sister of Chaos, Jaime also practised

swimming without using her legs, in case she ever needed to survive being thrown into water with her legs tied up. When she was done swimming, she started spinning and dancing, mostly with her eyes closed. She purposefully moved the water with her hands and though she was water bending. She was flooded with childhood memories of doing the same exact thing. She felt like if she spun enough and let herself go she would go into a different world, like the one in which she knew she was a mermaid. Jaime meant it when she joked with her brother saying, "I was a fish once." The pool helped her connect with that past life. She figured that she had been a special kind of fish, like a dolphin, because they were bisexual and mate for pleasure. She felt so connected to herself in the pool and while she was spinning. She wanted so badly to slip into the world that she felt she was almost in when she was dancing and water bending.

    Jaime felt that this was probably why some people got addicted to drugs – because they either felt more connected to themselves and their past lives, or because they felt like they were entering other worlds. She understood that many people were more consumed by who they wanted to be, or who they thought that they were, instead of who they needed to be.

    Jaime was lucky. She connected with her soul path every day. She was constantly flooded with inspiration for teaching. Connecting with herself in the pool helped reinforce what she had already known about wanting to learn how to teach swimming. Practising her modified freestyle, flooded with childhood memories, she remembered her dad teaching her how to swim the crawl and the breaststroke. Her brother, the frog, preferred underwater breaststroke. She looked forward to the days when she'd introduce her own children to a life of loving the water just like her dad had done for her. She knew that until then, she'd have other children's lives to impact. Jaime thought it was funny how a movement could trigger so many memories.

Jaime's New Life

Jaime created a new life, three thousand miles away from almost everything she knew. She knew her new city, well enough to want to live there. Jaime created a new life of continuous learning, in which she lived with four of her peers. Her new life was far from her triggers, but conversely her friends as well. Her new life gave her the space to practise, in every sense of the word.

Jaime could practise her yoga, as well as getting around without a car, navigating and getting to know a new place, studying, learning to live with new people, and taking care of herself. Jaime lived with three boys and a girl. She was the oldest one. Their youngest turned twenty in their first month together and was engaged, so he spent most of his time with his fiancé. Jaime had to learn how to live harmoniously with him, as well as Maja and the two boys who shared a name, Matt Sequoia and Matt Perianth. They were considered a mature flat.

Jaime had made a point to seek out the LGBT society at the university and met people online who were also starting at the school and queer. Some of them, Siobhan and Richard, lived in the same residence hall as Jaime. They moved in the day before Jaime's flatmates, after Jaime had been there a week alone.

The week Jaime spent alone in her flat before her flatmates moved in was the first time in her life that she'd ever been truly alone. She had no obligations that week, so she practised daily, socialised and made friends, talked to ghosts, and talked with herself.

When Siobhan and Richard moved in, Jaime invited them over. She was stoked that Richard lived above her, and thought Siobhan was beautiful and wanted to hook up with her. The first night they went to Jaime's, Siobhan asked if she could bring her flatmate, Finn. Finn and Jaime ended up getting along quite well, and going to bed together after they got back from the club, what sealed it for Jaime was Finn going to the gay bar with her and Richard. What helped was playing a drinking game in which Finn revealed that he had done things with guys before. Jaime had let him sleep over, and was pleasantly surprised to have slept next to him with ease.

    The night that her flatmates moved in, Jaime's new friends had spontaneously come over when she had only invited Finn, and they brought others with them. Two of Jaime's flatmates had wandered back to their flat and joined them in a drinking game. It was the boys who shared a name, Jaime's two Matts. The results of the game involved Richard starting an argument with Matt Perianth, getting a very deep kiss from Matt Sequoia, everyone stripping and Perianth getting totally naked at one point, and Perianth revealing his virginity at twenty one. Since everyone knew already that Jaime had slept with Finn, the game demanded she had to reveal the next person in the room that she would sleep with, and her answer was Perianth. One thing happened that night that Jaime wasn't comfortable with. The game required Richard and Perianth to kiss, and Perianth said no. Richard and Sequoia held Perianth's arms down so that he could not resist, and Richard kissed him. Jaime apologised to Perianth over and over that night, afraid that she had traumatised him with her friends.

    The next night she bonded with Perianth over hours of drinking, just the two of them alone together. She talked to him about how she thought it was respectable that he was still a virgin, and how she hoped that he did not have sex built up in his head as the be-all end-all best thing ever. She found him worthy of telling her secret to, and for a while he was the only one in the flat who knew, and was kind enough to be there for her when she was having flashbacks. Later that week, they ended up in bed together, and navigated friendship from there. Funnily enough, Maja and Sequoia slept together as well.

    Jaime took Finn as a regular lover, enjoying his company and his sexual partnership. Both Scorpios, they got on amazingly in the bedroom. Jaime was open with him about her polyamory and PTSD. Finn treated Jaime very nicely. He even took her to a feminist punk show. Finn liked going to the gay bar with Jaime and her friends from the LGBT society. Sometimes, he made out with Richard. Finn was open with Jaime about having worn girls' clothing before, and enjoying wearing makeup. He'd told her after he heard what she had done with Sydney that he would be down to try it. She helped him explore, and he liked what he found. They were ones to role swap and dress like their opposite, and still enjoy hooking up. Finn even suggested being called Fiona. Jaime liked having someone she could explore that with playfully, because with Sydney it had really only ever been painful due to Sydney's actions and attitude. Jaime walked away from great conversations with Finn feeling understood and connected. She also noticed that she slept well next to him, and rarely had nightmares. She slept well next to Perianth, too, who, on occasion, was nice enough to let her sleep in his bed. Over time, Finn agreed to try polyamory with her, after hearing how she related it to yoga.

"Punk Boi"

Jaime met another punk boi
But didn't Syd Vicious make
Her afraid of that type
So why in her right mind
Would she go for it
Another bi punk boi
Scared as she was
And suddenly, love.

"Mind the Gap"

He says his house has faerie doors
Seafoam aquamarine eyes
Shine as we discuss lore
Side by side in bed we lie

Hair of Amaterasu's rays
Glows like stars
In the warm, bright day

Both of us ruled by Mars

He thinks of places we should go
Breathe in and out
Inhale it slow.

"Mature, Well Spoken, and Sensible"

Sneaky respect
Some of the best
Unlike the rest
Passes the test

Eyes like the sea
Drink me in like tea
I was taken by the dance
Decided to take a chance

Lucky and blessed
Not currently stressed
Desire for your sweet sex
Your warm caress

Smiles and stories
What more can we share?
This electric lightning connection
With communication quite rare.

"Two"

Strawberry imprints on
Sensitive skin
Where bone protrudes
Provoking an inhalation
Pulling on the nerves
And maybe drawing blood
Exhale, the shape of teeth
Marks on fair skin
Crooked teeth,

Teeth that grind
A mouth that hurts all the time
A reflection of the madness in the mind
A mind that want to be over the past
But has deep scars that last
The past has changed the bones
A skeleton altered and left alone

Wracked with damage to the nerves
That's where stretching has a place to serve
Inhale, exhale, learn to breathe again
Learn to be again
Stones and scents to help
When the night comes black
And the fight for the sleep lacked
The warmth of another body
Only works when there is trust
Sometimes it exists alongside lust
As long as the arms provide a safe space
Does the heart race?
A warm body like a fire's base
Both soft and strong like the sea
Gentle and fluid, calming energy
Going and coming back to me
Trust, light like air
Love and trust, maybe not so rare
Warm as the sun
Light shines from one
The light of trust and truth
Gently reach a hand to feel
The other person is real

The Queerness of Sequoia and Perianth

     It was the teacher in Jaime that looked at her flatmates with a critical eye, not her ego. She was observing and assessing them, learning how they worked like they were her students. She was not judging them, but learning what they needed, and where they needed improvement. She was being just as critical with herself. She learned what made them tick, what they liked, how they learned, and how they lived. She was observing what she could offer them. She also learned about the masculinity issues that her Matts had.

Sequoia was put off by Jaime's sexual openness, perhaps threatened by it. He often made jokes about her promiscuity, saying that she was "always on the pull." Jaime knew that all was fair in love and banter in her flat, and she knew that it stemmed from his insecurities, so she didn't take it personally. Sequoia wasn't confident enough to go out to the club without being totally smashed. Jaime noticed the way that the Matts dressed to their insecurities. Perianth thought and got told that he was too skinny, and wore baggy clothes to look bigger. Sequoia thought and got told that he was fat, so he wore clothes that were tight enough to show off his muscles, but loose enough to leave something to the imagination. The boys wore pinks and purples, among other colours, and Perianth expressed himself with his socks, wearing pink socks and socks with funky patterns. Jaime felt bad for noticing qualities about the lads which she regarded as queer. She felt like it was mean of her, and like she was contributing to their masculinity issues. She felt like she was part of the problem, one of those girls as bad as their bullies from school. But she couldn't help seeing things through her bisexual lens, especially after having seen them both kiss boys on the first night. She had no doubts about their attraction to girls, but felt their attraction to boys was questionable. She never mentioned it to them, but thought it was more questionable how often Sequoia brought up what Jaime had done with Sydney.

Jaime noticed things about the boys like how they went to the gym together and how they liked to show off their bodies. Sequoia wore tight shirts and flexed, and Perianth walked around the flat shirtless and was always willing to strip for drinking games. It was almost as if they did it for each other, because one almost always had something to say about the other's body. Typically, it was

Sequoia telling Perianth that he was too skinny, or demonstrating what Perianth could do after "making gains" from the gym.

Jaime viewed everyone as potentially queer for the right person. She noticed the way boys felt the need to be "macho" with each other, a desire to fight, but also a desire to touch each other. One day, she was downstairs with her flatmate boys, Finn, and Sequoia's friend Sky. The boys had started punching each other in the arms and in the stomachs. Sky looked at Jaime and had said, "it's 'cause we're blokes." She also noticed the varied levels of queer in the boys she was outside with - one who labelled himself bi, one who straight-identified but acknowledged having done things with guys, and two who Jaime had seen kiss other boys.

Cigarettes and Fidgets

Some students needed fidgets. Some students were movers who got distracted by their need to stimulate. Like she would observe this in children, Jaime observed this in her flatmate boys. She paid attention to what kind of textures and sensory experiences that they liked and disliked, their body dictionaries, how they breathed, and what kind of sensory input they craved or gave themselves. Sequoia would put his key in his mouth, and Perianth liked little ping pong balls. Smoking cigarettes gave Perianth something to do with his hands. Jaime noticed this new forming habit through her teacher's eyes, but also through her bisexual eyes. She knew that lots of queer men took up smoking, as a habit that hurts, an excuse to talk less, and a way to hide. She worried about warning signs of a self harming lifestyle.

Perianth Things

Jaime wondered why Perianth thought she had romantic feelings for her, but she thought back to other people and noticed that they had also thought that about her. Jaime noticed that love was her natural reflex. She was going to love until she was given a reason not to. Yoga helped

Jaime work on those things that she struggled to love after she was given reasons not to. She tried to work on that so much that she had forgotten the way her natural love could be disarming. Of course she was going to love her flatmate, and she loved him as a person. She saw him, and she appreciated his energy.

    She knew he didn't understand the way that she worked, but he was trying to get used to it. She considered him too nice for her, too pure for her, and felt that he would have been good for her when she was younger. She felt bad about how their experience went, and wanted to try again, but knew he didn't want to. She did not feel bad about their experience because she trusted him and knew that he had been worthy of opening her body to.

    They became close friends, after a few complications. Jaime remembered being drunk with him, sitting and talking at two in the morning, practically crying about how she didn't know if she was capable of true romantic feelings for anyone ever again. He'd been so kind to her that night, assuring her that she would. She appreciated his kindness to her. She'd known from their second night together that she could trust him with her feelings and that sometimes he would not know how to deal with that. He was respectful to her as well, not making a move on her when he let her sleep in his bed, even though he knew he could. Jaime could not explain why they became as close as they had, but wanted to maintain the friendship. At the beginning, she often felt she was tiptoeing around him, because she was still learning him. He became one of her closest friends overseas, and even took her on occasional adventures. Perianth was sweet to Jaime, and she was ever grateful for that, because he was there for her during many times of need, and was a good flatmate to her. He helped her maintain a feeling of safety and comfort in their flat. They had a relationship where silence was no longer awkward, and where they could be themselves with each other. He was used to her doing yoga in the kitchen, and his presence did not distract her and put her off balance. He learned where to move so he did not get kicked in the head and he learned how to assist her when her sciatica was acting up. Jaime did her best to be a good friend to him, and to also give him his space so that he would continue to want to be a good friend to her.

"One Petal Flower"

If you think
She's beautiful
When she's just gotten up

Not when she's asleep
Because many people
Are beautiful in sleep

If somehow she makes
A smile creep
Across the lips she's kissed

Maybe it's something
Not to be missed.

If you describe her
like the sunset or sunrise
Only if you tell no lies.

"New Territory"

This is new territory
I don't know how this became normalised
For me, that friendship includes
Kissing and sleeping in each other's beds

When did I become this person?
Were me and the Ace girls like that?
F r i e n d s?
What does that mean?

My closest friends (at home home)
A former crush
Someone I slept with many times
My gay husband

Those are most of them
Where are the girls from my home home?
There are some in other places…

Mandie and Lizzi

     Mandie and Lizzi were two bisexual girls in a happy, loving relationship. Jaime knew Mandie and Lizzi from the LGBT group chat, and was pleasantly surprised how excited they were to meet her in person. Jaime had developed crushes on both girls, which she spoke to Glitterboii about, not wanting to ruin their relationship. The girls were still honeymooning, or maybe they were just perfect for each other. Jaime wondered if maybe she was just bitter. She didn't expect their relationship to survive university. But, she valued them as friends and people and didn't want to be the cause of their relationship ending, so she chose not to act on her crushes, even though she felt they made it quite hard for her. Mandie and Lizzi were comfortable enough around Jaime for one to undress the other in front of her. Later, Lizzi confessed to Jaime that she and Mandie were looking into polyamory. She asked Jaime for some advice on how to start looking for someone to join them. Jaime was glad to be able to talk to them about it, and equally glad that she could talk to them about what her and Finn did in the bedroom, which she had previously only ever done with Sydney.

Skylar and Emerson

     Sequoia had made two friends on his course. Jaime found it funny that both of these friends ended up being bisexual boys. They also had unisex names, and went by unisex nicknames, which Jaime liked about them. Skylar was Sky, and Emerson was Em. Skylar was the first friend, who stayed overnight sometimes so he didn't have to commute to school for morning lectures. He went out with them to the clubs, and hung out with them outside the flat, participating in physical activities. Skylar, however, put his moves on Maja, and ended up no longer welcome in the flat after Jaime's birthday, but remained friends with her and Perianth.

The second friend was Emerson, who played sports for their course's society with Sequoia. Emerson enjoyed a night out as well, and liked to dress dapper. Jaime had a gift for getting people to tell her about their sex lives, and Emerson was one of her victims. While she disagreed with his political views, he proved to be generally nice to women and looked after her in some ways when she was drunk on nights out.

Perianth and Em were both political conservatives. Emerson was a bisexual conservative. Perianth didn't want to share his political views at university, but they came out. Jaime wondered how they could be conservative when they seemed to have liberal attitudes and personalities. They did not view women as not equal to them, and were respectful in their treatment. They didn't condone disrespect to women. Perianth was cool with Jaime's queerness, her queer friends and lover, his own queer friends, and even accompanying Jaime to the gay bar on her birthday. He was the kind of guy who went to strip clubs and weed cafes in Amsterdam. Jaime figured that their families must be conservative or come from money. She had the foresight that they might experience a struggle with their conflicting values and lifestyles.

Jaime questioned if Emerson and Perianth were genuinely respectful. Emerson drooled over girls in the club and made come hither gestures. Perianth had to relearn not to make a certain kind of joke around Jaime or Maja. but Jaime used to laugh at those kinds of jokes, before she knew better. As time went on, Jaime learned that Perianth could be there for her if she needed him to protect her in the club. She hoped she influenced her boys to know better than the jokes they made. She hoped Perianth particularly, could learn from her, and if he learned nothing else, she hoped he learned to be less insecure about his appearance.

Emerson was afraid to be out as bisexual because of his conservative views. He knew that the duality of bisexuality threatens how society is organised. By challenging current assumptions about immutability of orientations and society's supposed divisions into discrete groups, bisexuality becomes a threat. People are also threatened by the refusal to choose. Bisexuals who profoundly maintain open options run the risk of becoming over diversified and spread thing, attempting to substitute "equal opportunity" and a lack of affiliation for genuinely ending oppression. The refusal to choose threatens the "us or them" mentality we are socialised with. This is because the refusal to choose has been linked to unpredictability. It is worth noting that unpredictable is not the same as unreliable. (Bi Any Other Name). Perhaps these reasons mixed with conservative views had something to do with why Perianth couldn't acknowledge the seemingly bisexual tendencies that Jaime and Finn noticed.

Yasmin and Oshun

Jaime and Finn met Yasmin and Oshun through Mandie and Lizzi, at a party. Yasmin and Oshun were a couple, who immediately got along with Jaime and Finn, and invited them to their flat at a subsequent date. Oshun showed Jaime and Finn incredible kindness, cooking for them and inviting them into a mutually beneficial friendship based on generosity. The girls were artists, and Yasmin wanted to teach art.

Yasmin was particularly active, and it piqued Jaime's interest. She introduced Jaime to the revolutionary concept of picking up litter whilst out for a run. Yas noticed the effects that intense exercise and the lack of intense exercise had on her mental health, and wanted to help others learn and understand about it. She was very health conscious, and

Jaime got to teach her about Ayurveda and eating for the different doshas. She understood the benefits of yoga, having practised before, and occasionally joined Jaime in practising or partnered up with her for a bit of acro yoga. Jaime was interested in collaborating with Yasmin in future educational projects.

Yasmin and Oshun provided Jaime and Finn with a safe and nurturing environment in which to learn and grow together, where they could share ideas and work on projects. Most importantly, they provided Finn and Jaime a space in which to be themselves, completely, without judgement. They were allowed to experiment, to feel, to speak, to relax in their bodies. Finn and Jaime held onto this and aimed to create such an environment for others in their other personal relationships.

Stevie

Jaime and Finn had decided to move in with Sky and a coursemate of his, and needed another person to fill the house they liked. Not knowing where to look, Jaime turned to the LGBT Society to see if anyone needed help finding housemates. A girl called Stevie reached out to her, and she and the boys met up with Stevie. Upon getting to know her, Jaime was thrilled. Stevie was so many things that she was looking for in a friend. She appreciated poetry, art, and she cared about the environment. She was also a great cook and had good taste in music. Jaime and Finn enjoyed Stevie's company, and Jaime felt fulfilled knowing she was forming a meaningful relationship with another girl, something that never came easily to her, but was with Stevie. Jaime instantly loved Stevie for accepting her, despite her previous struggles with making female friends, and felt immediately bonded to her through sisterhood. She was protective of Stevie, and knew that Stevie would be there for her when she needed. She looked forward to cultivating a "girly" friendship, where they could lay on each other's beds, laze about, chat, paint each others' nails, and make snacks. It had been a truly long time since Jaime had had a girl she could trust, and she felt like she could open her heart to Stevie. Stevie proved quickly to be a good secret keeper, and also a great conversationalist who was up for any topic. Such friendship was required for Jaime to continue to motivate herself to be the best she could be, and Stevie inspired her to live more sustainably.

Jaime's Jealousy

Jaime had to learn to deal with the twinges of platonic jealousy that she got when her flatmates were doing things together without her. She knew that ultimately, deep down, she would do what was right for her regardless of what her flatmates were doing. Yet she felt the social pressure to spend time with them and to like them. She worried that she was being excluded, and that relational aggression was being used, particularly by Maja. She worried that the Matts liked Maja better than they liked her. She had to deal with experiencing these feelings, and the feelings that she felt when they were all out for drinks without her, watching films in Maja's room together without her, or when she walked into the kitchen and they were all already hanging out. Jaime had to learn to accept these feelings and let them go as they came.

Love, Sex, and Fancy Things

In the essay *Love, Friendship, and Sex* from the book <u>Bi Any Other Name</u>, Wayne Bryant discusses sex between friends. Jaime experienced sex between friends in her new life with Finn and Perianth, having unique experiences with each boy.
"The big problem with relationships is that people often confuse love, friendship, and sex, which are three independent types of interactions, none of which automatically imply the other. Sex does not equal friendship or love, or mean that sex will happen again. There is no reason sex should ruin a friendship, and no reason one's lover cannot be their best friend. There can be love without

sex, and sex without love, regardless of friendship. Friends who can sleep together without the pressure of sex and commitment of love are invaluable" (Bryant, W. 1990).

This is represented in the book Anam Cara through the concept of space. John O'Donohue writes, "one of the lovely areas of love where space can be rendered beautiful is when two people make love. The one you love is the one to whom you can bring the full array and possibility and delight of your senses in the knowledge that they will be received in welcome tenderness. Making love should not be merely a physical or mechanical release, but should engage the spiritual depth that awakens when you enter the soul of another person. The soul of a person is most intimate. The world of touch includes the whole world of sexuality, this is probably the most tender aspect of human presence. When you are sexual with someone, you let them right into your world. The world of sexuality is a sacred world of presence and Eros, devastated by greed and contemporary commercialism."

There is the concept of carrying people we've slept with within us because they have touched our souls. Jaime was glad to sleep with Perianth because he did not carry anyone's energy with him besides his own. She felt that she did not transmit the energy of others to him because she used yoga to distance herself from the part of her soul which had been touched. She was able to bring her own energy to him and pay attention to him genuinely, but Perianth had become confused by this, thinking she had romantic feelings for him. He had to learn that for Jaime, friendships could exist within the parameters of hugging, kissing, holding hands, and sex.

"The Spaces Between Us"

There is space
Where the conversation dips
Where we understand each other
Through a stained glass window

There is space
Between your fingers
For mine
At any time

There is space
When we lay
In the sheets
Or when we're shaking them

There is space
Between us,
Between your shoulder blades
Where I like to kiss

There is space
Between us
Where I search your (sometimes stormy) eyes
And look for any words unspoken that I've missed

There is space between us
Containing a multitude of experiences
Shaping our lives
A whole galaxy of time

There is space
Three thousand miles of it
At some points
Keeping us apart

There is space
Shared between us
In a little box
Inside our hearts.

The space between us
Where you allow me to work
And to be myself
Is your greatest gift to me.

It was through yoga that Jaime managed all these new experiences, including being in her new location for personal, family reasons. She dealt with ups and downs, formal and informal learning, and all sorts of feelings. Yoga had prepared her with the skills she needed to go forth in life and succeed.

Safe Space

Jaime's ultimate goal was to create a safe space for her students. A safe space encompasses so many things.

The sad thing is that a safe space must be created from violence, and everyone from Jaime's preschoolers to her preteens have to be exposed to lock down drills because some people bring guns to school.

Dex argues that everyone needs to know what to do in dangerous situations just to survive.

Sometimes, Jaime tell the children, danger will be where you are and you will have to flee. Other times, danger will be outside of where you are and you will have to stay where you are.

Dex tells Jaime not to forget to tell them about the times when you will need to fight.

A safe space is somewhere where Jaime can openly read her Gay Witchcraft book without being judged or questioned. This place is not her home, with her family, though she loved them dearly. This place will be her future home, though, she vowed to herself.

A safe space is somewhere that a queer person of colour can openly read that same book without being judged or questioned. There are not enough of these places at the present moment. Jaime's future classrooms will be these places, she vowed to herself.

A safe space is somewhere for the young Peri, whose strict island parents forbid living with them after coming out. Peri had only been fourteen, and ended up in foster care. Peri got switched around from family to family as they discovered the truth. Peri needed somewhere to be a safe space after some foster families had given a much too enthusiastic send off.

A safe space had both an incredibly personal quality and a strong sense of community. You could be alone, but this was made possible by the power of the people around you. In turn, you contribute to the safe space, helping to maintain it.

Jaime was incredibly grateful for the safe spaces she had been a part of and absorbed the effects. She wanted to start some safe spaces of her own. She was reaching into creation. She had a positive force to radiate.

Jaime was struck by the Book of Qualities. She related to sensuality, who liked to make love at the border where time and space change places. Jaime also related to Whimsy in the Book of Qualities because she too colour coded her closet. Her brother was also a troublemaker. She too was unafraid to be outrageous, yet also shy. Coincidentally, Freedom was Whimsy's lover. Jaime believed her lover Le Feu to be the epitome of Freedom. Like her he was not designed to belong to anyone but himself. Lastly, she identified with suffering from the Book of Qualities, and was proud to recognise the value of the lessons she'd learned through her suffering.

Half Red, Half Blue (the Story of Jaime and Sean)

A sixteen year old girl with shoulder length brown curls waited in line for her bus home from high school. She looked around, bored. A blond boy wearing skinny jeans and purple eats headphones stood in front of her. He had a studded belt around his waist and then she noticed he was wearing a bracelet that said "legalise" on it. She tapped his shoulder, and he turned around to remove his headphones and reveal snakebite piercings on his face.

"What kind of legalise does your bracelet say? I've got a legalise bracelet too and I wanted to see which thing we've got in common. I'm Jaime, by the way." She beamed at him.

He introduced himself as Sean and rotated his bracelet so she could see it read "legalise love."

"So, you're gay?" she asked, as they climbed onto the bus.

"Bi, I guess," he said as he sat down, and scooched over to let her into the seat.

"Me too!" She was delighted. "I love making gay friends! Now, tell me everything about you, because I want to know why I haven't seen you around before."

Sean told Jaime all about his life in Massachusetts that he just left, his situation with his family, and what he liked to do with his time. They got off at the same bus stop, and Jaime demanded his phone number before they parted ways. She called him Snakebites, thinking already that his name was too typical for such a unique person.

They spent every afternoon on the bus together, and most mornings, blasting music, talking, joking, and laughing. Sean let Jaime come into his stage house, he showed her a woodcarving he'd made of his ex-boyfriend (the one who got away) and gave her a pair of watermelon coloured sneakers that the old owners left in his stage house. The first time Sean visited Jaime's house, they walked all over the neighbourhood together as she described her life.

He did a backbend on the bridge to the island at her hiding place. Something clicked about them. Jaime was naturally open, but something about her made Sean want to open up to her. They talked about absolutely everything, even swapped secrets. It's an understatement to say that they were fast friends. Syd, Jaime's most serious high school boyfriend, was threatened by their sudden inseparability.

"You want to fuck him, don't you?" Syd insisted.

"Sydney, he's gay. I have no chance," Jaime replied, as Sean had quickly changed his statement of bisexuality to one of pure homosexuality.

"But if he wasn't gay, you'd want to fuck him, wouldn't you?" Syd protested.

"Sydney," Jaime sighed. "I will admit that I find Sean beautiful, but you have nothing to worry about."

Often, Jaime was told she was too honest. Syd flew off the handle at her honesty.

"Of course! Of course you think he's beautiful, with his blond hair and blue eyes and skinny jeans. Of course! Beautiful Snakebites Sean!"

"Sydney, please. Can't you just be happy for me that I have a new friend who I really connect with and really like? I want him to party with us, so you can't be like this." Jaime's word about friendship was usually unmoving, she would never renounce friendships for her relationship.

The first time Jaime and Sean smoked together was out of an elephant bowl that Jaime had got from Warped Tour in the stairway at his stage house. The first time they had a sleepover was when Sean slept in her basement after the Homecoming game and afterparty. Back then they would not have expected that basement to become Sean's home for half a year.

For the Homecoming game, Sean partied with Jaime and Syd's crowd for the first time. Back then they also didn't think Sean would end up partying with a different round of Jaime and Syd's crowd with Jaime and Syd in a new relationship. There's a picture of them in red tinted lighting from that night, Jaime's wearing her devil horns and Sean's wearing blue. That night they'd ridden around in the bed of

Chance Pasto's red truck that he drove while drunk. They'd pregamed at Jaime's, then went to the high school. They stayed fifteen minutes at the game, got bored, and went back to party. After everyone left Jaime stayed up late with Sean talking about everything.

Sean attended Jaime's seventeenth birthday party. Her own boyfriend didn't even do that. Jaime could not have guessed that two years later he'd be throwing her birthday party or that she's spend her twentieth with him back at Syd's house. Jaime's extra-from-Syd crowd attended this birthday party, too and got to meet her new friend Sean. As your typical "straight dudes," they all made the same comment about him. "Sean's mad cool, Jaime, even though he's gay, because he's not like, in your face gay."

In the middle of Jaime's senior year, Sean switched high schools and then switched states. About a year passed by and he contacted her. He was back in town. Jaime was dating Julio, starting a new job, and doing school, so by the time she finally saw Sean he was living at Anabelle's house. It wasn't long after that that he was living in her basement and the two became inseparable.

Jaime and Sean were all about adventures. Sean started living with Jaime shortly after she'd gotten her license. Jaime recently acquired the family's mid-sized SUV after her small convertible's transmission blew on her way to school. For the summer she and Sean frequented concerts at an all ages nightclub since he had no ID. They spent long nights in her backyard, when the nights were still as warm as the stars were bright. They drove across state lines together, into each of the three states that theirs was bordered by (one of those states was where Sean used to live, where they had driven in Jaime's red car, when Jaime got to meet the one that got away for Sean and his original best friend). Sean spent his eighteenth birthday in Jaime's backyard, where she stayed up with him until four in the morning. Sean was Jaime's favourite person to drive with.

Sean was all about music. In high school he and Jaime would share headphones on the bus or blast music from speakers. He had always been all about music. Jaime's favourite early memory story of his was about how he used to spend his days with his original best friend, listening to music and using a fog machine. When he lived with Jaime, nights were soundtracked by his boombox, and for ambience sometimes he'd put a strobe light under her patio's glass table. They'd go at it for hours, never getting sick of the sound and light therapy. Sean was Jaime's ultimate copilot. He controlled the music, he controlled her phone – answering text messages from her parents, flirting with people, contacting whoever they were meeting up with-, and he controlled navigation when Jaime wasn't mapping from her brain. She would defer the passenger seat to him over anybody, even romantic partners.

    Music was a form of control for Sean. At a young age he learned that music could drown out anything, including any ruckus his parents wanted to cause. Sean lived for loud music. Loud music could drown out any jerk at school, too. And music was always there. Music was there when Sean had no parents, no friends, no partner. Music was there when he had to be with himself. Music could make anything bearable – school, work, travel. Sean was able to control what he heard and didn't hear. Even when his life was chaotic, he could still be in control of something.

    It has been speculated that Sean encourages bad behaviour (like Benji). Sean and Jaime burned bright, but they were a little crazy. A little risky as well. They had both gotten suspended for the same thing in middle school. Somehow, states away from each other, and experienced somewhat the same thing. They had many differenced among their commonalities, but there was something about them that made them think the same way about some things. This was the same something that allowed them to enjoy the movie Elephant together, songs about suicide and Columbine blasting in the car, and YouTube videos of planes crashing. This was also the same something that allowed Sean to ride along with Jaime when she would ask him to save her from crashing her car. This is why people would accuse Sean of encouraging bad behaviour. He was a little bit of know your limits and take no shit mixed in with a bit of (possibly hereditary) self-destruct. Sean and Jaime, they could smile their way into being crazy. Perhaps that's why they were devils in Anabelle's hallucination.

Somehow, they could smile their way out of it, too. After everything, Jaime and Sean were practically tough as nails and they never let the self-destruct button stay on for too long. They were high risk at risk youth, but they did things together that helped lower their drive to risk their lives. They shared being moved by music, and they shared a love of (and need for) movement. This is why they loved to go out and dance. As dance partners they rocked the floor. They were both blessed with good looks and out together would often be mistaken for a couple, which turned out to save them from a lot of nightclub creeps. They could dance all night totally sober and feel alive without much risk. They also spent time cooking together. Sean was moved by food. Jaime was eager to learn. Nights in with money spent on food saved them risk, stress, and served them good. Cooking let them cater to their health.

Instead of aimless driving, they occasionally drove to destinations. They had made day trips to several places. Instead of times to be super risky, these were times to enjoy things they didn't always see.

In the fifth year of their friendship, Sean had his own apartment for over a year. Jaime was not his roommate, as intended, but they were still the best of friends. They still had sickly sweet smiles and still kept each other in check. Sean lived at Kumo's house after Jaime's, until he had his own place. Jaime found herself ever amazed at his strength.

For the months that Jaime had provided Sean with a safe space, he provided her one at his own place, when hers became slightly less safe. They both knew what it felt like to be displaced.

In one of Jaime's favourite shows, How I Met Your Mother, there was a quote which said, "friendship is an involuntary reflex, it just happens, you can't help it."

Jaime felt that we are naturally inclined to align with others, which is why friendship is like an involuntary reflex for us. We want to keep the bonds we form and not burn our bridges. So, we keep the feelings of our loved ones in mind when we act. Our desires adapt to include our loved ones, and we aim to spend time with them to strengthen our bonds. We seek support and comfort in others, and like to know when people are around who would fight for us. It is a survival instinct. It is also related to Maslow's Love and Belonging, as we need to feel as though we belong

Rad Warriors Union

     He doesn't think of himself as an orphan. He doesn't think of himself as homeless, either. But the alcoholic woman he lives with is not his mother. She just quit her job, so he doesn't know how long he'll be staying. Her own children are taking her to court. He doesn't think she's an alcoholic. Not compared to his parents.
     He isn't homeless because he's gay. He just so happens to be gay and homeless. His parents said they always knew. No, he's homeless because of alcoholics. Circumstances. He's eighteen, but can't prove it. You can't get an ID without an address. But he's fine. Perfectly fine, don't worry about him. He's got this.
     None of them want to go home. Not even the one whose house they're at. She's totally checked out for the night. The colors are still moving.
     A few others around the table have experienced homelessness. One boy was kicked out and is back "home" now wishing he could've kept couch surfing. Another ran away once. So that made four of them. The gay orphan, the bi runaway, the punk who got kicked out, and the girl – bi and totally checked out.
     They were sitting in Jaime's backyard, congregated around her patio table. Jaime, Sean, Rorey, Sawyer, and Syd. Syd just Syd, he'd dropped the -ney part completely. And then there was the new girl. Or at least, Syd didn't know her. But to be honest, Syd didn't really know most of the people around the table. He had met Sean (Snakebites) before and hung out with him and Jaime, and Sawyer he knew from the beach. Other people would come to sit at this table, even

over the course of the night. For example, Sean Cruz, Rorey's boyfriend. Syd stared at the table. He had sat here many times before doing this same thing. He and Jaime used to entertain guests here. Back when they were he and Jaime.

So, basically, most of his friends were either on dope or dropped him completely. One day he opened his door to find Jaime, shaking and looking like she was about to cry. Turned out that one of her friends had OD'd. She went sort of nuts when she found out, turning up to see people she hadn't seen in years. Jaime had always been so emotional that way. But that's how Syd ended up sitting across the table from his ex-girlfriend, who would periodically look at him like she wanted to get back in his pants, and then she would make a face like she wanted to kill herself for thinking that.

Jaime. She was the only person he ever let call him Sydney. She loved his full name, loved that it was unisex. She was one of those weird girls who likes boys with girl names or boys who do other girly things, like wear jewelry or cook, or kiss other boys (and it just gets gayer from there). She never even let him call her by her full name. Jaimesyera. It sounded a lot prettier when she said it, anyway.

Syd enjoyed her company nonetheless, glad to have a friend and a place to go instead of home. And Jaime was always generous with her weed, though right now Sean was in charge of that matter. Nobody pushed him too hard here. Jaime knew better than to ask too many questions, even if she knew something was wrong. She normally knew what it was, anyway. She was always like that – she just knew things. He wasn't even bothered by all of her gay friends. They weren't the annoying kind of gay. They were just chill stoners. Yeah, Rorey's hair looked like a bird's egg, and Sean's hair was every color of the rainbow, but he still didn't find them to be a nuisance. Not even when Sean Cruz and Rorey showed PDA. Snakebites Sean liked to be in control of the music, but everything he played was fine and not obnoxious.

"Sean, I swear you play human silencing music," Jaime snickered, stirring briefly from her edible-induced trance. With her car being worked on, she had the hours to spare for the cookie. She almost never got to let loose like this.

Sean ate a cookie with her because she shared everything with him. For the past year, they had been inseparable. Syd was still unconvinced about Sean's gayness, and just as convinced as he was when they were dating that Jaime would love to be all over Sean.

Jaime couldn't deny it, and Syd wasn't the only boyfriend to get jealous of her friendship with Sean. They were kindred spirits, connected as soon as they met. All the time he had to move around didn't make a difference. They just picked right up where they left off. He lived at her house for half a year, in her basement, and had helped her through so much. He made her day when he called her his best friend. He was the copilot in her car and gave her the confidence to push herself and drive farther – first to the nightclub and then on road trips. They would constantly treat each other – to dinner, to concerts, to road trips, to weed... Even so, she was still uncontrollably jealous of how much he liked to hang out with Sawyer. She didn't find Sawyer as entertaining as Sean did.

Sawyer could be really nice sometimes. But she could also be really not nice, or really annoying. At first Jaime thought she was cute, but she didn't even think that anymore (most of the time). Sawyer wasn't unattractive, it was just her personality. She was a lovely caramel color, with a short haircut but big, poofy curls. She had her tongue pierced just like Jaime (copycat) and her nose. She wore snapbacks and was generally just a small person. She was, however, very loud, and could rarely control herself.

Sawyer resented Jaime herself. Jaime and Sean were the same sort of person. They were just good at everything they tried. Sean got a new job so quickly after he got fired, and he's already been promoted. Jaime doesn't think she's smart like Sean, but she is. She even goes to college. She would brush it off as community college, but she still goes, she still does her work, still makes good grades. She worked harder than most of her friends – with two jobs and all the classes she took. She was crazy enough to take summer classes, too.

Not to mention she could drive, and she owned her own car. Sean was the only person without a license she'd let drive her car. Figures. Sean just knew how to do things. He could dye hair, he could pierce people, he could change oil. He was an amazing cook. One time, he even took his boom box apart and hooked its speakers up to the TV ang got it to work. People like Sean and Jaime, they could just figure it out. They were gifted and talented. They were good at so many things – too many to count. Jaime could sew, Sean could mix music, they could both draw... Sawyer wished she was good at something.

Sawyer, her best friend Tiffany, and Jaime were young, attractive ladies who didn't "act like ladies" but wanted to be "treated like ladies" sometimes but also like to be in charge, spoiled people, and openly talked about loving riding dick – who went for girls too at varying degrees. If they all went out together they got stared at. They were focused on their own growth. Independent.

Rorey's eyes were closed. He always knocked out, even when Sean Cruz was there.

Music blared from Sean's speaker. Jaime grinned at the next song. Paper Planes by M.I.A. It was their song. The two of them listened to this song on many drives. It was mixed with the song Pumped Up Kicks by Foster the People. Every time the Paper Planes chorus came on, Jaime made her fingers into guns and sung along.

Jaime grinned at the music and held out her hand to Sean, who obliged and took it. They sat in silence holding hands with Jaime grinning as the music went on about guns and hustling, and she leaned back in her rocking chair.

"Sean, you gotta look at these stars."

It was a clear night; the stars were beautiful from Jaime's backyard. But for Jaime and Sean, they were moving.

In some ways, they were a band of misfits. Gay kids, hair dyed freaks, stoners, orphans, and runaways, the kind of kids who carried knives on them. Kids who drank, kids who tripped, kids who didn't make it out of high school. Kids who stole and kids who tried to kill themselves. In some ways, they were the kids your parents warned you about.

But in all ways, they were warriors.

Syd had a friend pick him up so the night wouldn't have to end. Sean Cruz took a taxi to the train station. Sunny, the new girl, drove Rorey and Sawyer home. And at two in the morning, when the colors had mostly stopped moving, Sean stood up, hugged Jaime goodbye, and took a walk for an hour to get home.

The Hardest Story for Me to Write (Sean's Tale)

Jaime didn't remember when he told her outright, when they talked about it.

She remembered he said he was eleven. She remembered the other boy's name, she thought, she thought she remembered how he knew him.

Sean and Jaime didn't feel the need to repeat conversations. Like the song by the Talking Heads says, "say something once why say it again?"

Jaime didn't remember how it came up in conversation. They just got there. It just became known.

She didn't know who knows. It's not like Sean goes around broadcasting that sort of thing. He wasn't about to give people reasons to feel sorry for him. But they didn't really talk about it, meaning Jaime didn't really talk about it, meaning Jaime didn't bring it up because she didn't want to trigger her friend.

Funnily enough, she can't recall his comments to when she told him about what happened when she was fifteen. She remembered he believed me.

Jaime believed him when he told her. You don't joke around about that kind of thing. You have to want to tell someone. You look around before you talk about it, you hush your voice when you say it out loud.

Jaime wasn't speaking to the mechanic when she first started hanging out with Sean, as per Syd's orders due to the reaction he had after she told him what happened when she was fifteen. The night she told Syd was the night after the vigil when Jaime decided he deserved her virginity and she told him because she wanted him to know why she was scared of sex.

Jaime didn't know if Sean spent time being scared of sex afterwards. It's tough, because Sean is always strong when he's scared. He doesn't let himself show any broken moments. Rage? Sure. But never sadness (despair) or fear. Jaime also know that she had many reasons to be scared that she had learned from her mother's values, Sean of course experienced life differently. Truthfully, Jaime didn't have the tools to tell Sean's story. She can only talk about him as she has experienced him.

The facts of his story are indisputably such:

Sean has suffered. Sean is also a survivor of sexual trauma.

Sean's family is not together.

Sean left high school.

Sean has lived at Anabelle's house, Jaime's house, Kumo's house, and Rorey's house.

Sean has incredible work ethic.

Sean hustled and got his own place with two cats and has lived there for over a year being strong, brave, and bright.

Sean is an inspiration. Jaime's favourite thing about him was that he didn't make her struggles less than his. He viewed them as equals on a level playing field, cooperating and not competing. Sean met you where you were. He didn't overtly try to comfort you if you were sad, he'd let you experience your feeling and help in subtle ways, like by being there and allowing you not to have to experience your feeling alone. He taught you that if you didn't put in the work to cheer yourself up you wouldn't cheer up, that no one was going to do anything for you but you. He expected similar treatment – you'd meet him where he was with no complaints. Sean was direct, in a very take no prisoners way. You were either helping him, or you were entirely irrelevant. And not in the using people sense, but more in the cooperation sense. If your goals didn't align with his in a meaningful way, you weren't necessary in his life and he saw no reason to tolerate it. Some called him ruthless, but I called him truthful. If someone couldn't help him learn and grow, he didn't bond with them. His mission was to help himself first. This was necessary, as he relied on no one. For the moment Sean's mission was continuous improvement, and that was no less ambitious than any goal to help others. His time to serve would come

Prove Them Wrong

Sean loved proving people wrong. His favourite thing to prove people wrong about was that they could like the things that they said they didn't like. Whether it was proving Jaime could like spicy food or chicken, or proving to boys that they could like other boys, it brought fiery Sean joy to prove a point. He liked to do this to show everyone how their tastes change with age, and how fluid everything is. He also liked to make people appreciate everything.

"Bishi Bestie"

Cuddling his kitty
my Sean looks like a bishi
from my favourite manga
right down to the pastel blue hair
just like Shin
with his tiny septum piercing
and skinny jeans
he gives me that Bishi smile
smirk and lets Binx go
his light, icy eyes know
I don't have to say anything
he knows the song my heart sings

my bishi bestie
replaced my old shoujo friends
who used to be all over each other
and it's funny
Sean and I have outgrown
frequent physical affection
we can feel it now
without needing to feel each other
and just like a bishi
he is so strikingly beautiful
for a boy
makes a dynamic duo
with the Magical Girl
everyone so busy staring at our
beautiful, moon kissed skin,
star drenched hair,
sun bright faces
they never see our power coming
he wins the upper hand for us, typically
but we always trade places

"Slay/Stay"

It's in the twist of our hips
the way we wear our hair
the curl of our lips
it's in our hazy air

we are two
sickly sweet and charming devils
the world cannot resist, it's true
but we are on interplanetary levels

nobody knows how serious we are when we sing along
to our favourite questionable songs
or what we've both done wrong
or how we made a family in which we finally belong

so you kill the lights
and I'll kill the hearts
we end the fights
there's no defense against our dark arts

we were born to be bad
and in the best of ways too
so try not to get mad
when we shine at everything we do

we love fast, hard, and deep
the best you'll ever get
take a leap
and it can't be a regret

for now we hold each other's hand
fingers laced and intertwined
two beautiful crooked trees in a faraway land
wondering what we will find

"What It's Like"

here's what it's like
to be in love with
your gay best friend
agonizing torture

he's the best ever
and yours never
but he keeps you company
and teaches you things

he takes care of you
he wipes your tears
but he's not true
it's all your worst fears

you get to watch when he
takes boy after boy
which you could never be
you see him use each toy

he loves you
that is not a lie
he just couldn't be true
to a girl over a guy

even though you pretend play
the two of you are in love
it's not real at least today
but still you're thanking above

for this wonderful friend
your partner in crime
a dynamic duo you never want to end

"What It's Like Pt. 2"

They're the kind of friends
who give each other all they've got
and over backwards they bend
even when there's not

anything left to give
they give each other
reasons to live

she has rarely seen him cry
(he's seen her tons of times)
but she knows when he has to try
to keep it all inside

she loves this boy
almost as much as the one she calls her own
he loves her too but he's so coy
might always be one to roam

she gives him candlesticks to break
for when he's mad
he gives her love to take
for when she's sad

and even when they fall asleep hanging out
from working too hard, they have a nice time
that's what friendship is about

she's happy for him and all he can do
and he's quite pleased for her too
one thing they share
is how they dare
to love someone of their same sex
and not care about opinions of the rest.

Sound Therapy

     Jaime most frequently experienced sound therapy with Sean. (though others knew of its power, like Liam and Karoline, who were moved to make music.)
Those who didn't know Sean very well and liked genres of music that weren't electronic got easily annoyed with the tunes he blasted, dubbing him as someone who exclusively enjoyed electronic dance music.
     While Sean loved the kind of music that contained sounds that could hurt his ears, he actually enjoyed a variety of sounds and genres. Most commonly Sean could be heard playing electronic music or rap/hip-hop, but he also enjoyed rock and roll, swing, jazz, and slow music. Sean was the type of person who could listen to just sounds, too. Sometimes, he and Jaime or he and Anabelle would listen to Tibetan singing bowls, Native American flute music, ocean sounds, rain sounds, or steel drums. Through morning car rides to work with Sean, Jaime learned she needed slow to appreciate fast, quiet to appreciate loud.

Therapeutic Light Crew (TLC)

     Jaime discovered flow arts through going to raves with Julio. She was given her first flow hoop by the girlfriend of a DJ who had driven her and Julio home from a show, after complimenting the girl's LED hoop performance. A few months later, Jaime bought her first LED hoop. Jaime was fascinated by the combination of colours, sounds, and movements, and had fun experimenting with her hoop.
     She knew people with other flow toys, like glovers she'd met out at the nightclub she used to frequent with both Julio and Sean. One of the glover boys could spin poi, another had an orbit. One nice glover boy, Dan Teller, taught Jaime a few tricks with her LED hoop. They called themselves the Therapeutic Light Crew.
     Jaime wondered why she did not see more male hoopers in the flow scene.

Gender Dominance in Flow Communities

Why does gender dominance take place in flow communities? The circle is one of the most feminine shapes with no lines, edges, or points. When you look at all other flows, they have a point, edge, and line. With this, these shapes use feminine circular motion, but through a masculine platform. Many of them relay back to a warrior instinct, which is masculine in its energy. This is one thought as to why less women are involved with other flows such as poi and staff. To be a true flow artist, scared mover, and body talker is to access the deepest roots of masculine and feminine, showing up for the self in a way which overflows unconditional love with each step (Dharam, D. 2017).

Friends are Music

Sean reminded Jaime one Christmas, "music is always there." Jaime knew this to be factual. Music had always been there for her in times of darkness.

Jaime started to think of her friends in terms of music. She noticed the frequency at which her friends vibrated, and saw the waves of sound and colour that they emitted. Some were music she could listen to all the time. Others were music she could only listen to at certain times.

Jaime found that, similar to music, some friends were always there. Ironically, many of Jaime's friends were either artists or musicians. Sean was an artist in the kitchen and an aspiring DJ. Liam was a marching band musician. Le Feu was an artist with his scooter. Anabelle was an artist with her body. Karoline was an orchestra musician. Syd had been a guitarist. Your art is your yoga, too.

These were the people here with Jaime through her struggles. They were there with each other through struggles. They watched each other grow.

As they grew, so did their knowledge and possibility of conversational topics. Hearing her friend say the word diaphragm blew Jaime away. They were twenty and twenty one, so experienced, smart, and so young. They were able to engage in a deeper conversation about proper breathing, which was deeply pleasing. The way you breathe is your yoga, too. It's different for everybody.

As an early childhood educator, Jaime knew children respond to music naturally.

A yoga teacher called Jeiken once said, "yoga should be different every day."

Music and Child Development

Jaime knew that children needed a variety of experiences to support musical expression. Jaime knew that music supported developmental milestones in language. When it came to such milestones, we could send subliminal messages through music, helping children learn about certain concepts by presenting them through song. As adults, music can help facilitate conversations, silence, moods, moments. She had learned that beat competency was something most children developed naturally (the ability to keep and follow a beat [i.e. patterns, which is one way in which math is related to music]). In relation to beat competency, Laurie Cabot wrote a moving piece in <u>Celebrate the Earth</u> about dancing. "Dance is a means by which we are bound to the past; it provides a reflection of our beliefs and faith. Dance is feeling the spirit. Most of us instinctively know how to dance. We have been dancing all our lives."

As adults, we can ask how to give ourselves a variety of experiences stimulating the senses as well as a variety of experiences available involving different learning and developmental domains.

Sensory Experiences

Sean was an auditory, visual, and kinesthetic learner. Because of his ADHD, he had a predilection for kinesis. Due to both of these things, Sean took great pleasure in engaging in sensory experiences. Sean was big on textures, and his tactile sense was easily bothered by certain types of clothing. The tactile sense was the sense which allowed us to do things like button shirts or pants, put belts on, and physical motions of that nature. The tactile sense was also that sense which helped us differentiate textures from each other.

Sean's favourite texture to touch was soft things, which is why he loved having pets, especially cats, to touch. Sean had a love for soft things, which he shared with his animals, which helped foster his love for animals. His favourite texture to eat was crunchy things.

The sensory experience that Sean engaged in probably the most regularly was cooking. This was an experience that he got to smell as well as taste. It was math and science, and physical motions. His use of recreational drugs was a close second on the list of sensory experiences. Sean liked to release his body from the pain he suffered from scoliosis, and he also liked gaining a new perspective.

A sensory experience could be using your body as an experiment, but it could be a negative experience when you have dangerous feelings about yourself. Drugs could be a positive sensory experience for the body, but also a negative one. For a while, it was Sean's favourite sensory experience, until he realised that he could not simulate true happiness through drugs. Many people do not realise this, though, and get stuck in an experiment gone wrong.

Sean and Scientific Inquiry

Much of the childlike creative wisdom that Sean possessed was based in scientific inquiry. Sean was proof to Piaget's point about children being naturally inquisitive. Besides loving to figure out what made people tick and how to get them to like the things that they claimed to dislike, Sean was interested in learning all that he could.

Sean watched videos on the internet to learn all sorts of random facts as well as to improve skills he already had, like cooking. Sean liked to experiment with what he could create with any ingredients, he liked to experiment with hair dye, art mediums, building things, and fixing things. There was a point when Sean took an experimental approach with drugs, when he was feeling low but still curious about how life could be worth living. He was almost at a point in his life where he was ready to consider experimenting with how to make his body feel better and improve his health.

      Sean utilised the internet for its ability to provide him with instant information. He made a point to become knowledgeable on a plethora of topics, including current events, and random, unrelated facts. He had watched many tutorials, researched many questions he had, and learned history. The internet was also where Sean found music. Jaime tended to use the internet for more specific functions, like specific research, music, photo uploads, or email. Jaime found herself too easily sucked into seeking information on the internet, she could be lost to a computer for hours if she logged on, and preferred to stay in the more natural, present world.

Bits and Pieces (Wi-Fi Connections)

      Sean used the internet to find boyfriends sometimes, including Sawyer the Selfish and his new, very dark-skinned boyfriend, Alo. Sean knew it could be unsafe to meet people from the internet, but he also knew the internet was a great place to seek community. Since Sean suffered from social anxiety, he found it easier to talk to strangers online.

      Alo was incredibly polite. His very dark colouring made Sean look even whiter. Sean loved most races and was unbothered by any differences between the colours of their skin. Alo told Jaime about wanting to become a registered nurse, and she was glad to see Sean dating someone with an ambition. In passing conversation, Alo mentioned how he had lived in North Carolina with his grandmother and that she had gone into his school and asked a random student if he was gay, and subsequently kicked him out before he was eighteen.

      Sean was a very straightforward person. It reminded Jaime of how Innocence in <u>the Book of Qualities</u> was "telling secrets in between her words but most people don't think they're secrets because she says them right out."

Sean said to her once, "I love being horribly straightforward. I love sending reckless text messages (because how reckless can a form of digitised communication be?) and telling people I love them and telling people they are absolutely magical humans and I cannot believe they really exist. I love saying, "Kiss me harder," and "you're a good person," and, "you brighten my day." I live my life as straightforward as possible. Because one day, I might get hit by a bus. Maybe it's weird. Maybe it's scary. Maybe it seems downright impossible to just be – to just let people know you want them, need them, feel like, in this very moment, you will die if you do not see them, hold them, touch them in some way whether it's your feet on their thighs on the couch or your tongue in their mouth or your heart in their hands. And there is nothing more risky than pretending not to care. We are young and we are human and we are beautiful and we are not as in control as we think we are. We never know who needs us back. We never know the magic that can arise between ourselves and other humans. We never know when the bus is coming." She found it inspiring, and continued to speak her truth.

Zen and the Art of Breaking Stuff (The World Inferno Friendship Society)

Sean taught Jaime a lot. One thing she never forgot is that he taught her that it was okay to break stuff when she felt destructively upset. He taught her to break things that made satisfying sounds – like candles, plates, or glasses.

Once, she brought Sean to her house and he was living with. Jaime situated him in her backyard before running inside and up to her room. She returned with three candlesticks in different colours and handed them to Sean without a word. He broke each candlestick multiple times and set them on fire. Afterwards, he smiled, and his first words to her were, "how did you know exactly what I needed?"

Jaime smiled and replied with how she had learned from him and he had learned from his grandmother. Sean smiled at Jaime's memory and cleverness. The situation had been diffused.

A year later, Jaime chucked a wine glass that Anabelle had left on her kitchen table for too long at the pavement in Le Feu's parking lot after her family made her emotional. Following up with pranayama, Jaime found herself completely turned around calm up in Le Feu's bedroom. As an adult Jaime had things available to her for breaking if in case she ever needed to.

Pranayama was incredibly powerful. Until reading <u>The Breathing Book</u>, Jaime had underestimated the power of the ujayi. She learned to breathe into different parts of her body, especially when she'd pulled a hamstring at nineteen. As a person with intense, breath-centred anxiety attacks, Jaime gained a lot of power in her body as she learned to control her breath.

Jaime found herself regularly practising breathwork (pranayama), usually coupled with meditation. In times of need she would go through her mental filing cabinet to try and pinpoint the breath work her body needed the most. Did she need energising breath, or calming breath? She found it so helpful that she attended a regular pranayama class at her home studio for a brief period. Had she known pranayama at age fourteen, her life might have been vastly different, however, she recognised the fact that at age fourteen she may not have been as open to focusing on her breath as she was five and six years later.

Crystal Children

"I believe in fostering the wellness of others through natural remedies and self-care practises," someone said to Jaime at her yoga studio, and it stuck with her.

Jaime and Sean used spells for sleeping. One of Jaime's was that she had sewn herself a dream pillow, filled with dried lavender flowers and rice (so it could become a warming pillow), decorated with stars and moons. This was one of her sleep aids, along with a crystal prescription, meditation music such as Native American flute music, rain sounds, or ocean noises, and sometimes a warm bath, hot shower, smoke in her lungs, or all three.

Dream pillows used aromatherapy, which made them a sensory experience. Jaime knew of using lavender with rice, flaxseed, or buckwheat to fill the pillows so that they could be warmed up in a microwave. She liked to make pillows with peaceful, dreamy patterns on the fabric, and she liked to weight them to make them effective sleep aids. These pillows aided aches and pains, cramps, and the calming and relaxing properties of lavender aided insomnia. She made hers big enough so that she could use them over her eyes, near her nose, or on her neck. She took note of how the weight helped with anxiety when placed over her eyes in the same way that weighted blankets helped calm anxious sleepers.

Natural Remedies

Sean could put Jaime to sleep no problem. As an empath, he could both receive and project emotion. An empath herself, Jaime's energetic receptors were naturally quite open. Sean worked early mornings, long hours, and hard days. Coupled with his constantly functioning pitta energy, he tired quickly, easily, and rightfully he and Jaime were capable of reading each other's minds on occasion because Jaime rarely closed the magical circle formed by perfect love and perfect trust between them.

"I'm gonna be invading your brain, so look for me there," Jaime said to Sean.

The connection formed through this circle allowed Sean to transmit his exhaustion to Jaime. When she slept at his flat, he put on peaceful music for her and as soon as he left the room he gave her half of his fatigue, and a full night's sleep. This magic did not keep him up at night or drain his energy. As a person who was naturally inclined to fix things and find solutions, Sean had created a remedy to reenergise his best friend. The connection formed by their magical circle also allowed them to walk between each other's dreams, sometimes in a lucid state. They could also share or swap energy. However, all magic comes at a price – for example, because of the open magical circle formed between Jaime and Le Feu, Jaime could feel it deeply when Le Feu was in emotional distress. An energy swap could leave one person drained.

Jaime had a spell on Sean's doorway which suspended any of her negative feelings there in the air so that it could not be absorbed by him. She could not protect him from everyone, but she could protect him from herself. She cast so many spells a day that she often forgot about many of them, including the one she'd placed Sean's entrance to his abode. On any given day Jaime placed protection spells on an array of family members and friends. Casting so many spells a day drained Jaime of a lot of energy, because that was really what spellcasting was – sending and directing energy. Jaime almost always cast only positive, helpful spells, mostly with the consent of the recipient, and very rarely cast curses, because she'd learned the hard way through cursing Syd that what you send out comes back to you.

Energetic Emissions

Jaime felt it was equally as important to block or shield the energy she emitted as it was to block or shield herself from the energy received. When she had sex with Le Feu, if she was ever feeling sad, she shielded him from absorbing her sad energy through their sexual contact.

Sometimes Jaime forgot to shield herself from energetic emissions and would later find herself wondering, "does this feeling belong to me?" She exerted so much energy daily functioning and casting spells, and absorbed so much energy, that she often had to perform energy cleanses. An energy cleanse could be performed by meditating on bathing oneself in white light, from head to toe. As an empath, Jaime's energy receptors were very open, and she sometimes became distracted from her own energy due to the energy of others. She felt without choice.

Absorption of Egocentrism

As an empath, Jaime had to be very careful of absorbing energy from other people. She usually cast spells to block the energy of others from permeating her field. One thing she was prone to absorbing, however, was egocentrism. As a preschool teacher, Jaime was exposed to a whole classroom of egocentric little people. Her family could also get egocentric at times, between her dad's illness, and her brother's mental state. Jaime worked daily to check her own ego.

Sean and Guided Sleep Meditation

Sean couldn't count sheep to get to sleep. When he was younger, he'd get distracted and sooner be listing different creatures and then he'd end up researching his future dream pets. Guided sleep meditation worked for him. It gave him something to focus on instead of everything else, and therefore allowed him to surrender control of putting himself to sleep. Highly affected by auditory stimulation, Sean allowed himself to be told what to do in order to be talked into a state of deep relaxation and sleep. He noticed that when he surrendered control over focusing on putting himself to sleep, his sleep was deeper and more relaxed.

Sean used sleep as a type of ishvarapranadhana because he was showing devotion to himself. Sean recognised that allowing himself to rejuvenate and rest, and that it was an incredible act of self-care. Though he believed in himself as a direct extension of that energetic force. He knew he was the maker of all of his miracles, he knew that he was in charge of his life. He knew he paid his bills as a legal adult and could make his own choices about all aspects of his life. A practitioner of Bhakti, Sean honoured his place in space and his journey. Humbled by his experiences, he took no day for granted, no bite of food for granted, no moment under his own roof out of the rain for granted – regardless of his predilection for irritability and crankiness.

He remained grateful for the gift of breath.

Jaime recalled a few comments about her voice from her yoga teacher training. Christine Christie had told her to watch out for her singsong voice (a trait she'd inherited from the world of working with children), and the whole class as well as Christine told Jaime that she had an incredibly calming voice for being talked into savasana, final relaxation. Savasana is a fully conscious pose aimed at being awake but in a state of complete relaxation and helps to relieve mild depression, high blood pressure, headaches, fatigue, and insomnia, and relaxes muscles, tense shoulders, and facial muscles. The energy shift she felt in the room teaching classes before and after she talked them into savasana was so noticeable that Jaime understood her classmates' comments to be true. She felt incredibly blessed to be gifted with the ability to help others relax.

When space is given, so too is time, typically. People who could cultivate silence together were good at giving each other space. Space to be oneself could be created even when there is no physical space between people. Jaime and Sean gave each other space sitting toe to toe on Sean's couch. Jaime and Le Feu gave each other space laying in Le Feu's bed. When Sean gave Jaime space to be herself like Harmony of <u>the Book of Qualities</u>, she knew that she would get better, and she became able to function. When they needed that space, when they felt overwhelmed, they sought each other out like best friends did and built a blanket fort out of space and trips across the universe.

Sean as Harmony relates to the quote, "if I sit in his kitchen in the late afternoon and drink ginger tea by the time I am ready to go home the contradictions inside my head are no longer shouting at me and trying to tear each other apart. He gives me space to be my whole self. A.A. Milne depicts Piglet giving Pooh space to be his whole self in the same way as Sean did for Jaime.

"I don't feel very much like Pooh today," said Pooh.
"That's okay, I'll bring you tea and honey until you do," said Piglet.

Sean could stand on his head, just like Jaime and Anabelle. He could also hang from a pole. Though he was rarely physical due to his standing job and early morning hours, he took care of his body. Jaime knew that Sean was good for her because he had the ability to turn her into a morning person. No matter how late they stayed up when they had sleepovers, Sean would gently wake Jaime up to drive him to work, and then once there, he would provide her with breakfast. Thanks to him, she started showing up early for work.

Sean didn't always listen to his body dictionary. Knowing this, Jaime learned his body's cues. She knew that Sean wouldn't say when he was tired, he wouldn't tell people to leave his apartment, and would only send himself to bed if he was about to drop. Jaime knew that because Sean was half red half blue, the skin around his eyes would change colour. His eyes would become swollen and his eyelids would turn red while his under eyes would become more of a purple shade. "You're tired, honey," Jaime would whisper to him as she handed him his pillow. Because they were both internally wired for nighttime, if they didn't actively make effort to try and sleep, they could easily spiral into a night of insomnia.

Jaime knew what Sean's body did when he was anxious, she knew he had nervous hands and a proclivity for tapping and shaking. She knew he also tapped when he got aggravated, and noticed that he tapped often around Ana. She could tell when he had a stomachache and knew his body when he was angry. Jaime knew Sean ran hot with his pitta constitution and even knew what kinds of sounds and textures he preferred. She felt she was a better friend by knowing these things.

"Sleepovers"

X.
He slept at her house once
with her ex-girlfriend
and wasn't sneaky
leaving his sneakers downstairs
following house rules

he slept in her bed
twin bed, kindred
twin buddies
while her ex-girlfriend slept
next to them

there's photo proof
and he's using his vape
they're laughing
at a crazy morning hour

the next day was sure something else

XX.
She slept on the couch once
where he lived for a while
before they took their
red car adventure

to see his old people
eat his grandma's cookies
and have a meal at Friendly's
photographed into forever

XXX.
He slept at her house once
when her ex-girlfriend didn't
when she stayed at his next station
and they drove her there together

it was when they lived together
a whole several months full of sleepovers
someone to always talk to
as well as someone to host guests with

XXXX.
Their first sleepover ever
her dad had no idea
and it was all so his dad
didn't freak out

they laughed at his shock
when he opened the door.

 XXXXX.
At the crack of dawn
I crawl into bed with my best friend
his whole apartment is watercolours
jeans half blue half red
(just like us, two sides of the same coin)
tufts of teal and indigo grace his head
long lashes lay closed
we sleep as the sun rises
for we have travelled far and we are weary
but we're in this together
neither of us can sleep flat on our backs
due to sacral problems so we're
curled to face each other in an open heart
energy formed a bond
so melted we can't be pulled apart
brought together by stars above
just from seeing "legalise love."

"When"

When Sawyer left Sean
Jaime was there
When Sean's sister called hyperventilating
Jaime was there
to hold his hand
so he didn't start hyperventilating himself
so he could talk her through her breathing
ten minutes after Sawyer came or his belongings
and Sean was on the phone with his sister
for three hours and Jaime was there
practising yoga, good vibes, and healing energy
that night she took him to get food
and burned him up on almost a whole slice
taught him hoop tricks
they altered his environment
talked about their plans to move in together
weak from stressful things, Sean made Jaime soup
they put on the Labyrinth, Sean's favourite movie
and slept on the couches
they woke at the same time multiple times
Sean asked how she was feeling and pointed out,
"you send a lot of positive energy out and that's draining"
on the way to work in the morning Sean eased
them into their music and marveled at the fact
that he was in a good mood in the morning
thanks to her.
The next day, as a thank you,
he used his powers to heal her ailments,
lending her his strength.

"Gravity Found You Here"

I looked into his eyes as he lost his mind
and watched him and Sawyer cry
"you'll do this with me one day," he said
who would've thought it would be in his own apartment
marble bathroom floor
beautiful mess of experiments
watercolour and hair dye
on his floor full of light
processing and transmitting sound and colour
saying happy birthday Jesus
never could be more proud
to know someone so strong
so this is our Christmas
(a time to spend with family)
and he managed to hide rainbows everywhere.

My best friend and I communicated telepathically last night
I've never felt more connected to someone before
sideways wavelengths
rainbow lotuses of peace
talking through coloured sound waves of energy
breaking apart – atoms
being put back together broken
pay for these dumb ass lights
no day but today
gravity found you here

Bowling

Sean was, to Jaime, pretty flaming. He was also a straight up savage. He was a 'spaz' like she was, with his random noises and little ticks. He was completely open about his sexuality, he didn't water it down for the straight people around. Jaime's "straight" friends knew that Sean both gave it and took it.

Jaime liked to mix groups. She took advantage of the fact that her "straight" boys got along with her gay boy. She took particular advantage of this when she invited Sean along for two dollar Tuesday at the local lanes.

There he was, in his button up shirt and skinny jeans, flaunting a neck full of love bites from his new boyfriend. Liam stared at Sean's neck for a while and thought about how those marks were from a guy. He was the only one of Jaime's friends to comment on Sean's neck.

"That's some bite mark you got there, Sean!" He exclaimed.

Sean didn't know what to say, so he just giggled.

The whole group had social anxiety and rarely went out. Jaime was out with Sean, Liam, Le Feu, Ver, Rocco, and a new girl she had a crush on. Sean and Nef were the type to encourage Jaime's bad behaviour. The three of them bounced off each other when it came to conversation. If Jaime and Sean were a dynamic duo, adding Nef to the mix made them a triple threat. Choosing not to participate, Sean and Nef watched people instead, and discussed their observations. Specifically, how queer Jaime's "straight" friends were in their eyes.

"So queer, Jaime, that they can hardly look at me or talk to me, and only one of them shook my hand," Sean told his wife.

"The sad part about that is that they all really like you," Jaime replied.

Sean and Nef encouraged Jaime's promiscuity. With Sean, Jaime took on the half joking role of the promiscuous one in the group. This puzzled her in a way, because at fourteen she had been torn to pieces by Dawn's slut shaming.

Perhaps it was because Sean and Nef could be promiscuous as well and she felt comfortable being open about it. It was the comfort she used to have talking about sex with Rosie and Glitterboii, and later with Benji. Jaime had thought at one point that she'd found that with Andie, Stella, and Logan, but it turned out to not be so. Jaime didn't bother trying to hide her promiscuity. Le Feu knew, and he obviously didn't care or they wouldn't have their casual thing. If people she was interested in minded, then she knew they weren't worth being interested in.

The same girl who used to be so open with Glitterboii and Rosie was also a girl who used to act drunk and stoned with them back when she was straight edge. She would get so excited that her eccentric personality would just bubble over and spill out of her. She was made of watercolours, a little messy and outside the lines. Somewhere inside her, that girl still existed. She started hiding when Jaime started getting panic attacks. Even people who had been in her life as long as Liam, Le Feu, and Sean rarely saw that part of Jaime. It wasn't that she didn't get excited or joyful anymore, but that she had learned to become a much more mellow version of herself.

Part of this was because of how strikingly different the group she joined with Liam and Le Feu was from the group she left with Rosie and Glitterboii. For example, save for Le Feu, she had no physical relationship with her boys, but her girls had had no boundaries.

Jaime was excited – she never got to see her three best friends at once in the same place. Making plans with so many people, Jaime had honestly expected a few people to flake or bail. Seeing them all at once brought out the eccentric excitement in her. The combination of that, the two margaritas she had, and getting to kiss the new girl provoked Jaime to get rowdy with her excitement, which for Jaime meant getting rowdy with her words. Nothing spiteful, all playful.

Back at Sean's after Jaime expressed fear that her other friends may have gotten annoyed with her behaviour. Sean had to remind her that she wasn't used to experiencing that emotion so fully and that she had cultivated a great joy I her experience.

    Jaime in her element was all summer sunshine, surf rock, and walking the nose on a glassy wave. These were all the things that one hundred percent Jaime, that she didn't get from anyone else. When she was truly happy and excited, she felt the surf stoke mixed with the fluttery excitement she felt when she kissed girls and boys, with a pinch of how it felt to be out dancing. Happiness made her feel alive, awake in her body, and she could feel it radiate out of her. For Jaime, the highest high was surf stoke. This is why she knew that what she could experience from chemicals would never be her highest high, and how she never fell into the trap of getting hooked on how good drugs could make a person feel. She believed in all-natural altered states of extreme joy – surf stoke and sex. (This is not to say she didn't enjoy recreational drugs, but when she cultivated joy, what she aimed to create was never what she had felt from substances.)

Tight

    It never made sense in Jaime's head how she and Sean became best friends. She knew all of the events that led up to it, but didn't understand how they just clicked, or how time bound them together holding hands into a friendship that could be described with one finger wrapped around another. They were tight.

    Jaime knew that when they met in high school they got along so well that she saw to making him her friend because she had no other gay friends at the time, and hardly had any friends in general because Syd was so controlling.

    It seemed sudden to Jaime that she was the one Sean wanted to talk to and be with after a rough day at work, or that she was the one he trusted with his spare set of keys. It seemed so sudden to Jaime when Sean meant so much to her and the thought of losing him was crushing. She was unprepared to be so close with a friend again. Upon losing Dawn and Rosie, Jaime wondered if she would develop such close friendships ever again. Suddenly, her and Sean weren't just friends, but they were seeing each other all the time, spending countless hours together, talking about everything imaginable. Suddenly, it was Jaime and Sean, Sean and Jaime, a pair, a unit, a boxed set. It was comparable to how when Jaime met Sawyer and Tiffany, they were always together. The difference was that Sawyer and Tiffany had been best friends forever, known each other all their lives, while Sean and Jaime had not. They were just tight.

Jaime remembered when they weren't for a short period of time. She feared losing Sean for real. He enjoyed cutting people out of his life. She did, too, but saw no need for them not to be friends. There had been a communication breakdown when Jaime's red car got wrecked by Freddie Pasto, due to which Sean thought Jaime hated Sawyer. Sometimes Jaime did things for fear that Sean would cut her out again. He had come back to her, though, she didn't have to beg, and she'd always remember that.

Jaime knew that they would always be tight because of the way they knew each other. The way they'd learned each other. No one else they hung out with made that kind of effort to learn how they operated and then regularly made use of that knowledge. She knew that they would always be tight when she was crying at three AM saying, "you're the one I'd miss the most when I go away to finish school, you're my partner in crime," and Sean smiled and told her, "you need to go, you need to get your second degree." She knew that they would always be tight when less than twenty four hours later, Sean was shaking asking Jaime if she would be mad at him if he up and left to start fresh by moving to California with Tess. She was so touched, she teared up in the driver's seat. "Oh, honey, I would be over the moon if you got yourself out of your situations. You don't have to worry about losing me."

"Why did God speak to me today about leaving, and why would it be so easy?" Sean pondered.

Jaime joked, "when you said you wouldn't move again for a while but you're suddenly realising-"

"It's been a while," Sean finished. "I've been through

enough in that apartment and at this job and with everyone I know and I've sure been up and down this strip of highway enough and oh my God it's time for living."

"The time is now, baby!" Jaime grinned.

"The time is now. This is huge."

And for the moment they let Jaime's Clyde car carry them home stunned.

The Seven Layer Haunting

Everybody knew that Sean's apartment was haunted. At first it was believed that there was only one spirit in his abode, but eventually he and Jaime came into contact with all seven spirits. They were ghosts reborn many times of the essence of the original Titans (the children of Mother Earth and Father Sky) who also personified the seven deadly sins. Though they were incredibly powerful and believed to be evil, they were actually there to offer help to Sean and Jaime.

Pride was there to help them gain confidence. He also represented the energy and powers of the Titans Coeus, Hyperion, Theia, Themis, and Kronus. One could shine with pride, but was warned not to get blinded by pride. In the same way that one could be proud of their intelligence, it was important not to become too proud. Many fell to their demise by being overly proud of their power, or by being overly proud of their morals, thinking that they were better than others.

Sometimes, Pride and Greed were best friends. Greed helped make sure that bills got paid. Greed represented the powers and energy of Kronos and Themis. He warned Sean and Jaime of the dangers of being greedy for power, as well as the dangers of a law and order system based in greed.

Rage often accompanied Pride and Greed in their endeavours. Rage could help Jaime and Sean breed strength. He represented the powers and energy of Rhea, Kronos, and Iapetus. Such energy included anger at death, anger at the powers of others, and anger at what one lacked. He taught Jaime and Sean the dangers of holding onto anger.

Envy and Rage were partners. Envy was meant to

give Jaime and Sean ambition, and she represented the powers and energy of Rhea and Kronos. She taught them the dangers of being jealous of what others have and their power.

Sloth was often lonely, though he was involved with both Lust and Gluttony. Sloth helped make sure that Jaime and Sean got down time, alone time with themselves, and helped them sleep. He represented the powers and energy of Tethys, Oceanus, and Crius. Though going with the flow and looking at the sky could be great, he showed the dangers of going with the flow too much. Sloth also showed Jaime and Sean the dangers of being too stormy, and getting settled by the storm, like being too depressed to function.

Lust and Gluttony were life partners. Like Sloth, they helped Jaime and Sean take care of biological needs like getting them laid, and helping them eat. Lust represented the powers and energy of Phoebe, Crius, and Mnemosyne. Gluttony represented the powers and energy of Kronos and Mnemosyne. Lust, though beautiful, represent the dangers of lusting after what couldn't be attained, the lust and romance of the sky, and falling in love with the muses of epic poetry, history, love, music, tragedy, hymns, dancing, comedy, universal love and holy spirit. In a similar manner, though he felt nice, he represented the dangers of overindulging in the inspirations of the muses, and well as overindulging in personal power.

Jaime and Sean knew they had a lot to learn from the Seven Spirits. By ayurvedic principle, the human experience is imperfect. Therefore, the sins are unavoidable, inescapable. Perhaps we die because we commit each of these seven deadly sins by human nature. Yoga helps us master the sins within like we master our senses, learning to do them less and less in each rebirth until we can get off the wheel of life by lowering our bad karma. Our physical bodies are bound by the sins, their urges, desires, and whims. Do our hormones make some of the sins happen? Lust, for example. Jaime found herself looking at the seven deadly sins through Rigby Wilton's comparative religion lens, asking herself about similarities, and how it applied to her life. Rage and Lust were two evils laid out in the Bhagavad Gita. "Hell has 3 doors – lust, rage, and greed. Rajo-guna (evil) – rage, and lust (ravenous and deadly) which hides the Atman, to prevent this one must control the senses." the Gita states.

    Queer people were sometimes regarded as highest sinners, though not just queer folk but everyone experiences them. Stereotypical examples were the proud "in your face" gay, the promiscuous gay, the gay who envied straight relationships, the rich gay who didn't help the community, the oppressed gay who hates the straights, the gay who is depressed about the orientation and doesn't do anything because of it, and the gay who feels bad about themselves and indulges often. By removing the sins, one becomes immortal and gets off the wheel of life and death. By doing so, the sins become immortal as well. Bringing virtues together destroys the sins. Jaime and Sean learned that where there was sin there must be virtue. They were just as vital as the sins were for balance.

    Where there was Pride there must be humility and kindness, where there was envy there must be kindness, admiration, and respect, where there was gluttony there must be moderation, where there was rage there must be patience and understanding, where there was sloth there must be diligence and activity, where there was greed there must be liberality and seva, and where there was lust there must be bramhacharya.

    The opposite of lust was previously abstinence or chastity. Jaime believed that brahmacharya was a better term. She had discussed with Glitterboii the differences between lust and love and why we all have different reasons for sleeping with someone. Lust was the desire for someone's body and what they give us without respecting them. Abstinence didn't mean to completely refrain, but caution us to consider why we give our bodies to others. Separating the word from the stigma is important. To abstain is to take control over impulses and truly reflect on a situation. If it's lust, it's worth abstaining from, and you conquer the sin by abstaining. If there's more to it, the opportunity will likely present itself again.

The spirits taught Jaime and Sean to truly understand the seven heavenly virtues. Pride taught them that it was important to be humble and kind. Greed taught them how important generosity was. Sloth taught them why diligence and activity were important, like Gluttony taught them to use moderation. Rage taught patience and understanding. Envy helped them realise that kindness and admiration were better ways to appreciate what others had. Lust taught them Brahmacharya, which was different for everyone but had the same basic principles – that it is guilt free, safe, involves trust, and especially involving consent. The spirits also taught Jaime and Sean that they lived within most everybody and that it often took people a lot of yoga to overcome their impulses to be ruled by the titanic energy of the inner sins and to live more virtuously. The spirits told Jaime and Sean that every saint had a past, and every sinner had a future. They also explained that the Bible said that Jesus had died for the sins of others, making it an act to free others from the limitations preventing them from entering Heaven, meaning that if we sin we will not be prohibited from Heaven.

The Gita mentions that some have divine tendencies while others have demonic tendencies. Divine tendencies were outlines as acts of sacrifice, almsgiving, austerity, fearlessness, charity, control of passions, studying and obeying scriptures, truthfulness, even temper, harming none, compassion, gentleness, modesty, unmalicious tongue, abstaining from useless activity, faith in strength of higher nature, forgiveness, endurance, clean in thoughts and act, tranquility of mind, and being free from hatred and pride. The Gita states that "pious men eat what the gods leave over," and makes mention of rituals and sacrifice. The person with acting according to their divine tendencies adores Krishna, is moderate in eating, recreation, activity, sleep, and wakefulness, practises yoga which makes their unhappiness go away, discriminates right from wrong, and their joy is inward.

Jaime decided for herself which qualities aligning with divine tendencies were most relevant to her own life.

Her choices were tranquility of mind, modesty, truthfulness, straightforwardness, even temper, abstaining from useless activity, moderation, non-harming, compassion, forgiveness, endurance, control of passions, inward joy, practise of yoga, acts of seva and sacrifice, and being free from pride and hatred. She felt that it was important to recognise that you could still be proud of yourself without becoming consumed by pride, by being proud of what you were blessed with that allowed the thing you're proud of to manifest. Jaime was proud to be blessed with the ability to connect with children, and such connections released her pride back into the akasha.

Jaime and Sean understood that living righteously involved a lot of continuous self-improvement, particularly including checking their egos. This was why yoga was so important. Whether falling out of a post helped them check their egos or if all they needed was meditation, some part of yoga made that process possible. One great example of how yoga allows for the ego to be checked easily is when Jaime and Feori practised together. Feori said to her, "did you see how much I was moving to hold that position?" To which Jaime replied, "you'll still be moving in any static pose, because you're always breathing and adjusting." Feori thought about her words and accepted them as truth by saying, "that's fair enough."

Since all of us were created in the image of the divine, we are all perfect in the eyes of the divine unless we do harm. We ought not lose faith in humanity because there are people who do harm, we must be understanding of the light and dark within all people as well as the whole world – the circle of life in which there will always be good and bad, and that those people doing bad things are acting according to their demonic tendencies and are not practising yoga for self-regulation. As Mahatma Gandhi said, "one drop does not dirty the ocean."

The Titans

There were twelve Titans who were the six sons and six daughters of Uranus (Father Sky) and Earth (Mother, Gaia). The Titans preceded the Olympians and got defeated by them. They were primeval and incredibly powerful.

Kronos is the god of time and ages, changing time, and the ruler of the Cosmos. He birthed Giants, and throwing his father's genitals into sea birthed Aphrodite. He married Rhea and swallowed all of their children but Zeus, who later makes Kronos vomit up Zeus' siblings.

Coeus is the god of intelligence and foresight, inquisitive attitudes, and the desire to learn. He births Phoebe, Leto (mother of Apollo), and Asteria (mother of Hecate).

Crius is the god of constellations and the father of a dragon. He births Pallas, Perces, and Astraeus.

Hyperion is the god of light , watching, and observation. He established rhythm of days and months. He births sky dieties Eos, Selene, and Helios.

Iapeutus is the god of mortal life span or death. He is equal to Kronos, defeated by Zeus, and is the father of Atlas, Menoetius, Prometheus, and Epimetheus.

Mnemosyne is the goddess of memory, inventress of speech and writings. She is the mother of the muses - Calliope (epic poetry), Clio (history), Erato (love), Euterpe (music), Melpomene (tragedy), Polyhymnia (hymns), Terpischore (dancing), Thalia (comedy), and Urania (universal love and holy spirit).

Oceanus is a saltwater god , the father of river gods and water nymphs. He was born alongside Gaia, and didn't participate in the war.

Tethys is the goddess of freshwater.

Theia is the goddess of shining, who birthed the Sun, Moon, and Dawn.

Themis is the goddess of divine law, order, justice, and morality. She is prophetic and the mother of the Fates and hours.

Phoebe is the goddess of prophetic radiance who was never involved in the war. She has a lust for mortal men.

Rhea is the goddess of fertility and motherhood. She is the Queen of the Cosmos, often pregnant but never a mother, and therefore often mad and angry.

Jaime and Le Feu

An experience involving the common confusion of love, friendship, and sex.

"It is very nice when friends can sleep together without the pressure of sex and commitment of love."

"I will not prevent an honest friendship to manifest itself sexually, no matter what sex the person is." -<u>Bi Any Other Name</u>

"Hey Sean, do you know why Le Feu is good for me right now? Jaime snickered.
"Oh, Jesus," Sean replied.
"When I feel needy for him, I sometimes don't hit him up, and accept that I am fine without the attention I want. Or other times, I do go hang out with him, and it is a nice reality check, because even though he doesn't give me all of the attention I feel like I need, it is still fulfilling." Jaime smiled.
After that Sean had to agree with Jaime. Le Feu was good in his book, even though he shook his head at some of Le Feu's actions.

Not Afraid to Touch

Jaime thought that all of her male friends had wonderful qualities. Le Feu, however, had a special place in Jaime's heart even though Liam was her best of best friends. Liam accepted Jaime for everything that she was, no questions asked, no judgement.
Le Feu was the only one of her male friends who wasn't afraid to touch her. He knew what she was and how she was but he didn't mind. They never dated, but he wasn't afraid to hit on her, kiss her, or go further.

Male Partners

Jaime's male partner at the moment is one of her most dear friends, and they are sometimes lovers. He knows her quite well. He knows her crying, shaking, panicking. He knows her smiling, happy, proud, excited. He knows her angry, upset, fragile. He knows her intimately. He knew how she liked to kiss, where she liked to be caressed. He knows her naked body beneath his fingertips. He knows Jaime's faces, the way she bites her lips, the way she dragged her nails across his back. He knows the sounds she makes, the magic of her climax. He is always kind to Jaime in bed even if he's rushing things.

He is okay with Jaime searching out girls. They have good communication. They openly discuss things with each other. Jaime was good at initiating discussions. They discuss what they would like to try, and how they practise safe sex.

They have good sex. They have more than good sex. They have passionate, intimate, connective sex. They make sex magick. They have great conversation, too. It's quite casual, but made Jaime not quite want to look for someone who actually wanted to date her. Jaime didn't know how she could have someone to take her on dates while fully understanding that she won't sleep with them (until or unless she was ready and wanted to), but that she would be having casual sexual experiences with one of her best friends potentially up until the point of someone asking if Jaime wanted to be their girlfriend, or if she asked someone to be her exclusive partner.

She loved him with his freedom.

For, as mentioned in the Book of Qualities, Freedom is Whimsy's lover.

Jaime had only ever made sex magick with Sydney. That is, until she and Le Feu started sleeping together.

Sydney had been her first boy, and their sex magick had been that of love. Jaime had only ever been in love with one person she'd slept with. What her and Sydney had had had been intense and powerful. Its intensity had scared them. Their love had been strong and fiery, despite them both being water signs. Though it burned out, their love had been real on some level. Though their sex had been magical, Jaime had never intentionally tapped into its power.

When she first started sleeping with Le Feu, Jaime became very confused because their sexual encounters were so powerful. At first, she thought this meant that they were meant to be romantically involved, but she soon was able to see the truth. She realised that their sex was indeed powerful because they loved each other, but that their love for each other did not have to be shoved into the box of monogamy. The first time around when they slept together, Jaime did not tap into the power of their encounters. the second time around, she did. Intentionally sleeping with him helped Jaime manifest things – for both of them. She used their power to manifest jobs, him passing his license test, and people signing up for her yoga classes.

While visiting her family in England, Jaime had gotten crystals for Le Feu. She happened to get herself matching ones, wanting what they could do for her. Green Onyx, for easing stress, feeling at peace with surroundings, bringing stability and permanence. Red Jasper for recalling dreams, providing protection, absorbing negative energy, and aiding determination and organisation. When she carried her twin rocks to his, she felt like she was carrying him with her. Due to their sexual connection, the connection between their brains remained open, especially since Jaime almost never dismantled their magical circle of perfect love and perfect trust. sometimes she could sense where he was, or he would pick up vibes from her to answer the phone for her. Jaime started being able to sense when Le Feu was not thinking about sex.

As a hypersexual being, Jaime found it difficult to relate to people who were not always in the mood. When she dated Syd, she found it hard to relate to how sexuality didn't matter to him like it did to her and how it didn't dominate his thoughts. She understood that Le Feu was similar. Though he was torn up about his own sexuality, Le Feu did not think of it at all much of the time. Though Jaime couldn't relate, she respected Le Feu.

Connections Between Dark Haired Bi Boys

Jaime wondered why she had only experienced connective sex with three boys – Sydney, Le Feu, and Todd. She had had two experiences with girls which had been somewhat special to her, but she hadn't had a connective experience with a girl. The closest she had come was kissing her Dream Girl, her Colombian Queen. She often dreamed of sharing it with Jolie, and hoped for it for real with someone one day.

She was with Todd first, but they weren't fully sexual. Jaime and Todd had a deep personality connection. Their families had many similarities. Their senses of humour bounced off of each other. Where she was creative, he balanced her out with a logical mind. They had explored but never had the full adventure. Later, Jaime had wished she did with him first. She contemplated telling people he had been the first. If she could count what she did with Courtney as the first time, why could she not count that same thing with him as such?

Le Feu she got close with next, chronologically. Their closeness came gradually. They were in each other's vicinity regularly, but at first only had specific friendship forming experiences. It was much later that they began to talk about everything. The talking did it for her, of course, being a word-based person. The words and the time fueled the connection.

Sydney and Jaime thought they connected but they turned out to be more like magnets – opposites that attracted. He liked Jaime's punk rock side, a side of herself Jaime didn't show often. They probably would have made good friends, but after seeing each other the way they had they would never know about being friends.

Jaime had had more junk sex than connective sex. Her experiences with more than half of her partners were junk sex experiences. However, some of those experiences were one-night stands, and some happened for a brief period of irregular frequency before stopping altogether. Because of this fact, it's possible Jaime had more acts of intimate sex than junk sex, due to the cumulative number of times she'd slept with Syd, Le Feu, and Todd. This number was not possibly countable, but may easily exceed her infrequent one night stands or short lived flings with partners. She felt very over sex with boys from binging on junk sex, and was leaning towards girls feeling unfulfilled in that department still. Jaime had even grown out of having sex because she felt badly about herself, and considered this progress. She knew how to choose to make it a good experience for herself, how to purposely use, but even doing those things, when she felt bad she learned that the wrong kind of sex didn't make her feel better. It made her feel new to not sleep around much anymore, though at times she didn't know what to do.

    Rick Batch suggested she shouldn't be so open talking about her sex life if she wanted to attract a mate because it was a turn off. To Jaime, openness about sexuality was a turn on. If they were open with her, then they were honest, unlike Sydney. She delighted in the open honesty of Todd and Le Feu. In turn, they allowed her her voice. Jaime did not know any way to be other than open, she felt it kept her safe. She found herself frustrated at Rick's suggestion, considering he had a reputation for being a "manwhore," or "boyslut," their body counts were close, and she was still willing to sleep with him after everything she'd heard and seen about him. He was lucky, she used to avoid boys with such reputations.

    Le Feu had been with Jaime for a brief period of time when they were teenagers, and she was the one he ended up going to when he was upset about Janae breaking his heart. Jaime answered the phone for him while she was in another country and listened to him cry. Their friendship was very unique in the way that Le Feu had healing through Jaime's sexual touch. Jaime had a tendency or sometimes a desire to help the hurting. She told Le Feu when he was upset about Janae that "the best way to get over someone is to get under someone else." What he found that she taught him was that he was more healed than he realised, and that he was healing every day.

Masculinity in Making the Moves

Something Jaime learned was that guys almost never knew how to respond to girls who were confident enough to make the first move. Since middle school, she had been the type to tell a boy she liked them or ask them out. Girls noticed her confidence and disliked this about her, as well as the fact that she chose not to conform to fashion trends and pop culture fads.

It seemed masculine in nature, being the one "on the prowl," so to speak. Some boys, like Le Feu, didn't care – if she asked for sex, he'd say yes most times, but it was on his terms, and there were plenty of times he asked, too.

Jaime took initiative to start conversations. A few of her guy friends, including Liam and Ver, expressed not knowing what to do or say if a girl came up to them and started conversation. This led Jaime to believe it was socially considered masculine to make the first move. Jaime's tendency to be the one to talk first was likely partly because of her genderqueer identity, and partly because of her sign ruling the throat chakra.

In her relationship with Le Feu, Jaime had been gifted by him the control of their communication. He was receptive to her discussions with him, and allowed her to control when they stopped sleeping together. Each time that they had started out hooking up, he had been the one to initiate it. But their subsequent encounters during the periods in which they were involved with each other were sometimes initiated by Jaime. Knowing that he was not afraid of a girl who was not afraid of making the first move made her feel hopeful. She wasn't afraid to ask for what she wanted or speak her thoughts and express feelings.

In her early anxious days, Jaime had been the confident girl who tried to chat up Liam when she thought he was really good looking. He had his own reasons for not being into her, but he definitely didn't know how to respond to Jaime being open with her feelings for him. She didn't know a way to be besides open. She thought it was interesting to know two boys who were so close and similar but also so different.

   Liam talked Le Feu up as a player. Le Feu did enjoy being the one to make the moves. He once told Jaime that he used the people he met online as people to practise conversation with. Since e Feu could, on occasion, be the player that Liam painted him as, he accepted girls who made the moves on him. Jaime was open with him about also being a player and he never shamed her for it. Le Feu maintained the socially masculine trait of making the first moves while allowing himself, like a chameleon, to display the socially feminine qualities of liking being doted on by romantic partners, and taking care in his grooming and appearance. It was considered a socially masculine trait to be a player, and Jaime had taken her cues from her boys. It was from Le Feu, in particular, in fact, that Jaime got some of her ideas on how to talk to ladies. Sean had always suggested that one thing Le Feu liked about her was that she was somewhat a guy.

Liam

   Jaime remembered Liam being appalled when she was casually sleeping with Julio before they started dating. Liam subsequently heard many of Jaime's stories about being a player. She was regularly seeing boys at times and typically chatting with girls, too. Liam was nothing like Jaime. He remembered how she had so openly told him she wanted to sleep with him when they were both virgins, and that she'd cried in their chemistry class when he told her about his first sexual encounter (they never talked about any of that, but both remembered). Liam hadn't been with many girls he hadn't dated. Some would call him aromantic. He disliked the hookup culture of their generation (typically the way girls felt about it). Jaime had found a way to use their generation's hookup culture to her advantage. As Glitterboii had put it once so eloquently to her, "some sex toys have batteries, others have first and last names." She also aimed not to get played.

   To Liam, participating in the hookup culture involved

stepping out of his comfort zone in many ways. It typically involved talking to strangers, being willing to unveil his own body, an exchange of energies, and detachment from feelings and expectations about the person and experience.

Liam got a lot of anxiety when thinking about hooking up with girls, because he never knew what exactly would happen. Ver also got anxiety about talking to girls. Jaime noticed that Liam and Ver's social anxiety was getting in the way of talking to, going after, or hooking up with girls. The unknown gave Liam fear, because in order to hook up with someone, Liam already had to step out of his comfort zone. Being the one to make the moves and put his hands on someone's body made him nervous, because he wasn't always sure that he was doing what they wanted, and he never wanted to be that guy who made an encounter awkward or awful. Being the one to make the moves and put his hands to someone made Liam vulnerable. So too did stripping naked in front of someone he was not close with. It took courage and bravery to be so vulnerable. Liam always thought of Le Feu and Jaime as being more brave than him because they were open and willing to be vulnerable by making the moves. Liam has asked Le Feu how he fucks without feelings, and probably got an answer about how Le Feu didn't lose his virginity to a girlfriend.

Liam asked Jaime and the boys, "how does it make me look if I turn down a girl who wants me when I don't necessarily want her?" and Jaime was reminded of their friend, Rocco. She didn't know if Rocco had realised that she was able to feel when someone doesn't want to hook up with her, and she thought about why boys might feel they have to. It was due to social conditioning. Rocco had been sending her naked pictures, and when they were alone together, even though she knew he didn't like her in that way because she was so much like a boy, she felt as though he felt the need to live up to the photos that he had been sending her.

Sean claimed to Jaime that Liam and Ver didn't go for girls because they were gay. Sean figured that if they stayed single, no one would find out, but they had no reason to go for girls. He was convinced that all of Jaime's male friends were secretly gay.

Jaime and Le Feu Against Toxic Monogamy Culture

Jaime learned that in many ways she and Le Feu were two sides to the same coin. They both fluidly drifted between the player and the loner, containing both masculine and feminine qualities and mannerisms. They thought of themselves as "selfish" because they were goal oriented. For them, relationships were viewed as distraction, heartache, drama, time, effort, money. She noticed negative connotations to being focused on yourself, and that the road to self love was sometimes found through being "selfish." Jaime and Le Feu were capable of finding fulfillment in things other than companionship, which was why it worked well for them to hang out when they miss a partner, they were in agreement about not being into monogamy. Their relationship worked because of Jaime's discernment at a young age of being a nonmonogamous person and their equal discernment of self focus being more important than companionship.

"It's funny when people assume that I'm into you in a way where I would want to date you because they mis-assume that I am interested in a relationship at all, especially not a monogamous one," Jaime would say to him.

"I'm not trying to date anyone, I need to use that effort for myself," he would reply.

Jaime and Le Feu were both whole on their own. They felt that they had "already been through" the toxic monogamy culture of their time. This was one in which there was a normalisation of jealousy as an indicator of love, the idea that sufficiently intense love is enough to overcome any practical incompatibilities and that it should cause one to cease to be attracted to anyone else. It also held the idea that the partner's every need should be met and if they're not then one party is either inadequate or too needy and the idea of commitment being synonymous with exclusivity. The ideas of marriage and children were the only valid justifications for being committed to a relationship. This culture had the idea that insecurities are always partner's responsibility to tiptoe around and never own responsibility to work on and that value to a partner is directly proportional to amount of time and energy spent on the other and it is in competition with everything else they value in life. This culture was also big on the idea that being valued by a partner should always make up a large chunk of how one values themselves. Jaime and Le Feu disagreed with this culture, and rebelled against it by being perfectly whole on their own, as well as by being polysexual and polyamorous.

"Burn This Letter"

I.
What do you know
about that?
Asked through pursed
unhappy lips and

the whole library
in your mind
opens up
but instead you decide

to keep your mouth shut.
(choose your response carefully.)

II.
when everything
you want to say
is the total wrong thing
so you settle for

thanks for not
lying to me
at least we know we
are clean

our bodies have tasted
heaven together
now I know you risk
as much on the edge as me.

It reminded Jaime of Hana-Kimi.
"So I'm the only one who knows the real you?" - Umeda
"That's right, so don't tell anyone, okay?" - Ryoichi

Online Dating

It all started with Benji (of course). He suggested getting a MeetMe to find girls when Jaime was in her nonmonogamous committed relationship with Julio. Of course it didn't work.

Or did it all start with him? As Jaime recalled, she used to meet people online before. Not dating exactly. First, chat rooms, but those were too sketchy and she was too young. Flash forward to the myspace days where you could talk to someone's profile. And then, to the days DeviantArt – on where she made several friends.

Jaime's favourite (Slam, the poet) commented on her fanart of a few books in one picture and began a lasting text friendship. They got to meet once. It was never romantic, though it was once potentially sexual, because we're both bisexual.

In the days of her Invader Zim fanart, Jaime made friends with a group of artists on the website, of varying ages and sexualities. They were quite talented. Jaime was mostly in it for the laughs.

The age of iPhones is a game changer. You can get dating apps and just have them for your boredom, or your fancy. MeetMe didn't last terribly long, though Benji found a temporary girlfriend on it at one point.

After MeetMe came Her – an app for girls only. That's how Jaime met Forest. And she actually met her! In company of Courtney from Cali, while visiting the City. Jaime got to kiss her, but they never got anywhere. Jaime didn't really know what happened. She thought Forest was so cool, and they had some of the same interests. They just lived states away, Jaime guessed.

At first Jaime wasn't down for Tinder. At first Jaime thought she was too good for Tinder.

It wasn't until Syd cheated.

Courtney suggested Tinder, so Jaime could find girls. Courtney and Benji can be two of a kind. (except that Benji is more clever)

Tinder pissed Syd off, though. And made him cry,

drink, and blow coke (so he told her). He's the one who cheated first, though. Twice. But Jaime decided, Tinder wouldn't last long.

When they broke up was the first time Jaime downloaded the app for both sexes. Talking to people online is crazy. You can be completely honest with someone, and they could be completely lying about everything. You could mess with someone. You have your boys who straight up ask you if you're down to bang, you've got your girls who don't reply, your couples looking for threesomes, and your people on it for attention. You've even got boys who ask if you'll peg them.

Her lover uses online dating apps and is a self-proclaimed "tinder whore".

And does she mind?
Not. One. Bit.
Why?
Because she knows everything.
Open, honest communication.
Knowing is everything.
Get yourself tested.
Be safe. You have the power.

Letters to Benji

Dear Benji,
    My boyfriend confessed he's fucked a guy before. He says he's not bi but I've known since he was thirteen.
    Best,
    Jaime

Dear Benji,
    My boyfriend let another boy kiss him in front of other people. It was wicked hot.
Best,
Jaime

Dear Benji,
    My boyfriend initiated a weird threesome with another guy on my twentieth birthday.
Best,
Jaime

Dear Benji,
    My boyfriend cheated on me with another guy. Bastard couldn't even do it while I was in England, he waited till I was back. Why couldn't he have just asked?
Best,
Jaime

Dear Benji,
    After my boyfriend cheated on me with a guy, he got upset when I wanted to hook up with a girl.
Bugger it,
Jaime

Dear Benji,
    I eat his ass and fuck him with a toy and it makes me feel like a real lesbian.
Best, Jaime

Dear Benji,

My boyfriend blows coke to cope with his bisexuality.

His lover has slept with someone we know who has herpes (slaggy Ziggy)..

I wish I could stop hitting him.

Best,
Jaime

Dear Benji,

I'm single again and I've been going on dates with none other than Posh Boy.

It's all thanks to you, telling me he's a bi swinger too. (Remember that day at the beach? I told him to wear that shirt he wore that day and he did.)
(P.S. You're right, he's a confirmed 1.5)
Kaboom,
Jaime
Dear Benji,
I wish my only threesome didn't suck.
Best,
Jaime

Dear Benji,

I found your abusive ex on Tinder all genderqueer and looking for a femme for fun with her and her boyfriend-after-you.
Funny how things change.
Best,
Jaime

Dear Benji,

All negative from my second STD scare. Grateful for good communication and honesty.
C   ome to find out that now since you there's been four other at risk boys like me and you. We are high risk friends (and both of us whores) (like us, again) (we should play the number game out like we used to at Toad's Place)

223

  Speaking of numbers, statistically speaking about four of my partners could've been carriers. I know you know this feeling. I am lucky. I think it's funny that that statistic and the number of high risk friends like you after you that the doctors would ask about too is the same number four.
Statistically,
Jaime

Dear Benji,
  Remember how close I felt to you after I found out?
(After you told me)
I feel that way again, now.
Bi-swing-you-ly,
Jaime

Dear Benji,
  I am in a casual full open swinging relationship and I'm low key in love.
Best,
Jaime

Dear Benji,
  I thought I wasn't in a relationship. As it turns out, I think I am in in one. Just a nonmonogamous one.
  Here I am living my swinging polyamorous dream- without even knowing it!
(Benji how did I not see it before?? We're seeing other people responsibly and with each other's consent.)
Now all I need is to find a girl to have a threesome with us then we'll really be swingers!
Best,
Jaime
P.S. Is this what happens when you start calling your "fuck buddie" your lover? (he is one of my best friends, not just my "fuck buddie")
P.P.S. Does this make me a grown up now? Being twenty one and acknowledging my recurring casual sex relationship with someone I share a deep connection with as a casual full open swinging polyamorous relationship?

224

Boys Against Gender Norms

    Last night Jaime hung out with Le Feu and Krus. Le Feu and Krus had gone to the mall together, and Le Feu had treated himself to clothes, shoes, and jewelry.
    After the mall is when Jaime came over. She sat at home in Le Feu's room and nearly cried laughing about how the boys discussed shoes at length for over twenty minutes. She laughed even harder as they moved on to discuss clothes, including name brands and how they wore their pants. She was impressed as Le Feu described how he did laundry. She nearly cried laughing again as he described his forty five minute shampoo and conditioner routine in the shower.
    She said nothing out loud and just laughed. Boys against gender norms, she whispered to herself in her brain.

Masculine Décor

    At twenty one and close to twenty two, Le Feu still had at least one wall of his bedroom plastered with pictures torn out from magazines. These pictures are of other men. Sporty men – men skateboarding, BMX biking, and scootering. Jaime had known Le Feu for over six years and his bedroom has looked like that for as long as she could remember. In the past two years, one picture from a magazine had been added – a promo for a skate company with a topless girl hiding her breasts.
    Le Feu had once described his platonic love for his closest male friend to Jaime in such an interesting fashion. He described his friendship like a relationship. Not many people would let him talk like Jaime does. He's verbally articulated that she is the only person he talks to like that, which means intrinsically that she had heard the deepest version of him.

The Unspoken Argument

When Jaime entered his bedroom, Le Feu fidgeted on his bed. He had words for her, but he did not want to say them. Probably the biggest difference between him and Jaime, despite them both being signs which ruled the throat chakra, was that where she was open, he was private.

Jaime, of course, could tell that Le Feu had words for her, and therefore sat in the chair across from his bed, leaned forward towards him with her elbows on her knees and her head rested on her hands. She sat in complete, expectant silence until he spoke.

"Jaime, sometimes I get a little concerned..." Le Feu started.

Jaime just widened her big, brown eyes at him, nodded her head, and made him finish what he started.

"Sometimes I get a little concerned that you have feelings for me." He had trouble looking at her when he spoke.

"Well, I do, Le Feu," Jaime said with a smile. "You know that I love you, but you love me too. That doesn't mean that I think we need to date about it." She changed her seated position to a more relaxed stance, leaning back into the chair.

"Jaime, what does that even mean?" Le Feu asked, and then immediately added, "are you sure you're not just saying that?"

Jaime exhaled. "You know, Le Feu, unbelievable as it may be and as much as I love you, there are reasons why I wouldn't want to date you besides because you're one of my best friends."

Le Feu sat with that for a minute, but couldn't help himself.

"What are they?" He inquired.

Jaime laughed.

"Why do you seem so surprised? Like you haven't got your own reasons why you wouldn't want to date me besides because I am one of your best friends." Before Jaime let Le Feu say anything to that comment, she added a question. "Do you really want to have this out right now?"

Le Feu watched a flicker of fear pass through her eyes as she asked that question.

"What do you mean?" He asked simply.

"I mean that we've never had this conversation before. Do you really want to talk about why we wouldn't date each other?"

Le Feu nodded.

"Alright, but please promise that after we will still be best friends. And, occasionally, best friends who sometimes touch each other." Jaime tried to sound calm, her eyes were pleading.

"Alright, Jaime. Deal." Le Feu was afraid, too.

Because they trusted each other, they walked through fear together.

"Le Feu. I wouldn't want to date you because I think you care too much what other people think and it's a turn off when you try to impress them, like when you pretend to support a president you didn't vote for who doesn't support you. You suck at answering the phone and I need frequent communication. I know that you can be a jerk sometimes even though you are mostly always nice to me. You'd break my heart. You don't go down on me as often as I go down on you, but I also choose not to ask because I don't want to fight you about it. And lastly, I think that you wouldn't want to date me because I am all of these things – like openly bi, an angry feminist, genderfluid, an open swinger, an activist... and I think it sort of scares you, maybe because you feel like you can't be open like me, or who knows why. But I could only date someone who embraced those things." Jaime took a breath. "And one more thing, though this is more of a side note, the way we hook up is mad corny, even though you're the best I've ever had – just because you have never taken me on a date. But since that was never expected, it really can't be commented on, and honestly doesn't affect things or how they feel or how I feel about you. Your turn."

Jaime almost never failed to floor Le Feu with her words when she tried. Sometimes he almost regretted asking her questions, even when he wanted answers. He held up a finger while he processed for a minute.

"Well, I can't say you're wrong," Le Feu started. "I wouldn't date you because you've cheated on people and that scares me. Other than that, there's really not much. I mean, you're pretty crazy, but we talked about I like crazy, because I'm crazy, and you're a lot better than you used to be." He exhaled, paused for a minute, and then started, "I feel like an asshole, though, for holding it against you that you've cheated before. Well, more like a hypocrite, because I have, too. Another thing is that I know you have trouble keeping your mouth shut about things in general."

"And that is perfectly fair," Jaime mused. She was calm, smiling wistfully.

"It doesn't bother you that I don't want to date you? Or why?" He could not help but ask.

"It doesn't make you love me any less that you don't want to date me. It's fair."

"Good God, Jaime, when did you grow up to be so mature?"

"Le Feu, you said yourself that I'm good because I know you're not looking for a relationship. Because we both knew we started this with an expiration date. Besides, it's more meaningful to me that you don't want to lose me than it would be if you wanted to date me."

Le Feu pulled Jaime into his lap.

"You're right. We better enjoy it while we can."

Ruling the Throat Chakra

As a Scorpio, Jaime was a sign ruling the throat chakra with Aquarius. Le Feu was an Aquarius, and they each represented an imbalance of excess and deficiency in the throat chakra. Jaime was the imbalance of excess, and Le Feu was the imbalance of deficiency. Leu Feu bottled up communication.

Jaime was amazed at how Le Feu actually wanted to discuss his orientation with her without prompting and how she got answers, she'd expected it to be like pulling teeth like it was with Syd. Jaime knew she talked too much (like Innocence in the Book of Qualities.) A perfect example was the story Jaime does not want to tell about how she told too much with having to tell much at all (featuring extreme guilt). She had the ability to tell things without telling them right out. Sean knew then guessed about how she found out, and Liam knew from previous but Jaime gave it away with her emotional words, "why does he want to make me mad when I know his secret?"

Skinny Love

One thing that Jaime loved about Le Feu was that they both had very low percentages of body fat. She preferred her "boys to look like boys, not men" as she said, and this meant aspects of their physical appearance like facial hair or physical size. Because her rapist had been a stocky, older man, Jaime felt threatened by boys who were bigger than her. Jaime did not feel threatened by Le Feu. She loved that he had visible hipbones for her to grab onto, because it helped her to think that he was just universe, soul, skin, and bones. She held him and thought, "I can take you. And you know that I am strong."

As Jaime lay in Le Feu's embrace, he talked about his relationship with his ex, Janae.

"You know, I thought I was being pretty cool, letting Janae hook up with as many girls as she wanted – just no guys. But I dunno."

"No, it is pretty cool. That's the dream – find someone like that and you hold on. She's missing out."

"I guess you're right," he said as he drew closer to Jaime.

A few hours passed during the night as they talked and laughed. Le Feu sat up in his bed playing on his console with Jaime curled around him, both clad in only hoodies and intimates. Jaime had a tendency to probe when she was bored and just in general because questions were how she got information often. She had gotten into a habit of jokingly probing Le Feu with serious questions when he wasn't paying attention.

"So," she yawned. "did you clean up your phone?"

"What do you mean?" he asked with a glance away from his TV screen.

"Did you hide all your secrets? "she snickered.

"Oh." He paused the game and leaned in the opposite direction. "I don't want to talk about that."

"That's fine," Jaime answered. "We don't have to."

Le Feu exhaled deeply.

"It really freaks me out that Janae knows. I mean, I don't think I want keep doing that. I'm not really sure about it all. It's weird. It's a whole weird thing."

Jaime wondered if he had ever talked about that before. In an attempt to make him feel better, she explained why she had bothered to come out, and then shared her most embarrassing stories about hooking up with girls. She even discussed how bummed she was that she felt like she was now bound to sleeping with people that she was both emotionally and physically attracted to, and the girls who made her realise it.

Le Feu was an overall good friend to Jaime. Even when distracted he tried to give her honest and thoughtful answers to her probing question. They were often asking each other about their goals, how life was going, and about work. He was supportive of what she did, how she expressed her feelings, and helped her through tough times. She, naturally, did the same thin in return. They had let an honest friendship manifest sexually and danced gracefully between those blurred lines. As it happened, as a Scorpio and an Aquarius, their signs ruled the throat chakra, and as a result they had exceptional communication.

Many boys were surprised that Jaime did not have close female friends, which they would find out when asking her to introduce them to girls. Though Jaime often just said that girls tended to be mean or make her nervous, the real reason she didn't have close female friends was because she felt that too quickly women started either bashing themselves, or others, including those around them. Noticing this, Jaime realised it was something she wanted to change for the girl world, and thereby the world in general.

Laying next to Le Feu, Jaime texted Sean. "We're the perfect couple, me and Sean." she mused. "This is my life. I'm married to a gay man and I have a nonmonogamous sexual friendship with my best friend. Goals." Le Feu laughed.

Like mentioned in How I Met Your Mother, their friendship was an involuntary reflex. Jaime felt compelled to explain to Le Feu the lack of need to come out, and how it didn't make him "less" to not, how coming out doesn't make anything more valid, how she knew it's not safe for everyone, and how he shouldn't feel forced to challenge heteronormativity. She knew he did not want to hear those things and instead talked to him about how coming out wasn't a single action but a daily process.

Jaime knew that authenticity as valuable and that where boys may seem forward they still hide who they are, and while girls seem to be confident in their sense of self but manipulate the way they relate to people. Finding someone capable of both was quite the feat these days. She felt honoured that their friendship was such a reflex for Le Feu that he could be his authentic self around her.

Just a Title

For some reason, in Western culture, compassion for animals and vegetarianism/veganism were socially considered feminine. Le Feu started talking to Jaime about considering vegetarianism because of his compassion for animals. He told her that he didn't want to give up chicken, and Jaime explained to him that he could be a pollotarian (which she'd learned from Rosie). After a short conversation, Le Feu said, "well, it's only a title." Jaime smirked and said, "yeah, just like orientation and relationship status." The two had a laugh about that.

Le Feu had a persona he put on, particularly on the internet. To Jaime, it was the most unattractive thing about him. He put on the socially masculine air of not caring about anything – from girls to the environment to animals to his own life. Of course, he really did care about all of these things. But compassion was socially for girls – ambition was socially for boys. Le Feu (and many other boys) received messages that the only thing he was meant to do was be successful, and the only way of being successful was making a lot of money, and the only way to do that was to not care about anything except themselves, their job, and their success. These are dangerous messages for young boys to receive. This is the hate culture in which our children are being raised. The media directs our impressions and have taught us that it is cool not to care. Le Feu fed into the hate culture because he wanted to remain accepted by society, relating directly to meeting his love and belonging needs on Maslow's hierarchy. It would be a radical notion to reteach how cool it actually is to care, and how much more valuable love and kindness are than hate and apathy. When he talked to Jaime about his mixed sexuality, Le Feu made sure to specify that he was "not anymore, not this year." He did this out of fear, in the same way that he pretended he was a Trump supporter online, thinking he needed to protect his reputation. Jaime knew that if he really wasn't "anymore" then he would've deleted the app. He was still paranoid about his phone, no matter who the person looking was.

Le Feu's Label (Le Feu's Answers)

It took Jaime a long time to realise that Le Feu preferred to keep his business private because at one point his throat chakra was too open. Like Jaime, as a sign which ruled the throat chakra, he spoke his mind, and was open about his business. Because of this, he got in a lot of fights for "talking trash" and usually ended up pretty beat up. He changed. Adapted. Grew. Transformed.

Jaime knew she would never forget the first time she heard Le Feu label himself. He used the same label she did. She was slightly taken aback when he'd used it, not thinking she'd ever hear it out loud.

Coming out is an ongoing process. There will always be people who don't know. In some situations, it is better that way. It is difficult for many young people because they feel a desire to communicate their truth, yet as we grow many of us would like to stop coming out as we realise the danger it might put us in. As we age many of us also tend to wish that we didn't have to keep coming out to people. Some of us decide to stop and just allow others to find out organically. When we have to keep making effort to come out, people sometimes have us feeling as though our queer identity is our only identity. Regardless of how large or small of a part of identity that queer part is, it is important to remember that it is only a part of our identity and that we are made up of a collection of selves and experiences.

Coming out is not a requirement. Not coming out does not make anybody less queer or valid. Coming out is not a safe option for everyone. Coming out does not make anyone any more valid. It is more than a single action, but a daily process, which can become exhausting. Do not feel forced to challenge heteronormativity if it is not a safe option – being a chameleon is necessary for some. It is not up to anyone to decide for you, but an incredibly personal choice. Survival comes first, your community will be waiting.

Authenticity is incredibly valuable. Boys may seem forward and open with their speech, but often still hide who they are on the inside. While girls may seem confident in their sense of self and appearance, but manipulate the way they relate to people and will show different sides of themselves to specific people. Finding someone capable of being authentic in both speech and sense of self is quite the challenge. However, not coming out because it is not safe does not decrease one's authenticity. Not coming out because it is an aggravating process to be involved in does not decrease one's authenticity. It meant something to Jaime when Le Feu, SLB Benji, and Rick Batch all discussed their mixed sexuality with her because they were bravely baring their most authentic selves to her and she valued that.

"Let me see if I have a Dutch," Le Feu said, and he reached across Jaime. She laughed.
"That wasn't a move, by the way."
She snickered and stated, "if you wanted to touch me, you would touch me,"
"You're right," he smiled, and put a hand on her thigh. Now this, this is a move.
They shared a laugh about that.

After Le Feu shared his answers with Jaime he rolled over and announced, "alright, I'm going to bed!"
Jaime rolled onto her side and embraced him as the little spoon. Within seconds he rolled back over to kiss her deeply, one of the rare few treasured special kisses that did not lead to sex. Every time Jaime got answers from Le Feu, he brought it up organically, all of his own accord. Jaime usually listened and let Le Feu talk, regardless of the topic.
They had conversations – meaning she talked too – but she tended not to interrupt, question, or pry. She let him get out whatever he needed to first. Sometimes after Le Feu brought up the subject, Jaime would lay little "traps" by nonchalantly tossing in a sentence or a question. But only after he brought it up, because once she found out, she had been prepared to never bring it up to him again. The fact that

he came to her to discuss it and spoke openly about it on his own spoke volumes to Jaime about the true nature of their friendship. She felt the deepest honour each time he opened his mouth about it, despite him expressing his fear that she knew almost every time he spoke about I t.

Once Jaime heard all the answered she needed from Le Feu, she tore them up and burned them, in hopes of forgetting the truth, for fear that she might accidentally tell them, like how she made herself forget about Liam's experimental secret.

She was, however, driven mad by the way he'd mentioned that something happened at a young age, which he returned to visit as he got older. She knew he had said, "they were my age though so it was straight," and she knew she had laughed at how "straight" had become synonymous with "it's all good," or "don't worry about it." Still, she wondered if it was okay for someone to touch someone else if they're the same age? When she researched it, she found that the conditions were if they had an ongoing mutually enjoyable friendship, if they were similar size/age/social/emotional, and if it was lighthearted and spontaneous. Jaime didn't like when stories got told but it is unclear whether consent was obtained. It reminded her of Syd's story involving Drake, in which there were drugs and intoxication involved and in which Syd refereed to it as "traumatic." Upon each retelling, Sydney had given conflicting descriptions of "it was straight?" as well as "it was traumatic."

The healer in Jaime checked for answers to the questions "are you wounded? Are you broken? Do you need to heal from this?" in Le Feu's story. She was a natural healer – like Benji – since Scorpios both sting and heal. Jaime's tendency to try and fix the wounded directly related to her soul path of being helper and protector of mankind, which she acted on in the way of helping and protecting the children.

As the "mom friend," Jaime's bear instincts gave her a strong tendency to attempt to help the hurting. When Le Feu was expressing his pain about Janae breaking his heart, that was the instinct which activated in Jaime and prompted her to tell him, "the best way to get over someone is to get under someone else." When Le Feu lamented about who would want to sleep with him, Jaime giggled and said that she knew he had a best friend who would. Jaime offered him healing through her sexual touch. It worked for them, because Jaime never aimed to make him hers. She knew that he was not hers. She knew people could not be owned (for everyone she'd loved and wanted had left her). She aimed only to make him feel better, like he had for her long before. She said to him one day, "you are more healed than you realise and you are healing every day." He smiled when she said things like that, because he knew she could not help but tell the truth.

    Jaime couldn't figure out why she wanted to talk to Le Feu about Benji after she found out. She and Benji didn't even speak anymore. It wasn't until Le Feu told her, "not this year" that it dawned on her why she was reminded of Benji.

    She yearned to ask Le Feu, "do you use boys like trash?" and tell him about the boy who did.

    She worried that he let himself be used like trash.

    She thought about telling him how she used to use girls like trash. She thought about telling him how she used to use boys like trash. She thought about telling him how she used to use sex when she felt like trash, how she used to let people use her like trash. She wanted to talk about how it's sometimes okay to use people for sex or to use sex for something. She thought about how they used each other, and decided to keep her mouth shut.

    Jaime put Benji's song 25 to Life on her iPod, and any time it came on in her car, if she could handle it, she wouldn't skip it, despite when her friends made fun of his shaky flow at the beginning.

    "You try rapping about that," she'd say. She wanted people to hear it, people like Syd, Le Feu, and Sean. Songs like that proved it does happen to guys, too, this is real life.

Le Feu asked Jaime one day, "so, this other guy you see sometimes, the one with the nice car, is he better in bed than me?" He was half joking, but Jaime felt bad when she saw him struggle with his ego and esteem.

"No," she answered matter-of-factly. "He's just more out than you."

"What do you mean?" Le Feu asked immediately, and then it registered. "Wait, Jaime, do you only sleep with bisexual men?" Le Feu's jaw dropped.

"At the moment. Though I'm sure that's subject to change." Jaime replied.

"That's sort of sick." For some reason it made Le Feu queasy.

"Everyone's got preferences," Jaime shrugged.

***

"Jaime, you keep romanticising these bi boys, but all they do is cheat on you," Sean said one day, in Jaime's car on the way home from work.

It was not the first time Jaime had been told that she romanticised male bisexuality. She had also been accused of fetishising bi boys. The way she thought of it was that she had a definite preference for bisexual people in general, because she felt that they would be more understanding of her, and therefore more accepting. She knew that she thought it was hot when two boys kissed, but she also knew that she felt that way about when two girls kissed, so she ruled that out as just kink of voyeur. She also knew that she had extra love for bi boys because many people hated or erased them, but she ruled that out as a type of admiration (with respect) and not fetishisation. It was a real thing, though, bisexual males get fetishised. Some bisexual males can't help but enjoy being fetishised because for them someone is accepting that thing about them which society won't, but sexuality is something which needs to come second when seeking partners after physical and mental attraction based on personality traits and characteristics.

Sean unfortunately perpetuated the stereotype of gay boys who didn't like bisexual boys because they felt like bi boys could not be trusted. Sean had dated a bi boy before who had a girlfriend while he dated Sean, and eventually left Sean for her. Sean said it was easier for a girl to trust a bisexual boy because they'd revert to their socialised heteronormativity. Jaime never thought to ask Sean if he thought bisexual girls couldn't be trusted. She loved her bi boys a little bit extra for the gay boys who didn't.

Wristcutter Game

In a typical display of "telling secrets in between her words but most people don't think they're secrets because she says them right out" like Innocence, Jaime opened everyone's throat chakras.

"Hey Sean, what are the odds you tell us what made you first want to kill yourself? Like the game in Wristcutters – what was your method?"

She thought of her own reason, being twelve years old getting bullied and her first boyfriend dumping her for not being "cool enough."

"I'm not gonna tell you why," Sean started to answer Jaime's shot at playing What Are the Odds. "But I will tell you I tried to drown myself in the shower."

Jaime almost couldn't contain her laughter, not thinking that possible.

"And you, Jaime?" He countered. "What are the odds that you tell us your preferred method?"

"Count me down, love." Jaime was playing by the rules of the game, in which the players must count down from three and say the odds simultaneously.

"3, 2, 1." Sean counted down.

At the same time, they exclaimed, "one hundred per cent!" and laughed.

"You got me! Semantics," Jaime started. "I'd crash my car. Easy question."

She spun the bottle and it pointed at Le Feu. "Same question for everyone; what are the odds you tell us?"

Le Feu shook his head, undid his belt and slipped it off, then mimed a noose with it. He pointed at Ver.

"That's all you, boy. What are the odds?"

"50/50 with an overdose." Ver casually laughed it off.

Jaime mentioned a memory of the girl in the movie who stuck her head in the oven, and Liam said, "I don't like this game anymore. I never actually wanted to die when I wanted to kill myself. You guys are bad," he said. "You all had plans."

"Nah, baby. We're broken. But it's okay, we've all learned to breathe." Jaime winked at Liam.

Jaime clung to her kula of people who shared her pain. They kept her sane. In a slightly sick way they could all relate. She sought to heal them all, as they had all healed her. Anywhere she was that belonged to her they were welcome, always.

How Jaime's Boys Differed

Jaime noticed that her boys seemed to have the language to discuss their problems to some extent (or could duke it out hand to hand and be fine afterwards) that her group of girls had lacked. Her boys did not revert to the coping mechanisms of dark humour, targeted relational aggression, and acting "fine" that her girls had. Jaime wondered whether it was a matter of age and maturity (as her boys were older when she got close to him than her girls were when she was close to them), or if it was because her male friends had been socialised to be more vocal. She had always appreciated the similarities between boys and girls as a bisexual person, but getting close with a group of boys really helped Jaime to appreciate the differences between boys and girls. As she looked for more girls to befriend, she sought out those who also associated predominantly with boys or those girls who "acted like boys" like she did – like Sawyer. She wanted girls who weren't afraid to be vocal about their feelings. She loved how Sawyer spoke her mind.

Jaime and Le Feu's Past

Le Feu had once been a bully to Jaime. When she had gotten suspended for an overexaggerated situation in which she'd threatened her bullies, she was made to apologise to her bullies. Naturally, her bullies were also made to apologise to Jaime, but most of them did not take it seriously. Le Feu had given Jaime a genuine apology, recognising that he'd been bullied before, too, and never bullied her again. Le Feu had in fact been suicidal at one point after being badly bullied. As adults Jaime noticed how much he cared about what other boys thought of him. Le Feu saw Jaime's spark in middle school with her old friends. He knew her baseline. Some people didn't. Her boys regularly saw her spark fluctuate through adolescence and adulthood. After being badly bullied for so long, Jaime cultivated a lack of care for what other people thought. She cultivated enough of an appreciation for herself that she cared only what she thought as she evolved.

    One thing that was important to Jaime about Le Feu was that he was the only person she knew who truly understood what she went through with her dad. He watched his mom battle sickness for much of his life. When Jaime was freaked out about her dad or down because he didn't feel well, Le Feu was literally right there with her. Remembering this often in dark times, she regularly sent light to him.

    Jaime knew other cultures had a very different relationship with their elders. The Japanese, for example, believed it was the duty of the family to take care of each other with age, and many other cultures shared this belief. Jaime noticed that American culture tended to involve putting beloved family members in the care of others, instead of taking care of them together as a family. She believed that this was meant to help people detach from their feelings surrounding sickness and death, but in her opinion the actual effect of this practise was that the people became more desensitised to people who needed care and compassion. She felt this directly related to why she felt unequipped to deal with everyone's feelings (and especially her own) when her family members were placed in care facilities. Among many things, Jaime worried about the treatment of her family members as they were being cared for. She felt the necessary shift was for humankind to recognise the importance of respecting our elders, our wise ones, as we care for them through age and dis-ease, and guide them eventually out of this realm, as all must one day go. This involves the recognition of the collectivity of selves – including the self in old age, and the dying self, which related to the archetypical maiden/mother/crone goddesses in Wiccan religion and how she is within us all – such as the Celtic goddess Morgan. The triquetra symbol represented the inner trinity. This also relates to the Ralph Waldo Emerson trifecta of self, nature, and god, for death is where the self meets god and returns to nature, and the self is an expression or manifestation of god itself.

Honto Ni?! (Jaime, Le Feu, and the Truth – a Most Unhappy Threesome)

If Le Feu's story must be told, so too must this one.
The thing about Jaime and the truth was that she pretty much always ended up telling it. Even when she didn't want to, and even when she didn't mean to, and even when she knew she shouldn't. Even when she spoke in other languages, or wrote it down. This had always gotten her into trouble.
Jaime knew she shouldn't have let Sean guess what she'd discovered, but she knew he already knew the truth and that was just confirmation. Jaime didn't mean to get mad at the bar and tell Liam that she didn't understand why Le Feu made her mad since she knew his secrets. She didn't mean to answer when Liam immediately guessed what exactly she meant. Jaime knew she could tell the truth without outing him entirely. "My primary male partner," she'd say, omitting his name. Or sometimes she'd refer to him as her lover. She tried to remain cryptic about sleeping with him to people who were not in the know, unless it became absolutely necessary, because that was what he wanted.
Jaime knew that she would have to live with the truth of the fact that she told his secret, regardless of how she was feeling. She struggled with the truth that she would probably lose her best friend if he ever found out. The truth was, she knew she should tell him. It was the one story Jaime never

wanted to tell. Cover to cover, she had messed up. The road to Hell is paved with good intentions, they say, and she felt it was starting to look that way.

    Is there anything to be said for all the times that Sean would be in conversation with Jaime and call Le Feu gay, and Jaime would exclaim, "no, stop, he's not"? She did say it because he wasn't. It was still the truth. But is there also anything to be said for all of the times Jaime spoke out of emotion and agreed with Sean? Did neutralising her words and actions actually do anything? Thinking about this story sometimes made Jaime sick.

Root Chakra
Muladhara
"The Earth is what we all have in common."

The Root or Base Chakra will show stories of displacement and stability. The Root Chakra involves those we trust for immediate survival. The Root Chakra represents those moments when we say, "I am." The mantra for this chakra is "I am safe, I trust." The Root Chakra is located in the coccygeal spine, and is represented by the colour red. When healing the Root Chakra with colour, red should be used, or if the Root Chakra is overactive green should be used followed by a small dose of red. The Root Chakra embodies the element of earth and represents the direction of North. The Root Chakra is ruled by the planet Mars, and its ruling signs are Gemini and Cancer. Cedar atlas, cinnamon, juniper, vetiver, and ylang ylang are essential oils which affect the Root Chakra, and one crystal which can be used for the Root Chakra is Red Jasper. The Root Chakra is grounding and represents the physical body, and one pose which resonates deeply with the Root Chakra and can be felt in the whole body is Virabhadrasana II (Warrior 2).

When someone's Root Chakra is balanced, they would be grounded, safe, self sufficient, and financially stable. When the Root Chakra is in excess there is anxiety, and dependency. When there is a deficiency in the Root Chakra there can be reckless choices, and even homelessness.

Ana, a Personal Account

I was never entirely sure if I wanted to be them, or if I wanted to be with them. The way they were so strikingly beautiful. The way people loved them. The control they were in. Nobody ever wanted to be with me.

I probably used to walk down every hallway like it was a runway once. Conjuring fantasies of dreamy hunks to sweep me off my feet. And maybe sometimes of beautiful babes, too. Back before everything was so competitive.

But then you had to be the best. The best at whatever you did, the best looking... so I tried to be the best Anabelle I could be. I worked hard to perfect myself. Still, though, nobody wanted me.

Not ever my parents wanted me. They would send me back and forth from house to house. I don't think they ever even knew about my mixed sexuality. Still I wanted to be perfect for them, anyway.

I had had sex or done sexual things. Never really felt right with anyone. I just want love.

I think I wanted love when I dragged Jaime into the bathroom at Sean's job, and I think I wanted love when I started kissing her and then ripped off my clothes.

But she pushed me away and I banged my head against the cold, metal hand dryer and she said, "I'm sorry, Ana, but you're not really my type. You kind of look like a skeleton."

And I had never felt so fat in my life.

Jaime introduced me to yoga. At first, my eating disorder ran my yoga lifestyle. The desire to practise was driven by the desire to remain thin. Jaime had told me that if I discovered a physical hobby I enjoyed, I'd be able to eat food and stay thin. I practised obsessively. Driven by the desire to be flexible and strong, I drilled myself for hours at a time. In no time I was sticking my handstands and forearm stands, thanks to muscle memory from when I was a competitive gymnast. Gymnastics was where my eating disorder had begun.

Everyone was impressed by my practise. They discussed my strength, my amazing skill. They marveled at the way my body looked. Someone even anonymously paid for my teacher training.

It wasn't until later I realised the way yoga had helped me. My depression was getting better. I was eating more and purging less. I began to teach, and I got a job as a receptionist at a studio. It wasn't until later I realised that my yoga was more than just my physical practise. My yoga was my art as well. My yoga could be a special cup of tea to calm my anxiety. My yoga was for my recovery.

I suffered from borderline personality disorder, characterised by unstable relationships and an inability to recognise feelings of love that others have for me, as well as schizophrenic psychosis, episodes of which included visual and auditory hallucinations. At the peak of the episodes, I was hearing voices telling me that I was a terrible person who was worthless and deserved to die. I heard voices telling me that I was stealing from people, or trying to kill my dad. While having sex with someone, I hallucinated that Sean was a blue devil, and Jaime was a red devil, and that they were telling me I was going to Hell for my choices. I spent many occasions in the psych ward at various hospitals trying to overcome my mental illnesses. Managing my disorders was a daily difficulty.

Sean had to explain to me that my magic wasn't meant to be like anyone else's. He said this when I was talking about how I wanted to be prescribed the kind of pills that my sister was prescribed. I didn't realise that maybe I might need something different to work for me. Yoga is part of that something different that works for me. It helps treat my brain. Many of my difficulties come from deep root chakra imbalances, due to being moved around a lot as a child between my parents' houses, losing my brother, and the unstable relationships between my family members. My basic needs of trust, shelter, and safety were slightly compromised, and from that I am learning to recover.

Some Words on Ana

Because Anabelle had borderline personality disorder, words of affirmation was her primary language of love. Ana would twist words around and take things the wrong way all the time because of her disorder. She relied on tone of voice, facial expressions, and body language, but often entirely misinterpreted the things people were trying to say to her. She depended on words to reassure her that she was loved, worth, and special, even if she didn't believe them. When people didn't talk to her it brought out paranoia and self depreciating thoughts of being worthless. Anabelle's thought process somewhat reminded Jaime of Ugliness in the Book of Qualities, where she was trying to steal back her sense of belonging, yet felt that that which came easily to her was worthless.

Anabelle had incredible tapas when it came to her physical asana practise. However, her tapas was lacking when it came to motivating herself to work on the project which was herself. Head often in the clouds, she seemed to think that things would eventually fall into place and work out in her favour.

Sean said to Ana, "I wish you would realise that you have to work to keep the pieces where they belong," in response to her talking about how she expected that everything would "fall into place."

What Sean really meant was that it wasn't going to fall into place, because you have to put the pieces in place. Sean, Jaime, and Nef all knew that you needed a realistic plan with attainable goals in order to be able to get what you wanted. They each mapped out their course of action and carefully made well thought out moves. Ana had a tougher time grasping that. She did not know what steps to take or where to seek guidance for how to attain her desires. Jaime, Sean, and Nef knew that life must be maintained, and that there really wasn't a point at which one could just sit back and admire how neatly and pretty all the pieces were in place. There was always something to be done. They had a hard time explaining this to Anabelle. Due to her BPD, she often took it the wrong way, responding with comments like, "you think I don't do enough?! So now I'm a horrible person because I'm not always doing anything?!"

Ana's borderline personality disorder also clouded her judgement when it came to being able to discern whether or not people could be trusted (whether or not they were sketchy, shady, schemers, or otherwise questionable characters). She always assumed everyone had good intentions. This got her into many scary situations in which she thought she could trust people who wanted to take advantage of her.

Ethereal Green Beans

There was a visiting hoopdance teacher that Jaime's favourite hoopmaking company had connected her with, a beautiful Afro-American called Ciel who was from the West Coast. Jaime was inspired by her flow and eager to collaborate with her.

Ciel said to her, "I haven't found my sense of peace yet. But the world goes quiet and everything is just a little bit brighter when my hoop surrounds me. To relax and kind of breathe, I'll sit and hug myself, Remind myself I'm a human being and am worthy of all things wholesome. Then I discovered hula hoops. Yeah, those things you played with as a kid. They changed my life."

She talked in depth with Jaime about being pansexual, and what it meant to fall in love with a person's essence and energy, as well as what it meant to her to help eliminate the internal queer community bi and panphobia. She wanted to help individuals work on offering others more acceptance and support. She was a deeply emotional person, who could only form romantic connections after platonic bonds had been built. Her deep running emotions helped her to be empathetic towards others.

In her hoopdance lessons, she spoke to her students about the collective consciousness, the universal frequencies we all share, and how we can tap into them through dance, because our bodies are wired for movement. She discussed love, and self love, believing that we are mirrors, and that the way in which we love ourselves is how we end up loving others.

"Your circle is a circle of love," she told her students. "Love is safety and wholeness. Love is universal, warm, and can be felt everywhere, especially if you know where to look. Love is a child in a park observing a sunny day, or a dog jumping in a puddle. Love is all around us, and you can feel it in your circle."

Ciel took her students through slow, meditative hooping, and gradually brought them into a faster paced flow. She gave them opportunities to explore and experiment with their bodies, and to feel the music. She also let them flow silently for periods of the class time, to explore emotion.

"My ethereal green beans, you must ground yourself to some thought of nature within your circle at some point, because nature is the safest place, it is a powerhouse that will rejuvenate the earth. I invite you to explore your circle with bare feet in the grass, sand, dirt, or water, to feel the breeze on your face, or the sun on your skin. I invite you to hoop in the rain. I invite you to experience this life as fully and openly as you can. I can only hope that this circle will be a tool of self discovery for you. My instructions are only the beginning, for this is your journey," she would always say at the end of a class. "I invite you to empower yourselves by changing your perspective. Notice how different your situation or emotions might feel once you are spinning around. Drink it in, and hydrate your soul with experience."

Ciel had moved around a lot in her youth, and found her stability in her practise. Wherever she was, she was safe, whole, and loved in her circle. Wherever she was, she was free to experience her emotion, attraction, and free to experiment - as long as she had her sacred circle. Ciel let her yoga dance.

"Black and Blue Tapestries"

Black and blue tapestries
hung over each window
across from the bed
each given from a different friend

the girls must think alike
since they each gave the boys circles
as if to say
let your love last forever

the boys smile at each other
fingers slightly intertwined
amidst the rest of their white walls
and kitchen fixins

they both work jobs
they're not the best
but they pay the bills
they put food on their plates

and the boys like the same sort of music
and both had mostly girl friends
as they climb into bed each night
to snuggle up across from their tapestries

they can rest easy
for here they are making it
metal in their mouths and smoke in their lungs
they did this themselves, together.

Before I Was Theirs, a Personal Account

Before I was theirs, there was the white couple who raised me. People looked at my brown skin and my white parents and struggled to pronounce my Latino name.

Before I was theirs, I came out to the white couple. They said I couldn't be a girl. So, they took me back to the foster home.

Before I was theirs there was the black couple who wouldn't let me grow my hair. "Your curls aren't nice enough," the woman said. "You can get it shaved instead."

Before I was theirs, the black couple let me go because they said I was too expensive and they had to downsize. I understand.

Before I was theirs, the white guy who wanted a kid beat me when I grew my hair. He used his belt when I said yes, I did want to look like a girl.

Before I was theirs, I was stuck in the foster home for a while. All the younger kids got fostered first.

But then, they showed up, and they wanted to foster me. My gay foster parents, Neil and Dom. Recently never have to go back to the foster home. No more bouncing around from family to family.

That means I have my own family, and one that accepts me for who I am. That means I've got a shot again. I told Jaime my story when I met her, and in return, she opened her studio to me and helped me find another family, a family within the queer community, and even a family within a yoga class.

Birth Order

Courtney was the first person to ask Candy her boy name.

Candy's first question to someone she was interested in when finding out she was trans was, "do you have a preferred name?"

Courtney dates a transguy. Somehow, after everything she's been through, it's right up her alley. Courtney was girl all the way.

Candy was in between. Once, Candy had a crush on a transguy. She knew it was possible. Now, potentially interested in a transgirl.

"You look just like your brother," everyone always told Candy.

For the longest time she didn't see it. Probably around when she started noticing she did look rather like her older brother was around when she wanted to be like him.

But Chaos was difficult to be like. Chaos took risks, Chaos lived on the edge. The best Candy could do at age twelve was to wear Chaos' old clothes and listen to his music. Why would Candy want to be like Chaos, though? Chaos practically terrified her. Chaos took too many risks in Candy's opinion. Yet still, she strove to imitate him in some ways. Chaos was the only one she felt she had around to look up to.

Courtney always used to say that she wished she had siblings so that she wouldn't be so lonely.

Chaos was exactly his name as well as aggression and rage. Their older sister was always faraway. Candy watched his mind show through his ego and his solar plexus. She learned rage and feeling insane as well as what not to do.

Candy learned to navigate both loving women like Chaos did, and also not treating women the way Chaos did. She learned by example the way she felt and spoke about women, and watched the way she never wanted to be treated. She wanted to be much kinder to women than Chaos was. Yet, just like Chaos, she adored their bodies.

Candy learned to walk the fine line between feeling aggressive and insane, and not acting like Chaos. She could never let her big brother come out from inside her. He was too untamable, fully wild.

Jaime was her boy name. No one will ever know who Jaime Alexander really was. Jaime found out that her parents thought she would have been born a boy, and the top name they had picked out had been James.

She never thought she would a boy, but she wondered how she would've turned out had she been born one. Having a brother, she had a frame of reference for what she would have looked like. She thought that she would have been bisexual anyway, which is why she thought that as James she would have gone by Jamie. Turn James into Jamie and it's spelled like Jaime which means I love, which was how she always sought to be act out of. She figured Jamie would've kept his hair long like Dex (Chaos) does, and that he would still have gotten his tongue pierced and tattoos. Switch a few letters around in Jaime and her identity is protected. She, however, could change her name over and over and become someone new each time, in this new and changing world.

Boy Sawyer

Boy Sawyer was Guatemalan and had gone to a different high school than Sean and Jaime. Sean met him online – they had shared interests in music, chilling, and pizza. But, Sawyer's mother did not approve of him being gay.

Sawyer had a group of female friends. He was going to the state school and working tech for the phone company when he got kicked out. Sean happened to not be able to take it anymore with Kumo's mom Veronica at the same time.

Sawyer had good credit, part of why he and Sean were able to lease a apartment. Sawyer didn't talk or visit much with his family, and his mother had never been inside of their place.

Sawyer's friends were his family. He loved to party with them. A commonality between Sawyer and Sean.

Sawyer lost his best friend. She never made it to twenty, thanks to a car crash.

Sawyer became incredibly codependent. He clung to Sean, didn't want to be without him ever. He wanted Sean to hang out with him and his friends who were left, and he wanted to be with Sean when he was with his friends.

Sawyer's anxiety was constantly on the rise. He had to drop out of school and work full time to afford to live. He went through periods of frivolous spending.

Sawyer got a kitten for free and uses her a lot to help cheer up. He is still searching for ways to manage his root chakra deficiency imbalance.

Those Three Boys

     In seventh and eighth grade there were three boys who gave Jaime trouble – Benji Rod, Alberto Tilanda, and Kasper Ethyk.

     Jaime had "dated" Alberto first, in seventh grade as a rebound. Her second boyfriend ever, who taught her to make out. They used to talk on the house telephone. His mom would answer the phone with "Bueno." He told Jaime that he had witnessed abuse within his family. When they were together, he still had a lot of his baby fat, but after they broke up for about a year he dropped down to his bones. He had been close with both Benji and Kasper. When he was thin, he tried to get girls to have sex with him.

     All three boys have self-harmed.

     Karoline had dated Kasper for a lot of seventh grade. They were Polish together. She told Jaime he once tried to unbutton her pants and she stopped him. He told Jaime a lot of stories about him and Alberto hooking up, in great graphic detail. He told Jaime these stories over the internet, of course. She thought they were totally believable. The boys wore skinny jeans, kept their hair longs.

     Benji Rod is the first Benji Jaime knew, not the fun one she writes letters to. Benji Rod was her third Latino boyfriend. Benji Rod was the first person she came out to on New Year's Day. He said, no way. It was just after they broke up, but they "dated" again. Benji Rod was Jaime's first biphobic boyfriend. She couldn't believe that she tolerated a second. "You're going to cheat on me with a girl," he argued. Karoline, he thought. Benji Rod had divorced parents. He and Alberto, though friends, had anger issues and controlling natures, possessive tendencies, and a desire for acceptance.

     Again, all three boys have self-harmed. They were often causing a ruckus with me, any one of them, telling Jaime about the harm they were doing. Why these boys self-harmed was always unclear. Why did Jaime's bisexuality bring out possessive biphobia in Benji Rod? Was there any truth to Kasper's stories? And what of the friend that Benji

Rod made in the Chinese new boy who would send Jaime pictures in his mother's underwear? What indeed.

Benji the Biphobic

      Benji's biphobia came out in several ways. When he couldn't go on a field trip with Jaime, he asked Alberto to watch over her. He wanted Alberto not only to watch over Jaime but to stick close to her, to try and keep her apart from Karoline. Benji never expressed a reason for his lack of trust. A second field trip, he still wanted someone keeping an eye on her. Again, he was asking for her to be kept away from Karoline. It made Jaime nothing but angry.

      Benji requested she stop keeping company with her queer friends, like Glitterboii. He called her queer friends extraterrestrials. In an act of absolute mania, he outed her to her mother with intentions of getting her kicked out of her home. Benji the Biphobic was a ball of destruction for Jaime, though after she left him, she went straight to Karoline. She recognised his reason to worry. Still she resented him for his biphobia and its lasting effects on her.

"To Her Apartment"

in which I learned firsthand
love is that "mutual weirdness"
I've read about
where you can display your weird cuteness

watch what you like
house your library
mostly the books you've
read before and you say

it depends when I ask
how often you reread them
will you ever know
the impact of the experiences

you allow me to have
within and throughout
your own sacred space
and this is how she

shows me she loves me
after the not-life
we've shared
thanks to our creators.

"Visiting Sister"

she has dad's fingernails
I have tighter curls than her
but our brother wins
the best hair award

her fiancé used to have
long hair too
and they're basically
married anyway

she made the dough
and he made the dinner
and the sweet pet to
perfect the show

it was hanging out
in their bathroom
and feeling finally old enough
for your sister's secrets

my cister?
Maybe, but I'll
never clarify
mine or about my own

it's wondering
about a black
moleskin notebook
in the desk drawer of the small room

filled with a list
quite like your own
and an answer in your head
to never asked questions

she doesn't have dark
circles under her eyes

and she knows how to
wear makeup if she wants to

she likes Sherlock clothes
(tweed) and jeans
I don't care for pants like that
though it's funny

I recall her taking the piss
when my younger self said
I felt like stretchy tight (gym) clothes
were meant for dancing

now I wear tight stretchy clothes
when I'm not being genderqueer
and dance in my hoop
while dad asks why there are dark bags

under my eyes

Root Chakra Connections

Yamas are the limb of Patanjali's yoga which deals with ethical standards and integrity. Niyamas are the limb of Patanjali's yoga which deals with self discipline and spiritual observances. Several yamas and niyamas relate directly to the root chakra. Other limbs and yogic practises also relate directly to the root chakra, outlined as follows.

Ahimsa (non harming)

Ahimsa is a yama and refers to non harming, no shaming, clear boundaries, physical and emotions. Ahimsa is the ultimate expression of respect for others, because it means non-harming. When one has respect for themselves cultivated through recognition of their divine light, they are able to have respect for others. This is the meaning of the mantra namaste - "the divine light in me recognises the divine light in you." The non-harming referred to by Ahimsa includes both physical harm and that which is inflicted emotionally and verbally. To truly practise ahimsa, one must use kind words instead of harmful ones, and one must be just and non harming to themselves as they are to others.

Aprigraha (non hoarding)

Aprigraha is one of Patanjali's yamas. There are multiple translations for aprigraha, including non hoarding, non greedy, and non attachment. This yama applies to the root chakra because much of it relates to the physical world, like when it teaches us not to hoard material objects, for example. When it comes to aprigraha, the ultimate truth which must be discerned is that happiness is not derived from material objects. The only reason that anyone can understand the concepts of non hoarding and not being greedy is because they are in understanding of the fact that material objects are not everything. Everyone must discern on their own what things fill their lives that becomes everything through which happiness, fulfillment, and contentment are cultivated, but they will never be anything tangible.

When we look at aprigraha as non attachment, it means letting go of what you hold onto. Sometimes this means letting go of what we hold onto in each pose – some people practise with blindfolds for this reason. Other times it refers to letting go of feelings, people, anything that we may be attached to. It is said that "holding on to anything is like holding on to your breath – you will suffocate." "Let it go and it will be yours forever." Sometimes, aprigraha even means letting go of our limitations or boundaries.

"You don't have any limitations at all, you are just addicted to them" - Kyle Cease

"Familiarity is our most dangerous comfort." - Jo Thyssen

Asana

The word asana literally translates to posture or pose. Asana is the word as the end of the Sanskrit name of every pose

Asana is simply physical posture, the physical practise of yoga. Asana is you on the mat. It is said that no matter what we are doing, we are in some form of asana. The "main" asana is typically tadasana, a standing pose, which means mountain pose. In yogic thought, we are able to find tadasana in every pose. All asana are meant to be active in every pose. Always we are breathing and therefore our pose is always moving.

"Counting is the syllables of movement" Kendall Sturges

"It doesn't matter if things aren't perfect, practise is a time to feel alive, loved, and free." Unknown

"The study of asana is not about mastering posture, it's about using posture to understand and transform yourself." Uknown

"Sound when stretched is music. Movement when stretched is dance. Mind when stretched is meditation. Life when stretched is celebration" Ravi Shankar

"Movements are like waves – you have to go with them" - Sandra Sabatini

"You can't stop the waves, but you can learn to surf." John Kabat-Zinn

"In an asana, the mind has to reach inside the body to find a quiet space until a point comes where perfect balance is felt" - Geeta Iyengar

"Bring peace to uncomfortable feelings by going inside them and seeing them for what they truly are.. just feelings" - Aaron Bjorn

Astya (non stealing)

Astya is directly related to Aprigraha. Without greed, there is hardly a need to steal. The only time in which stealing is acceptable is when it is a matter of survival (i.e. Jean Valjean stealing food in Les Misérables, or Aladdin stealing bread). Which material objects must not be stolen, there are also non tangible things which should not be stolen, including time and credit. Credit must be given where due, and ideas which are not original cannot in good circumstance be called such. It is also important not to steal the lovers of others. Above all else, we humans must refrain from attempting to steal control of this planet from our Earth Mother, for she will always overpower us and it would benefit us better to work cooperatively with her instead of work against her, guided by greed and misconceptions of truths of humans being superior to nature.

Astya and Appropriation (giving credit where due)

Cultural appropriation is a form of stealing. It is important that we give credit where it is due. Jaime did not claim any yoga magic as her own, she simply borrowed from the prakriti. Jaime felt that it was important to appreciate other cultures, and if we became so moved by them that we wanted to adopt certain practises as our own, it is important to do so with the deepest gratitude and respect.

Bandhas

The pelvic floor is a diamond shaped area from the pubic bone to the rectum. Everyone has a pelvic floor. Everyone's pelvic floor expands and contracts with their breath. This is most noticeable from cat/cow positions, where there is no weight on the pelvic floor and the breath can be felt freely. The mula bandha holds the breath in the pelvic floor, and is the bandha most useful for inverting.

Bandhas are energy locks, we lock the energy in certain parts of our bodies by holding our breath there. The purpose of bandhas is to hold and cultivate the energy from a specific body part. They help us to achieve longer holds in various asana. When you master the locks, you master the practise – outside you're flowing through asana, holding for long periods of time as well as managing new positions, while inside there is consistent, directed concentration, steady and long breaths, and a calm, clear mind. When we release a bandha, the energy floods strongly through the body.

The four bandhas are:
Mula Bandha, which locks the energy in the pelvic floor.
Uddiyana Bandha, which is the lifting of the diaphragm by holding the breath out.
Jalandhara Bandha, which closes the windpipe and esophagus by pressing the chin against the chest, in or between the collarbones. In this bandha the breath is held in..
Maha Bandha, which is the act of holding all three bandhas at the same time.

Bathing

Showers and baths can be used like spells to do things for people's bodies like heal injuries, ease one into sleep, wake a person up, or ease stress (among many other uses). Children must learn to take proper care of their physical bodies, which includes learning hygiene. Children must be taught bath time as a fun, sensory experience so that it can become a thing of enjoyment for them. As they grow older, they learn to appreciate bathing as an act of self care, and an opportunity to explore the self, their feelings, and discern truth while thanking the body, as well as healing it and recharging its energy.

Body Breath

One of the things people tend to find the hardest in yoga is connecting with their breath in such a way that they are able to actively breathe into all parts of their bodies. The breath doesn't just reach the chest. Each cell in the body breathes, and therefore the breath reaches every part of the body. Being able to recognise what that breath feels like takes lots of self study (swadyaya) and practise, and learning how to direct that breath is a skill based in honing that recognition. Jaime learned to recognise her body's breath and hone the skill of directing that breath when she pulled her hamstring at nineteen and had to breath into it to heal it and help it be able to handle being in certain positions.

Body Isolation and Awareness

In asana we can isolate muscles for isometric movements, and in art modelling there are ways to move without moving. Jaime and Dex were very body aware siblings, for the sake of taking preventative health measures. Jaime learned about the Proprioceptive Sense which keeps us from bumping into things, and helps us understand where we are in space.

Body Poetry

We can use asana as a language the body speaks. Sex is another example of how bodies speak to each other. Dance is another language of movement.

Jaime found herself writing poetry about girl versus boy bodies, curves versus lines. She was not the first to use poetic body descriptions – colours, flowers, nature references of beauty to talk about body.

Erikson's Trust vs Mistrust

Erikson theorised about stages of development that we all go through during our lives. Like emotions, we cycle through these stages of development despite the fact that there is an age they each specifically relate best to. The first stage relates to the root chakra. The first stage refers to infancy, but we cycle back to it constantly throughout our lives. This stage is Trust vs Mistrust, in which we learn whether or not to begin trusting our world, when we learn things like if our needs will be met when we cry as a baby. We learn whether or not our family will come back when they walk away, and these things form our initial concepts of trust or mistrust. Later in our lives, as we get older, we learn through many experiences who we can trust and why, as we pass back through Trust vs Mistrust. This concept relates to the root chakra because establishing this trust helps us to feel safe in our worlds, and safety is a big root chakra concept.

Mudras

Mudras are tools to help draw yourself inward. Typically, mudras are hand gestures used during meditation and asana. Mudras have specific goals for channeling the flow of energy in our bodies. There are over 100 known mudras. Many reference the hands as holding energetic points for the five elements. The thumb represents akasha (space or ether), the index finger represents air, the middle finger represents fire, the ring finger represents water, and the pinky finger represents earth.

Two of the most common mudras are Anjali Mudra and Gyan Mudra. Anjali Mudra is when our hands are together at our heart's centre, and represents honouring and celebrating the moment. Gyan Mudra is when we touch our thumb and index finger in a circle and leave the three remaining fingers flexed. The intention of this mudra is to improve concentration and sharper memory. Many people use Gyan Mudra during their practise to help them concentrate on balancing poses.

Physiological Needs and Safety

Maslow's most basic needs are our physiological needs and our safety. Every human shares the same physiological needs – the needs for air, food, water, shelter, and (for some) sex. Having these needs met directly relates to the root chakra. The need for safety that all humans have relates to the sense of trust and mistrust continuously revisited in the root chakra. The root chakra is the foundation, and is all about stability. When mistrust leads to unstable relationships with others, the safety of the self is compromised.

The Physical Realm

The physical realm includes feeling comfortable and secure in one's physical body. A person with a balanced root chakra accepts their body as the thing which houses their soul, and they treat it with care and respect.

It is possible to experience breath in every part of the body. Each cell is breathing, and once trained, the breath can be noticed and intentionally directed. Breathing into different areas of the body can easy ailments, especially when accompanied by colour healing breath techniques.

Physical Touch

One language of love involves physical touch, which includes things like hand holding, hugging, cuddling, kissing, and sexual contact. Perhaps people whose primary language of love is physical touch feel the energetic vibrations of love greater through physical touch. These people may also likely be very tactile based people and kinesthetic learners.

Jaime's third language of love was physical touch. This could be involved with how Jaime felt she was a bodily kinesthetic learner and a touch based person. Being a touch based person did not always go favourably for Jaime. The slightest touch in a certain spot could instantly turn her on. This was why learning hand to hand combat as a means of self-defense was incredibly hard for her. Learning dance styles involving a partner was also a challenge for Jaime for the same reason.

Pratyahara
"You cannot change what you are not aware of."

Pratyahara involves the internalisation of perceptive senses. From a child development, the perceptive senses are the five senses along with our proprioceptive, vestibular, and tactile senses.

The proprioceptive keeps us from bumping into things and helps us to understand our place in space. The vestibular sense refers to the water between our ears which keep us balanced. The tactile sense involves being able to tell textures apart as well as being able to do small motions involving putting on clothes like fastening buttons, snaps, or zipping zippers. The five senses are our senses of sight (perceiving colours and shapes), sound (hearing music and words), touch (involving the physical body), taste (involving food), and smell (involving aromas). The author of the book Balanced and Barefoot has discussed the way that children seek out the movements natural to them for development of their vestibular and proprioceptive senses, explaining things like why children can be seen randomly spinning in circles or bobbing up and down.

Ahara (food) refers to physical food for nourishment, impressions which nourish the mind, associations, which are the people we hold at heart level who nourish our soul and affect us with gunas. Pratyahara often referred to withdrawal from the wrong food and impression, while simultaneously opening to the right food and impressions. The right diet and relationships yield control over mental impressions, control of withdrawal of sensory impression. A healthy mind resists negative sensory influences like a healthy body resists toxins and pathogens.

In Ayurveda, Gunas are used to define the mental state – the mind is harmonious if it is with Sattva, heavy if it is Tamasic, and Rajasic if it is agitated. The mind is balanced and clear sighted if the three gunas are harmonious, but Sattva manages everything as the "right balance."

The Gunas are 3 fundamental qualities of Prakriti

(our original nature). The Gunas are found in Hinduism traditions of Sankya, yoga, Bhagavad Gita, and Ayurveda referred to as factors of illness which are sometimes healing. This makes the Gunas types of energy.

Sattva represents stability, harmony, virtue, light, and brightness. Sattva provides development of the soul, enlightenment, and brings joy. It is the principle of all intelligence. Yoga and meditations were designed to increase sattva.

Rajas represents turbulence, movement, motivation, and passion. Rajas can create selfishness which leads to disintegration, pain, suffering, emotional fluctuation (fear, desire, love, hatred). It is the principle of energy.

Tamas represents dullness, darkness, and inertia. It hinders and hides, is a passive force blockage, causes degeneration and death, gives illusion leading us towards ignorance and attachment. It is the principle of materialisation.

The Laws that manage the Gunas are as follows
- Alternation – the Gunas are constantly in dynamic interaction as interconnected forces
- Continuity – gunas maintain specific nature during specific time when they are dominant
- Night (Tamas) becomes sunrise as Rajas, Rajas passes to day as Sattva – gradually and alternately

Elements and Gunas relate to each other in particular ways. Ether comes from Sattva, clarity. Fire comes from Rajas and energy. Earth comes from Tamas, inertia. Air comes from Rajas and Sattva, lightness and movement. Water comes from Rajas and Tamas, movement and inertia.

Practise pratyahara so as not to get disturbed or distracted when practising meditation. Pratyahara incites us to cultivate an awareness of the breath travelling through our body and we accept awareness of what our bodies feel like. With this we cultivate an awareness of limits, learning not to push too hard, not to push ourselves over the edge. We know our bones can only bear so much weight, our muscles can only stretch so far. Pratyahara helps us to understand that we are not invincible and provides us with ego checks as we develop respect for body's limits (including eating limits, when we shouldn't eat to fullness, but instead eat to ¾ fullness). Pratyahara helps us with honouring our self and our journey by allowing and accepting pain, fatigue, illness, stress, weakness, off days, etc. Perceptive senses can also be sources from which to cultivate joy. Depending on ability, the perceptive senses allow people the sights of the sunrise and set, colours of which can be incredibly healing, the sounds of music and nature, which also have healing properties, the tastes of many foods, the touch of soft pets or a lover's body, and an assortment of smells, some of which stimulate memories

Types of Pratyahara

Indriya-pratyahara – control of the senses
Karma-pratyahara – control of action
Prana-pratyahara – control of prana (life force)
Mano-pratyahara – withdrawal of the mind from the senses.

Ayurveda beliefs say that "sensory impressions are the main food for the mind." Some ways to practise pratyahara include ceasing in taking impressions in without closing off the sense organs, like sitting with eyes open while directing attention within, or using visualisations.

Wordless Music

Most people have difficulty performing two cognitive tasks at once. This is why texting and driving is such a dangerous distraction, because texting and driving are both cognitive tasks. Sensory perception can also affect one's ability to perform cognitive tasks. One example of this is experiencing sensory overload. Sunshine and Katara experienced the overstimulation of their perceptive senses by things such as misophonia, which sent them into sensory overload

Another example is how Jaime had to learn to drive to wordless music at first so that she wasn't distracted by trying to sing along. One can become distracted by sounds,

smells (especially foul, pungent ones), tastes, and textures.
Through pratyahara (release of the senses and control of the senses) we can hear the sounds from within. Recognition of real versus imagined stress comes to us along with recognition of tension in our bodies, and the recognition of the reason and if the reason is valid, asking ourselves "is this my stress?"

Receiving Gifts
One language of love involves cultivating meanings from receiving gifts. This language represents validation of feelings of affection when someone gives them gifts. However, when a relationship is solely based around receiving gifts, it will likely perish.

Scientific Asana
An amazing thing about the body is how movement is an exact science. It takes just the right amount of force, pressure, and concentration to achieve any particular posture, as well as having each body part placed in perfect alignment and cultivating balance. The ability to breath comfortably in any posture is a miracle to be respected and not overlooked. It is in these moments of combined effort, realisation, and joy for basic life can be cultivated.

Unveiling
Do you have a ritual for unveiling your body? Do you ritually unveil other bodies?
Can you be with yourself naked? (sky clad) The unveiling of the body promotes self acceptance, especially when recognising the body as a vessel for the soul. Through Bhakti we can use the process of unveiling our bodies to take time to appreciate and thank the physical body for housing our soul and for all that it allows us to do. Some rituals are practised sky clad, like spell work or sex.

In the poem "I'll Never Forget the Girl in the Mirror" from the book <u>Intimate Kisses,</u>
Sharon Olds describes coming across herself after the

unveiling process, as she sees herself in the mirror during sex. She discusses the orientation of her body, her haunches, flanks, and breasts. She describes herself as an animal who looked so directly that she knew she belonged her and was living her true life. Seeing oneself unveiled can be transformative. This, of course, can also relate to dysphoria. Yoga directed at the root chakra could be a way of working with dysphoria.

Sacral Chakra
Svadisthana
"We have the same strength as water."

      The Sacral Chakra (or Spleen, Belly) Chakra will show stories of fluidity, sexuality, and trauma. The Sacral Chakra involves the ability to relate, physical contact, and trust. The Sacral Chakra represents those moments when we say, "I feel, I want." The mantra for this chakra is "I accept and forgive myself" The Sacral Chakra is located in the sacrum, and is represented by the colour orange. When healing the Sacral Chakra with colour, orange should be used, or if the Sacral Chakra is overactive, blue should be used followed by a small dose of orange. The Sacral Chakra embodies the element of water and represents the direction of West. The Sacral Chakra is ruled by the planet Mercury, and its ruling signs are Taurus and Leo. Bergamot, clary sage, mandarin red, and patchouli, are essential oils which affect the Sacral Chakra, and one crystal which can be used for the Sacral Chakra is Tangerine Quartz. The Sacral Chakra is grounding and represents fluidity of emotion, and one pose which resonates deeply with the Sacral Chakra and can be felt in the whole body is Malasana (low squat).

      When someone's Sacral Chakra is balanced, they would be able to fluidly navigate life. When the Sacral Chakra is in excess there are poor boundaries. When there is a deficiency in the Sacral Chakra there can be emotional walls.

"VHS Tape" Response to "the Laundry Room" by Simone Parker

As soon as she discovered
what would elicit a squeal or a shudder
she climbed out of her skin
and got under mine

she got all cozy
like she was in bed
or like I was the backseat
of her family's minivan

I never even thought about what it would be like
until she asked,
even though I knew I would get there

when the snow fell
we got to leave school early
my heart melted like the snowflakes on her nose

I remember the Lion King was on
but I don't remember when we stopped watching
we never felt like we were in my basement

I couldn't even hear the sound of the furnace
over the sound of my heart
and when she leaned into me
there was no water running through the pipes

and no unfinished ceiling
there was just her hair
and the way if felt to know
that I definitely liked that.

(and I definitely liked her)

Girls Make Boys Cry (Sometimes I Think I Deserve This)
A memory in Jaime's Journal

    It's New Year's Eve. I stand between my first two ex-girlfriends in my crop top and skirt. Someone snaps a Polaroid for us. They're both wearing black and their faces are both caked with makeup. They think they look good. I don't wear makeup. In the middle, I am the focus of the photo. I am the prettiest one. It's a bit weird to have them both around at the same time. They both make me sick.

    We are all awful bitches. Let me say that one right out as a fact. All three of us girls in that Polaroid picture can be pretty effing terrible. Some people would look at that photograph and think that all three of us are good looking, but we each have an evil side and a reckless side, through which we become dangerous girls. We have all made boys and girls cry. Obviously, we have all also been hurt a lot and are pretty messed up so it's hard to tell if it's really our fault that we are bitches. We each have our own special brand of crazy.

    We each fall somewhere different on the Kinsey scale which is just a bit funny when you remember that it is almost as though we all slept with each other It's even funnier to think that I dated the one on my left first and she dumped me because she was only into guys, and then years later, I dated the one on my right, and when she came to visit and met the other one for the first time she saw her naked. They didn't do anything but it's still a funny story to tell.

    There's also less funny stories to tell, like what an awful thirteen year old I was trying to force my first girlfriend to come out. She wasn't my girlfriend at the time, and to this day she refuses to label herself. I tried really hard to get with her too at her fourteenth birthday party and truthfully to this day I don't remember if she resisted or not and that troubles me. I remember her being super into my mom's Victoria's Secret catalogues (I don't blame her there) and teasing me and seducing me.

    Or the time my second girlfriend slept over, and I

274

didn't want to do anything for fear of waking my parents when we were fifteen and she just did it anyway. Or when we went camping with her family and a friend and she was kind of mean to everyone, and I was too annoyed with her to want to sleep with her that night but she did stuff to me anyway. Both of which were unfair occurrences as she was on her period and I couldn't do things to her.

One dumped me and I dumped the other one. I lose both friends, after maintaining friendship for a long while, and after adjusting to the funny weirdness of having my two ex-girlfriend best friends in a room together. I have that photograph hanging on my wall. I cry every day but I don't call them.

I fade away.
Erased, they move on.
I try.
(They don't call, either.)

"Friends?" – Jaime and Stream of Consciousness Writing Therapy

Sometimes, it's like, make all the lists. Remember all the things. Other times it's like, remember nothing. Don't remember what things happened.
Which list do you make?
And how do you know what counts?
I think it's weird that different people can count different experiences. Nobody ever teaches you how to make sense of it all.
How do you organize your gained information? Or do you even at all? Do you just let it sit there or does it come up to show again?
I don't think anyone warns you about the way that life eats away at you. In school you learn about how your body is made up of cells and how often the cells replenish and you learn the effects that aging has on the body but nobody ever tells you about how people will cling to your heartstrings and tear them out as you try to walk past.
Nobody warns you about the way people can make you sick in more ways than one even though they warn you about the spread of germs or sexually transmitted diseases and infections. You can't wash your hands of other people.
Sometimes you feel them on your skin or on your lips and you remember the way they laughed or something that they did. Sometimes it makes you want to rip your skin, it makes you cringe, it makes you wish you could effect a change somehow.
Can you believe that you became a stereotype and it's your genuine character?
They never tell you about how someone can be your entire world and then suddenly, not part of it at all. Or how you could be ready to die for someone they mean that much to you, and then you realize that you have died for them, that you're not even living, and that they're still trying to kill themselves anyway.
They do not warn you about the ways that you will rip yourself apart, from all the not good enoughs, the not

helpful enoughs, the ways you will recount every single thing you could have done better. The way that you will be disgusted with yourself and try to wear your insides on your outside. They will not tell you about the screams that echo behind your ears, inside your head, the way your heart beats out of your chest making you rush to catch your breath. They do not tell you how you will take everything to heart when you tear yourself apart – the things they said, the way things were, the way that you will resent yourself for everything they said they liked about you almost more than you will resent yourself for all the things they hated about you.

They do not warn you about who will be here for you through those times. Generally, they will be quite important. They will love you when you are at your hardest to love, and you in turn will want to love them, too. Sometimes you will surprise yourself. Sometimes that person will be you. Sometimes, battered and bruised, all you have is you. You will be amazed at all that you go through. And if you survive, which I hope you do, sometimes you will wonder how that miracle happened.

Trigger Warning

The following story depicts an individual's story of trauma resulting in damage to the sacral chakra. This story may trigger traumatic memories for individuals with similar experiences. The example presented is extreme and potentially disturbing, but is still a realistic problem our community faces.

Boys Too

Hari was tall and slender, a swimmer on his high school team. Sometimes he wore contact lenses, sometimes he wore glasses. Regardless, he was stuck seeing, and was in the locker room twice a day – for gym class and swim practise. The locker room became a problem area for Hari.

One day after gym class, an older boy called Zaire caught Hari staring at him as he pulled his jeans on.

"Like what you see then, faggot?" he sneered.

Hari stretched and looked away.

"I mean, you know, yeah," he answered boldly.

"What are you playing at, gay boy? Got a crush on me or something?" Zaire demanded.

"Oh no, I don't get crushes," Hari replied.

"Whatcha mean you don't get crushes!? You're over here starin' at my dick."

"Oh I'll have sex with anyone but I don't experience romantic attraction." Hari had no idea why this was the moment that he chose to be honest about that fact for the first time in his life.

Zaire drew closer, and suddenly Hari thought that he was about to get hit.

"Oh you'll have sex with anyone? Then you must just be wanting to suck me off, huh?" Zaire continued to close in on Hari.

"N-no, not particularly." Hari answered shakily.

Zaire backed Hari against the wall of lockers.

"Well that's just too bad then, gay boy." Zaire started, as he unzipped his jeans. "Because you're about to."

Zaire pushed Hari to his knees and choked him until he opened his mouth. Zaire shoved his manhood into Hari's mouth and thrusted into him until he reached his orgasm, forcing Hari to swallow all of it. When he was finished, Zaire pulled up on his jeans and spat on Hari. Hari left the locker room much later than Zaire had.

After school and after practise, Hari and his friend Lily went to a cafe, like they usually did. Her afro was out today, and she had on tight fitting jeans with a cropped t shirt. She clung to his arm and smiled.

"You know, Hari, we've been spending an awful lot of time together lately," she started. "I was wondering if maybe you'd want to be my boyfriend?" She fidgeted anxiously, awaiting his answer.

"Oh, Lily. You're beautiful, and really cool, but I don't experience romantic attraction. We can have sex, if you want, but I just have no desire to be in a relationship, possibly ever." He felt bad breaking it to her, not knowing (or not noticing) she'd developed a crush on him.

"What do you mean?" she asked, slightly hurt.

"I just think the idea of being romantically involved with anyone is undesirable. I don't want a person to do everything with, to be close to, or to cuddle. I like being alone. I think having someone close to you like that is kind of gross, breathing all over you and stuff." he trailed off.

"But you can have sex?" she inquired.

"Yeah. Sex is fine and fun when I want it." he answered matter-of-factly.

Lily pressed herself close to him.

"So, want to come to my place and have sex?" she smiled. "Of course you do. What guy doesn't?" She pulled him to follow her.

In her bedroom, when she pulled down Hari's pants, she complained that he wasn't hard yet.

"Don't worry, just start," Hari insisted.

Lily used his body to help herself reach orgasm, and then complemented his performance.

They returned to the cafe afterwards, never having made it inside earlier. When Lily went to the bathroom, Hari noticed a sign on the bulletin board which read, "yoga for survivors of sexual abuse" with a date, time, place, and phone number. Discretely, Hari took a photo of the sign. He paid for his and Lily's drinks and walked out, walked all the way home.

At home, his moms made sure he had dinner and did his homework. In the bathroom before bed, Hari threw up his dinner thinking about the day's events.

The next day at school, Zaire spotted Hari. After classes, he followed him out of the building with some friends. Hari started heading home and they followed.

"Look, it's the gay boy who sucked me off yesterday! What's the matter gay boy, didn't you like it?!" Zaire got up close to Hari. "Aren't you dying to do it again?" he sneered.

"No, I'm really not."

Zaire slapped Hari across the face.

"That's not very nice! And I've brought you a treat! I've brought friends!" Zaire laughed. "Boys..." he signaled, and his friends came closer.

When Hari returned home, he checked the photo on his phone of the sign from the cafe. The class was that night. Not knowing what to tell his moms, Hari slipped out while they were cooking dinner. He walked to the location of the class and took it. After class he asked to speak privately with the instructor, and broke down into tears, telling them everything.

Eventually Hari was able to talk to his moms about what happened, as well as the police, thanks to the help of the yoga instructor from that first class he took.

Posh Town Boys

Rigby Wilton and Jacque Luke Chauncey ("Party Boy Jacque") lived within miles of each other, and were at one time quite close. They shared a lot of the same partners. It was spoken about that they had likely gotten off together as well. The boys were friends of April, and Jaime had met them through Julio.

They each had a known reputation with girls. They also had their own variation of a story of depression and drug addiction in their younger teen years. They were in recovery and were said to be suffering sexual addiction in their coping process.

Rigby was perhaps the more sought after one of the two. His family was wealthy, but it may not be his family's money that drew people to him like moths to a flame. Rigby Wilton was incredibly charismatic. He was as slick as Billy Flynn, the lawyer from the play Chicago. Rigby's charisma made him easy to talk to, whether you were a boy or a girl. He was a natural flirt, and many of his girlfriends got jealous when he talked to other girls because of this quality. He dressed nicely and knew a lot about a plethora of subjects. Rigby's main draw, though, was that he was genuinely a kind person and treated his lovers with respect for the most part, and held no ill will toward anyone once they parted. He usually stayed friends with his exes and he always treated partners well and made sure their needs were met.

Party Boy Jacque, on the other hand, was mean and abusive – at least emotionally and verbally. Jacque and Rigby were both considered to be good looking, but while Rigby had unique physical qualities, Jacque was more "typically" good looking. And while Rigby was sexually responsible and regularly got tested, Jacque was not. He could not provide you with an exact number of people he had been with, and he did not get tested. In fact, he had herpes, and let it spread like wildfire to several young and beautiful women. Jacque was very much a "go to the gym," beer guzzling, macho kind of guy.

Jacque liked to prey on girls with low self esteem or problems at home. His recipe for success included complimenting them and charming them at first, before proceeding to tell them how worthless and ugly they were. And somehow it worked. Even when girls watched him do it to their friends, they fell victim to his sick spell. When he was rejected, which was rare, he would be even more mean.

Both boys fell somewhere on the Kinsey Scale between a 1.5 and 3. it varied depending on their mood and possibly their level of intoxication. They were both quite fluid. They were both European, and that seemed to hold some reason to their fluidity. Jacque would ruthlessly use boys as trash as he desired, including Marcie's friend Philip. Rigby would openly flirt with boys, like SLB Benji, though nothing usually came of it. It is speculated that Rigby had male friends he had experimented with, including Philip, Jacque, Rick Batch, and Hudson. All boys who got around regularly, apparently got around with each other as well.

Rick Batch's Place (and Porsche)
"Date With Posh Boy"

He wants me to look
like a real girl
as in wear a dress
mirror twirl

he only asked once
but I wear one every time
he dresses nicely too
so I guess it's fine

and truth is I don't mind
the dress
just like I don't mind
that he's a bit of a mess.

"He and I"

We share an
ex-girlfriend
which reminds me of
how my friend,

the fiancé of
his friend
almost shares an ex
with me

save for lack
of date
and his boyfriend
fucked my boyfriend

and somehow
I always end up
back there

no matter what

at least this bi guy
isn't lame and corny
is responsible
and self aware

"Conversations with Rick Batch"

"Leave it to me
to pick the most
bisexual seeming guy
in the room
to go home with,"
Jaime snickered

"it's starting to sound
a little sick,"
laughed Rick

as he lectured her lightly
about her sexual openness
and how it was a turn off
and even though she wondered

why she bothered getting in a car
with someone who'd text
while driving a stick shift Porsche
yet she walks away feeling better
and wonders why, too

she knew Rick
couldn't really call her sick
without being a hypocrite
as a recovering addict.

"She Said Please"

She wanted to experiment and have fun and that's exactly what I needed.

She said, "you could just go for it."

She said, "I'm sorry I know it's weird."

She asked if we could stop because it was too much for her.

We sat and talked. I shared stories about my experiences.

She said, "can we continue this conversation with our shirts off?"

She said, "I want to kiss you again."

She said, "maybe this is what I like the best."

She said, "I can try, but I can't promise it'll be any good."

She asked if I could, "for maybe a few minutes."

She said, "I might stop you."

I said, "that's okay."

She didn't stop me a second time. She loved it. Then, she thanked me for helping her. We talked about poetry. She took herself home. I smiled all night.

"November"

I was attracted
to my rapist (before he was my rapist)
when I found out he used to
wear dresses and flirt with boys
(on separate occasions)
and I wish I
never told him that.

"The Face in the Mirror"

Who is this person
who lurks in mirrors
and in windows
who are they?

For they are not the same
as the girl with the
flowing mermaid surfer curls
and juicy frame in skintight clothing

all flowers
and flowing dresses
she is soft
and summer warm

summer sun kissed golden
not that cool blue pale boy
all beanies and baggy sweats
and English boy lips

Blue cold like the colour
of my childhood home
like snowy starry winter
nights that fade to purple

purple cold has spirit
and helps you through the night
gives you the pride
to dress like that in public

not like red cold
the colour of being stuck in that truck
shaking in my boy sweats
getting forcibly fucked

and orange cold

for waiting outside tow trucks
the kind of cold that sneaks up
on you even when it's warm

but yellow cold
is back to gold
back to the sun kissed smiley girl free
in the slight salty breeze

green cold
for the solace
found in summer rain
when you learn to love yourself again

it's a bit like Mulan
to not know your reflection sometimes
stare into your own eyes
which appearance lies?

But they both feel right in ways
sometimes a mix of the two
and screw what everyone says
I'll wear what I want to

Sacral Chakra Connections

Agender Yoga

Yoga knew no gender, and did not discriminate with who it touched. Lord Shiva, who Sage Patanjali watched dance the dance of cosmic ecstasy, and from whom the yoga sutras were transmitted, was depicted as androgynous as well as gifted with the ability to shapeshift – which meant sometimes switching gender. Ardhanarishvara is the name of the androgynous form of Hindu God Shiva and his female counterpart Shakti.

Bramhacharya
"When the prefrontal cortex fails to make you happy, promiscuity rewards you with the needed flood of dopamine." - The Big Bang Theory

Bramhacharya is a yama which means appropriate sexual behaviour. Originally, the intended meaning was chastity and abstinence, but in the 21st century (with an anarchist feminist approach) appropriate sexual behaviour
-runs on a personal agenda
-feels confident
-feels secure
-is safe
-is guilt free
-is pleasurable, satisfying
-involves trust – perfect love and perfect trust, are in fact the two ingredients needed for casting a magical circle. When perfect love and perfect trust are in sexual behaviour, a magical circle can be cast and the sexual energy will be incredibly powerful for the working of magick.
-involved thought, discussion, and exploration
-is body positive and sex positive
-includes a knowledge of desires and limits
-includes an awareness of the absorption of a partner's energy through sexual acts and a willingness to carry them within a personal energy field.

Sex Positivity

Sex positivity must be taught alongside bramhacharya. We must understand that sex is okay, and that it okay to feel good or to feel sexual. We are not taught [that it is okay] to make ourselves feel good – if we can make ourselves feel good what do we need anyone else/anything else for? We must not buy into it, our frequency and energy is being controlled with media and portrayed attitudes. Anarcha feminist ideals but should be normalised (why are these values such a drastic category?) Sex positivity reinforces safety first, because safe sex is good sex. Bramhacharya teaches us that all sex starts with consent from each party involved. Sex positivity says to us "if it makes you feel good, do it" within reason, after weighing the "why not?"

Part of sex positivity for some may be using sex as a protest. As stated by Chrissy in the Punk Chick episode of That 70's Show, "if we can make ourselves feel good what do we need the establishment for?" Some people need to remind themselves over and over that "the body is not a temple – temples can be destroyed and desecrated – let your body be a forest, growing back over and over again no matter how badly devastated."

The Trouble with Teaching Abstinence Only

Many sexual education classes teach only abstinence and about the dangers of sexually transmitted diseases. What should be taught in sexual education classes is how abstinence can help to understand and recognise one's personal value of sex. Abstinence is usually shown as the only option to avoid unwanted pregnancy and sexually transmitted diseases or infections. However, when young people are adequately educated on contraceptive options and barriers from sexually transmitted diseases or infections, they are provided with a much more valuable resource than when they are taught about sex from a sex negative perspective. This will only breed feelings of guilt and shame as people go on to engage in sexual activities, whereas when people are encouraged to enjoy pleasure, they are more likely to feel good about sexual experiences they have. Abstinence has its place in a sex positive curriculum, because abstinence is a perfectly acceptable personal choice which many people choose for various reasons including religion and asexuality. It is important that abstinence is just not taught as the only option in sexual education classes.

Similarly, there must be detachment from expectations of sex, because it's not going to look like porn, and we all have to be okay with that. Much of what we learn about sex comes from the hallway curriculum, that which we learn from our peers and the internet. What's important is the naturality of it, how the body will know what to do. It is up to each individual to discern truth of what it means to them.

Consider the withdrawal of the senses, and desire – control of the mind when it is turned on, withdrawal from action driven by desire. Withdrawal from expectations of what sex is "supposed to" look like, feel like, and mean.

Does it add value to have sex? What does it do for you personally to remove it? Personal experiment. Everyone must choose what personally feels best – everyone has different adhikara for bramhacharya. For example, the hookup culture of millennials is not appropriate sexual behaviour for Liam specifically for the reason that it did not make him feel good. Bramhacharya as appropriate behaviour for Jaime and Le Feu means the way that they hook up with people, because they made active choices to let it feel good (Jaime started making that choice when she was with Julio and having the "it won't mean anything if it's not Syd mentality and toxic cultural concepts of virginity). Why is virginity valuable or precious? Virginity is a heterocentric social construct, and doesn't define one's worth. Virginity doesn't exist (it is an imaginary concept) but the hymen does and it could break in many ways. Part of appropriate sexual behaviour is that you get to define what sex is to you personally.

Saying "not anymore" was appropriate behaviour for Le Feu at the time because it wasn't making him feel good.

There is much to be said about the inappropriate social conditioning of boys to believe something is wrong with them if they reject the advances of a girl, asking themselves "how will I look?" Liam felt this way when his coworker hit on him, and then Rocco and Keith both experienced these feelings about Jaime. Rocco ended up feeling the need to live up to the pictures he had sent her.

Porn culture has made sharing intimate pictures a norm, and each person is responsible for determining their personal appropriateness for sending nudes. It is definitively inappropriate if underage, and it is difficult to determine the appropriateness in a culture of mistrust and mass circulation. Some people suffer from inappropriate behaviours of immature laughing and shaming when it comes to sexually explicit photos or videos and the general rule in that case is that if you can't be open with communication or accepting of others you probably shouldn't be having sex.

It is important to teach people that they are able to feel energetically when one is not wanted and how it is inappropriate behaviour to feel a need to go through with what one doesn't want, and how the unwanted action is inappropriate. If it does not come naturally and has to be forced, then it is inappropriate sexual behaviour. We are in the midst of a necessary shift towards appropriate normalisation of sexual behaviour and desire, including orientation. Appropriate sexual behaviour is when it is meant to be an act of respect, it is inappropriate if it is not, for there must be respect for the act.

Appropriate behaviour requires knowing personal limits, safety and communication, sex positivity. It relates to developmentally appropriate practise, which was age appropriate, individually appropriate, culturally relevant.

Jaime noticed a habit in herself of looking for validation about her worth in physical connections, recognising that that desire for intimacy could be either appropriate or inappropriate sexual behaviour. She must recognise types of intimacy separate from sex and understand that it is important to not let intimacy versus isolation drive inappropriate sexual behaviour. Jaime often found herself too easily turned on when learning self-defense, which related to her being a touch based person, and it was bramhacharya for her to not act on every impulse of desire.

Sacred Sexuality

"Sex and art are the same thing" - Picasso

"Sexual love has the ability to transport us into new realms of experience – physically, emotionally, and spiritually – realms in which we come to better understand who we are as sensual, caring creatures on this earth. Like the arts, sexual love offers limitless possibilities for human expression and pleasure."

"Real religion – affirmation of life, reverence, spirituality, the honouring of mysteries – is profoundly and positively connected to sex." <u>Intimate Kisses</u>

Sex magick involves using sex as magick for spiritual enlightenment, to reach levels that less conventional routes of magick can shortcut, like drugs, for example. Sex can also be used as magick for spellcraft when it is mixed with love, because "all magic is love, love is the strongest emotion. All magic should be performed out of love. (<u>Magical Herbalism</u>) Part of what makes sex magical is how it can be anything (mean anything) Sexual rites were part of the ancient ceremonies of the Celts (oak and mistletoe gods, holly). Sexual combining represented the power of the Sky God fertilising Mother Goddess. Many other religions used sexual rites in their ceremonies as well. The book <u>Gay Witchcraft</u> describes how sex magick was magick for spiritual enlightenment, to reach levels like drugs, less conventional routes of magick. It was magick for spell craft (all magic is love, love is the strongest emotion. All magic should be performed out of love. [<u>Magical Herbalism</u>]) Sex magic is a type of "Sympathetic Magic". Sometimes sexually religious acts were practised in newly plowed fields to entice crop fertility. Sex magick honoured the creative life force of mother Earth. Sex magick works best with personal intimacy and asks us to first give. The power of sexual energy and sex magick can usually be felt within the whole being.

The book <u>Gay Witchcraft</u> tells us that the Aztec deity Xochiquetzal, a Goddess of love revered sexuality and sensuality as an art form.

Mai/Maj (May)

May is a month of sensuality and sexual revitilisation, in which our senses are particularly sharp (Cabot, L.) month of sexual freedom in honor of Great Mother and Horned God of woodlands. Trial marriages could be contracted at this time for a year and a day, if it proved unworkable both partners could go their separate ways peacefully. Children took the mother's name. Two times the dowry was paid for women previously married or with children. Abortion and choice or change of mate was a woman's right. Virginity was not prized among Celts because a family was important to them – sexual activity was encouraged, especially at Beltane. Children conceived at Beltane were considered very lucky.

Celtic Deities of Sexual Acts include Cernunnos, Macha, Morgan (a triplicity goddess), and Queen Mab.

Sacrum Problems

Sacrum problems are common for the modern human body as so many people are sedentary for much of their days or only use a few planes of motion instead of all available planes. Sadly, due to the prevalence of sexual violence, many people also experience sacrum problems as a result of trauma. Trauma from sexual abuse is stored in the base of the spine (the sacrum) and affects the sacral chakra, which rules sexuality as well as emotions. Jaime suffered from sciatica as a result of sexual abuse, because her left hip had been pushed on in a way which left her sacrum misaligned. Jaime learned in her teacher training that often people who could not enter savasana with their legs straight out were victims of sexual abuse, and she realised that she was one of those people for whom laying flat on her back with her legs straight out aggravated her sacrum and she chose to take savasana with her knees up and her feet flat on the floor.

Sexual Education and the Hallway Curriculum

The sad truth when it comes to sex education for the LGBT+ community it is often not learned in school health classes. We usually do research on the internet, and learn secrets passed down to us from our older, queer friends.

Queer youth need to learn proper sexual education. They need to learn about how their bodies work, how their bodies interact with others, and what will harm their bodies. Transboys need to learn how to safely bind if they so choose, and how to deal with their periods, to say the very least.

There are also specific healthcare needs for bisexuals – mental, physical, sexual – which need to be addressed in schools as well as in the healthcare field. According to the 2011 Williams Institute report, around half of the LGBT community identifies as bisexual. One third of LGBT men are bisexual. Bisexual adults are at a higher risk for cancer, heart disease, obesity, STIs, mental health problems, depression, substance abuse, self-harm or suicide attempts. Bisexual women have highest rates of cancer, obesity, emotional distress out of the general population of women. Bisexual men are disproportionately affected by HIV, HPV, and other STIs. In studies done on bi women it was found that 64% had eating problems, 37% self-harmed, 26% were depressed, and 20% had anxiety issues. Bi men are 3.2x more likely to have any lifetime mood disorder (including depression, anxiety, panic disorder.) Despite sexual imperialism, 40% of LGBT people of colour identify as bi. 27% of bi youth reported living with very accepting families, while 26% of bi youth experience homelessness. Bisexual people can earn 15% less than heteros in their lifetime, living on less than $30,000 a year. Many bisexual people suffer from partner abuse which gets blamed on their bisexuality. 47% of bi students reported one or more incidents of sexual assault.

The National Intimate Partner and Sexual Violence Survey 2010 indicates people who reported experiencing rape, physical violence, and/or stalking by an intimate partner –
61% were bisexual females while 37% were bisexual males
44% were lesbians while 29% were heterosexual males
35% were heterosexual females while 26% were gay males
This survey also found
26.6% of bisexual women had PTSD
and that there was a 46% lifetime prevalence of rape for bisexual women.

      The only way to prevent these issues is to educate the youth. Many of these issues have psychological causes besides lack of education. Bisexual people are often rejected by both the straight and gay communities. Straight communities erase bisexuality by viewing it as experimentation, or by saying that bisexual people are greedy and can't pick a side. Bisexual men are often told that they're just secretly gay, and bisexual women are often over sexualised. Rape culture and biphobia combined with the oversexualisation of bi people pose a threat to bisexuals. Bi men are also fetishised – where someone loves most about them the part which most fear (this is sometimes referred to as "Bi fever" and is all based on preconceived notions or stereotypes about bisexuality in men). Any of these reasons and more contribute to why bisexual people are at such a high risk. By educating our youth, we hope to bring the risk down.

Bi Positivity

"All identity labels are umbrella terms to some degree, but this term 'bisexual' is not only serviceable, but it is sufficient. And yes, it brings together a bunch of people who are maybe shades different from one another. And maybe that's the beauty of labels that they force you to be with other people and see the difference." - Charles M. Blow

"I like beautiful people whether they're boys or girls" - Akiha Hara – <u>Hana-Kimi</u>

Akiha – I love being with both men and women
Ryoichi – I don't mind being with men or women (depending on who it's with)
(<u>Hana-Kimi</u>)

"Maybe the simple diagnosis of either hetero or homo is misleading. Maybe there's just sexuality, and it's bendable and unpredictable, like a circus performer." - <u>Nick and Norah's Infinite Playlist</u>

"We are moving toward sense of androgyny/bisexuality as we balance polarities" - <u>Gay Witchcraft</u>

"I do not in the least underestimate bisexuality…I expect it to provide all further enlightenment" – Sigmund Freud

"The moon goes through phases each month, yet no one ever says that it is no longer the moon. The moon reminds us that it is okay to change. The moon has phases but sexuality does not. For many queers, being straight was their phase. Perhaps their similarity to the moon makes queer folk celestial beings. Purple is half red, half blue, but it is still called purple, even when shades are more red or more blue. The same applies to bisexuality. With cells in our bodies that are constantly functioning, breathing, and regenerating, humans are very sentient beings. Consider the fact that we are made of stardust and one has quite the house for their soul." - Unknown

One of the French terms for bisexuality is "voile et vapeur," meaning powered by both sails and steam.

The book <u>Bi Any Other Name</u> brings to our attention the opinions of Freud, Kinsey, and Mead. It also brings up Dr. Jay Paul (an out bi psychologist) whose 1985

"Bisexuality: Reassessing our Paradigms of Sexuality" article discusses fluidity and variability in sexual patterns. This article mentions that the biological and environmental origins of sexuality are still debated. Dr. Paul presents us with a "flexibility model" where the male and female are presented as variations on the theme of life and diversity instead of as opposite sexes. Trained from birth to think of ourselves as either/or and indoctrinated in sex-role conditioning, we are led to tend toward "compulsory heterosexuality" based on and rooted in male supremacy. (Rich, A. 1980)

  Sean lacked some bi positivity when it came to boys, because he always got to telling Jaime about how bisexual boys would end up reverting to heteronormativity. He told her that they would choose going back to girls because it was easy and less scary.

  Elisabeth Badinter said in The Unopposite Sex men and women are growing more alike in the modern age and humanity's basic bisexuality will be revealed. Through such a realization, we can discern truth as a group (humankind) and pull away the veil of uncertainty. The hostility and misunderstanding toward bisexuals and bisexuality must be addressed, understanding that hostility comes from and unconscious acceptance of good and evil, us or them mentality. Bisexuality threatens dualism by representing a continuum. How can we change this? One way is to start in education, with gender creative students and an inclusive curriculum. An example of a starting point in education is the use of intentional language. Bi positivity also means representation. One example of a positive representation of bisexuality in the media is Deadpool. The disturbing lack of bi positivity is one of the many reasons why bi boys like Syd, Le Feu, and Rick Batch feel like their sexuality is not part of their identity.

Ritual Dress

"You ever think that our group is the same as any other group like the football team? And the only real difference between us is what we wear and why we wear it?" - Patrick, the Perks of Being a Wallflower

"In order to produce energy there must be opposites" – C. G. Jung

"The unlike is joined together, and from differences results the most beautiful harmony" - Harclitis

"A tendency towards consciousness and a basic tendency towards a counter position exists from the beginning, just as when muscles expand and contract." paraphrased from Marie-Louise von Franze

"a person may come to sense two kinds of movement taking place within (as they pray) pushing away and drawing nearer, knowing it is only for the sake of their return, accept it in love." Hasidic Prayer paraphrased

"Female surfers have taken up the subculture 's most fundamental offering: to bend the rules of normative gender while experiencing oneself in everyday ways, as both connected to local/global ocean environments and to one's own physical intelligence and strength."

"Surfer girls were about ocean-going physical power and the serious mental game it took to sustain that. They trained not at the university, in leftist organisations, or at public demonstrations, but rather in the coastal outdoors." (Surfer Girls in the New World Order)

"Many who cross-dress (gay or straight) view the process of transformation as a ceremony" (Gay Witchcraft)

Ritual dress is a means of personal expression and can represent freedom (why dress can be a "big deal" for some.) One's method of dress is how you're seen, how you present yourself, how you love your body. Some people choose clothes for mood boosting, colour healing, or use clothes as a house or shield for soul (body). Our clothes can also show a relationship with the selfishness. When it comes to ritual dress, there is also the act of worship through wearing certain clothes or none (being sky clad). In many forms, ritual dress involves a transformation ceremony.

<u>Parabola: Myth and Quest for Meaning Androgyny Vol. 3 No. 4</u> uses many different texts to describe an inner wish to deepen understanding of selves when at a crossroads inwards, recognising our inherent duality. The book incites us to accept, include, and reconcile opposites. In hope of unity and reconciliation; we must find meaning in a sense of singleness and wholeness. We are wanting unity and having duality. The essence of our holiness has at its disposal both forces of good and evil upon our realisation of being creation. The gods have said to us, "you are made in our image, after our likeness." We must accept the emptiness of plentitude. We must accept that vulnerability is only way to safety. This book views androgyny as an achievement to be attained, with the original conditions of our soul. Everyone recovers their original androgyny and individuality. In many senses, we are shapeshifting, stepping between the binary boundaries imposed upon us. It is normal to shift to fit the shape of the part which we must play in any given situation. We adapt, we know where to camouflage, we know where we can stand out. Ritual dress plays a part in all of this. Some ritual dress does not involve clothing, but makeup. Other ritual dress involves the way of presenting oneself, the dressing in a cloak of personality to create an effect. For example, the surfer girls mentioned in quotes above would dress themselves in their cloak of toughness to be recognised not just as girls who could keep up with the boys, but girls who were in a league of their ow next to boys as strong forces of nature. Wearing this invisible cloak of character was part of the ritual of surfing for these women.

the Virginity Myth

    One of the texts used in <u>Parabola</u> is written by PL Travers and discusses the connection between the zodiac signs Virgo and Scorpio, as well as the myth of virginity. Virginity is seen as a social construct, because the "sexualisation of women is only accepted when it's nonconsensual." When a statue of a woman is given a mirror, she is called vanity instead of beauty for looking at herself, "morally condemning the woman whose nakedness you had depicted for your own pleasure" (John Berger, Ways of Seeing). Women are taught that their value is determined by how many people have touched them, and it is important to mention that being touched by other people doesn't make you worthless. It is worth mentioning that you are not a flower, you may have a hymen which can break in many ways, but virginity is not tangible.

    Travers suggest the similarities between Virgo and Scorpio based on how their signs are symbolised. Their symbols look like letter Ms with tails, each pointed a different way. Travers argues, "would not the sexes use their weapon in different ways?" Same tail, same sting. The personalities of Virgo and Scorpio possess a sting, a feminine quality. This referenced a verbal sting, and Travers mentions that when it comes to scorpions, both males and females have poison in their tails. When the tail turns outwards, it is to touch, to sting, to remind. Travers argues that stinging is a feminine activity no matter which does it. Jaime and Sean possessed this sting, able to cut people into pieces with their words. Jaime was a Scorpio, and Sean was on the Leo/Virgo cusp.

    Travers also brings up that when the tail is turned in, it is because it is hiding something. She suggests this is the grace of Virgo, hiding an unravished secret seed of the self, teaching us that some part in all should be kept intact. Because, after all is given, what is left? This brings up the question of virginity again, because don't males have something to give? Virgo asks a lover, "where is that in you that is not meant for me and is, for that reason, precious?" Virgo asks, "do you want their energy? Do you want to give yours?" Virgo teaches respect for "that of yours which is not for me."

This particular section of <u>Parabola</u> inspired Jaime to get involved with teaching children body ownership. Teachers are trained to protect the "virginity" of children by not letting them explore each other's bodies, kiss, or look at each other. Jaime felt that it was equally important to teach children that hugs were not mandatory, that they did not have to kiss their family members, and that touch was on their terms. She knew to ask children if she could pick them up or hug them, and knew it was important to show that she respected them if they did not say yes. It was just as important to teach boys body ownership as it was to teach girls body ownership. Jaime felt it taught them about what was theirs and not for anyone else.

Benji could say, "I lost my boy virginity before I lost my girl virginity as a sort of sick joke (just like Sean could) and follow up with an explanation of why he can't leave a virgin he sleeps with. Even with his alleged 256 (and counting) sexual partners, he must have at some point realised that there was some part of himself meant to remain intact, because he stopped sleeping around and giving himself to everyone, leaving himself with nothing (because you can't pour from an empty cup), something to keep for when all else has been given.

Benji's words were always chosen carefully. As a Scorpio, he possessed the stinging tongue speaking scathing words capable of bringing tears to the strongest eyes. The feminine sting showed through his love for gossip.

Raised by a feminist, Jaime had been brought up believing the best part of herself was the part which was unlike anybody else. This was the part of herself which was unlike anybody else. This was the part of herself which she was never meant to give up or to anyone else. The things which made Jaime unique were the things that were special to her, and therefore not meant for anyone else.

Solar Plexus Chakra
Manipura

"We are what we repeatedly do."

The Solar Plexus Chakra will show stories of empowerment, power, and self love. The Solar Plexus Chakra involves our ambition and self esteem. The Solar Plexus Chakra represents those moments when we say, "I do." The mantra for this chakra is "I am confident and worthy." The Solar Plexus Chakra is located in the lumbar spine, and is represented by the colour Yellow. When healing the Solar Plexus Chakra with colour, yellow should be used, or if the Solar Plexus Chakra is overactive, violet or purple should be used followed by a small dose of yellow. The Solar Plexus Chakra embodies the element of fire and represents the direction of South. The Solar Plexus Chakra is ruled by the planet Jupiter, and its ruling signs are Aries and Virgo. Bergamot, grapefruit, lemon, and rosemary are essential oils which affect the Solar Plexus Chakra, and one crystal which can be used for the Solar Plexus Chakra is Citrine. The Solar Plexus Chakra is powerful and represents our inner fire, and one pose which resonates deeply with the Solar Plexus Chakra and can be felt in the whole body is Navasana (boat pose).

When someone's Solar Plexus Chakra is balanced, they would be confidence. When the Solar Plexus Chakra is in excess there is controlling behaviour, bullying, and eating disorders. When there is a deficiency in the Solar Plexus Chakra there can be compulsive overeating, and low self esteem.

Sakura Pazina

When Jaime worked at Yooso (Elements), she met Jeiken's best friend, Sakura Pazina. In fact, she trained Sakura for the receptionist position that she worked. They worked in harmony, as Sakura was a quick learner and hard worker. When Jaime left Yooso after disagreeing with Christine Christie, she and Sakura remained close. When Christine left Yooso after disagreeing with the owner, Sakura asked Jaime to come back.

Sakura had a serious practise, likely based in her interest in healthcare. Or did her tapas in her yoga practise help her discern her desire to mix her two passions – healthcare and travel. Sakura was aligned with her truth to heal others. At twenty, when Jaime met her, she had already started on her course. Sakura had been to Morocco before working at Yooso, and after working at Yooso she travelled to India to begin practising medicine.

Jaime admired her work ethic, tapas, and organisational skills. Sakura was the type of person that Jaime wanted to surround herself with to continue to be inspired.

Jeiken

Jaime met Jeiken through Anabelle and Yooso, she took his classes and loved them, was moved by them, and went religiously. They were coworkers, though she met him as Anabelle's old friend from school. She decided to befriend him.

Jaime learned that he was born in Colombia and lived there until age twelve. He went to an all boys' Catholic school and was fluent in Spanish. He moved out of his parents' house at eighteen but was living out since he was sixteen. Being in Colombian Catholic environment Jeiken experienced silence and negativity or ignorance about his homosexuality. He felt people were not moving on from old views (i.e. negativity and stigma around sexuality and gender expression, racism) and that blocks us as human race from unity and coexistence. Yoga helps one realise nobody is better than anyone else. Jeiken believed "how I treat you is a reflection of how I treat me." He expressed "feeling different" around age five but lacked the language to describe or understand why, at nine he was first showing signs of his homosexuality. He came out at fifteen, was outed at home and school. He experienced an inner explosion of needing to communicate truth of himself while experiencing tumultuous feelings about that like freaking out, crying, being afraid to say it, but was always happy and confident in sexuality and didn't let others' reactions mandate his emotions about himself. He became the president of the GSA at his high school, volunteered for GLSEN, and was active in queer community. He felt that "the people who need yoga most are those who are disconnected, sad, who need to align, connect, blossom, and flourish into the best version of themselves not connected to negative thoughts and low vibrations." He felt that lack of teaching emotional intelligence and management to people was to blame for those people's actions. He knew he deserved a full life experience, he was aware of a universal force or energy and chose to go with the flow, trusting everything is going according to plan. He thought it was the nature of things to flow (like water), and didn't believe in control.

  Jeiken discovered yoga at eighteen after end of a bad relationship. He was in a bad mental place, was living with friends and wasting time, and he noticed he was getting out of shape. He started off self-taught from a video and didn't want to go to classes. He felt limited and wanted to learn inversions. His practise became a life changing lifestyle. He asked himself, "who was I? Who am I?"
Once he started practising, he immediately knew he wanted to teach yoga. He became certified in Kripalu, it took two times of applying for him to get accepted into a teacher training program in Massachusetts. His teaching style combines different types of yoga. He was a practitioner of Kripalu. To him, Kripalu was very compassionate, introspective, mindful. It contained a different alignment and different sequences. Jeiken believed in asana as tools for self

discovery. He loved being able to discover the body again and again in many different postures, planes of motions, with many different breaths. He also loved the spiritual approach Kripalu takes. He felt it taught conscious communication – how to talk and listen, how to be a good person, manage self inside and out. Kripalu yoga opened him up to a shift in mental alignment and showing light in way true to self, trusting inner wisdom. The physical practise focused on longer holds, and stretching the comfort zone. It was made to make one feel "I am so powerful and connected" while also being not a particularly demanding practise. It helped Jeiken see past the mental clutter. He felt that yoga taps into the subconscious. He also believed that yoga was you off the mat. He felt that yoga was your reactions to world around you and that everything was a mirror – what you put out comes back.

Jeiken offered ears to listen, understanding, support and reason. He loved art and painted a lot, though he had experience with other mediums, He was fascinated by creation, constantly creating. He said to Jaime, "there are so many pieces waiting to be created, I am just a vessel." He believed that yoga was art, everything around was art. He said, "yoga is the language my body speaks."

When it came to nature, Jeiken thought, "I am nature." He knew nature as the one true home, but thought people were so oblivious to it and thought they were separate, while actually being a representation of nature expressed as an individual. He felt his human nature aimed to coexist with the rest of the world, to help it thrive. He knew nature was more than just the planet. He was vegan for the sake of nature. He felt that it was very grounding to have a relationship with nature. He thought that sexuality and nature were so not one or the other, so not black and white, and that it was primitive to consider it as black and white, because there were so many ways of expression.

Jeiken was a wonderful teacher, standing firm in his power and truth. He had realised the magic of yoga, and let himself be changed by it.

Moonage Daydream Rest in Paradise David Robert Jones, 8 Jan 1947-10 Jan 2016

Eiwob Divad, space god. By that we mean none other than the Goblin King himself, Ziggy Stardust.

He touched us all with his song. We were all one once. We have all also felt like none, and maybe that's why he touched us. Tons of people were touched and inspired by Bowie and got to make money off of his effect because they were talented or available at the right time for the right opportunity with the right means to thrive. They were lucky, but we were luckier still to be in his musical presence. His legacy will live on, but those of us who were lucky enough to exist in the same time as him are the most lucky.

He paved the way for us. We were all rock 'n roll suicides, we were the rebel rebels, we were heroes. We were earthlings basking in his superhuman glow. It is still hard to write about. It is still so fresh. One day, there will be more evidence of the lives that were touched, when it is less fresh and more musical history.

There is speculation about this next statement, but it is widely believed that David Bowie was many firsts in rock and roll, and many members of the queer community claim him as a trailblazer. Bowie wrote and performed songs with lyrics that used the word "queer," discussed levels of androgyny and varied attraction among genders, as well as music that blatantly described same-sex sexual encounters. Bowie performed in drag, with makeup on, or with a generally androgynous look about him and appeared this way regularly. He was also openly bisexual, getting with other rock and roll legends, such as Mick Jagger, Marc Bolan, and Lou Reed. Many musicians then and now took their lead from David Bowie.

The stardust is in all of us. All we need is to hear his voice crawl from our speakers or headphones, hanging on a line from Rock N Roll Suicide, promising us - "oh no love, you're not alone! No matter what or who you've been, no matter when or where you've been." And even when the music's over, we know we'll be okay, even if we're "under pressure."

"Brian Molko Wouldn't Break My Heart" Jaime's Journal Entry

It all started when I started smoking cigarettes. I was fourteen and so intrigued by cigarettes that my newfound obsession drove me to go on LimeWire and search the word smoking and download every song that came up on the list. That's how I found the song Ashtray Heart by a band called Placebo. The second song LimeWire had to offer me by Placebo was called, "This Picture," which contained the lyrics that started the song saying, "I hold an image of the ashtray girl, of cigarette burns on my chest." I was as fascinated by the singer's voice as I was by smoking cigarettes.

The band was good and fit into my eclectic music taste. I was raised on classic rock and some English punk rock and eighties hair metal and glam rock. I got some love of nineties grunge from my older sister and had role models like Australian Shirley Manson of the band Garbage and Gwen Stefani of the ska-punk band No Doubt. I developed a love of ska and reggae from my brother and could never really call most music I was into my own because someone else showed it to me. Placebo became my own since I found them myself. There were heavy riffs and loud drums, but it was the vocals and the lyrics that kept me intrigued. The singer seemed to moan most of the words to the songs. The singer moaned so much he sometimes sounded like a girl.

I was used to moany singers. Like I said, I grew up on class rock. I grew up with Robert Plant sounding like he was getting off into the microphone over Jimmy Page's godly guitar riffs, I grew up with David Bowie's unique voice, I grew up with Marc Bolan moan singing beautiful nonsense, and Steven Tyler hanging on his words with us. So his voice was nothing new to me. Yet still I loved it, possibly somehow more than my old faithful favorites.

When I discovered Placebo, the summer had just begun, and at fourteen as an emerging smoker my life became a whirlwind of people to see, places to go, and no time to download music or research bands. The research did not begin until the autumn of my sophomore year when so many people abandoned me and I had so much time to be alone. At fourteen I was already an out bisexual and by myself in my loneliness began to research my orientation. I didn't research more about bisexuality, but I researched more bisexual things – movies to watch, music to listen to, and on a website called NNDB I found a list of noteworthy people who were all out as bisexual. As I scrolled through that list I found many people that I knew and loved – David Bowie, Lou Reed, Gerard Way, Kurt Cobain, Janis Joplin... There were also historical figures, like Alexander the Great and Julius Cesar, and others like the poet Lord Byron. That's when I found him. His listing said, "Brian Molko, front man of Placebo." I clicked his name and saw his picture for the first time ever. I had never seen such a beautiful face in my life.

Brian just smiled out at the camera, looking slightly coy in his low v neck black top and blazer. His blue eyes looked piercing, his black hair longish. The listing told his son's name and birth year. I could see Brian's birthdate and birthplace. It also showed me that Brian was in a film called Velvet Goldmine, which I made a note to self to find and watch. Then, I began the rest of my Brian research. I Google Image searched his name to see his face and so many of the photos were beautiful. He was slim and lean, his hair was long in some of the photos, his facial structure was rather attractive to me, he wore makeup and nail polish, and he sometimes dressed in drag. My thing for Brian began as just a fangirl's crush. On NNDB, I liked that list I found because it made me feel like I wasn't alone. I knew I wasn't the only bisexual person in the world, I knew other bisexual people personally, but the length of that list had just made me feel so much better.

I took my research to YouTube, where I discovered one of my favourite Placebo songs, and likely one of their most popular songs, Nancy Boy. The music video was a little weird and freaky, as were most of their music videos, but the lyrics spoke to me with their themes. Brian was ballsy for so much – his words, his voice, his appearance. In my research I think I watched probably every music video that Placebo ever made. Naturally, I had to download the songs I liked the most. Picking a favorite was so difficult since so many of the songs spoke to me. To name a few, I fell in love with Every Me Every You, Pure Morning, I Do, For What It's Worth, Teenage Angst, and Meds. The music was just the right angsty mix for me, with words that made you think sung by a voice that made me weak at the knees and with rhythm and beats that made me want to thrash around. Like that Placebo became my music. It was both my happy music and my sad music. It was my angry music and music that eased my anxiety. Brian wrote and sang about things that I thought and felt.

    I started watching and reading interviews with Brian. I did not long to everything about him, but I wanted to know his personality. He was cheeky and hysterical. I loved his advice to young bisexuals - "keep your options open and don't let the people with small minds get you down." Brian spoke about drug addiction, about dressing in drag and wearing makeup, about bisexuality and sexuality in general, about his promiscuity, about getting through suicidal times, about his youth, and about music. I came to the conclusion that Brian Molko could not break my heart (except, of course, when I thought about his age and how unlikely us ever meeting would be, and the fact that he had a child.) I decided that if I were to be with a boy, I wanted a Brian Molko boy.

    I got to the live performance videos. There was Brian, in all his glory moaning over the microphone. Again, there was Brian shredding on guitar and moaning. The more live videos of performances I watched, the more ridiculous they would get. Brian would pretend to do dirty things with his bandmates while he sang or played guitar as they played. There were even videos of Brian kissing his bandmate Stefan Olsdal. Those ones drove me crazy. I never knew why, but I *had always been that kind of a girl. Before I knew I was gay I had a little thing for boys who were gay or doing gay things. I couldn't explain why seeing boys kiss made me feel the way it made me feel. I had officially fallen in love with Brian Molko. I loved him so much, I could gush about him in French and Japanese as well as English.*

I did not expect that I would find a boy exactly like Brian Molko. I knew there were certain traits I'd have to be willing to compromise. Just like I had to be okay with the fact that if I ever was lucky enough to see Placebo live, it might not be everything it was in the videos because Brian is older now, he doesn't moan quite so much when he sings anymore, he's not always making a scene in drag or kissing Stef. Some might say he's grown up.

Brian helped me unbeknownst to him for five years. He helped me through his music, his interviews, the covers he did, live performance videos, and his role in Velvet Goldmine. I regarded him so highly. He was one of my top five musicians. I felt that he had a song for every situation. Brian made me feel less alone in my orientation and gender identity as well as my school of thought. Whenever I need a hand, I just turn him on and listen to him sing like he is turned on. Lately, his version of a Beatles song "Across the Universe" has been helping the most when times get tough, because there's nothing like hearing him moan "jai guru deva om" and then beautiful sing, "nothing's gonna change my world" and I remember that nothing needs to change mine.

Dancing with Molly

    Jaime had heard tell of Molly and her beauty, but for Jaime she had been spoken of but never seen. Jaime didn't really know about her until she was seventeen and the boy she was interested in (and all of his friends) knew her quite well. They had all been out dancing with her many times. That particular ex-boyfriend brought her to a party he threw the ay after Jaime graduated high school, but Jaime didn't meet her, because she vanished when the cops came to crash the party.
    The people she hung out with knew miss Molly rather well, they were always going out out with her or inviting her over, but she was never around when Jaime was around. Julio didn't see her the whole time they dated, so Jaime didn't either.
    The first time Jaime met Molly was Sean's eighteenth birthday. Jaime picked her up for him as a sort of surprise because he had had a good time with her once and wanted to see her again. Jaime didn't know much about her, but she spent twenty dollars to go get her. The night Jaime met Molly, she was wearing a short, white, lacy dress and had white blond hair. Jaime was nervous in the car with her until she picked Sean up from work. He was so excited to see her.
    Sean lived at Jaime's house back then, and they brought her to my backyard. They listened to music and Jaime played with her lights and that night that Sean hung out with Molly was the first time Jaime had ever been kissed by her gay best friend. Sean and Molly stayed up later than Jaime could, and he assured me that Molly would find a way home and that he would lock up. He said it was the best birthday ever and Jaime was glad to give that to him.
    A few months later, after Jaime's nineteenth birthday, Sean and Jaime went out to the club with some friends, the second show they had seen in a week. Sean found Molly at the club and brought her over to meet Sawyer, Tiffany, Cody, and Tony. They all fell under Molly's spell but Jaime did not, however they danced all night with her and everyone and each other. They all wanted to kiss, except Sawyer. She just

wanted to dance. Sean kissed Jaime and Tiffany kissed Jaime and Sean kissed Cody and Tony and got them to kiss each other and Tiffany kissed Cody and Tony. It was a whirlwind of dancing bodies, lights, and kissing. And Jaime just danced because Molly didn't interest Jaime like she interested the others. Jaime stole a leather jacket from the club that night to keep her improperly dressed friends warm.

  Sean and Jaime didn't see much of Molly until it was nearly summertime. Back at the club, it was just Jaime and Sean one night, and he found Molly again. Jaime still didn't know her like Sean did, but when he pulled us on stage to dance, Jaime started to understand. As Sean shook his hips in his tight, black jeans and studded belt with the hilariously obscene buckle and danced like a stripper, Jaime got her first glimpse of what Molly was really like. She was just like us. She covered her wrists in kandi to hide her scars and danced the night away to forget the pain. She felt the beat of the bass and lived for her loved ones. She loved you however you were, too, if you were a boy or a girl or in between or neither. As they stepped off the stage, Jaime started to think that maybe Molly wasn't so bad, and maybe she would like to get to know her.

  When Jaime got to know Molly for myself, she was on the way to the casino with Syd, my ex-but-maybe-will-be-my-boyfriend-again and his friend Bruce, and two of their mutual acquaintances, the famous dynamic duo of Marcie and Phillip (that's Phillip, not Phil). Marcie and Molly were quite close friends. They were all dressed super fancy. Syd wore suspenders and a pinstriped suit jacket with colourful shapes on the inside. Jaime wore a low cut white dress covered in flowers. Molly wore a little black dress. That was the night gay marriage became legal across the states.

  Syd, Molly, and Jaime broke away from the other three and walked laps around the casino talking about life. Molly loved getting people to talk. After that night, Syd and Jaime became inseparable again for a brief period of time.

  The thing about Molly is that, like most people, she always leaves you. Except, a lot of people get really, really sad when she leaves, because of the way she makes you feel.

It's too easy to fall in love with the way she gets you to dance and talk and the way she makes you feel so open and full of love. Some people spend the rest of their lives trying to find Molly again, but she comes and she goes, and no one thinks about just trying to be like Molly. She made Jaime want to find a reason to dance and she made Jaime want to remain open and loving to many types of people. Jaime has met and gotten to know Molly, and she did love her, but she doesn't need to go dancing with her every night to have a good time. Jaime would be just fine.

Trigger Warning

The following stories depict individuals with imbalances of excess in their solar plexus chakras, and who also experienced deficiencies in their solar plexus chakras by way of suffering from low self esteem. The examples presented are extreme but are still realistic problems our community faces.

Suicide Note

To whom it may concern,

If you're reading this, I've killed myself. Well, presumably. It's possible that I ran away, or maybe I failed to actually off myself which would make sense since I am such a useless failure.

To whoever found me, I am so sorry. I have thought about this for half my life. I couldn't take it anymore.

Though it is likely that I have been committed, if I am actually dead then these are my wishes.

You must take my cell phone and unlock it. The passcode is clit, because I am that gay. There are two numbers you should take down and contact.

The first is C.C. There's a skull next to her name. It's a 505 number. Tell her I've always been sorry I couldn't be there for her. Somehow, a part of me never managed to stop loving he and it never stopped hurting.

The second is P.B. There's a purple heart and a palm tree next to her name. It's a 619 number. One of the only ones in my phone. California. She's still in my favorite contacts even though we haven't spoken in months. Tell her I should have called. Tell her I should have apologized. Tell her I'm sorry I was stubborn. Tell her I thought I deserved to be where she got to go because I worked harder than she did. Tell her as it turns out I didn't deserve anything, not even my own life. Tell her she said she wanted to stand up for her girls but she didn't stand up for me, instead she lied about me, was mean about me, made fun of me, and didn't take me or my feelings seriously. Tell her that's not what friends do, especially when they've gone through something similar. Tell her I would never have done that, no matter how mad I was at her. Tell her I hope she's happy with her new best friend.

Yes, I want you to contact these people and tell them what I did and said, even though they did not miss me, not once, not ever. You see, that's part of the problem. Anyone could leave me and would never miss me. I would always miss them. I was always the only one who suffered. I was never able to stop loving them or stop wanting to call them. It tore me to bits. They never once looked back. I couldn't chase them. They wouldn't have wanted me to. They didn't care. I always cared more. I always tried harder, I always made the effort. It got me nowhere. Caring and worrying about others was the biggest and worst mistake of my life.

Another thing was that I always felt like I was living a lie. Even though I was out I didn't feel like I was accepted. I could never bring girls home. You'd hate me if you ever knew some of the things that I did.

So, I've decided to end my life. Or at least try to.

I will miss every one of you. Even the ones I hated, because that's just who I am.

A very rare few of you will miss me.

Peace Out, A.P.

Revenge

Why did they want to do this to everyone? What caused it? People looked into their character, their past after the event.

Adrienne Wyatt, age fourteen, was arrested the night of the event, and is currently residing in a psychiatric hospital until she turns twenty one. Cole Trymoor, age fifteen, was arrested the night of the even and is being held in custody in a detention facility until he turns twenty one.

Cole Trymoor was dark haired and olive skinned. He kept his hair slicked back and wore black wife beaters tucked into dark cargo pants. He had a lean frame which he occasionally showed off by wearing unbuttoned shirts over the tank tops. He had a pierced ear and a jumpy personality. He looked the part.

Adrienne Wyatt did not. She had long, ash blonde hair that she always kept up in a ponytail. She was always wearing athletic clothing, like gym shorts and tee shirts. She was a small girl who loved sports. They kept her busy.

They met skipping gym class. Why would a girl who loved sports want to skip gym class? Every time she went into the locker room, all the girls who wore jeans and thongs or dresses and lacey panties would see her change from sweatpants to gym shorts, out of tee shirt to tee shirt in her sports bras and boyshort underwear. They called her mean names like lezzie, dyke, and muff muncher. They would push and shove her around the locker room. They also tried to throw themselves at her, with questions like, "what, don't you like that?" Since then, she skipped gym class. The day she was arrested, she was wearing a black, lacy dress with her hair done in curls.

Cole could not be bothered with gym class. For starters, he preferred to smoke cigarettes behind the bleachers. For seconds, he didn't care to change for class, because that would mean potentially revealing the weapons he carried to school. It's not that he didn't like sports, he was quite fit. He was also all about strength, endurance, and agility. It was more about how everyone at school called him queer for the funny way he did things.

People called his hairstyle gay, as well as the way he dressed and the way he walked. People at school had been calling him queer for over a year. Boys used to beat him up, tape signs to his back, trip him and all that. Because he could speak French, because he was good at math and science. Because he used to make good grades and be good at fixing things. Because he had to arrange things at his desk just so, and because he read books for fun.

They liked to jump him in the locker room. Sometimes they would just beat him, but other times they would be more obscene. He knew that he wasn't gay, he wasn't a fan of any of that. He had cut a list of reasons why into his arms and his thighs.

Adrienne chose to run the day they met. Gym class was being held in the weight room, and she walked out of the building to run around the bleachers. Cole sat beneath them and watched Adrienne make two laps around before joining her on her third.

"Why do you keep running?" he asked.

She stopped in her tracks, shocked by his presence. Her expression became panicked.

"You're not going to tell anyone that I'm skipping gym class are you?!" she was breathless.

Cole smiled at her for the first time and she felt her heart skip a beat. His eyes and his smile were so cool they were ice cold.

"Right there with you, cherie," he said and she fell.

He was the first boy to ever treat her like she might actually be into boys.

"My dad is sick with a heart condition!" she burst out

"...and, all the girls in my gym class call me a lesbian and that's why I'm skipping but I love sports because they keep me from thinking and, and that's why I keep running and that's what you asked and now that I've answered that I'm Adrienne and I'm not a lesbian and who are you? And why are you skipping too?" She shook a little as she spoke and then Cole asked her, "do you smoke?"

She shook her head and he said, "these are like my meds." He held them up for her to see and smiled as he said to her, "I think you're like me."

She didn't know what to say but he didn't stop there. He told her about his experience with gym class (not all of it, though). Then he flashed her that smile again.

"I think you should hang out with me during gym class every day. It's nice to have company. What do you say?"

Adrienne blushed and quietly replied, "that would be cool, I'd love to."

"For the record, the sporty look is cute, not queer."

Adrienne beamed up at Cole and that's how he got her hooked.

Adrienne and Cole became somewhat of a couple. They were seeing each other both at school and outside of school. Cole was great with Adrienne's parents. He buttoned up his shirts to cover up his wife beaters and ate all of their bland, heart healthy food with no complaints. He always made sure to talk about math or French in front of them.

But all the fun happened at Cole's house. Adrienne met his divorced mother who wasn't around much, and explored his house as well as his expansive wooded backyard. Cole introduced her to drugs, alcohol, and sex. He let her walk around in his mother's dresses and jewelry and told her how beautiful she was, regardless of what she was wearing. He gave her presents, like bracelets and earrings he stole from the department stores at the shopping malls.

Then he started asking questions. "Wouldn't you like to show everyone who bullies us? He'd whisper. "Wouldn't it be cool to get them back?"

Cole taught Adrienne how to fight. She loved it the way that she loved sports. They went running together, too.

That was how it happened.

Cole got the guns for his birthday. He'd asked for them for hunting. He shoplifted Adrienne's lacy black dress and told her when to wear it. He told her the plan. They went running with the guns. He told her no one would hurt her again when they were done.

When they walked into the pep rally, Cole kissed Adrienne in front of everyone.

"Just so all of you assholes know," he projected as he raised his weapon. "Neither of us are fucking gay!"

Adrienne stood there with her gun as people screamed and started running.

Cole fired three shots that missed the crowd and injured one football player with two bullets in different places before he was tackled to the ground. Adrienne sat down on the gym floor and let the noise and the problem consume her, and for the first time in her life she did not run.

Cole broke down to police about how he had convinced Adrienne into his whole plan. He also informed police that the only person he injured was a football player who had jumped him in the locker room and then proceeded to abuse his mouth. Adrienne told police about how Cole had convinced her to seek revenge.

The town decided after the event to educate the high schoolers on tolerance and against stereotyping and bullying.

The two are currently in recovery in separate juvenile detention centres, forbidden to speak to each other. Jaime's studio runs a program for the youth in prisons and juvenile detention centres, separate yoga classes for the boys and girls. The intention is that these classes will help make it easier for convicts to assimilate back into civilian life after release.

Some Notes on Adrienne and Cole

Did Adrienne really have long blond hair, or would she be labelled as a product of a bad neighbourhood, a thug, a religious terrorist, or a communist? Did Cole look as described or would he otherwise be labelled as well? Did it matter to the point of their story, or did race compromise the other details? Would it make a difference if instead of shooting others they shot themselves in front of the school? Would it elicit a different reaction? Would the youth still get labelled? Columbine was a suicide, and there was gay bullying at Columbine. Why were children violent instead of being taught how to deal with bullies and why aren't children being taught not to bully – are we taught violence because dominance is "masculine"?

Regardless of physical appearance, Adrienne and Cole both had their solar plexus chakras compromised, which is why they ended up with such a frightening imbalance. Since their self esteem was attacked, they had acted with their ego. They were seeking for a self esteem boost, mistakenly thinking that they were better than their bullies. What they were projecting was their self-hate absorbed from bullies telling them to die. When people hear things enough, they start to believe it.

In the Bully Society, Jessie Klein investigates the motives behind the many school shootings in America. The motives she found were anti-school attitudes, violence against girls, dating or domestic violence, masculinity issues and gay bashing, status, racism, or gang related issues. She found that masculinity issues made up nearly 50% of school shooting motives, with gay bashing making up 10% of motives, and violence against girls making up 20%, totaling 80% of school shooting motives. The boys who committed the Columbine shooting were victims of bullying about their masculinity, got called gay often, and were taking revenge on girls who had added to their masculinity issues.

Additionally, Klein found that young people were considerably more stressed out due to high stakes tests, a highly competitive environment, scheduled time, time valued over social encounters and connection, a culture of therapy, meds, depression, anxiety, and other mental illnesses - ultimately, a culture of misery. Young people are bombarded with perfect images and are encouraged to pursue their own success at the expense of others. With a media deregulation in advertising there is no concern about impact just moving products, or using sex appeal. what are we doing with our economy to our human experience? Hypercaptilism is breeding hyper reliance, independence is becoming an economic value, and we are dismantling social support systems. We are refusing to participate in instrumental relationships. Why are conversations so scripted? Why do we talk about products? This only breeds social despair, social isolation. It also promotes systematic cultural problems – making us self blaming, self fixing, and well adjusted to injustice. One of these systematic problems also involves the culture of slut bashing – boys or girls who reject themselves or who are rejected by their peers.

Another systemic cultural problem Klein found was how young people experienced an imposed identity due to the gender police. From very young, children are offered the ideals of princess versus superhero, and taught "what girls and boys are like." Non empathetic girls are seen as catty versus nurturing, compassionate, gentle, and kind. Being human and discussing feelings is seen as being feminine. Does this make empathy a masculine or feminine quality? In addition, being smart seemed to equal being gay, and often resulted in gay bashing. Young people were also subjected to relational aggression, and were under a great deal of social pressure. Klein recognised a universal human needs to be seen, heard, and connected with, and claims that humans are born to love. She suggests developing a meaningful philosophy of life, in which love is the ultimate goal, and where there is a focus on sharing emotion, knowledge, thoughts, and experiences. She also suggests the need for help for the students, the bullies, the parents, and the bystanders to make an environment in which school shootings would occur less frequently.

Wrong Room

When Zia woke up in a hospital bed, zir wrists were all taped up. Ze was hooked up to an IV. There was a bright red paper bracelet that read, "allergy" dangling from zis wrist. Zia remembered what happened and shook zis head. Someone must have walked in to zim passed out on the bathroom floor from loss of blood.

"Whoops," Zia thought to zimself.

A man in a white coat and a crisp, blue button up shirt with a tired but cheerful face walked into the room Zia was in. Zia guessed doctor.

"Ah, Zachariah, you're awake," he said, smiling.

Zia cringed at the use of zis full name.

"Is something wrong?" the doctor noticed Zia's dark, Israeli features start to look stormy.

"I prefer Zia, not that name. More fluid." Zia could barely look the doctor in the face as ze said it, but the doctor crossed out Zachariah on his clipboard and scribbled Zia in its place.

"I see," the doctor mused. "Zia it is then. Well Zia, welcome to the teen psychiatric ward at the Bayview Hospital. We're not happy you're here, but we are happy to help you. You are here today because approximately twelve hours ago someone found you in your bathroom and wanted you to live. You'll be with us for at least the next two weeks. Your school has been notified. My name is Dr. Felner and I'm in charge of this ward of the hospital."

"Excuse me, Dr. Felner, but could you please tell me who exactly found me?" Zia interrupted.

Dr. Felner looked down at his notes.

"You were brought here by a Miss Taryn Irtis."

"Oh, Jesus," Zia sighed. "Of course."

"Someone special?" Dr. Felner's eyebrows were raised.

"My...girlfriend....or something... maybe not anymore... I don't know. She's just Taryn. Much simpler than me."

Dr. Felner gave Zia a warm smile.

"You can talk to Dr. Joyce about that tomorrow at 4pm if you'd like. I've got a list for you of all scheduled activities and your required therapy sessions as well as meal times. Lu is going to be your guide for today."

Someone appeared at the door.

"Ah, there you are, Lu, right on time. This is your new friend, Zia. Show Zia around and be nice," Dr. Felner instructed as he took Zia off the IV.

Lu smirked. Zia took note of Lu's short ginger hair, hazel eyes, and dark chocolate skin. As Zia followed Lu, ze took note of the big hoodie Lu had on and Lu's cargo shorts.

Lu walked backwards and told Zia all about the teen psych ward, and then led Zia to a room.

"So this is your room.. your roommate is... somewhere right now. Her name is Kim Starr."

"I'm rooming with a girl? That's allowed?"

Lu smirked, contemplating a response. Did Zia need to know what Kim Starr was? Maybe. Lu wouldn't want it to weird Zia out if he found out on his own. Before Lu could start, Zia happened to be staring. Lu followed Zia's gaze. The sleeves of Lu's hoodie were rolled up past the elbows. Lu's eyes narrowed.

"Hey, that's not very nice. You don't see me staring at your wrists. What, are you wondering which one of them got me here? Because if you are you'll never figure it out."

Zia seemed startled but also mystified.

"Which one got you here, Lu?"

Zia looked right at Lu's face. Ze found it pretty, but ze couldn't figure Lu out.

"A whole bottle of Vicodin mixed with a bottle of rum got me here, thanks." For some reason, Lu grinned.

Zia was stunned. "Jesus."

"Actually, my sister got me here. She's the one who found me passed out in our backyard and got my stomach pumped. What about you?" Lu still had an eerie grin.

"My girlfriend... or whatever she is..." Zia sighed. "Hey, Lu... can I ask you a personal question?"

Lu laughed. "Like, 'which cut got you here?' isn't a personal question. Gonna ask why I did it or what? Sure, Z, go ahead."

Nobody had ever given Zia that nickname before. Most people just called zim Zack.

"No, no..." Zia took a breath, gathering zis courage. "Lu, are you a boy or a girl?" Zia could feel zis cheeks getting red hot.

Lu looked Zia in the eyes.

"What do you think?"

Zia looked down, because ze did not know.

"I'm Lu," Lu said, and grabbed Zia's hand. Lu unbuttoned the cargo shorts, and guided Zia's hand down the front of the, Then Lu moved Zia's hand up, inside the hoodie, under the shirt, and over and across the ace bandages on his chest. Lu dropped Zia's hand and rebuttoned his cargo shorts. "Boy or girl? You decide."

Zia's mouth was wide open. Lu contemplated leaving before Zia could respond.

"Boy," Zia whispered.

"Thanks," Lu beamed.

"But you're like... like really good looking." Zia wasn't sure about using the word "pretty" to a girl who wanted to be a boy.

Lu came close to Zia's face and whispered in zis ear

sensually.

"Sure, Zia, good looking. Wouldn't you like to do me so hard that I want to be a girl again?"

Zia got flustered.

"No, no, no... I don't think I'd care w-what you were... I'd probably still want to do you." Zia nervously trailed off.

Lu's expression softened.

"So, you're bi?"

"Dunno. Could be. Haven't gotten it all figured out yet." Zia looked down.

"What's there to figure out?" Lu inquired.

Zia went quiet. Then ze took a deep breath.

"Okay, if I can't tell you, who can I tell, right? I'm not sure if I'm a boy who likes boys and girls or if I'm a girl who likes boys or... or what. It doesn't... uh... it doesn't always feel right."

Lu noted Zia's long hair and name and smirked.

"Oh. I get it."

"What about you, Lu, do you like boys or girls?"

Lu continued to smirk.

"I like whatever I want."

Zia smiled at the reply.

"I like that," ze said.

"It's called fluid," Lu clarified. "Or flexible."

Lu leaned into Zia.

"Have you ever been with a boy before, Z?"

Zia looked away from Lu.

"Just kissing."

"Tell you what," Lu propositioned. "If you let me do

you like a boy, I'll let you do me like a girl. Should be a good way to figure out if you've got the right parts or if you're in the wrong room, eh?"

Zia was taken aback. Ze did not know how to respond to that offer. Ze thought briefly of Taryn. Was she crying at home, praying to Allah, worried about Zia? Or had she given up to get off with someone else?

"No offense, Lu, but if you don't have a dick how exactly would you d-do me?" Zia finally asked.

"OH MY GOD ZIA, YOU MEAN I DON'T HAVE A DICK?! Wow, I had no idea!" Lu exclaimed. Lu was grinning so Zia figured ze wasn't in trouble.

"You know what, Lu? I think what I really need is just a friend to listen to all of this for me. Do you think you can be that for me?" Zia had mustered up the courage to say it.

Lu's face softened.

"Of course, Z. Of course. Offer still stands as long as you're in here, though, cutie."

Zia blushed.

"Yeah, I'll let you know when I figure out what's going on with my girlfriend."

"Sounds like a plan, Wristcutter. Let's go over to arts and crafts. I can't wait to see what kinds of things you like to make."

In the following week, both youths discussed their first encounter separately with their therapists in the ward. Zia was given resources to understand language identity a little better, and Lu was talked to about having a lack of boundaries and what that meant, as well as whether or not it was a good thing. Jaime's yoga program for troubled teens came and visited the hospital several times a week, where Jaime met the youths and learned their stories. Jaime brought them yoga twice a week while Ana brought her own class through Jaime's studio to the youths at the hospital, centred around art, eating disorders, and recovery. Ana and Jaime became good friends and mentors to Zia and Lu, helping them not only through tough times, but helping them to develop skills they could carry through their lives into tougher times.

One With the Mat

Ten toes wiggled in the air. Slowly, with precision and control, the toes lowered, the legs rested on biceps, and Aris Otono rose from a headstand to a fallen angel to a side crow and held it for five breaths. Smiling, Aris dismounted. Yoga was a place to feel sane.

Toes stood naked in the grass, soaking up the sun's rays toes attached to legs, and legs to... maybe hips? Sometimes. There were thighs and quads and hamstrings, and there was a tummy. Something in between. There was a torso, and tough abdominal muscles. There was a strong back and maybe sometimes a butt. There was a chest and biceps and deltoids and forearms. There were hands, and Aris was capable of standing on them. There was a neck and a head and a face.

Aris' dirty light brown hair was choppy between chin and shoulder length. Long enough to be pulled back when desired, and long enough to hang over the face. Aris' almond shaped eyes were light green forest canopies. Crimson lips on caramel skin, sprinkled with freckles. Sometimes, Aris was full of smiles. Mornings blessed with a yoga practise in the sweet sunshine were the kind to smile about. Just Aris and the yoga mat, breathing and working through physical asana.

Sometimes Aris wore loose clothes, sometimes tight workout clothes. Aris accepted the fact that sometimes in yoga, everything would show. Any binding equipment will show when shirts don't stick to a body revolved in space. That was acceptable. The price of showing not always passing was fine for the benefits that came from yoga.

Aris used yoga for many reasons. Yoga was an escape from the mind, a way to slow down time. A way to be able to focus on the body, without focusing on all of the less liked bits, and become aware of what was going on in the body and how it felt. And it felt good to be aware. Aris used yoga as physical meditation on some topics. Focus in school and good grades was something Aris frequently dedicated energy to meditating on through yoga. An intention could be set and an entire physical practise could be devoted to the intention. Afterwards, the mind might be cleared. The emotions might be more settled. One might be more ready to function. Aris meditated through yoga on depression, anxiety, and gender identity as well.

Aris was a kindhearted soul who cared for animals and nature. Aris enjoyed gardening, cooking, and reading books. A quiet person, but talented with musical instruments. Sometimes, Aris was well-adjusted. Sometimes it was the right kind of therapy and Aris was confident in dress and presentation.

Other days, Aris didn't have a clue where ze stood. Ze didn't always feel quite like a girl which is why ze kind of thought ze was a boy. But sometimes, Aris liked light blue flowy clothing or wanted pink highlights. Some days were for snapback hats and funny faces and others were for beanies and big hoodies and hiding away. But some days were for tiny ponytails, braids, or buns. Aris enjoyed binding and boy clothes. The unisex name had been given, not chosen.

Aris chose to be strong. Aris chose to be able to lift up on zir own, to have the muscle to support weight and sit in postures. The strength gained from some practises could be used for other things. Strength became a skill, something that could be learned, refined, utilized, and maintained. Finding a way required strength. Aris developed yoga routines as fluid as zir gender. Whichever ze was, ze could feel good in zir body.

"How to Kill Yourself"

Step One
make friends
watch others in the locker room
fall in love

Step Two
come out of the closet
get outed
be in middle school

Step Three
date your best friend
get your heart broken
lose your friend

Step Four
get a new best friend
watch her try to kill herself,
try to save her – fail.

Step Five
lose the friend
lose yourself
come out to someone you can't trust

Step Six
date someone long distance,
date someone who hates your orientation,
date someone who makes you jealous

Step Seven
lose the love of your life,
twice -get cheated on,
stay through the cheating and lose them still

Step Eight

get a job
come out
get a job and don't come out

Step Nine
fill your lungs with smoke
run a lavender bath
and try not to fall asleep

Step Ten
make friends with people
watch them kill themselves and
go to prison.

Try to go on.

"How to Live"

drink tea,
a little potion
helpful to me
for any emotion

move your body
bend, don't break
even when
your life begins to ache

kiss to stop time
watch the clouds and the stars
take moments to align
drive around in different cars

make friends
with people who are interesting
and people who
actually care about you and about things

go for two am joyrides
cuddle, learn, and grow
stay up all night dancing
but learn, too, how and when to say no

read books
tend a garden
learn to cook
get lost in these worlds

make music or sing
find a way to create
learn to be thankful for things
learn how to wait

give yourself sleep
and rest
give yourself time to relax
treat yourself best

practise your breathing
realise your power
breathe in and out
don't panic, don't pout

carry crystals to protect you
even on the days
when you say you want to die
the crystals will help you survive

eat your vegetables
and your fruits
regularly get tested
make sure to learn how to shoot.

the Story of Dawn the Destroyer

This is the story of Dawn the Destroyer. This story is incomplete because it is not being told firsthand. But, this is still her story.

Dawn was a Turkish Muslim. Jaime didn't know if she was still a Muslim, but she was still Turkish (you can't get rid of that). Jaime only knew her from when she was an eleven year old ballerina until she was fifteen and rebelling.

Jaime could recall Dawn expressing feeling a sort of oppressed by her Muslim religion at an early age. Jaime remembered going in Darcy's hot tub with Dawn and learning that she couldn't shave her body hair because she was Muslim. Jaime also recalled that Darcy's slumber parties accommodated Dawn's dietary restrictions because they would have turkey bacon instead of regular bacon. Once, Dawn stayed with Rosie for three whole days at Darcy's house over the summer when she was thirteen and that was when the girls first found out that she felt very controlled by her parents, particularly by her dad.

(Jaime guessed that was how she liked her girls because Karoline felt that same way, but this is Dawn's story, not Jaime's. She'd tell Jaime to live in the moment anyway.)

Dawn did the unspeakable those days – ignored every single phone call and text from her parents. Of course she got in trouble for it later (even though her parents were in contact with Darcy's parents and knew Dawn was fine), but Dawn was having her first experience with control.

Dawn grew to love control. She learned exactly what she could control – herself, her body. Dawn had always been naturally thin and lean, had a naturally athletic build, but she started messing with her nutrient intake. Jaime didn't know what exactly her relationship with her food became, but she kept herself rib and bone thin.

Dawn learned how she could control her friends when she told them, "I want to kill myself." Immediately they were at her service. Did she need anything? Was there anything they could do for her? Suddenly, they were all letting her know they were there, they cared. Suddenly, everyone was going out of their way to do things for her, or to hang out with her. Suddenly, she had so much power. She had even more power once she started cutting and burning herself. At first she wore long sleeves to hide it, but then she realised her friends had stronger reactions once they saw the marks on her arms.

Dawn chose to destroy herself to be in control. Of course, she lost control.

(and no one blames her, she was depressed.)

Dawn was so out of control she used sexuality to manipulate and control her friends. She told stories with the help of Abraham D'Lacey of kissing girls and got her female friends (Jaime and Rosie) to kiss her. She hung all over them until she no longer wanted anything from them.

Dawn was a colour stealer, and she sucked all the colours out from Jaime. Jaime had always liked black. But she had always liked colours, too. Without Dawn, life for Jaime felt blacker than black, it felt empty, and she felt the darkest of blues. How did Jaime learn to make so much paint at Dawn's house? Yet Dawn had always needed to use hers. And Dawn never gave them back, either. Jaime had to find new colours, learn how to make them.

Being a colour stealer made Dawn an energy vampire, when she learned to use her powers for evil. The way that she used up Jaime's energy was ultimately why Jaime left Dawn. Dawn suffered karma for her dark ways, and Jaime was left pondering the risk she ran with being too flexible in life with people (how she got walked all over, manipulated, and taken advantage of). Later in life, Jaime related this to the hypermobility she held in her body.

Dawn was the reckless one. She hated herself so she didn't care what she risked. Glitterboii and Jaime were the ones who cared. Jaime got called the mom friend of the group because she was the one who was careful and wanted everyone else to be. Jaime was the mom friend for other reasons, including her protective nature. Jaime was the mom friend because it was in alignment with her life path which was to be a helper and protector of a humankind. It was the spirit of the bear in her which helped her along her life path, and as a protector, she was naturally inclined to take care of herself and her loved ones. Because Jaime was a defender of humankind, she had the protective instinct to find out if her kind were wounded. This was why she sought answers from Sydney and Le Feu about their encounters on the other team.

Dawn got so out of control she was going to school drunk and stoned.

It is unknown how Dawn the Destroyer became Dawn the Different. She got sober. She began living gratefully. She practised moving her body.

It is unknown how Dawn the Destroyer's story began or how it ended. It is simply recorded for the sake of the solar plexus. It shouldn't have come as a surprise to Jaime that Dawn discovered yoga. Jaime didn't know how she discovered it or how often she practises, but Jaime knew she was doing her handstands and counting her blessings. She's better now, she says. She learned to count her blessings. Dawn found that Allah loves her during her practise despite being brought up to believe that as a queer she wouldn't be loved by Allah.

She knows Jaime's new friends and that's weird for Jaime, and it used to bother Jaime that she was into yoga too, but more yoga taught Jaime to understand that Dawn found yoga because she needed it.

They don't speak now, but she's welcome in Jaime's studio should she ever need it. Though Jaime doubted she would ever show up.

Youth Groups

When Jaime was twelve, she stepped foot through the glass doors at the old Triangle Community Centre back when it used to be over by My Three Sons (KiddieTown). She was just twelve, with her older friends, at the beginning of eighth grade. Jaime was the first of the younger friend group to go. It was Jaime, Rosie, and Glitterboii. Rosie and Glitterboii were in high school. Jaime didn't remember which one of them had asked if she was interested in going. She remembered why she had been interested in going.

It was after Nature's Classroom and holding hands with Karoline, after all those slumber parties at Darcy's, after knowing Akiko/Oliver. It was after watching straight, lesbian, and twink porn with Karoline over the summer. Jaime's eyes were wide open. She was wide open.

When Jaime was twelve she took in the light blue paint on the walls, the leather couch, the black chairs, the coffee table, the shag rug, the black bookcases brimming with books, the table and chair set, and the framed painting of the rainbow flag outside the doorframe. When Jaime was twelve she was introduced to a community of young people and adults, people who'd imprint upon her and stay within her, including Fayne Wasano who'd introduce Jaime to the joys of cigarettes just roughly two years later, Erika who roughly two years later Jaime would fall for and who also would tragically pass less than ten years later, Thor and Howard the facilitators who would become Jaime's business contacts and references, and Kenzie the lesbian facilitator who made Jaime laugh so hard.

When Jaime was twelve, Glitterboii pulled her aside by one of the bookcases to ask her what she was. She said she didn't quite know yet.

Jaime attended meetings nearly every Sunday at that centre from when she was twelve until she was nearly sixteen. It was a place to go to laugh, to learn, to share, to discuss. It was also a place to go to cry, to hide, to whine. Jaime attended game nights and other organised events in those four years, including the first vigil for the Children of September, at which she publicly came out on a live television newscast in front of City Hall declaring that she didn't care if her dad heard her. It was a place to cultivate that strength.

More of Jaime's friends joined the group and fluctuated in and out. They watched the older kids get accepted to schools and we celebrated with them. They watched people get into relationships, they met other people's friends, they watched facilitators come and go. They started a book club. And they listened to everyone's stories. They shared their own. They asked questions. They grew from the circle group.

When Jaime was thirteen she stepped through Ms. Ratatano's door for her first meeting of the group-whose-title-accommodated-the-allies-first (the gwtataf). It was part of her high school. Jaime only stayed until she was sixteen, then Syd didn't want her to go anymore. That group, though, was more just one of the groups she went to – it was slightly less helpful and slightly more dramatic – but nonetheless a group she was thankful to be a part of.

When Jaime was fourteen they took the train to Fairtown and walked to the attic up the stairs in the church for the group that would later become too big for the attic and move to the basement. Jaime stayed with them until she dated Syd, though she attended an event held by them while she was dating him. That group was beautifully structured with discussions and debates.

When Jaime was fifteen, Thor and Howard, the facilitators from the Sunday group started a Saturday group in another church. When she was fifteen Jaime was able to spend time Thursday through Sunday being with her people.

Thursday through Sunday they spent time empowering themselves. They spent time cultivating strength, and destroying fear, shame, and guilt. They could have made another choice, but they made the right one for them. They made the choice for growth.

Convicts and Crazies

This story is recorded from many retellings, Jaime did not experience it firsthand. At first, Jaime only knew Marcie. Phillip was spoken of, but never seen.

Marcie and Phillip (Phillip not Phil) were best friends. They happened to both be from different lands. Marcie travelled with her family to several countries after her homeland before settling in this one. Phillip had been adopted as a toddler.

Marcie was the oldest in her family. Phillip was the youngest in his. They were best friends freshman year, about fourteen. These were two friends on a strangely electric plane. They felt deeply affected by the outside world and other people.

Marcie was manic depressive, but it is unsure if it was known at the time, and Phillip had borderline personality disorder.

They let the weight of the world get them down and they got into drugs. Marcie had the access. Phillip had many of the provisions. They were fourteen. Phillip had the idea.

Phillip stole his brother's car, and picked Marcie up one night.

"Where should we go Mama Mar?" he asked, grinning.

"Just drive. Just. Drive."

It wasn't until they hit Indiana that the cops pulled them over. Those Indy police found everything they had. They spent a night in jail and every time Marcie told the story she made sure to talk about how they never gave her her wallet back.

Phillip's mother grew to despise Marcie after this event. But Marcie's mother still adored Phillip. Phillip and Marcie were still inseparable as ever. Phillip was Marcie's gay best friend. They were both pretty sexually open. They tried to befriend everyone.

For a period of time, Phillip and Marcie had an apartment together. That's when Jaime met Phillip. He came to a meeting at a group Jaime went to (when she was revisiting group after a length of time) and later that night we saw each other at a party. Phillip and Marcie often let other people party in their apartment when they weren't there, like Rigby Wilton.

Phillip accepted money for sex. Marcie got into heroin. Their friendship burned forever. Years passed and Marcie beat her addiction. Phillip was able to get his own apartment, far away, in Milwaukee. Phillip started college. Marcie dumped her user boyfriend when he got himself sent to prison and got herself a job.

Their lives improved as they acted less on their impulses. They each used the help of strict diets to help regulate their impulsiveness.

Ace of Magical Girl Swords

Jewish, Puerto Rican, and Native American, with a degree in religion, Katara was an interesting and slightly mysterious young editor. Katara was super into cosplay, and used it as her escape from reality. She made her own costumes almost entirely from scratch.

Katara managed to function highly – she had an apartment with a friend and a degree, she had a job. But she suffered from bipolar mania disorder, among other anxiety disorders.

She could go through periods of time where she would engage in frivolous spending. Money could be run through easily and spent on items of whimsy.

Due to previous experiences, Katara was asexual. She was attracted to women romantically, though the thought of sex was generally repulsive to her. However, sometimes her mania would raise her libido, even towards men. Katara worked hard not to act on manic impulses.

Katara spent time writing fanfiction and writing activist posts because she felt the need to use her given voice. She worked out both for endorphins and to maintain her body for the cosplay arts. Katara channeled her passions into impulse control.

"It's never too late to transform yourself," Katara's Sailor Moon poster read.

She often felt her bipolar disorder made her life so much harder, especially with the complications that libido hypomania could bring her. As an asexual lesbian, she was only into girls romantically, although if she ever did experience sexual attraction, it was towards a lady. Hypomania put Katara's world into a less intense version of a manic episode. It could make her feel hypersexual, but she wouldn't be actively going out and getting laid. The hypomania could sometimes drive Katara to flirt with boys, even though her true self wasn't interested. It could make her spend money, but not exorbitant amounts, but enough for her to feel guilty about frivolous spending. Manic episodes could be so severe that they could lead to hospitalisation, but hypomania was the step between feeling fine and feeling manic.

Coupled with anxiety, depression, and PTSD, Katara often felt weighted down by mental problems. These were the things from which she would like to transform herself. Katara learned that when she was done searching for love in painful places, it was best to start searching for her self love in healing places. She wondered at first, how could yoga be a transformative practise?

She learned in relation to breaking habits. One could not change what they are not aware of, a matter of pratyahara because the senses helped raise awareness to what these habits were. She learned that asana was a tool for self discovery. She asked herself, what can one do when they find themselves slipping back into habits? Practise asana – but which one is relevant for the habit to be addressed? She learned that a habit was the nervous system recalling a pattern. She learned she had a lot to learn.

Positive

Stella found out she was infected when her boyfriend passed away. Everyone thought it had been an overdose, but autopsy revealed a terribly low T cell count. Overdose, maybe, but it had been suicide related to his disease. How could Stella think about getting tested when she had to think about burying her boyfriend.

She didn't get tested until a month after his passing. She waited the two weeks and didn't cry when she got the phone call.

"That's what I guess for sharing needles I guess," she thought to herself.

Once she thought of needles, all she could think of was getting her fix. She called her dealer and it wasn't until he was on his way that she remembered she was out of cash. Luckily she knew she could get what she wanted in other ways. Stella didn't care if he got infected, she figured he probably already was.

Two months passed and she suddenly remembered the random sexual partners she'd had to cope with the death of her lover. She felt possessed to tell them all, yet terrified, and she felt horribly guilty for it. For three days she threw up.

Stella continued to go to parties and use with other users. She would get so strung out that she'd forget she was infected. She took herself out to get a tattoo for her deceased lover, too.

Stella never told any of her lovers, past of present, even though she should have. She couldn't say it out loud. She never told any of her junkie friends, of course, either. She got careless with her using, and people pushed her to recovery.

There she discovered yoga, at first intrigued by the difficult physical postures. She wanted to get good for the pictures, and she practised with another girl who loved heroin. The only physical activity she'd previously enjoyed had been longboarding. She was amazed at how she connected with her body and began a deeper practise. She found somewhere to attend classes instead of remaining self-taught. After a few classes, one savasana brought Stella to tears. She approached the teacher when class was over and asked, "can I please tell you something I've never told anybody before?" Her teacher nodded and Stella whispered, "I'm HIV positive."

Solar Plexus Chakra Connections

Ambition
     To seek ambition is to seek a fire. Ambition is a driving force, and one must be prepared to be in the car with ambition for quite a while. Anyone seeking ambition or already working with it must balance it with patience, and use tapas to help feed it. If not properly cared for, Ambition will wallow away into Daydream Nation.

Energy
     Not only do people contain energy that they send out to the world, but they also contain an energy level. A person's energy level is an idea of how much fuel someone has for their day. Food can give energy while things like studying and exercise can take energy out of a person. Yoga can help renew a person's energy, even if only practised for ten minutes a day, or if only practised through daily meditation or pranayama. As beings made of energy and full of energy, it is important to attend to our energetic needs. Since beginning her practise, Jaime's energy improved, which had been previously shattered by a laundry list of disease.

Energy Osmosis
     It is said that one becomes like the five people with whom they spend the most time. Like we absorb the habits, language, and mannerisms of others, we also absorb their energy. When surrounded by successful people, we tend to want to become successful ourselves. Contrarily, when surrounded by lethargic people, we tend to become lazy ourselves. Jaime experienced energy osmosis when she slept at Sean's and absorbed all of his sleepy energy (among the many other forms of energy osmosis she regularly experienced).

Chi Blocking

A character in a show Jaime used to like was trained in the art of chi blocking. Her name was Ty Lee, and she was also an acrobat, chi blocking was Ty Lee's primary method of combat. She described it as "hitting weak points." By blocking someone's chi, she stopped their flow of energy, preventing people from directing elemental energy (i.e. water bending, fire bending.) What Ty Lee was really doing was hitting pressure points.

Pressure points are areas of the body which are more sensitive due to a large number of nerve endings grouped together. Acupuncture believes in using needles to stimulate the pressure points, making blood and chi flow more freely. Conversely, applying pressure to the points can stop or temporarily block the flow of chi in someone's body.

There are several ways to play with one's chi, including the chi ball, Tai Chi, or dancing with the chi and directing it. Directing chi can be like spellcasting, as it is a method of directing energy, like an elemental bender in the show Avatar. Yoga is a way of physical spellcasting, since it is energy direction with the whole body. Entering a yoga practise with an intent helps us to harness the energy of the day and the energy in our bodies, helping us utilise it to the fullest extent and make the most of our gifts as we move the energy through our bodies.

Chi blocking can also be achieved by directing energy to go against another's emitted energy. Any negativity created by anyone returns to them threefold. More positive methods of chi blocking through energy direction are to energetically create a shield from the unwanted energy or to send intentions of neutralising the unwanted energy. Blocked or imbalanced chakras are an example of how chi can be[come] blocked in one's own body. Dex had shown Jaime and many others an easy way to visualise chi – by taking one's hands shoulder width apart and pulling them closer together, stopping when energy is felt, not letting the hands touch. Once the space between the hands is smaller, the hands should slowly circle the space as if it were a ball. The motions should be fluid, based in thoughtful exploration.

Erikson's Autonomy vs Shame and Doubt

Autonomy vs shame and doubt is a stage of development we first experience in toddlerhood (ages two to four) when we are learning how to do things on our own. Negative impressions gained from attempts at autonomy were from where shame and doubt came from. We struggle with autonomy through many ages, but it is our society's general consensus that we will one day become fully autonomous adults. Words of affirmation compliment the attempts at achieving autonomy, because encouragement is usually needed so that people understand they are acting correctly.

Industry vs Inferiority

Industry vs inferiority refers to the stage of development of school age children (ages five to twelve) in which we are able to do many things, learn many things, and produce a great deal of work. If someone does not do many things, learn a lot, or create things, they tended to feel inferior, or sometimes were socially viewed as inferior. It is important to work through feelings of inferiority as we pass through all ages.

Initiative vs Guilt

In the initiative vs guilt stage of development, children must be encouraged to take initiative in their learning and in their world (preschool age). Their interests must be valued, respected, and utilised as to further their development of a desire for discovery. If the children's interests are not valued, the children end up suffering guilt for being interested, or shame for being enthusiastic or energetic. Typically, these children are learning through their bodies and methods like project approach work quite well for them. When children suffer guilt and shame, it negatively affects their self esteem. We pass through other opportunities in life in which we want to take initiative regularly and may sometimes struggle with guilt related to the desire to take initiative. We must learn to take the lead sometimes. One example relates back to the masculinity in making the moves.

Maslow's Esteem

Self esteem must be cultivated on its own, as unrelated to thoughts and expectations of others. What raises and lowers anyone's self esteem is different for every person. It is important to focus on positive forces which raise self esteem and to eliminate the negative ones which lower it. Self esteem is directly related to one's self concept. It is integral to the development of children to grow up with self esteem, in order to feel capable of achievement of tasks and success in life. Bullying is one force which negatively affects self esteem.

Self Defense

Dex got into becoming classically trained in martial arts when Jaime was between eighth and ninth grade. When she was fourteen and fifteen, he taught her to fight. Jaime did not believe in violence like he did, but she felt that it was important for people to have a chance by knowing what to do out in a world in which people try to steal from, strike, or touch others in unwanted ways.

When she got assaulted in school for her orientation, Dex made her weapons she could wear in her hair. After school he started teaching her how to shoot a bow and how to throw shuriken. He taught her hand to hand combat, and enjoyed practising things on her hypermobile arms. She liked to try and plank when he would hip throw her. Punching bags hung in their backyard that she could hit when she was experiencing feelings. Dex maintained his body and strength for survival's sake – to win in hand to hand combat. Always thinking someone was out to get him, survival was his ultimate goal. For Dex, self-defense was a necessity. To Jaime, it was a practical life skill. Jaime offered self-defense at her studio to empower people to protect and stand up for themselves and others. She made sure each of her teachers were accepting and inclusive of all students, to offer a safe space for them to learn to defend themselves from a world less accepting. Jaime tried to offer a variety of teachers, as well, so that all students could be comfortable. Learning fighting had been tough for Jaime, at times it could feel too sexy to her, regardless of the gender of the instructor (what she begrudgingly remarked as the perks of being bi) and she often had great discomfort when learning from male instructors.

Swadyaya (Self Study)

This yama is required for true discernment. Discernment includes knowing what is best for oneself, and being able to tell whether or not messages received from perceptive senses and emotions are blocking clarity. By utilising discernment people can intentionally participate in the gift of life by making the choices which cause them to align with their most true self and purpose.

"Reflection requires both considerable flexibility and sufficient attention to purpose to ensure that over time all participants recognise the value of the time they devote to it." (Eraut, 2004)

Tapas (self discipline)

Tapas is one of Patanjali's niyamas. Much like how everyone learns differently, everyone has a different adhikara for tapas in all the different aspects of life. Some people have more natural tapas when it comes to schoolwork, others when it comes to working out, some when it comes to spiritual rituals, just to list a few. One can use yoga to cultivate more tapas in whatever area they desire, just like yoga can be used to direct any other energy. Tapas is the energy of ambition.

Heart Chakra
Anahata
"We are all love."

The Heart Chakra will show stories of love. The Heart Chakra involves those we love. The Heart Chakra represents those moments when we say, "I love." The mantra for this chakra is "I am lovable, I feel compassion." The Heart Chakra is located in the lumbar spine, and is represented by the colour green. When healing the Heart Chakra with colour, green should be used, or if the Heart Chakra is overactive green should be used followed by a small dose of pinks or reds. The Heart Chakra embodies the element of air and represents the direction of East. The Heart Chakra is ruled by the planet Venus, and its ruling signs are Pisces and Libra. Eucalyptus, rose bulgar, and spearmint are essential oils which affect the Heart Chakra, and one crystal which can be used for the Heart Chakra is Rose Quartz. The Heart Chakra represents all love, and one pose which resonates deeply with the Chakra and can be felt in the whole body is Urdva Dhanurasana (Full Wheel).

When someone's Heart Chakra is balanced, they would be able to give and receive love with healthy loving boundaries. When the Heart Chakra is in excess there is clingy and possessive behaviour, and a fear of being alone. When there is a deficiency in the Heart Chakra there can be apathy, a lack of empathy, critical behaviour.

Japanese Love Letters

At fourteen Jaime was blessed enough to study abroad for two weeks as part of a class trip. It was a trip she was supposed to take at thirteen, but that was the year swine flu broke out and their sister schools pretty much asked them not to come. Of course, Jaime cried her eyes out about that because she had been so excited, but she got to go as a freshman in high school. She left early from school one Friday in May, went to Junior Prom that night with another girl, and left the next morning with classmates and teachers for the airport, headed to Narita aeroport in Japan. After a fourteen hour flight (awful for Jaime since she hated flying), they had arrived safely, and after a few train rides they arrived at their sister school in Tokyo, weary from travel, but excited to meet their host sisters.

Jaime's sister school was an all-girls school, her first time ever dealing with separation of the sexes at school, and also her first time ever having to wear a school uniform – not to mention one that required her to wear a skirt. She loved it anyway. The way that school worked in Japan, at least in the school Jaime went to although she was pretty sure that this was quite common, was that the students were assigned a homeroom and the teachers would move through the different classrooms teaching different subjects at different times. They usually rolled a cart around the school.

She was in Jaime's homeroom. Jaime noticed her because she was sleeping in history class. When Jaime looked closer, Jaime realized that she was white and not Japanese. That was when Jaime became confused, because she had not come with her school group. Plus, she had a uniform that actually came from the school, not one from home like Jaime's which was meant to look like their uniforms did.

Jaime later found out everything, when she turned up with two other white girls to join the things that Jaime's school group was doing. The school had three long term foreign exchange students – two came from a sister school in

New Zealand. And then there was her. Her name was Jolie, she was from Belgium, and came to Japan through Rotary International. She was seventeen and her name suited her for it meant beautiful and she was so truly beautiful, inside and out. Jaime was able to speak to her in French, as well as in English and Japanese.

  Jaime could not explain how she fell for Jolie except that it was all at once. Many of the girls who came with Jaime's school could tell that Jaime was keen on Jolie from the way that she always tried to be close to her. As it happened, she actually was interested in both men and women like Jaime, and for some unknown reason Jaime feelings were actually somewhat reciprocated.

  There is a photograph of them beside one another, dressed up in kimono that the special women had put on for them, and they're making hearts with their hands. Jaime is cheesing something fierce, because the feeling she had in Japan filled her from her crown to her toes. Jolie has pigtails in the picture, and Jaime's hair was gingery colored at the time and down with loose curls. They are about the same height, Jolie might be an inch or so taller, and had similar builds. Her smile was contagious. Jolie had a face that looked like she spoke French, which intrigued Jaime because she had learned about this phenomena in French class through which children who grow up speaking French have muscles in their face which develop looking differently than those who grow up speaking English due to the different sounds that they pronounce.

  There were quite a few things that attracted Jaime to Jolie so genuinely. They were quite similar – Jolie loved photography and travel. Of course, as she was older (and probably smarter) she was a bit more professional than Jaime, with her nice Nikon camera and her travel program. It was more than just her good looks, Jaime was attracted to her intelligence, how strong she was by being able to just up and leave absolutely everything she knew and live in a completely different country and learn the language, her silly side, and her genuine kindness.

There is a photograph of the two of them beside each other with bright yellow flowers in their hair, smiling wide. It was taken after they learned about flower arrangement, at the going away party for those of them from the States. Jaime cherished the photos of the two of them together in the same frame because there were not many. There's one a classmate took during the tea ceremony where you can see in their eyes and our smiles the love that they shared for each other. In some of the photos they're even making the same face. Jaime took about as many photographs of strictly her as she took of strictly Jaime.

Jaime went to Japan for two weeks. School over there went from Monday to Saturday. Jaime spent the last two days of her trip in Hiroshima. She only went to school in Japan for maybe nine days. Which means she only knew Jolie for maybe nine days.

It is hard to tell which one of them started the note passing. It could have been Jaime, since she had memories of writing her a little love poem in a mix of French, English, and Japanese and somehow coming out to her. She vaguely remembered a line sort of like, "tu es grande mais je suis petitite" to express how highly she thought of her ("you are big but I am small"). She wrote Jaime back such lovely notes, in pink marker, folded up all pretty, signed with hearts and kisses. Jaime remembered her asking in a note that she did not tell her host sister about Jolie's bisexuality because she did not know how people in Japan might react. Truth be told, unless Jaime looked at those treasured love notes, she could not tell you what they wrote about. She just remembered being totally smitten with her.

Jaime's love for Jolie was unrequited. Nine days in Japanese school with her, hugs and outings, cheek kisses, possibly hands held, and notes passed. Jaime had a boyfriend at the time. Nothing serious. She cheated on him with so many girls that year that to this day she could not fathom why Jolie was not one of them. Luckily, they keep in touch.

Jolie, ma cherie, n'oublie pas bisoux pour moi, Jaime thought.

Bright Yellow

The couple was first spotted in the nightclub in matching bright yellow tee shirts. One had light gloves, the other a pacifier in her mouth. Her skirt was too short, and her panties could be seen. She was a dancing whirlwind, and her man would give everyone he passed who intrigued him a surprise light show. The two danced the night away and went home to their young son. They were not married, nor did they always live together.

They were next spotted at the same venue for another electronic dance music show. They were in a group, the whole group was quite close friends as well as frequent visitors to a local music venue. The group members were all kind to other ravers, the girls consistently saving other girls from creep guys, and the boys protecting their girls from the dangers of dance clubs, which included but were not nearly limited to mosh pits, thievery, sketchy drugs, and getting lost.

They were a dreadlocked duo, the girl white and her man Puerto Rican. She was a hairdresser, or to use the word which describes her degree, a cosmetologist. We'll call them Krystal and Manny. The couple lived in two different states, New England states which bordered one another. The cities in which they lived were only about half an hour away from each other. He was a landscaper.

They each had their own funk and unique sense of style while maintaining an aligned belief system. The two had been together for at least five years.

Krystal was bisexual. Manny believed that all humans were bisexual. He himself had never had an experience with another boy. Krystal missed girls.

Their quest was simple. Krystal and Manny were seeking a second girlfriend. They wanted to open their relationship, but only to someone special. They wanted someone to grow with, to learn with, to play with. They believed in polygamy and free love. They were free spirits. They believed sharing was caring.

However, as it turned out, they found it was not such an easy and simple thing to find. Girls that they approached were not quite so open and free. Some were disgusted, others afraid. Some were intimidated by the length of their relationship. Some girls did not want to risk putting their relationship on the line in case things like jealousy came up, even though they swore it wouldn't.

"It's just a lot to get into," girls would say to the couple.

So, for the moment Jaime experienced with them, Krystal and Manny treasured their relationship and their small son, and held out hopeful, waiting for the one.

Losing Manny

Jaime wore bright yellow and lime green to the wake, at request of the family – yellow for the first night she ever saw him and Krystal, shining bright as the stars, and lime green because it was his favourite colour.

Jaime could picture the conversation between Krystal and Manny.

"When I die, I don't want people to wear all black," he said, laying with Krystal. "You have to tell them to wear colours for me to celebrate my life."

Jaime could also see Krystal crying and screaming to Manny's parents. "You have to let people wear colours for him! You can't make everyone wear black! He told me he doesn't want that!" Jaime felt the moment of conversation hit her like a ton of bricks when she read the notice about the wake. She knew she had to make the drive up to his service after not being able to go to Erika's service. Funerals were very hard for Jaime, being a heavy crier and someone who talked to the dead. Not a single person turned up to the wake in all black, and she knew Manny was pleased.

She met up with their rave family to carpool to the wake. No one was prepared to go alone. Everyone had done something or brought something to make it special and easier for them all. Lime green glow stick bracelets, Pikachus, sympathy cards, the smokey quartz he had given

Jaime. Jaime's dream girl was at the service with her beautiful baby in her belly. She was the first person they all saw upon arrival, standing outside to make them stronger. Inside they waited in line together. Girls held hands and went up to say goodbye together. The tall boy with the full beard and ponytail broke down into hyperventilating tears while praying for him from the chairs in the room with the casket. Jaime grabbed his hand and they went up to say goodbye together. Kneeling up at the casket, he told Jaime what Manny had meant to him, and kissed his forehead. Jaime cried, "I never thought the last time I saw him would be the last time I saw him." She looked at him and said, "you were light. Your light will live on, through all of us and your song. Thank you."

    They all went out to eat and then to a house after. They shared their favourite Manny memories. Jaime drew a picture of him that everyone added to, and showed them the children's book she'd made for school about counting hula hoops which featured Krystal, Manny, and her other friends. She talked about how Manny had given her hope when she found out that he and Krystal were polyamorous as well, they were the first people who didn't make Jaime feel like she was wrong for what she liked. She mentioned how he and Krystal had invited her to get involved with them and the boy with the ponytail laughed about having received the same invitation. Jaime could still close her eyes and be back on her patio with Manny as he said to her, "I believe everyone is bisexual." She could still feel the grin she grew from meeting like-minded people.

    Manny connected Jaime and ponytail Ash that night. When death strikes, often we don't know what to do besides to hold each other close. Manny told Jaime and Ash to cuddle that night, he connected their lights. Ash told Jaime he could see the light in her and that she had calming eyes. Manny told them to show each other the love they had for him by hooking up, to make each other feel good instead of shaken up and sad because he loved them both.

    The last thing Jaime had to do immediately was hoop for him to her suicide songs and Stairway to Heaven. After that, she finally knew that he was at peace, but would always be with her. She knew she could make time and space to talk to him, and he'd listen, and perhaps even answer sometimes.

Aprigraha and Polyamory

The combined effect of Manny's wake and Pride on Jaime was the realisation that she was polyamorous because she was made for so many people and was made to connect with so many people. People fell for her easily because she was always connecting. She understood that there might be some people she'd rather be with more, got sick of less, or connected better with than others. Jaime didn't know any other way to be besides open. She had always been her genuine self. People had always been charmed by her. Benji would say it was their Scorpio charm. Some have said that it was because she was a witch.

Jaime meant it when she said, "I swing both ways." In the same way that she felt limiting herself when it came to gender was unnecessary, she felt that monogamy was another useless constraint. She saw no need for such limitations. It was because she was open. Jaime could articulate what she wanted and didn't see why she couldn't have it. She was liberated by her sexual freedom and stood firmly in that power. Her ideal partner would be openminded in the same ways that she was. Being openminded to Jaime also included being open to the possibility of eventual monogamy. She always reserved the right to change her mind, for as Pocahontas sang, you never step in the same river twice.

Genuine Jaime was so openminded that she was convinced that she was meant to love all and serve all. To Jaime it was yoga. It was why she could not hate Sydney, Phillip, or Freddie Pasto. It was how she healed Le Feu. When bad things went on in the world, Jaime found it more difficult to love everyone. Still she tried to remain open to the good within everyone and within the world.

Manny saw Jaime's true self and he was open to it and open with her. He encouraged her to stay open, and to be herself. He helped her know that there was nothing wrong with her identity, nothing wrong with connecting. He inspired her with honesty, he lit the fire with talk of free love. She loved herself best with her freedom, a gift most precious. Manny helped Jaime know that other people could love her with her freedom, too. In her soul Jaime felt she would always be open and free. Standing in her truth, Jaime could breathe easily. Sex was not her enemy. She was picky with her lovers now, and pickier with her partners. Still, she kept connecting, like the synapses in her brain. Her heart song knew the wait and search would not be done in vain. Very comfortable with her truth, it rarely caused her pain – only when she tried to work on confronting guilt and shame. She's been out for years; some things never change. Manny and Pride helped bring out the Jaime that's always been out the same, and snuff out the one the unaccepting world drove insane.

Jaime knew that no person could be hers. She knew that no person could belong to her. No lover or future child, for they belonged to themselves, and to the world. Being with Sydney had taught Jaime that the tighter she held on, the more it made him pull away, and the crazier and more jealous Jaime got. Jealousy and obsession were no good for the soul. The tighter Sydney held on and the more possessive he got the more it frustrated Jaime. She knew that she could have no one forever, and that even if she eventually got married, one of them would eventually die and get returned to the Earth. She understood impermanence.

When Feori discussed his polyamory, Jaime felt strong in her truth. *If they can never be only mine permanently*, she thought, *then why should I stop them from loving whoever they want and doing what makes them happy, when they love me as well, and when I wouldn't want my freedom taken away, either?* After dating Syd in high school, Jaime had sworn off jealousy, which had mostly been successful until she got back together with him. As a polyamorist, Jaime did not suffer from romantic envy. Therefore, she felt polyamory was the yogic way for her.

The Erika and Manny Listening Club

Every two weeks a group met in Jaime's studio called the Erika and Manny Listening Club. It was a support group for people who had lost a loved one to suicide.

When Jaime had lost certain friends to suicide, she didn't even want to tell people that she was grieving because she didn't want to explain how they had died. She felt embarrassed, and she also knew that as soon as she told anyone they would be at a loss for what to say, because there was nothing to say.

The only thing Jaime knew how to do was to reach out to others regularly, checking up on them or talking about what was missed. Often, many people whose lives had been touched by suicide could see why their loved one decided to leave. Jaime started a group which connected people experiencing this with each other. The group also took its members out for hikes, retreats, meals, sports, events, gardening, yoga, and crafts, so that their minds would not be full of sad thoughts. The idea was that the members would eventually heal enough to be able to help others through their healing process. Jaime felt that this kind of group was an important service to offer the community and did research to make it work efficiently.

"Your Little Pastry"

My dainty little croissant,
he called you
as you went out for
your weekly date

my sweet little muffin
he called you over text
as he was describing to me
dirty details of your sex

my sweet strudel
he called you
because he was bothered
by honey and baby

and he wanted to be different
he said you were different
and he was so into you
he loved that you were bi too

my lovely doughnut
he called you
as he told me about your love
of bowling and your family

but then he told me that
you were "more bisexual"
than me
because you had been with more girls

I held back my tears
as I pushed away my curls
haven't seen him in years
but still think of his words
regarding me and girls.

"Poetry for Bookish Bounty"

I can write poetry about anything
I swear it's true
I used to write love poems about cigarettes
so I can certainly write poetry for you

I don't know if you like rhyme
or free verse
the inability to foresee reactions is a curse
but if you've got the time
how would you feel
about accompanying me for dinner and wine?

We could speak French
hold hands on a park bench
when I met you I knew you had the looks
more interesting knowing you're into books
seeing you full of pride I could breathe your stench
your queer pheromone
that only we can smell
the one they claim sends us to hell
so do you care to moan
in my ear as I whisper haiku
about all the things I'd like to do with you

I can write poetry about anything
including how your body reflects nature's beauty
with your moonglow skin
blessed I'd be
if you were to let me in

And even just someone with whom to practise French
and talk about books with
is valued as highly as crystal gems.

"Same Name as my Surfboard"

she came right up to me
out of nowhere at the club
and asked for my number

she had the same name
as my surfboard

we'll call her Sunny
just like her hair
golden waves
for sunny days

and she was down to
drive down to see me, so long
I said I would go up next
but I was wrong

liked her
but not exactly enough
to do something about it
and then it was too late

broken car meant I couldn't go
see her and I felt too bad
to have her come every time
but it was fine

ended up with someone else
but she was one of those
could have beens
can't help but wonder.

"Dancefloor Sweetheart"

Blond hair
dreadlocks
tiny body
slim waist

dancing whirlwind
black pants, black boots
music stops
and she's gone like smoke

on a hunt
to find miss mystery
the internet
brings us together

we meet at a show
same venue,
months later
to trade kandi

dance together
with kind and beautiful girls
our boyfriends let us kiss each other
it was laser eyed love

we only saw each other
a few times
before our lives changed
when can I see you again?

Wear you on my wrist
reminds me of the times I miss
one day we will be together
even if we end up staying just friends.

Dream Girl

    She was Jaime's dream girl. The girl who saw Jaime dancing alone and came to dance with her. She was the girl Jaime only saw once in a while, once in a blue moon, the girl Jaime only saw when they went out. She was the girl Jaime dreamed about.
    As an eighteen year old without any concrete experiences past kissing with girls, Jaime couldn't help but dream. She wondered all the time what beautiful girl would be her first. As soon as Jaime saw her, she was smitten. She longed so deeply for it to be her.
    It was not her. They both had boyfriends, and they lived quite far away. She travelled the world, born in Colombia. Jaime admired her from afar, cherishing every dance they'd shared. Jaime still dreamed of her. Jaime wore her gifts as though she could wear her around town, take her company to all her tasks.
    Jaime couldn't even explain why she was her dream girl. As soon as Jaime saw her she fell head over heels, love at complete first sight, without knowing anything about her at all. Jaime was not normally like that, and her pretty face crushes didn't normally last. Jaime barely knew her and yet wanted her as a girlfriend though they both had boyfriends (but why not have one of each? Jaime thought).
    She wasn't Jaime's typical type appearance wise either, so Jaime really couldn't explain why she had fallen so hard. Jaime had a thing for girls like her – girls who looked like her, girls who did things she liked to do, girls who acted like her. They had the same body type in the sense that they were both small girls, blessed with voluptuous booties, but she was much smaller than Jaime – both shorter and slimmer. Different hair, sort of. She was just different. She stood out. Striking and stunning. Didn't know her likes and dislikes. Jaime couldn't help it, though, she was simply twitter pated. She made Jaime's heart soar.
    The best thing about Jaime's dream girl is that she turned out to be real. Real in the sense that she was raw and

open, and she was genuinely kind and sweet. She was a real person, with real problems, and a real life, real thoughts and ideas, real dreams and goals. The most attractive thing about her was that she had real passion. And Jaime's dream girl turned out to be her real friend, and even though Jaime still wanted her, she couldn't ask for anything better, couldn't even dream of it.

Silk Street

As Jaime was driving home she saw someone standing in the road as the traffic light at the bottom of Sophie's hill turns red and she decided to take a quick right turn detour to avoid the person and the light and turned on to Silk Street. She was driving over the speed bump when suddenly there she was. It was Erika, sat cross legged with Rosie. She's got her brown harem pants on and a huge grin, braces showing. Her short brown hair framed her face. Rosie's all curls and smiles. Erika had just punched a boy outside Sophie's for trying to steal her money.

Jaime was not sat cross legged on the speed bump laughing with them. She was in the road, following her boys. She stopped and beckoned them to get up and come with her. As Jaime beckoned them, the ghost of the memory beckoned to Jaime to stay longer. But she had a car to drive, and missing one person always leads to missing another.

From time to time Jaime still hung out with Erika, funnily enough considering that the other few friends from their group are still alive. Sometimes Jaime will be in her bedroom reading or writing and she'll stop by, just to strum her guitar from Jaime's bedside.

Jaime was attracted to balls of light. Erika was an angel on earth before she went to heaven. A ball of light is the best way to describe her. She always wanted to help people who were down become cheerful. She was generous and open. She helped others realise their own divine light.

Jaime thought met her in April, when she was fourteen. Jaime's hair was long and ginger curly at the time, she was very much a girl, wearing jeans and a pink tee shirt. They sat together at youth group in front of the TV. Erika's short brown hair was curly, peeking out from her knit beanie. She wore a plaid vest over a graphic tee and jeans with writing and pictures all over that she had done herself. Jaime didn't know if Erika's clothes ever matched. Jaime asked for her phone number and Erika wrote it on Jaime's foot after drawing some pictures. Somehow Jaime loved it. Whenever you know, you know. Jaime liked Erika before she was shallow. For the short time during which Jaime smoked cigarettes, they would do that together when she came to Jaime's city, and they'd ride their bicycles and play guitar or go swimming. A summer love that was too long distance for either of them as young people, so nothing ever came of it.

  Jaime never knew Erika long enough to know if she was like Karoline or Dawn – balls of light that burnt out, exploding on themselves. There was no doubt about Karoline and Dawn projecting their divine light. They knew ow to make you feel special and see your own light. They knew how to create a good time. They knew how to light up a room. But they also knew how to make all that light go away, how to snuff it out. Jaime could not speculate on whether or not the way Erika died reflects if she was a light that burnt out. Jaime chose to see only the light in her, because she chose to only see the light in Jaime, and because Jaime never experienced Erika as anything but light. She knew the meaning of namaste, without ever practising the yoga craft. She simply was.

New Clothes for Simone

She asked Jaime to write to her about favorite clothes. So, Jaime sat down to write.

What makes something your favorite?

Well it starts simply enough. Maybe it's your favorite color. Or maybe it's the comfiest thing you own. Or maybe it's got your favorite logo on it – a sports team, a band, a brand. Maybe it represents a place you've travelled.

At some point it becomes about the memories infused into every thread. Maybe it's from the first university you got accepted to – or, the way you saw it, the first university that wanted you. Maybe it's the times you wore it out dancing with friends and it makes you think of who kissed you while you wore it. Maybe someone special gave it to you. Or maybe, you're homesick, and when you slip it on it takes you there.

You find yourself wearing it a lot, quite often. Even if you have a fair amount of choices, you find yourself going for the same thing over and over. That's how you know you've got a favorite. You begin to get too concerned, worrying about wearing it too much, that something might happen to it, or thinking that you haven't been wearing your other clothes much, and you start to wonder whether or not they are worth keeping in your closet or dresser.

Suddenly, you wonder when you became so materialistic. How could you care so much about an article of clothing?

Except, it's sort of the same way with people. We begin to like someone for simple reasons. Something about them was attractive to you – looks, personality, perhaps a shared interest, or perhaps a special talent or something they could teach you. As we try them on, we have experiences that form a bond to them. We begin to get sentimental. For any number of reasons, we go back to certain ones we've tried on. As we continue to try them on, we begin to find that some, for any number of reasons, do not fit so well anymore.

We begin to toss them from our closets and our dressers. Or we might pass them on to someone else. Shockingly, we feel bad. We feel guilt and regret for ever even trying them on at all. We feel a sadness and a longing for the experiences. We miss their addition to our life.

Maybe we begin to refer to people by the month in which they became relevant. Clothing begins to fall into the same category as songs, dates, movies, books... everything reminds us of someone.

Jaime's favorite clothes have been more than just hoodies, t-shirts, and jeans. Jaime's favorite clothes have been best friends, ex-girlfriends, ex boyfriends, and distant memories of distant places and people who never cared just the same. How she used to strut in her ex-girlfriend's shirts, or the panties she gave her. How it used to feel to wear her best friend around as Jaime wore her hand-me-down jeans.

Jaime's favorite clothes have been comfort, style, and functional. Her favorite clothes have been repeated crowd stoppers, jaw droppers, and stolen kisses. Her favorite clothes have been her gay flag socks or conference shirt, and even the uniform from where she used to work.

She asked Jaime to write to her about her favorite clothes and she said please.

The Girl I Never Write About

Shall we call her Sam? Since she looked like a character called Sam in a Nickelodeon show (oh, Nickelodeon TV crushes). Or shall we call her April? For the month in which they dated. Perhaps November? The month in which they were both born.

Jaime had a block of art in her room on her bookcase that she got from the Metropolis cafe where her sister lives. It's an eye, open, peering into you. Jaime got her the same one. Jaime thought she'd like it. She did like it. She was artsy. She felt like she'd spoiled her when she went on that trip, though Jaime only remembered two things she bought her.

She said she was interested in science experiments, so what did Jaime get her? Jaime bought her a piece of lightning from the Museum of Science and Industry.

She was on vacation too at the time. She sent Jaime pictures of her shooting. Jaime thought there wasn't much hotter than her in those pictures.

Never was Jaime not into her, but never did she get to touch her. These days she works in hospital and lives on her own with her man and fur babies.

Heart Chakra Connections

Erikson's Intimacy vs Isolation

Intimacy versus isolation is a stage of development in early adulthood but also experienced in other stages of life. It involves moving past the fear of being isolated through discernment of truth that you will never be alone, for you will always have nature, the universe, and the divine within you. Discerning truth of what intimacy means to each person – intimacy does not equal sex, cultural/media portrayal of sex as ultimate intimacy, how that is inappropriate and toxic, filling us with wrong expectations and impressions surrounding intimacy and sex. Normalising other forms of intimacy and the value of them is important, as well as being aware of the different types of intimacy for different people and situations like sexuality, intimacy is adaptable and fluid, like a circus performer.
Different types of intimate relationships (with doctors, lovers, friends, family)

Love and Relationships

The deity Neptune's highest form is unconditional love. It is from Neptune that we may gain much insight about the magic of love.

Jaime, being wordy nerdy, gained insight from various books she had read. She compiled several quotations which she felt adequately described some of the magic of love.

The manga Jaime loved, Hana-Kimi, had taught her about many things. There was valuable information about love in those books, and she found Akiha Hara and Hokuto Umeda particularly interesting. In one quotation, Akiha's ex-wife, Ebi, told the protagonist all about him.

Ebi said, "Whether he's dealing with a man or a woman he can find the person's true essence. I think he probably photographs whatever it is he sees and feels without worrying about technique. When he finds someone he immediately tries to provoke them."

She explained that Akiha was the first man to treat Ebi like a person – she was not being seen as a real person when she was told she couldn't do something because she was a girl, and that Akiha helped her gain an understanding of the real her versus being seen as just a girl. Ebi said, "even if we only love each other as friends now it's still love, right? Even when two people are in love there are times when their internal signals just aren't on the same wavelengths"

Later, Akiha described to the protaganist what it's like to experience the magic of love through the art of photography.

Akiha said, "There's a constant exchange of signals between the photographer and the model. In order to take a good photo, the one thing you need most is love. When you're photographed by somebody you like, you're able to relax more, and that helps bring out your natural look. The same is true for the photographer. If he likes the model, then it's much easier for him to capture her natural beauty. That's what all the signals are about. Without the signals there would be no depth and beauty. I'm constantly seducing models with sweet words until the perfect moment can be captured, almost as if we're in love or lovers."

There were a couple of quotes from Jaime's favourite character, the school doctor, and one from the creator of the manga, which Jaime related to.

Love is kind of like a car crash, you never see it coming. - Hokuto Umeda

There comes a time when that desire to truly know a person

evolves into true love. I'd never really thought about it that way before. – Hokuto Umeda

You never know who you might fall in love with. – Hisaya Nakajo

In one of Jaime's books from the gay book club that she had started, <u>My Heartbeat</u>, the main character, Ellen, described the bisexual boy that she fell in love with and the way that he felt about other people. "I get that the thing that matters to him is what he can have with somebody. Be it a girl, a boy, a man, or a woman. This doesn't make him straight, but it doesn't make him gay either."
James, the bisexual boy, said, "I'm not an expert, but I don't think sex is the thing that makes someone gay. It's more whom you love. The how and why of it. And if what you get back is worth what you give up." Later in the book, the boy describes what he gets from the protaganist, Ellen, as, "love, attention, bouts of intensity."

The last book Jaime included was <u>Naomi and Ely's No Kiss List</u>, which always reminded her of her time with Karoline. One character in the book declared, "it's bullshit to think of friendship and romance as being different. They're not. They're just variations of the same love. Variations of the same desire to be close."

Words on Relationships

Dex once so wisely said that you have a relationship with everything. "I have a relationship with both the door and the toilet, though I think I've got a more intimate one with the toilet."

Maslow's Love and Belonging

"We love because we first were loved (by the divine)" John 4:19

One of the needs in Maslow's hierarchy, represents the feelings of belonging to and being loved by a family as well as a community. These feelings help reinforce the second need on the hierarchy, the sense of safety.

The Importance of Kulas

Kulas are groups of like-minded individuals which help to serve as places in which people can cultivate those senses on Maslow's hierarchy of needs, safety, love, and belonging.

"Friendliness is not the abolishing of distance but the bringing of distance to life." - Walter Benjamin

Friendships are important because they are a support system, because they are people with whom to play, and because learning is a social process. How do you play with friends as adults?
Friendships are ideally voluntary and reciprocal. Children ask, "will you be my friend?" How do you do that as an adult? Friendships can be used as social capital for resources, to facilitate access to learning networks, social trades (helping each other, for example with homework), or defending each other. Bordieu describes friendships as, "durable obligations built up through networks to maintain togetherness, feelings of inclusion (and exclusion) and belonging." For example, it is widely accepted that if you don't accept the rules you can't play the game.

In his book, <u>Anam Cara</u>, John O'Donahue writes about friendship and spirituality.
In Celtic tradition, Anam Cara (a Gaelic word) means soul friend, someone to whom you can reveal the hidden intimacies of your life. This friendship is an act of recognition and belonging. Such a friendship cuts across all convention. Love is the continuous birth of the creativity within us. A friend is a deeper and more sacred connection, a loved one who awakens you life in order to free the wild

possibilities within you. Your noble friend will gently and very firmly confront you with your own blindness. you must depend on the ones you love to see what you cannot. Your noble friend complements your vision in a kind and critical way, forming a creative and critical friendship willing To navigate awkwardness and uneven territories of contradiction and woundedness. One of the true tasks of friendship is to listen creatively and compassionately to the hidden silences. Often secrets are not revealed with words, but told through the silences between words. Jaime felt this Anam Cara relationship with Sean and with Le Feu.

When we speak of an individual, we speak of their presence. Presence is the way a person's individuality comes toward you. Presence is the soul texture of a person. In a group, presence is referred to as atmosphere or ethos. That which grows needs space, though, and in order to preserve your own difference in love you need plenty of space for your soul.

One of the greatest enemies of spiritual belonging is the ego, which does not reflect the real shape of one's individuality. It is a fake self born out of fear and defensiveness. It is a protective crust that we draw around our affections. The person is not a simple, one dimensional self, but a labyrinth of soul. What we think and desire often comes into contradiction with what we do. To be natural is to be at home with your own nature. When you acknowledge the integrity of your solitude, your relationships with others take on a new warmth, wonder, and adventure. Each experience that awakens in you adds to your soul and deepens your memory. You may wish to change your life, but your vision remains all talk until it enters the practise of your day. However, you should never fully belong to something that is outside yourself. Where you belong should always be worthy of your dignity.

Perfect Love and Perfect Trust

"The things we love tell us what we are." – St. Thomas Aquinas

Perfect Love and Perfect Trust are the ingredients for creating a magickal circle. Creating a magickal circle is typically required for any spellcasting to successfully occur. These ingredients may look a little different for each person, but they follow themes of representing safety, calmness, compassion, affection.

Pranayama
"I meet my self in stillness and we breathe." – CureJoy Yoga

"You cannot breathe deeply and worry at the same time. Breathe. Let the worry go. Breathe. Allow the love and intuition in." - Sonia Choquette

Pranayama meant breathwork, which was related to the heart chakra because the heart chakra is in charge of all of the inner body workings of our hearts as well as love.

When it comes to the breath, there are 3 major nadis, which translate to rivers, or channels. The nadis start at the base of the spine and go up to the nose. In the centre of the body there is the first nadi, the shushunna at the centre of spine. The other two nadis are crisscrossing and go up from the pelvic floor to nostril, and every intersection of the nadis is a chakra, a spinning orb of energy vibrating at its own frequency. One channel is the Ida which ends at the left nostril, meant the lunar channel. Its energy is calming, cooling, relaxing, grounding, settling, feminine. The other channel is the Pingala which ends in the right nostril, and meant the solar channel. Its energy is energising, stimulating, quickening, lifting, accelerating, heating, masculine.

<u>The Breathing Book</u> by Donna Farhi teaches us that habit is the nervous system recalling a previous experience.

Paying attention to our breath helps with differentiating between real and imagined stress, as well as real and medicated, diseased reactions, emotions, or stress. By tuning into our breath, we become more able to make nurturing to our body choices. To know what we are feeling and what is important to use, we must inhabit the body. We feel the body through medium of the breath.

There are correlations between sensations in body and emotional states. By paying attention to our breath, we can create a body dictionary.

Some types of breathwork are ways for us to manipulate our breath. The following are some of these types.

Kapalabhati – an energising breath, pumping the breath out from the belly.

Surya Bhedana (piercing breath)/Nadishodhana – a balancing digital pranayama, using the fingers to alternate nostrils.

Lovemaking Breath (from the Breathing Book)

A lovemaking wave movement – a polymorphous sensuousness (whole bodied experience) in which the capacity for aliveness and pleasure permeates each and every cell of body. When it is a whole bodied experience we can multiply by 100x our capacity to love, be loved, feel pleasure, give pleasure, and experience ourselves as a whole rather than a part. Effort, force, and willpower will sabotage spontaneous breathing. Breath follows a natural cycle – desire waxes and wanes, allowing necessary periods of solitude, self reflection, without which deep connection is impossible. It is important to let wave of desire develop on its own. Through the intense kiln of relationships, we come to be transformed. Living, breathing, allowing awakened consciousness to merge with the breath (as both human and divine) is like merging with a lover.

In relationships we can get stuck in an endless struggle to gauge and decipher feelings, emotions, and motives. Working with another person can help you develop the very same quality of attention you need to give yourself. Working together can help to heighten sensory awareness in a way that will help create and sustain a healthy relationship.

Soul Mate Friendship

Everyone wants to be loved and respected for all they are naturally, all they come with, and have to offer. Everyone wants to be loved for being unapologetically themselves. This is a part of honouring our own journeys and even decolonising yoga. It is what friends do for us. At least, good friends.

When we find that soul mate friendship, it is a true friendship equal to love, and love is the highest vibration, making friendship a beacon of that divine light of love. Friendship can be used as self care. Sometimes, it means leaving toxic people, not staying in friendships just to have friends, and empowering making nurturing to the self choices.

"Friendship as radical practise. As listening. As healing. As unexpected. As a blooming bouquet. Protection. Defense. Arms. To carry and hold." - H. Melt

Yoga for Recovery

Yoga for Recovery involves creating a new life. What this new life consists of depends on what the practitioner is recovering from. Yoga is used in aid for recovery from drug addiction alongside other services, and for this type of yoga one creates a new life where it's easier not to use. Yoga is also used in aid for recovery from eating disorders alongside other services, where the patient also must create a new life where it is easier not to put themselves at risk. This may involve cultivating joy from smaller, natural things – i.e. daily breath, meals, sunsets/rises, nature, etc which would be using a Bhakti approach to yoga. Creating a new life through restorative yoga may encourage the practitioner to be empowering themselves to feel good, filling their life with meaningful things. The Tantric approach to yoga for recovery would help harness the day's energy and emotions, and encourage the discernment of the truth of the desired change for the self and the world. Tantric yoga for recovery would look inward deeply.

Learning to be yourself in a world that tells you not to – what does that mean to you? SLB Benji learned through recovering from his past to be cool with his unshaven body. He encouraged loving yourself at your worst (because who else will?) and owning uniqueness, differences, experiences. Through Tantric thought, Benji was the only one who could determine what he wanted to change about himself and act on it. He changed himself because he loved himself, in order to become better. Jaime created a new life for herself where it was easier not to panic, and it included hoopdancing. Jaime embraced her hoopdance flaws by imagining that Erika would tell her it was beautiful anyway. Jaime's Tantric-Bhakti yoga for recovery included making nurturing to the body choices, and allowing for movement snacks daily.

Yoga for recovery involves keeping away from low vibration people. These may be other users, negative people, energy vampires, and distractions, and it requires tapas to stay away from them successfully. Keeping oneself safe in the social world requires a cycle of shaucha and swadyaya – a discernment of the truth of people, self awareness, breaking habits, and retraining the self into more positive habits. It begs us to replace these people with positive people, and requires being able to be alone with ourselves. It is said that "loneliness means you are in need of yourself." Yoga for recovery encourages open ended thinking, and helps us with discerning what is worthy of our time. Through yoga for recovery we may also discern why we retreat into behaviour needing recovery from.

Change must be driven by the desire to not waste the

gift of life, and there must be recognition of gift of life. Through a pavritti approach, we embrace emotions, allowing all feelings. Yoga for recovery allows a tenderness with the self, allowing us the right to feel. Through this pavritti approach, we begin to create a new culture, as we are creating a life where it is easier not to use. This new life and new culture allow us to engage in acts of self love and self care.

Throat Chakra
Visshudda
"We all emit sound energy."

     The Throat Chakra will show stories of finding our voice; activism, communication, and hope. The Throat Chakra involves the ways in which we communicate. The Throat Chakra represents those moments when we say, "I speak." The mantra for this chakra is "I communicate clearly and compassionately." The Throat Chakra is located in the cervical spine, and is represented by the colour blue. When healing the Throat Chakra with colour, blue should be used, or if the Throat Chakra is overactive, orange should be used followed by a small dose of blue. The Throat Chakra embodies the element of ether. The Throat Chakra is ruled by the planet Saturn, and its ruling signs are Aquarius and Scorpio. Chamomile, cypress, geranium, and peppermint are essential oils which affect the Throat Chakra, and one crystal which can be used for the Throat Chakra is Blue Topaz. One pose which resonates deeply with the Chakra and can be felt in the whole body is matsyasana (fish pose).
     When someone's Throat Chakra is balanced, they would be someone who doesn't beat around the bush, and speaks the truth. When the Throat Chakra is in excess there is aggressive communication, silent discomfort, too much talking, and a lack of listening. When there is a deficiency in the Throat Chakra there can be an inability to express or speak up for themselves.

What Does God Look Like?

Jaime recalled having met Nev in sixth grade gym class, and complimenting them on their huge, brown eyes, and their unique name. Jaime and Nev had always been cool with each other but never close. Nev had been to Jaime's house a few times to cyph or party.

Nev was most aligned with their throat chakra. Nev identified as an androgynous Afro Latina, and was a very vocal activist. They had many things to fight for. Nev was incredibly musically inclined, and channeled their throat chakra alignment into singing, guitar playing, and rapping. Nev also made a great slam poet.

When their nieces asked them what god looked like, Nev told them that they are made of god, and that when they look in the mirror that it is god. They told their nieces that every time they act with kindness, love, and compassion, they are channeling god. Nev told them, "this melanin is god, this brown skin is god," and actively works towards empowering other people of colour to love themselves so that they can teach their children of colour to love themselves in a world of racism.

Jaime desired to form a closer bond with Nev because she found Nev to be an inspiration, and many of their community goals were aligned. Jaime felt like she had many things that she could learn from Nev, if Nev was willing to teach her anything. She understood that Nev had ownership of all of their knowledge, and had no obligation to share any of it.

Anya

Jaime met Anya while working at the children's museum, they were coworkers and became friends. Later Jaime found out that Anya was also bisexual, and even later she discovered Anya was on the autism spectrum and had nonverbal learning disorder. Anya was nine years Jaime's senior. Jaime was dazzled by her artwork.

One of the last things people learned about Anya was that she was on the autism spectrum. Her parents had responded to aspects of her disability abusively, and as an adult she kept her distance from them, resolving to never five with them again. Moving out had seemed insurmountable for Anya, but she moved in with her boyfriend when she was twenty two. Though her father had bigoted beliefs and abusive behaviour, Anya had developed Stockholm Syndrome and hero worshipped him. She told Jaime that is was very common for abused children to get closer to their abuser. She never came out to her parents, thinking of it as a beating she didn't want. Though her parents were homophobic, Anya felt that her father harboured secret homosexual feelings. She told Jaime that he would comment on the appearance of males but never females, and that she felt he was overcompensating with his obsession with the military and being "manly." She was convinced that despite her father's racism, he was in love with a black man who hated his own race.

Anya rated herself a three on the Kinsey Scale, and was in an eleven year monogamous hetero relationship. She resisted temptation and dealt with the disappointment of things that weren't going to happen. She recalled liking girls before she liked boys, having a crush on a girl in kindergarten. At sixteen, she was involved with a girl without a label for herself, and started coming out at twenty-two. Anya said, "bisexuality scares people because bisexual people notice more in general." She felt that love was giving, not sacrifice. She felt that love was giving yourself, parts of yourself, and caring about their life and growth. For Anya, love was feelings and actions.

Anya wanted to offer recognition for others who

experienced her disability. Since getting her article published, a ton of people reached out to her, thanking her for vocalising what it feels like. She got rejected the first time she submitted her article, but never gave up. She said, "visibility makes a difference." She thought it was important that people knew not to attack others for this.

Nonverbal learning disorder left Anya with topographical agnosia, or place blindness. She lacked an internal map and could get lost in a store, or even somewhere she was familiar with. She tried learning to drive for two years but it proved to be impossible for her since she lacked the ability to make quick decisions needed for driving or understanding where other cars were on the road. Her proprioceptive sense was affected by her disability, she recalled always having trouble with space perception, being that child who was often bumping in to people in line or standing too close to others.

Anya used art, writing, and blackout poetry to help herself relax. She also enjoyed swinging and listening to music, the rocking being a soothing motion for many people with autism. She explained that being able to draw with her learning disorder was very unusual because of spatial reasoning – being able to fit shapes into other shapes was tricky for her. Anya always drew with an idea, stuck to abstract art, and often used real life references for drawing spatial things. Her medium of choice was coloured pencil. She let Jaime read her poetry, and Jaime was most moved by a line which said, "the colours were ripped out of me." Anya saw nature as inspiration, and felt that everyone should have that grounding relationship with nature. She grew up with lots of pets, currently had a cat, and enjoyed hiking and camping. Art was spiritual for Anya, since she wasn't particularly religious. She had been raised semi Jewish, but her family had been less observant, and she recalled learning stories of Judaism through her grandmother's intricate art and puppet shows. In her early twenties, she tried Christian Universalism, which was a kinder, more generous version of Christianity with no belief in Hell. Though she preferred the idealism, she couldn't fully believe. She wanted to believe in an afterlife and a good force. She believed that we saw small glimpses of God when there were moments of understanding, or when things came together.

Anya saw the online community as her support system, and had goals for both the queer and learning disorder communities. She felt that oppression was both personal and systemic, because it was possible to be oppressed in one's personal life while not being oppressed by society, or vice versa. She also thought that people could hold themselves back and be their own oppressors at times. She wanted the queer community to be less dismissive of the bi and trans communities, as well as those who were not straight and not white. She wanted to see more representation. She wanted more people with learning disorders to speak for themselves so that the neurotypical people weren't taking their voices away. She also felt like there needed to be room for disagreement, because no singular voice could represent a community. Anya hoped to get more of her work published, to get her art displayed, and she hoped to eventually have a self sufficient career.

Anya's husband ran a trauma focus group for children between the ages of five and fourteen. They believed in medication, and looked after their health. Anya knew that hearing a lot of negativity could make it tempting to give up, but she knew that people could achieve more than they thought, and if things weren't working out, they eventually would. She realised that it was okay to set personal projects aside. She loved and empowered herself by creating things, working as hard as she could on creating things, working as hard as she could on creation trying to do her best, and by speaking out about things that were important to her. Jaime found Anya to be thoughtful, perceptive, extremely intelligent, and someone who had vivid memories.

"What They Never Tell You"

We learn at school
some way or another
how to share,
how to be nice

but we don't know
how much effort it really takes
to maintain friendships
and, oh, how we try

because the times are so nice
and it's true that sometimes
they could be better
but they're all that we've got

not to mention that they keep our secrets
and we keep some of theirs
if they let us
but we never know what might come out

and some way or another
we learn too
to be careful with what we give
since we may never get it back

still we give each other company
conversation, attention,
affection
and most of all time, effort, and care

we give we do
and we dare
as we pray they stay true
about what they never tell you.

Ash Supernova

Her name was Ash today, she was twenty, a Scorpio, and wore a red dress with black polka dots and black trim that made her feel like Rizzo from Grease. She was engaged in moving meditation, thinking about performing in drag with her hula hoop as a fun gift for her old youth group, and maybe – who knows – other events. Ash was Jaime, in disguise. Ash was Jaime's alter ego used for when she chose to dress in drag.

She faltered and dropped her hoop. It's not the sun in her eyes. It's not her leather jacket in the way. It's not her tired body. It's what her professor said at college yesterday. "They won't hire you if they see you..." She tried to reason with herself. "The professor said stripper. You're not going to be doing that," she told herself. But her anxiety got the better of her sometimes. She knew that she did want to learn pole fitness, and burlesque dancing for fun and to add to her desire to be a hoop performer. These are not reasonable jobs, though, so you're not meant to put a lot of money into it. You're told you can do those kinds of things in your free time. Since she did have a sensible passion, she strove for it. She worked hard and didn't have a lot of time for these other things you like, even though they are so good for her. They helped her let a lot out. But she wondered – do I have to give these things up for my future? It frustrated her because she wanted these things in her future.

It was like this. Jaime used to be an activist. That sounds bad, but it's like, back then she actually went to things. She used to go to those groups, they used to hold and attend events. These days, she had work and school. And she'll be graduating with a degree to work with kids. But why is it that a lot of people think that if you are involved with a cause like human rights or gender expression or anything involving the word gay in it you must keep it far away from children?

Jaime was told that she was supposed to be an activist for children now. This is true. Teachers are mandated reporters. They are supposed to care. But there are some kids out there who are gay kids, homeless kids, trans kids, depressed kids, and anxious kids that Jaime cared about a little bit extra. She wanted to be some support for those kids. So why must her two passions collide when they could connect?

Why would it be considered so bad if Jaime, a bisexual genderqueer girl, dressed up in attractive drag to give a hula hoop performance for an LGBT youth group or event? Would it be so bad? Has it been done before? Did she dare? She was inspired until she asked herself, would my boyfriend leave me if I started dressing in drag again? Even just for performances? He didn't know Jaime when she used to do that regularly. Would he, her boyfriend who earned her sixteen year old virginity after accompanying her to an LGBT vigil at which she made a speech, leave Jaime for performing as a boy? Would he, her boyfriend who used to accuse Jaime of cheating with girls, who later came out to her after cheating on her with a guy, leave Jaime for dressing like a guy? Would he, Jaime's boyfriend who let her do him, leave her for appearing in drag? That was a question she had no answer to and she was fearful of. And why did Jaime want to? Was something wrong with her here? If her boyfriend protested her choice of dress would she fight? Would he?

Jaime placed her hoops by the side of the house and walked inside. She did not know anything. She did not know any answer to any question, including whether or not she respond to hunger cues, how much her workout helped her anxiety, what she would wear after my shower, if her boyfriend was good for her, or where she was going with her life.

This is called blowing up.

Lavender Lights

In September of 2010, there were nine suicides within two weeks committed by teenagers aged thirteen to eighteen. All of these teens were victims of bullying targeting LGBT students. Not even all of these students were gay.

Each day it seemed like the suicide count increased. Our hearts dropped with each one. People made songs for them, the President even made a video for the It Gets Better Campaign. But nothing could bring them back.

Youth groups and school clubs organised vigils to honor the departed angels. The color purple was chosen to represent them; the color of spirit. Candles were lit. music was played. Speeches were made. We felt strength in numbers. We huddled close to one another, feeling broken and afraid. We checked up on each other often.

Voices were heard that had never been heard before. People were so moved by the events or other people's speeches that they stepped up once the mic was open to make impromptu speeches. People cried over the microphone. People dragged their close friends and loved ones up to hold hands and show support. People in the crowd held candles and held hands. One girl publicly came out in front of news cameras declaring, "I don't care if my dad is watching and hears this." People signed their names to show that others were not alone.

Some vigils became annual. People came every year to offer words of support and encouragement. People tried to be strong. They were unified on one thing – nothing is worth your life.

It is amazing how we felt compelled to do something though not all of us knew the victims.

However, what is more amazing is the way that even though people know about the suicides, they still ask why we need support groups, or why we think we're so different, or what the point is in caring about your orientation. Even some who belong to the community say these things. They must be lucky enough to not have had any experiences in which they were bullied, harassed, or assaulted for being who they were.

"Erika's Song" dedicated to Erika Goodman, who died 22.03.15

I love you
if you have scars
all over your arms
and legs

I love you
if you tried
to hang yourself
and I love you

if you used to
cut shapes into your body
or if you
burned holes in your arm

and I love you
if you swallow a cocktail
of pills every morning
because a doctor told you

it will make you normal
I love you
if you tried to drown yourself
or if you tried to starve yourself

I love you
if you're damaged
and you're not broken
I promise, you're perfect

I love you
if you've made it
and if you didn't
I know you love me still

I know you haven't really left us
you're the voice guiding
the sad but strong souls
singing softly - "be loud, be proud, be out, be yourself"

guiding angels across the rainbow
away from Hell
toes in the sand,
ukulele in hand

singing, "it's all right"

We Thought We'd Never See the Sun
in loving memory of Erika Goodman, resting in paradise since 22.03.15

    If you're ever feeling sad, love, think of me. Turn up the Beatles, and think of me singing.
    You might feel fat, you might feel greasy, you might feel cheap, and you might feel easy. But at least you're alive, love. Remember, you're not like me.
    I could have been a singer, I could have been a chef. I could have been an actress, or a famous ukulele teacher. I know sweetie, you agonize over why I had to OD. I'm sorry I can't be here for you more than the clouds could come down from the sky.
    But you are here darling. Even if you're unable to sleep every night, love, you are able to watch the sun rise every morning and watch the sun set every evening, you can watch the stars light up the sky. You can sing in the shower and you can dance in the rain. You can make your own food, you can play with your friends.
    So, don't ever think, not even once – just for me – that you want this beautiful gift of a life to end. It will one day, but hopefully not like mine, so abruptly and unfinished.
    You must create the world for me. Create a new world, full of love. Be full of light and cheer like a bird's song.
    Do whatever it takes, darling. Watch your favorite

movie over and over. Make new friends. Save your money. Lose people. Set goals. Read books.

My name on this earth was Erika. I was an open lover. Stay open and stay loving. I know it gets hard. But you are there to notice the clouds.

Notice what you see. Paint a picture of how it feels. If you can't paint, learn some chords and play how it sounds. Say what you think, what you feel, and mean what you say. Wear what you want and do what you love. Live intentionally, with purpose. Be cheerful. Rejoice. Treasure the world. Allow yourself moments of wonder. Be free. Love who you want, rainbow children. Dare to be full of love, and dare to give love – especially to those who need it most.

When you're free, you might even help or save someone like me. Plenty of us rainbow children feel the way I did. Many think I got to escape. Create a world our kind won't need to escape from. As a human, be an ally to all. Help others be free.

Let it shine like a gift, from you to me.

"There is Only Prey"

First of all,
I'm wondering how I even remember
what pet that this boy has
when we're not even really friends

(but I've known him forever)
so I ask him nicely
"would you please bring your snakes
into my preschool class?"

and he did
and everyone loved it
I tell him how nice he cleaned up
and that he'll be getting a thank you note

but for some inexplicable reason
I'm compelled to ask him
about a rumor I heard
and I ponder my words

I decide to just ask outright
open and blunt
"are you bi too?"
and afraid for the answer

afraid of messing up
a new friendship that
hasn't even started yet
but my question is met

with an honest answer yes
so we chat about what it's like
to be our kind of mess

and I've heard people say
how can boys and girls just be friends?
Especially bisexuals
for whom "there is only prey"

truthfully I don't know what to believe
since in a way it's like that
but it's more like
for either team we could bat

in a way we could have anyone
or more likely have none
can't make friends
when your orientation makes it end

but I've got a new friend now
with loads to talk about
half for his pets that made my class say wow
and half because we're both out.

Rated R

Benji came across first as very "metro-sexual" because most times people met him, he was attached to a girl, but had a quite unique voice and talked about things like whether or not someone's outfit matched.

People would ask girls who dated Benji if their boyfriend was gay, and they would get very upset and defensive. They knew he was into girls for sure, and he had a track record to prove it.

"I've slept with two hundred fifty six people," he would brag, and some girls thought nothing of it. Benji always made sure he said people.

Some people didn't know if that was really his number. Benji had the charisma that made some of his stories seem believable, but he still was considered questionable. He proclaimed that he got tested every six months for all sexually transmitted diseases and infections. One of Benji's famous stories was that he had Chron's disease (it could have been true but there was never any proof of any of his stories) and he got tested at that frequency because if he got an STD his Chron's disease would be affected.

Benji was quite a personality. His eyebrow and tongue were pierced, his ears were stretched, one of his arms was tattooed. He had tattoos on his chest and ribs, his nipples were pierced, and at one point he swapped the eyebrow ring for a nose ring. He was always found in skinny jeans.

"Your pants are tighter than mine!" girls would whine, and he would make jokes about the pants looking better on him, anyway.

Benji could be loud and he talked about obscene things. Often, he said things that made people uncomfortable. He was extremely open about his sex life and often engaged his peers in laughable conversations about bedroom things. Sometimes, all people could do was laugh when he said things.

One of Benji's stories was that he used to be successful in the music business as a rapper. He spent money on his friends saying he had money in the bank because of his rap career.

Benji masqueraded as a straight boy who got around with a lot of girls, but he was really bisexual. He was somewhat out, and a lot of bisexual girls he slept with knew. Most of the girls that Benji hung out with he had slept with. Benji claimed not to sleep with boys anymore. Benji was a womanizer and seemed to be a user of guys as well.

Sometimes Benji flirted with guys who couldn't tell that he was flirting. Benji was proud of his "game" and claimed that he could get anyone he wanted if he tried.

Benji may have had his genuine steady friend group or he may have floated around many different groups of friends. He was a bit of an enigma. Some people that knew each other knew some things about him. For example, they may have known people he slept with. Several girls met their "Eskimo sisters" through him. They may have known cars he drove – the Saab, the Saturn, the Passat – all stick shift, of course. They may have known some of the ink on his body – the Scorpio symbol with the number fourteen (his birthday, and his best friend tattoo with one of his homies), "believe" across his ribs, the flag of Germany looking fiery on his arm, his mother's initials in stars behind his ear, the microphone, the Notebook quote – claimed as his favorite movie – or the letters on his arm, conveniently the initials of a particular ex-girlfriend of his though he swore up and down that they stood for "sober living beautiful" to mark the long time he went off drugs for lots of reasons. Some people might have known one or both of his houses, his dad's in one town and his mom's about an hour away. They may have known jobs he had – mechanic, EMT, kids' soccer coach assistant. They may have known schools he went to or any of his career dreams from rapper to pastor. Or maybe they recalled his music taste.

Some people learned from Benji. He could teach how to drive stick or how to pick up chicks. He could teach how to back in park or geography. He was definitely a smart guy, though he bragged about all the schools he got kicked out of. Apparently, he used to never back down from confrontation. He may have grown out of it.

Benji loved to make people laugh. He loved to have a good time in general which is why he was always up for anything, whether it was tossing a ball around, driving for two hours, or just sitting and watching movies. Benji loved to talk and always spoke in his particular voice, and usually said things for laughs or reactions. If it would make people laugh, Benji would probably do it, like cutting his favorite pair of white skinny jeans into daisy dukes and prancing around the house, flashing his thighs to a friend's mother.

Benji used to be the kind of guy who would drive forty five minutes each way just too see his friends for a few hours. He was also the kind of boy who would have mostly female friends. He could make friends with guys but he seemed to have different groups of girls who were friends as his friend groups. Allegedly, he had made his way through most of them in the bedroom. Benji was the kind of guy who would take girls out on dates more often than their boyfriends, and he was usually friends with the boyfriends. Allegedly, he got in many fights for being "Mr. Steal Your girl."

Of course, Benji's story had a dark side. He spoke of things that made some cringe and listened to music that should have come with a trigger warning. Since you were not around for Benji's younger days, you do not know anything regardless of anything that he has ever shared with you. Some found that frightening, intimidating. Others were fascinated by the mystery. Some who had heard and believed his stories saw him as broken and wanted to fix him.

Benji confessed that he too wanted people he could fix sometimes. He felt that it was fulfilling to fix someone. He declared himself crazy for what he had been through, and he said he liked his partners crazy, too. But he had a type of crazy that he liked best, and could rattle off a list of qualities he found desirable and why. He told shocking stories of people he had experienced.

One experience joked around with him afterwards.

"They asked about you when I went to go get tested."

Confused, Benji reply, "what?"

The girl quoted the doctor. "Have you ever had sex with a bisexual boy?" and grinned.

She had always seen right through him. All she ever said about his lifestyle was encouraging sexual responsibility. Benji was known to encourage bad behavior sometimes. Somehow, he could just charm everyone, even those who didn't find him attractive. She was one of those people. He saw through her, too, seeing exactly how bi she was. She was the typical half of a couple that he hung out with. For some reason unknown but typical to his character, Benji got along better with the girl in the couple. They were two of a kind. Bi Scorpio freaks. They thought the same way about human sexuality. They were both swingers. Benji encouraged the swinger in her. The three would go out to clubs, and Benji and the girl would have contests to see who could pick up more girls. So, it somewhat made sense that once the girl was single she got off with her friend Benji, but neither was ever actually into the other, so it didn't work.

Any of these characteristics could be why Benji's new girlfriend does not let him speak to other girls, or perhaps to girls he has slept with. He did always say he fancied a short leash, so he may not mind.

Benji was interestingly aligned with his life path to help people. When he was with Andie, he had a desire to be a pastor. Benji also expressed interest in wanting to be a psychiatrist, but how it would become easier to become a nurse. He later became an EMT. Benji had told Jaime about how he had developed Crohn's disease in his late teens, and how he had to be careful because of it. Sickness always helped people understand the value of helping others.

Jaime remembered getting her tongue pierced with Benji. He got his nose pierced. He was supposed to have gotten his downstairs pierced, but Julio's friend's dad the piercer was unwilling to do that for him. He ended up getting his nose pierced. Jaime was getting her tongue pierced to subtly show girls that she was into them. After getting it pierced, Jaime realised that pulling her tongue ring against her teeth a certain way was the quickest way to remember she was alive. Feeling quick pain that didn't hurt too bad reminded Jaime not only that she was alive but also that life was worth living. Benji felt similarly about piercings, as did her friend Sean. Getting tattoos was somewhat of the same experience, all the while adding art to the canvas of the body.

Every time Jaime was driving on Route Seven and she passed that seven-eleven, she remembered that rainstorm in which they crashed into that telephone pole in Benji's Saturn. They were perfectly fine, they had been wearing their seatbelts, and turned immediately to each other to ask if the other was okay. There was no real reason for them to have crashed into that telephone pole, and there was minimal damage. A broken headlight, and Benji standing out in the rain in his black and white plaid pajamas, as Jaime called Julio to tell him what happened.

Mr. Fix-It

SLB meant sober living beautiful, which was an anagram tattoo on Benji's forearm, and also initials of an ex he had. Allegedly, he had been terribly suicidal and into drugs at a point. Through music he discovered the beauty of living sober. He was so moved by sobriety that he got the tattoo, though six months later was smoking and drinking again but not doing hard drugs.

Benji liked girls he could "fix," and he favoured those with eating disorders and suicidal tendencies, but especially anorexic girls. He liked to feel helpful or important by getting these girls to eat again. Because of this he fell for Anabelle at first sight, and Sean for similar reasons. Benji's attraction to Anabelle and Sean was the reason for Jaime and Benji's only ever less than mediocre sexual encounter. That encounter also marked the only time she had ever met Benji's father, which later she cringed about, since his father was not a good man.

Sweet Songs Were Wrote for You

Sweet dreams were made of car rides with sing alongs and trigger happy songs. Sweet dreams were made of midnight laughter and thanks for the ride home. Sweet dreams were made of "can you please drive, I'm too high" and sweet dreams were made of just getting by.

Sweet dreams were made of besties, that's what they called themselves. Only for a bit more than a year, but that was long enough. Sweet dreams were made of swapping secrets and sharing sexual stories. Sweet dreams were made of treating each other for tiny times that felt like dates. Sweet dreams were made of the smiles they shared when Jaime would wait for the verdict on whether or not she successfully matched an outfit together (most of the time the answer was, "no, silly, your clothes do not match but you rock it anyway" or she'd change my mind and tell him, "oh, what do you know? You're colorblind anyway.")

Sweet dreams were made of Jaime and her bi best friend. Two Scorpio freaks, birthdays a week apart, and a few years. Two of a kind. They got along like two peas in a pod. And on top of their many similarities, add another one. They were both writers. He wrote music, songs, poetry of sorts. Jaime wrote stories and poems – poetry and prose. He called himself a rapper. He called his songs raps. Instead of verses, his songs were made up of bars. He had pretty clever bars, thanks to his quick wit. After he came out to Jaime, he expressed a desire to write a rap about what it was like to be bisexual and film a killer music video for it. So, it was only natural that he asked Jaime to write him some bars for the rap. The rap was set to the rhythm of "Sweet Dreams [are Made of This]" by Eurythmics and included the chorus. His repeating verse or bar went as follows:

"How can I understand my life

when it doesn't matter if I find a husband or wife

if you haven't guessed

I'm bisexual alright"

      Jaime's bars included one of his choruses at the end.

"Hold my hand

while you get me off

send me to another land

but you better know that I am the boss

I get off on you

getting off on me

I'm the type of lover who

you need to let be

in my dreams are a boy and girl

I'll break free of your ties

in my dreams is a conquered world

I'm choking out all the lies

I love it when my lover makes me bleed

show the world we've done the deed

I'll give you what you really need

cause it's your (o) face I wanna see

how can I understand my life

when it doesn't matter if I find a husband or wife

if you haven't guessed

I'm bisexual alright."

It was great fun, but he never recorded the song.

25 to Life

When Jaime found Benji's remix online, she felt a twinge in her heart. Her heart consistently ached for friends she didn't see or speak to anymore.

It was two AM and Jaime had been searching the web for music she wanted to download. After getting through celebrity songs, she got to songs by a local artist and friend of Benji's whom she had met. From his channel she ended up unearthing Benji's old channel from before she even knew him. There were only two videos on the channel. One was a song that she knew because he used to play it in his car. The second was a video in which he rapped a remix to an Eminem song, and Jaime had never watched it before.

At two AM laying in her bed, Jaime watched a four minute video of her friend looking like skin and bones from when his Crohn's disease was bad, rapping about traumatic events from his past. Before he started rapping, while the intro played, he was biting his nails and fidgeting, looking like he couldn't believe what he was about to say. When Jaime showed Sean the video, he said that Benji looked like he would make another suicide attempt after he posted it. Jaime thought that he might have.

When Benji came out to Jaime after the queer movie double feature (and, thereafter, the only time she had ever been granted control of Netflix at Julio's'), he told her about all of the things that he rapped about in the song. She felt bad for not believing some of his stories since they seemed like such tall tales, even though she believed his serious ones. Seeing him on video say all of those things shook her up.

She could imagine him saying that was good, and that he wanted to shake people up with what he was saying.

In his song, Benji discussed the effects that sexual abuse and divorce of his parents had on his life. Jaime was glad it existed, despite his flow with words being a slight struggle. The fact that it existed meant others could hear it too. In many ways, music was Benji's yoga.

Benji told Jaime that he had a tendency to "use boys as trash" because of the abuse that he had been subjected to. This was part of why Jaime wanted to talk to Le Feu about boys like Benji, not letting himself be used like trash, and male bisexuality in general.

"Maybe We Had More Than We Thought"

I remember everything

from the music Benji liked

and the cigarettes he smoked

to the hand with which he wrote

I remember everything

I knew about Benji

from his black and white

plaid pajama pants with the pockets

that I always wanted to steal

to the way he told me that

when he gave head he swallowed

and I decided to be just as real

because if he could do it,
then I could, too
and I remember the way he liked to get hit
and how there was nothing he couldn't do

I remember everything
including all the trades
we made
shirts and pants and shades

I remember how I gave him
skinny pants that belonged
to an ex of mine
and I remember the time

he had a music video to film
for a friend and
got me and this other girl
to dance dance dance

I remember how
he did something and
I have no idea how he did it
but I know somehow it was him

somehow he got
this one guy's girl
to give me head

in my boyfriend's bed

while him and two boys
watched and sent me
the evidence
we laughed about it later

we wondered where
he got his charisma
he even made it enticing
to spring across the parkway

I remember everything
like the love bites he left
I had to cover with my seashell necklace
after I tricked him

he got into my friend
and my friend's female friend
and I tricked my man ho
goofy boy

I never even
was into him
and vice versa
but I remember when we gave it a shot

we gave it

a one shot wonder
and it was a
total silly blunder

because somehow it came out
with us not getting to speak
anymore – what's that about?
When it's not romance (or sex) I seek

I see him sometimes
in my dreams
or are they my nightmares?
We bat for the same team

or should I say swing
and that's what I miss
besides the humor, the wit
it's the way he helped to bring

out my inner truth
and just like him
turned out to be a ho
and he is here no mo.

Nefertiti

Nef was an activist for social justice when she wasn't waitressing or travelling. Colombian, Italian, and Dominican, Nef was blessed with good looks and a youthful appearance into her mid twenties. Nef was a bisexual feminist, anarchist, and supported the Black Lives Matter movement. She loved intellectual conversations as well as debates, though she had a reputation for being a bit of a hothead with a short fuse and she had a weakness for gossip. One day she wanted to be a nurse, tapping into the healing energy of her true self. Once the goal was able to be discerned, Nef could begin planning a path on which to chart her course.

When Jaime and Nef got close, they had a lot of open discussions about sex. They often got vulgar or graphic, and because of the way they connected at the throat chakra, Jaime felt as though she'd found a new Rosie, because Nef talked with her like Rosie used to. Jaime recalled feeling this same way about SLB Benji for the same reason.

Jaime and Sean were naturally nice, until they had a reason to be mean, unlike people like Nef, who were naturally mean as a defense mechanism. You had to spend some time with Nef to see her be nice, she's do it in subtle ways, like compliments or being helpful. If Jaime or Sean were mean, they could be terribly mean, but only when provoked by something important.

"I Could Make a List of Reasons Why Mechanics Isn't for Me"

It's boring
I don't care to be the
tool girl
I've spent too much time
watching someone fix cars

it's dirty
too greasy
those hands are the worst
what a mess

it's too mathematical
too much science
too much that I
just don't get

it all smells
like him
definitely not
an aphrodisiac

it takes too much time
and I'm too impatient
for time is a valuable resource
and I could be doing better things

I didn't do my yoga yet
I didn't do my hooping yet
I didn't move my body
so I just can't

someone else could
do it better
they could do it for me

it's too much stress

too much liability
too much of everything
too much to handle

I'm not strong enough
he was too strong
he didn't like my girlfriend
and I was dressed like a boy

the day I started to hate
mechanics and car problems
and working on cars
and all that comes with it

Throat Chakra Connections

Communication and Social Interactionist Theories

The purpose of communication is persuasion, debate, sharing, explaining, information, instruction, cultural understanding, entertaining, and social contact. Great conversations leave people with feelings of having been engaged, inspired, understood, and connected. What are communication inhibitors and communication enhancers?

At least 70% of communication is nonverbal. Nonverbal communication includes kinesis, through which the body conveys meaning, para-linguistics which include gestures, intonation, pace, and tempo, proxemics, which involves the use of space, and we use our five senses to give and receive communication.

Social interactionist theory involves others affecting our self awareness. Socialization is the process of learning how to behave in one's culture. Cooley developed the concept of the looking glass self, in which our self image is developed by our feelings about our perceptions of others' evaluations of us. The looking glass self affects our socialization. It can, however, be influenced by future interactions. Is this a limiting view of how our self image is developed?

George Herbert Mead theorised that only certain people can influence self image and only during certain periods of time. He spoke about the egocentrism of young children, and how our beliefs about how others perceive us become more important as we grow. He came up with three stages; the preparatory stage in which children engage in social interaction through imitation, the play stage in which children start becoming aware of social relationships and are focused on taking the perspectives of others, and the game stage in which children's understanding of social interactions becomes more developed, and they begin to understand the attitudes, beliefs, behaviours of the generalised other (society as a whole). He theorised that people perform in ways based on what they personally believe and what society more broadly expects of them. Older children begin understanding the taking on of multiple roles, like for example how mothers are also workers, daughters, sisters, etc. Older children start understanding that other people have opinions on them which are influenced by their own actions and words, and start being influenced by the perceptions and caring about the reactions of significant others in life. Mead also theorised that each person has an, "I," and a "Me," and are an amalgamation of both. The "I" is the response to the "Me," while the "Me" is the social self.

Feminism and Yoga

Feminist yoga invites us to harness the day's energy, sift through mental junk food, and question our choices by asking ourselves, "is this adding value?"

The book Sexy Feminism offers a lot of insight on being a good feminist in the 21st century. Feminism is always intersectional, and based upon lifting our sisters. One must be a good friend in order to be a good feminist. They must understand that not everyone has the same expectations, they must be flexible, dependable, understand that friendship changes but they don't have to, make efforts to understand the lives of others, recognise that it is not all about them, know their limits, and have some kind of mother love (whether for their own mother, themselves as a mother, other mothers in their lives, or mother nature.) Women are too often seen as competing with men or not doing their jobs, and many women even hear things said about if they are close with a female friend (socialised with indirect aggression – see Odd Girl Out). Girls must be taught that the good girl ideal is not the only feminist option, and that being "nice" will not always get you where you need to be. There must be an option for psychological stability and confidence as opposed to popular girl models of self-loathing "Ophelias," hypercompetitive queen bees, and destructive mean girls.

"Generation Y girls want to be the kind of female who doesn't settle, who will pursue, in and out of a sport, a no-matter-what philosophy of life. They are locating their desire to go beyond what girls have been told to wish for. This means, among other things, to embrace other girls and value "girl-ness" at the same time as one aims to achieve at the highest level – a balancing act that requires young women to refuse the social pull to become athletic to prove themselves more than or different from being "just a girl"

"Surfing is a place for girls to develop strength, flexibility, confidence, face fears and push limits, and surfer girls don't go it alone or compete with other girls but instead deepen their connections with both friends and the environment."

"How do girls grow up strong? Where does courage come from? How does girls' ability to play sports and to win improve their life chances to flourish and thrive?"
-<u>Surfer Girls New World Order</u>

Feminism and Sex

We already know about the existential crises sex poses for both genders: how internalising of repressing arousal displays the virgin/whore dichotomy, and manhood equates to sexual desire. Feminism promotes sex positivity over slut shaming. We are bred to feed on guilt. Sex positivity allows us to feel good and recognise pleasures of life, and helps us to use pleasure as empowerment. Feminist sex is when sexuality is run on a personal agenda, not a male agenda, and when there is trust, thought, and discussion involved. Sex positivity encourages us to know what we like and our boundaries while inviting us into feeling sexy, confident, secure, and safe in a pleasurable, satisfying, guilt free environment. We can use it as a type of adult playground - exploring things that scare us in safe ways. Lastly, feminism encourages us to love our bodies, and be body positive. This encourage honouring ourselves and others by eliminating negative self-talk and gossip about others through ahimsa. When we consider harming others, we must also consider karma and the threefold rule what goes around comes around. We must be kind to get kindness, and we must not shame ourselves or others. All of these ideals line up with aspects of the yama Bramhacharya.

The Dance of Anger as it Relates to Yoga

The book The Dance of Anger shows us strategies for using anger to create new, more functional relationship patterns. We are put in a position of strength by making statements about ourselves through anger, because it helps guide our determining innermost needs, values, and priorities.

We must observe the characteristic style of managing anger – that of our own and others. Learning to observe and change behaviour is a self-loving process that can't take place in an atmosphere of self-criticism or blame. We must not get distracted from power to change the self by trying to change others. We must move away from ineffective fighting by realising we can only change and control the self. Silent withdrawal or ineffective fighting and blame are no match for the threat of self-change.

We are constantly dealing with daily hurt, anger, betrayal, jealousy. We are also always gaining clarity to discover the causes of those feelings There must be an expression of feelings, and we must use positive ways to express feelings (i.e. art, music, dance, writing, movement, talking). When we are absorbing anger, and voicing anger we must eliminate the fear of loss due to conflict (detachment) by eliminating all assumptions that conversation will end with conflict when it comes to voicing those feelings. This fear of loss due to conflict relates to separation and togetherness, where loss creates a fear of separateness and a desire to control reactions of others. It can create separation anxiety based on discomfort with separateness and individuality, which is rooted in family history.

After we accept and honour our anger, we can let go

of it more easily. We learn how to let go of feelings when we take a nivritti approach, but it is also important to be discussing with ourselves the right to feel those feelings. We must also accept feelings as fluid and smaller than us, and determine how our body reacts to those feelings. It helps us to observe and interrupt nonproductive patterns of interactions and to anticipate and deal with reactions of others.

For an expression of feelings, we must tune into the true causes of our anger and clarify our position. We must listen to our anger, and there must be clear communication. We can ask ourselves, "what do we currently do with anger? What could we try differently? What are we (not) responsible for? We must be careful if we find ourselves being compelled to do more of the same thing, thinking that repeating the same fights protects us from anxieties accompanying change.

Jaime's Feminist Yoga Goals for Girls

Jaime aimed to help girls build their sense of trust by learning to trust themselves, their bodies, trusting the practise, trusting the teacher, and through practise helping them gain the clarity to discern who to trust.

She wanted to inspire them to lift others, by telling them to be the vibe of the tribe you want to attract and act through ahimsa. She also wanted to help girls understand that when we do not put our primary emotional energy into solving our own problems, we take on others' problems as our own, and that it was important to learn how to not be helpful, recognising not having all the answers or solutions to anyone's problems. She hoped her classes helped girls to think about situations rather than remain victim to them.

She wanted to help girls to make the choice of living their authentic natures beyond social conditioning which privilege males by teaching them to view the self as a container of many possible selves or forms which including self-focused forms such as the self which was passionate about health or a career.

She knew that promoting feminist self love posed the threat of a conscious consumer. By radically loving and caring for self, by seeking information, by radically deciding we love our planet as well as ourselves, and loving those we cohabitate with this planet with, the world can be saved. Jaime was a part in raising a generation of more conscious youth.

Jaime felt that Girl Scouts helped to teach girls valuable life skills and wanted to partner with the Girl Scouts because she felt that the life skills gained through yoga of calming distress, emotional regulation, and gaining clarity aligned with Girl Scout values of honesty, respect, exploration.

Yoga was a valuable resource for recovery, for many things including addiction, depression, anxiety, eating disorders, and PTSD. Jaime often found herself getting asked if she cared about the environment, animals, and if she's an activist for those things. She either had to or didn't want to explain that for her, those things take a backseat, because she was focusing on the children – particularly LGBT youth. To protect the earth, one must teach the youth to respect the earth. This will only happen when we humans don't want to kill ourselves.

"Instead of putting all your energy into thinking about death, how about putting some energy into your own life?" - Hana-Kimi

How to Tame a Wild Tongue by Gloria Anzaldua

"I will no longer be made to feel ashamed of existing. I will have my voice: Indian, Spanish, white. I will have my serpent's tongue – my woman's voice, my sexual voice, my poet's voice." This quote is relevant to the throat chakra because no person should be made to feel ashamed of existing, and should have their voice, their voice that encompasses all of their vastness, all of their selves.

Intentional Language

Many teachers had begun to use the phrase "[my] friends" in place of "boys and girls" when addressing the children as a group. In some ways, this was to be inclusive of gender creative students. In other ways, the language is altered to avoid phrases like, "you guys," and to not but one gender consistently before the other so as not to send messages that one was greater than the other. Other uses of intentional language include referring to job titles with gender neutral words, such as "police officer" as opposed to "policeman," instead of "fireman," and "mail carrier" in place of "mailman." This is to encourage children that they can take on any career they want, regardless of their gender. It is incredibly important for children to see posture representations of people of all genders in all roles, both in and outside the classroom.

Mantras and Aum (ohm)

A mantra is a sound or word repeated, typically to aid concentration in meditation. Mantras can be intentions, and can therefore become very empowering, and easily taken out of the meditative context. Mantras are given, traditionally, not typically created.
Aum is a traditional mantra which symbolises the totality of all. It contains the first and last letter (sound) in the Sanskrit alphabet. Therefore, it means all that could ever be said, all that has ever been said, and all that will ever be said.

In the book <u>No Mud No Lotus</u> by Thich Naht Nich, we are given mantras for transforming through suffering. They include:
I am here for you.
I know you are there, and it makes me very happy.
I know you suffer, and that is why I am here for you.
I suffer. Please help.

This is a happy moment.
You are partly right.

Satya (Truthfulness)

> Satya is the yama of truthfulness. Satya and Ahimsa go hand in hand. One must be truthful, for lies and rumour cause harm. A lack of being truthful can also cause harm, because misconceptions can be formed or conclusions can be jumped to, but the lied can also become a internal burden. Satya refers to both truthful words and being in tune with one's own personal truths and aligned with their paths.

Words of Affirmation

> This language of love involves deriving value from words, either about being loved or telling someone how important they are. People who are auditory/linguistic cognitive learners tend to rely on words of affirmation as their primary language of love. Some say that math is the language everyone cane understand, but these people believe that that language is love and that it must be conveyed by using language. Jaime called herself "wordy nerdy" and had vivid memories of learning other languages at very young ages, writing poetry all her life, and writing quotes of funny things her best friends said in middle school.

Brow Chakra

Ajna

"Sight is not the only sense",

The Brow (or 3rd Eye) Chakra will show stories of what we see in our world, stories of change and growth. The Brow Chakra involves recognition of our place in our world. The Brow Chakra represents those moments when we say, "I see." The mantra for this chakra is "I am connected to my intuition" The Brow Chakra is located in the medulla, and is represented by the colour indigo. When healing the Brow Chakra with colour, indigo should be used, or if the Brow Chakra is overactive soft orange or peach should be used followed by a small dose of indigo. The Brow Chakra embodies the element of light and darkness. The Brow Chakra is ruled by the Sun, and its ruling signs are Capricorn and Sagittarius. Frankincense, myrrh, and patchouli are essential oils which affect the Brow Chakra, and one crystal which can be used for the Brow Chakra is Sugilite. One pose which resonates deeply with the Brow Chakra and can be felt in the whole body is supported balasana (child's pose).

When someone's Brow Chakra is balanced, they would be a visionary. When the Brow Chakra is in excess there is lots of fantasy or nightmares. When there is a deficiency in the Brow Chakra there can be a lack of common sense and forgetfulness.

Sunshine Soul

Jaime met Sunshine through Dream Girl, Krystal, and the raving and hooping communities. Dream Girl and Krystal were the type of girls to empower others by sharing their selfies.

Sunshine was someone who gave others the benefit of doubt, acted through compassion. She supported those struggling with self love and acceptance (a hard thing to do in a world that makes self-hate so easy.) She offered a listening ear and open heart to all, something she knew that queer people of colour were in need of this alliance.

Sunshine had a belief in everything and nothing, the spectrum of reality. She felt that love was the highest vibration, but it both hurts and heals. Sunshine believed in moving mediation as reflection, moments of self realisation, channeling untapped inner strength, embodiment of spirit. It was a time for her to channel energy, fluidly and freely, while sharing her creative gifts. She had a dream of incorporating her work into a more fully immersive experience which allowed self expression as well as an exploration of creative capacity through multiple mediums. For her, these moments mapped all that is (a part of you) true and powerful; reminding you to breathe – as that breath is guided it's used to reignite the inner fire. The success and well being of her loved ones brought her peace.

Sunshine was learning how to give herself care, through things like dancing, singing, listening to music, writing, yoga, meditation, hooping, bubble baths, reading, playing with her cat, or snuggly companion. Her current companion was a boy, but she felt that she had "no orientation" it didn't matter, she liked what she liked. Becoming herself was a transition from orientation to overall state of being. She felt that coming out was coming into yourself, into who you always were beneath who the world wanted you to be. She recognised different aspects to sexuality – including promiscuity, intimacy – and felt it was important to express herself in healthy ways and exploring sexuality is a huge part of who you are. She felt that an intimate/sexual relationship with the self was key to finding confidence, self esteem, and self love.

She believed in meditation and connecting with her body to rekindle a feeling of being happy with herself and her appearance empowering her to love herself. Her goals were being fully happy with herself and not letting societal standards affect her self views. She was in a time of serious mental, emotional, spiritual growth with herself and her art. Her hair helped her feel connected to body and divine spirit, as did expression without words. She was a fan of brain and body workouts (i.e. hooping doubles). She believed in her planet as her god. She knew she needed world peace (what everyone needed.) She found mentally, emotionally, and physically transformative energy cultivated through yoga. She said that after three days of daily practise felt a mind and body difference – a positive mood, muscle fluidity, her flow didn't feel forced, she felt happiness with herself and her body, and she felt more motivated. She felt a gratifying connection with her body developing

Sunshine felt the she had a terrible relationship with her body. She was in constant pain, but was working towards creating a better relationships with her body. Screw gender, she thought, I'm human. She felt gender labels segregate groups of people into categories.

Sunshine grew up Hispanic in the states and predominantly white high school. She was an indigenous Latin Native American (Taino.) She felt as though she had had to fend for self, and had no support system. She became an activist, but was uncomfortable with the activist title, due to lack of involvement because of social anxiety and sensory overloads. She fought for justice in moments when injustice is witnessed or experienced. For a while, Sunshine was involved with a QPOC kula in Northampton, MA. She felt that oppression was someone taking away the freedom to be herself, and that people should focus more on themselves because everyone should be able to believe in whatever they believe in without harming anyone. It was important to her to give a voice to those unwilling to speak.

She currently felt that she belonged to the festival community though she felt that that particular community was susceptible to artificial people who didn't really care for you. She was a part of the hoop and online communities, but felt a bit like she was living in artificial "like for like" world. To her it was all fake bullshit she was sick of. Sunshine thought everyone should be themselves.

How To

"Shit," Pandora thought to herself. She had caught her eyes again down Blake's shirt.

Pandora could barely help it. Her new friend, Blake, was wearing a V-neck tee shirt, and the tops of her perky breasts were peeking out just enough to be distracting. But Pandora didn't want to blow it with her new friend by being caught checking her out. It was bad enough that Pandora had practically begged Blake to be her friend.

Pandora had a hard time making friends with other girls. At some point or another, she ended up creeping them out with her orientation. And she didn't even have to hit on them for them to become creeped out. Sometimes it was just complimenting them. Other times she got caught staring. Or it was the way she talked about other girls. It frustrated her.

Sometimes girls thought it was funny to tease her about it. They would be straight and act like her friend but then pretend to be bi-curious by coming onto her. Just like her friend Sean's sister Stacie who came to visit from the South, who teased Pandora by strutting around Sean's apartment in just her bra. Pandora was not sure how to tell if girls were going to be nice or not.

This is why Pandora had trouble making friends who were other girls. Blake was her new friend, they took a class together. Pandora thought Blake was such a clever girl and they seemed to share some interests. Pandora was excited for her new friendship. But still, so scared. Because she caught herself in moments like this, when she was staring down her new friend's shirt.

Blake noticed the darker skinned girl staring at her. She laughed. It made her feel curious. Why did the other girl look at her like that? What did she want to do? Blake wondered to herself. She started asking questions aloud.

"What do you want to do, Pandora?" Blake asked, drawing out her words.

"What?" Pandora looked forward as she blushed.

"Why do you look at me like that?" Blake asked.

Caught off guard, Pandora tried to explain to Blake

that she found her incredibly attractive, but was trying not to think of her in that way because she assumed that Blake did not swing that way.

"What if I did?" Blake countered.

"Do you?" Pandora ventured.

"I don't know," Blake confessed. "Nobody's ever asked me before."

Pandora smiled at Blake, and chose her working carefully.

"Do you notice girls?" she inquired. Blake stared openly at Pandora's perky, brown breasts displayed by her low cut, magenta crop top, and her kinky, fudge coloured curls.

"I don't know. I am noticing you right now." Blake offered. Dark brown eyes peered into Blake's baby blues.

"Do you have any idea if that's because you know I'm noticing you?" Pandora waited with bated breath.

"I don't know." Blake admitted.

"Well, you figure that out," Pandora smirked. "And let me know."

Boys Don't Cry

Boys self-harm. Boys have eating disorders. Boys try to kill themselves. Boys get bullied and bashed, too. Boys can be scared of the dark. Jaime's friend Le Feu used the flashlight on his phone. Her boys Feori, Syd, and Julio carried knives, in case someone tried to jump or rob them. Boys have things to fear, and some choose to take precautions. Boys get hit by their girlfriends, or boyfriends. Boys get raped, abused, and taken advantage of. Boys need help, too.

Jaime knew these boys. She went to school with these boys. Boys like Alberto Tilanda, who went to her elementary school. In seventh grade, Alberto Tilanda had anorexia. They were twelve years old. He straightened his long, black hair, and wore black skinny jeans. You could see his ribs. He got called "a fag" for looking like this, and tried to make up for it with a promiscuous reputation, having short lived relationships with girl after girl. He was sensitive and emotional and cut his wrists with blades. His dad was in jail at the time.

Wren Kumo, a skater Jaime knew when he was thirteen was the nicest kid around, did anything for anyone. Kept his hair long. Giggled, often and loudly, and sometimes randomly to himself. He definitely got called queer for his sense of humor somewhere at some point. His girlfriend put him in the hospital for bruised on his face. None of his friends knew how to help him. They don't teach you these things at school.

Boys like Jaime's brother, who would call Kumo a "pussy" and tell him to "man up." Even though they act like there was never a time in which they were vulnerable, having anxiety, and trying to kill themselves. They need feminism too, regardless of how disgusting some of them have become due to the male misconception that they must make females their slaves. They need feminism so that they are not conditioned to be these barbarian robots and can show real emotion.

Freddie Pasto, who Jaime met in second grade ended up addicted to heroin. At thirteen he went through a black nail polish phase which included hair straightening and occasionally trying on dresses. As he got older, he would wear items of girlfriends' clothing or jewelry. People found it to be amusing and soon he found school to be worthless. No one bothered to find out why he kept dropping out of school year after year. He turned to drugs to try and take away the pain of his problems. He is now in recovery, after serving jail time. He wrecked Jaime's red car while on drugs.

Boys like Sean and Benji, who were sexually abused in their youth. Boys who remember the names and faces of their abusers. Boys who wear skinny pants and pierce themselves and love to feel pain – who turned out to like boys despite having been abused by them. One who "used boys as trash" and one whose current boyfriend tries regularly to get with him while he is sleeping, who chooses to find creative ways to avoid his boyfriend's affections including spending all day cooking in order to be too busy to kiss or cuddle. Boys who once needed a cocktail of pills to be considered "normal" or "functional." They're all boys who need feminism.

Boys need feminism because Jaime was a girl who has hit her boyfriend before and even though she didn't leave marks that was not okay.

"Children of the Internet"

I must admit
we found it to be beautiful
to watch the way we could kill
ourselves
like when smoke filled our lungs

and in our reckless youth
no one could tell us it was never
beautiful
just
a part
of our culture

grateful for the sunshine
grateful for the power line
though it disrupts the pretty sky
but for the ability to connect
to try to convey
what I see through my own eye

we have grown up
broadcasting our lives
Children of the Internet
tournez-vous, lever la tete

but you can make friends
on the internet
the list of people you could
find on the web never ends

Like Slam the Poet
and wouldn't you know it
we had liked some of the same books
and we both liked to write

turned out to be on the spectrum, too
just like Kiki the forest girl
found her online and didn't know what to do
thought I'd give dating apps a whirl

but nothing came of it
but someone to send messages to
when you don't have anything
better to do.

"What's the Difference?"

Jaime didn't remember if Rosie went from being bi to pan or if she had always proclaimed herself pansexual, but she did remember a conversation they once had.

"What's the difference, anyway?" Jaime asked her, while nibbling on some food.

Rosie gave Jaime that look like she should know better.

"The difference," she sighed "is that I can be attracted to anyone."

Jaime rolled her eyes at Rosie.

"Yeah, me too, Ro."

She narrowed her eyes.

"No, you limit yourself to boys and girls."

Jaime became exasperated. Jaime wanted to say to her, "well what else is there?" but she knew better. Since I was eleven thanks to the Rocky Horror Picture Show and the internet she had an understanding of transvestites, and at thirteen she began to understand the meaning of transgender.

She understood there was an in between area between girls and boys. People these days refer to that as "non-binary." Personally, she felt in between girl and boy. She explored crossdressing and binding my chest. Jaime made an attractive boy, but didn't like binding.

The same year Jaime made her first real trans friend she began to consider herself genderfluid. She was fifteen. The decision was within only weeks of meeting him, and knowing him didn't affect her personal exploration and discovery.

His name was Elliott. He was the most beautiful boy Jaime had ever seen in real life. He had great style, an interesting and quirky personality, was a man of many talents. Jaime totally had a crush on him, and even though he was gay she got to kiss him twice. They went swimming together once, and even with his chest wrapped up in ace bandages Jaime still thought he was a beautiful and wonderful boy.

Therefore, she did not rule out people on the lines in

between from her pool of potential suitors, lovers, or crushes. But she still didn't really see the difference between bi and pan or the need for a new label. she saw people as people. If they were beautiful, inside or out, then they were beautiful. If they weren't, then they weren't. To her it was that simple. Like in books she had read, she fell for beautiful people.

Jaime didn't really know how to bring that point up to Rosie. She tried my best to explain, but Rosie's reply was, "so you're pan."

For some reason, that made Jaime's stomach turn.

"No, I'm bi. That's what I came out as, so that's what I am."

"But that's not what you have to stay. Isn't it great to figure out what you really are?"

"Ro, I recognize that orientation and preference can change, but I can tell you for certain that I'm a Kinsey three and I just don't really think pansexuality is a real thing. I mean I've always been bi and I've never noticed a difference between boys and girls and anyone in between."

Rosie didn't like that at all, because she told Jaime that she was panphobic. Jaime couldn't say her opinion changed after anything Rosie said.

Jaime had used her orientation as a way to feel comfortable with the fact that any kind of person could catch her eye and that she wasn't a boys-only girl. She stopped seeing the difference between boys and girls when she stopped seeing the difference between herself and a boy. Boys could wear makeup and dresses and skirts or lingerie or heels... and boys could kiss boys, and girls could kiss girls, girls could be womanizing, girls could do boys... the list goes on. For Jaime, it usually came back to one of two things - "what's the difference?" and "why not both?"

She still can't tell the difference between if she's panphobic or if pansexuality is kind of an unnecessary label. Rosie didn't stick around long enough for Jaime to find out. When someone declared that their identity, she normally smiled and said, "okay, cool," and thought to herself, "what's the difference?" because she kind of thought that all beings were somewhat fluid anyway.

Jaime's conversation with Rosie reminded her of one she shared with Le Feu when he was discussing getting off of eating meat. He had talked about how he wasn't ready to give up chicken, and Jaime suggested to him that he could be a "pollotarian," which was a vegetarian who ate chicken, similar to how a pescatarian was a vegetarian who ate fish. Le Feu laughed, saying, "it's just a title." Jaime laughed harder than he did, someone who was so concerned about his own title getting out would still shrug off a different type of title as meaningless.

After research, Jaime discovered that transphobia was creating a biphobic idea of bisexuality. Trans people are not meant to belong in the "other" category, that's for nonbinary folk. A transphobic and biphobic idea of bisexuality results in tension between bisexual and trans/nonbinary communities and constant fighting between bi and pan communities. What was needed was the reduction of fighting and tension between pan and bi communities and bi and trans communities. What people failed to have was acceptance and recognition of pansexuality falling under the bisexual umbrella, both polysexual orientations. The bi and pan communities are constantly fighting monosexism. There is no reason why single gender attraction should be the standard when there is so much mixed sexuality in other species.

Jaime recognised pansexuality as maintaining liberal socio-political ideology regarding gender about being between the binary. If Rosie was still around, Jaime would have said all of those things to her.

When she got older, Jaime started to think of pansexuality as relating to the god Pan – who had the power of wild things, nature, music, creativity, poetry, and sexuality. Worshipping him could sometimes cultivate abundance. Through yoga and her worship to the god Pan, she was able to
discern truth behind the veil of the ways people with mixed sexuality should stand together, through acceptance of

pansexuality as a subset of bisexuality, recognising that the spectrum of gender was similar to the spectrum of sexuality. While Jaime had discerned her truth at a young age about her true self being a non monosexual and nonmonogamous being, she recognised that a big difference between her and other polysexuals was that not all polysexual people were polyamorous like she was.

One day, Jaime happened to find a button with bi pride colours which read
"We are here to awaken from the illusion of our separateness" - Thich Nhat Hanh
She took it as referring to how polysexual folks have awakened from the illusion of separateness between genders and between humans.

The book <u>Bi Any Other Name</u> makes excellent points about this. One of the many authors of the compilation remarks that "many see bisexuality as threatening our acceptance of good versus evil, us versus them dualism. If it is possible to like males and females then it is possible to be both good and evil." The Japanese slang for bisexual translates to "one who uses both souls," or "one who wields both swords." One French slang term for bisexual is "voile et vapeur," which translates to being powered by both steam and sails. Some people cannot handle the concept of duality within individuals. We do not have to be either or, when we can be both and. Many polysexual people operate very much in concepts of duality within the individual, and as such, some experience "gender confusion – bisexuals sometimes do not feel or define themselves as wholly male or female – men and women being variations on a theme, not opposite sexes." Often polysexual people are reprimanded for their refusal to choose. Many see this as a way of giving themselves equal opportunity. Polysexual people, bi and pan alike often get the short end of the stick by getting inner community hate as well as outer community hate – the queer community tries to shut them out for their "ability" to "pass" as straight, but the straight community shuts them down for being "greedy." For this reason, the bi and pan communities truly must stand together.

Yoga helps us to awaken from the illusion of our separateness from the rest of the world, when we realise that we are one with the Atman. For Jaime, polysexuality was the way of the Atman, awake from the illusion of separateness and loving of all.

"Always a Center Kid"

It's days like these
that remind me
of when we used to walk
to the bridge after class

bikinis were on at school all day
sunshine begging us to come away
it's hard to believe that it was
simpler then

but when
I strut down the only hallway
in high school that I liked
pass the junior Japanese class on speaking test day

traded my keys
for a visitor's badge
can't stop these
lips from this great big grin

remembering when I was the one in
this hallway taking my test
and some of the things that I remember best
wouldn't be allowed now

like when you'd see a former student
just sneak into your class
out in the zen garden
face pressed against the glass

I guess things were different back hen
but it should be no surprised
that I drove to the beach when
I left my old high

I was only gonna look at the waves
but then the best Beach Boys song came on
and really brightened my day
just like it would've down that special hallway

back in my day
we had to be afraid
some of us could come out and play
while others got played

back in my day
you might not have known
everyone who was gay
some people never let it show

maybe when it comes down
to the things that are different from these
days in this town

I can hope that how it is
in high school has changed
for every child of the rainbow
where gay is okay

cherry blossoms bloom
and love is in the air
the sun and a tune
give me hope that it's fair.

Election

Thousands, possibly millions, of LGBT youth will be worried until tomorrow night. Possibly, depending on who gets elected, the next four years will be filled with worry.

At twenty one on Election Day, this is Jaime's first experience being able to vote. Living in a city surrounded by small towns full of rich, white, "self-made" cismen, there are plenty of Trump supporters around. Every time she saw a Trump/Pence sign outside someone's house, she felt physically unsafe – even though you'd never know where she falls on the LGBT spectrum.

Jaime's first experience voting took place at her middle school – a place she had gotten suspended from after threatening her bullies, and a place at which she'd been forced to apologise to them. There were ten Trump signs outside and zero for Hillary. It was probably the first time Jaime had been inside since she'd graduated eighth grade. She recalled being thirteen on election day and terrified for who would win – to the point of contemplating suicide. At twenty one she now faced a candidate who posed a threat of conversion therapy for LGBT folk.

When you're young and LGBT you don't get into politics for fun. You get into politics because your rights are being threatened. Jaime has been into politics since she was thirteen.

The election was called, Trump won. Plenty of people are incredibly angry. There is plenty of hate around. Jaime's mission is to protect the youth.

We must also remember that even though there is so much hate in the world there is also love. This is an important time to not discredit the love that some of our families have fr us as well as our friends.

It is perfectly okay and reasonable for us to be angry. We have the right to be furious. We have the right to protest. Especially with threats like conversion therapy.

But things are already getting violent. They want us to be angry, violent, and full of hate. They want us to forget about the love. We must cling to the love. The love helps cultivate hope. We must love each other more because this is our shared struggle. Through love we will create and maintain our safe spaces. Through love we will protect our youth. We must hold each other closely.

This means – don't abandon the guy your ex-boyfriend cheated on you with, and don't abandon the ex-boyfriend, either. We're all gay. We can't afford the inner community hate. We can't be torn apart. As a community, we must not be broken. We must show them – their hate will not break us. We have love. We must show them love is stronger. Love is love, and love will win.

We may be angry and that's okay. We're angry because we have love – love for ourselves those of us who worry for our own rights, and love for the people in our lives whose rights we also worry for.

After the election, in response to the president-elect's beliefs, there were many Women's Marches around the globe, which was the largest nonviolent protest since anti-Vietnam protests in 60s and 70s. There was worldwide participation of 4.8 million people, with 673 marches worldwide.

"We have to commit to what aligns us, standing together steadfast and determined, it's the only way we stand a chance of saving the soul of the country." – America Ferrera

Try Not To Mention It

Kal woke up as he usually did, next to his boyfriend, Kenai. Kenai was still asleep, an arm draped across Kal's chest. Kal smiled, he loved the way they looked together. Kal's skin was dark like chocolate, and Kenai had lovely caramel coloured skin. Kenai's long, straight, black hair was pulled into a messy topknot with an elastic, some loose strands of hair had escaped and were across his back or falling around his face. Kal's own kinky curls had been tightly braided last night into cornrows.

Every morning, when he woke up, Kal prayed. He knew that there were many people who were not as lucky as he was. He prayed for all of his Afro and Latinx brothers and sisters who came out to families who were not accepting of them. He prayed for all of his Afro and Latinx brothers and sisters who were too afraid to hold hands with their partners in public. He prayed for all of his Afro and Latinx brothers and sisters who were brought up by such religious families that they were too afraid to come out. He prayed for those same Afro and Latinx brothers and sisters – kids – who thought something was wrong with them, who cut themselves or starved themselves, who clung to any little positive sign they could if they had any. Kal prayed for all the people of Kenai's culture and all the other cultures he didn't belong to – for anyone oppressed or discriminated against, he prayed for peace. Kal wished for some way to help the children of this world, so he prayed for that too.

Kal's sister walked in, clad in her scrubs. She knew how late Kenai slept.

"Kal, baby, they need me in early at the hospital today. Can you please take your niece to her first day at her new preschool for me?" Her question was not really a question. She knew that her little brother would say yes. Kal dressed in his khakis and a purple polo, actively deciding to make a good impression. Kenai rolled over and inquired why his boyfriend was getting dressed so early on his day off.

"I've got to take Taz to school for my sister," Kal

explained, planting a kiss on Kenai's salmon coloured lips. "I'll see you when I get back, my love."

"They're going to know you're gay in that shirt," Kenai joked, but Kal took it as a warning.

As Kal drove his niece he asked her, even though she was four years old, if she could try not to mention to anyone at school that someone in her family was a boy who had a boyfriend.

"Okay," she agreed. "But why?"

Kal thought for a minute, changing his original answer from 'some people don't like that' to "Because not everybody's family is like that."

"Oh," the little girl said. "Okay!"

Kal walked with Taz to her classroom. Her teacher had a long braid going down her back, and was wearing leggings that had all the colours of the rainbow on the sides with symbols in spots of colour and a t shirt with the word "family" printed across it with each letter a different colour of the rainbow. Kal smirked. The teacher widened her legs and squatted down to speak to Taz, careful to make sure her knees did not go over her ankles.

"Good morning. My name is Jaime and I'm going to be your new teacher? What's your name?" Jaime had a bright smile, but Taz still hid behind Kal's legs. Kal pulled Taz off his body and got her to quietly introduce herself as Tazlynne.

"And I'm her uncle, Kal."

Kal shook hands with Jaime and she handed him a stack of papers.

"These are for the family," she started. "I'm hoping that families will get involved with the learning experiences of their children. Illustrated are the methods I'll be using. We're going to have a wonderful year."

As Kal walked back to his car he read the papers. The teacher described including in the curriculum meditation and mindful movement such as yoga, as well as swimming, gardening, and cooking. Kal smiled. He thought Taz would have a wonderful year. He prayed for more teachers like Tazlynne's.

"Becoming Glitterboii"

don't get bitter
find the glitter
make it better
write your future self a letter

make your project extra bright
to shine like long blond hair
billowing out in to the air
make sure you do the makeup right

teach all your friends about being queer
tell tales of living elsewhere than here
open up people's heart brains and peer
around to see what's near

get people talking
enjoy the steps of walking
put sparkles on the story
retell it till you're forty

make sure people know
help them find a safe place to go
listen when people feel low
and always put on a show

Teaching Lil Lars and Twister

For a short while, Jaime taught a very impoverished demographic of preschoolers. In this class, Jaime taught a Little Twister and a Little Lars.

These were two beautiful little boys, with big eyes, and long lashes. Little Twister was light haired and had eyes that changed from brown to green. Little Lars had a darker complexion, and curly hair. They were not related, but they fought like brothers. Each of their families spoke Spanish exclusively.

In some ways, these boys displayed bisexual tendencies at the early ages of three and four. Little Lars loved art and dancing. He also enjoyed dramatic play in the kitchen. None of these are indicative of any kind of orientation, but if Little Lars developed these hobbies into his older age, he would get called gay. I don't know why, it's just like that. Culturally, he might get steered away from the arts and steered towards sports as they're more "manly" hobbies.

Little Twister was slightly more obvious. He too enjoyed dramatic play in the kitchen as well as in the dollhouse. But Little Twister tended to hug boys more than girls. Little Twister enjoyed dancing, but his dancing was mostly in his hips, Little Twister liked to shake his booty. Little Twister also liked to dance with his young male friends, holding their hands. Little Twister had an edge – he cursed like a sailour. But he also had a soft side, it was by no means rare to catch him crying. The kicker with Little Twister is that he would grab other little boys by the face and kiss them on the mouth. I witnessed this one day as he pulled away and he looked up at me and just grinned. I merely grinned back, since you wouldn't catch me stopping that.

These boys will experience plenty of troubles. As if their language barrier wasn't enough to frustrate them, to be able to foresee these boys getting bullied for their interests was heartbreaking.

Jaime hoped to change this with future generations. The best she could do for Little Lars and Little Twister was

444

encourage them to keep dancing, painting, and playing in the kitchen. And to hug them a little extra, on their tough fighting days.

Eyes On Our Kids

We've watched the growth of many. We've helped plant seeds that grew into flowers. We've helped to create strong and capable adults.

We have eyes on the world. The big picture as well as our personal bubbles. We've got eyes on everything going on, so we know what to protect our children from.

We see all these kids and we see them completely and respect them. We see what they experience and we see exactly how much we can or can't help them.

Our service is invaluable. We facilitate their youth group. We create their safe space. We provide them with education and materials that they're interested in and start education and materials that they're interested in and start discussions and debates on a plethora of topics.

These kids were invaluable. They each had their own unique spirits and gifts. They each had their purpose in the world.

We felt with them as they shared. We rejoiced with them, celebrated with them. We watched as they got jobs and got accepted to colleges, we saw how their circles changed and stayed the same. We were sad with them, anxious with them, hopeful for them. We were angry and frustrated with them when there was injustice. We learned with them, for we were not experts. We cultivated strength with them. We watched them as they left the youth group's circle of seats to go live their lives. Some came back, others we watched from the sidelines. We saw who moved away, who became busy with work. Sadly, we watched some of them go into hospitals, prison, or heaven as well.

Somehow, we realised we had helped them as much as we could have. They had grown up before our very eyes, and with our help. They were on their own now.

We see when it is time for it to be their turn.

We have served our purpose

Nobody Forgets Their First Lesbian

Jaime saw that there are people, even within her own community, who will tell other people's business and out them without permission.

She saw that she was one of these people sometimes.

She see that as a community we are imperfect.

When Jaime was in seventh grade, and her Girl Scout troop met under her church, Ebeneza outed Akiko to Rosie and Jaime. It was one of those times where the word lesbian was whispered in the way they had discussed at the Alliance once. Neither Rosie nor Jaime really cared, except that when they finally met Akiko, they thought, "oh, that's the lesbian one."

Akiko was Chinese, adopted by white people. Jaime had hung out with her alone once and been slightly afraid. Who really knows of what. Akiko wasn't the type to out anyone.

Akiko later became Oliver, a transition no one was particularly surprised about, but one he got to out himself about.

Jaime saw that there were still many problems to fix.

Akiko's First Girlfriend

Akiko's first girlfriend was a Latina girl called Andromeda. Dromi was someone attracted to strong minds, and she had a strong preference for women, though she was open to guys, too.

Dromi had been hiding her relationship with Akiko from her family. Her mother caught her on the family computer sending messages to Akiko, and she'd ended up with a black eye. Eventually her family grew to accept it. Dromi came from a family in which males were present, and though she'd grown up dressed in dresses, she'd also been allowed to play any sports she'd wanted to.

Dromi had her own ways to relax, like riding her motorbike, going to the batting cage, or going to look at the water. She enjoyed the warm weather and admiring art.

These were all pieces of her yoga.

Like many high school relationships, Dromi and Akiko's ended. Jaime and Dromi attended a prom together, and after high school, Dromi went into the marines. Dromi and Akiko remained friends into his transition to Oliver.

Brow Chakra Connections

"I talk to the moon and she tells me it is okay to change" - Lauren Eden

"No society wants you to become wise, it is against the investment of all societies. If people are wise they cannot be exploited." - Osho

"If you've witnessed a truly compassionate being you've also seen a truly wise being and a wise being isn't going to be taken advantage of. Wisdom and compassion are like the front and the back of a hand; they go together." - The Gift of Well Being

Anarcha-Feminist Yoga Empowerment (the Threat of Conscious Consumers)

     Some people fear the power of yoga. Some religions consider yoga heresy. I think that people are afraid of what could happen when you become empowered. What if we did something radical and loved ourselves? Industries would lose their power. What yoga does, among many things, is to help you recognise your divine qualities. As you focus on your body's alignment, you become more aligned with your life path or soul purpose. As you focus on your life force or prana (your breath), you begin to realise the beautiful magical gift of life.

     This is threatening to the establishment. If we don't hate ourselves, then what can they convince us we need? If we are self fulfilling, then how will we believe that material items will fill a void in our lives? Imagine what happens when you learn to self regulate. When you learn to focus on your breath and your body and learn to meditate, you become in control. When Jaime learned to self regulate, she felt much better about her anxiety disorder.

     The practise of yoga asks you to consider what you put into your body as well. Imagine what conscious consumers would do to society, even if only when it comes to food. Imagine still if we decided that it was no longer beautiful to slowly kill ourselves with the sweet smoke of cigarettes. It is no wonder that people fear the power of yoga. But yoga is nothing to fear. Yoga is the practise of training your body and your mind, through which you become empowered as you discover all of your divine qualities.

What Fuels Your Feminism?

Is your feminism fueled by helping schools to overcome the gender bias and teach good relationships and consent, reducing domestic and sexual violence, supporting women to go into business, public life, and politics, women in poverty, or challenging the objectification and pornification of women? A handout Jaime received from a group called Feminist Fusion advertised that if any of these causes appealed, "join your energy to ours."

Anarcha-feminism generally views patriarchy and traditional gender rules as a manifestation of involuntary coercive hierarchy that should be replaced by decentralised free association. Anarcha-feminism is an anti-authoritarian, anti-capitalist, anti-oppressive philosophy with the goal of creating an "equal ground" between both genders. Authoritarian traits and values correlate to a "masculine model" of domination, exploitation, aggression, and competition. These qualities are integral to hierarchical civilisations. Anarcha-feminism advocates for a society based on cooperation, sharing, solidarity, and mutual aid without the imposition of binary models, opposed to traditional concepts of family, education, and gender roles that may submit women to abuse and restrict all from their basic rights to personal and social freedom (Feminist Fusion, 2017).

Anarcha Feminism as Discussed in <u>Bi Any Other Name</u>

"Like bisexuality, anarchism poses a challenge to the categorical way we think. Anarchism as a political philosophy places a high value on diversity, individuality, and self-identification."

The main principle of anarchism is that hierarchical authority is unnecessary and harmful, and humans realise their full potential through freedom. Anarchists believe that a just and organised society can be achieved in nonhierarchical and participatory manner based on voluntary, cooperative, decentralised groups. Here we can draw a connection from the book <u>Balanced and Barefoot</u>. "Play is guided by mental rules. When children get together they form their own rules (Gray, 2013). They are likely to assign roles to each other. Oftentimes in the woods at TimberNook, children create societies." (Hanscom, A. 2016) From this quote we can discern that children naturally know how to form voluntary and cooperative groups, yet another reason to listen to the child inside.

Anarchism is open to new ideas and adaptable. "This openness to change makes anarchism a natural framework for those excluded, ignored, despised" (i.e. bisexuals, feminists, lesbians, gays, trans people) (<u>Bi Any Other Name</u>) Anarcha-feminism focuses on not losing women's voices in revolutionary politics and ideally hopes the values of feminism will be infusing anarchist organising, process, and goals. Often, people become politically aware because of their orientation and being a victim of oppression, Jaime included. Oppression tended to bring an awareness of interconnections among various forms of oppression. Openness brings the realisation of the ability to refuse to adhere to hierarchical, sexist, heterosexist, and sex-phobic tenets one has grown up with and explore a variety of social and sexual alternatives. An awareness of anarchism and feminism seems to encourage people to question their assumptions about sexuality and relationships.

Anarchist activists are committed to changing society as a whole and creating a more equitable world where diversity is accepted and celebrated. They do this through reforming the system, finding ways to build strength and diversity by organising locally, emphasising education and exploration of creative tactics, devising ways to avoid despair about confronting capitalist society (i.e. yoga), demonstrations, and conferences or organisations.

Anarchism, feminism, and bisexual liberation are complementary. Our experience of each value system enriches and deepens the other two. Anarchism and feminism advocate the end of the domination of men over women, and some forms of feminism share with anarchism the desire to end all hierarchies. Anarchism and bisexuality challenge established categories and encourage us to view the world as fluid rather than compartmentalised. Bisexuality and feminism challenge traditional sex roles and notions of gender, as well as often addressing the politics of reproductive freedom.

Carpe Diem

A boy in his early twenties died abruptly and it shook the town Jaime grew up in. She had known the boy in elementary school, and her boys Liam, Le Feu, Ver, and J. Emballer had all been very close with him. Sean's friend, girl Sawyer, had known the boy and his younger brother, who was in critical condition. Jaime and Sean's friend, Nef, was friends with the gay older brother of the boy, who Jaime had met on her most recent lunch date with Nef. It was death of people as young as this boy and Jaime's friend Erika which offered Jaime the perspective that she must seize every day, and that life was something not only to be grateful for, but to be honoured. Jaime herself had difficulty with the death despite not having known the boy very well, because she had chosen the way he died as her preferred method of suicide when she still thought about suicide in realistic terms.

Seizing the day was often the topic of Jaime's meditation. She sometimes found it difficult to feel as though she was seizing the day when she had menial tasks to do like work or chores. Through meditation she was able to cultivate the understanding that seizing the days included the little things like enjoying a warm cup of tea, watching the sky change colours right before her eyes, a drive soundtracked with music that demanded motion, and curling up with books when the snow piled high outside.

Covens and Wise Ones

"The blood of the covenant is thicker than the water of the womb" (an idiom which refers to the importance of chosen relationships)

Covens help to reinforce concepts like safety in numbers and forming communities (kulas). The creation of covens usually means finding those who accept you, people to be with for support, people to be with in general. Covens help create relationships and bonds with strangers who share our interests. Covens also help teach us respect for elders as we learn from the wise ones.

Created Queer Culture

When Jaime did not know the answer about something related to queer history or queer culture, she turned to Glitterboii, who as a member of an older generation, was meant to guide Indigo children like Jaime. He knew much of what he knew because he did research in order to challenge Ms. Ratatano, their GSA leader, who felt the T must be separate from the LGB.

Society has buried original queer culture. We existed since the beginning of time but are only gaining language for different forms of existence in the present. Shame brought us down, but pride lifts us up. A united front is the goal, removing harmful stigmas and teaching pride in place of shame. Our history is rooted in hiding and uniting, and cultural erasure.

Pride is the ability to exist as exactly who you are, regardless of race, religion, sexuality, gender, etc. Queer is all encompassing, and stigma is the fault of oppressors. Regardless of how the world views us, our community came together to overcome adversity, which most previous movements failed at. The queer culture is about inclusion and coming together, as well as self discovery and the ability to love and accept someone unconditionally, the desire and ability to love and learn, and to make each other feel okay about life.

Queer culture is at the intersection of many cultures – black, women, trans, queer – and makes for difficulty discerning a true culture. To say something is ours and nobody else's is incredibly flawed, which is how people got left out of movements for change.

Decolonising Yoga

There is a disclaimer for Jaime's views on decolonising yoga. There would be those who tout Jaime's being and teachings as appropriation with her "dreads" (Celtic faerie locks) and yoga (as a "white hippie"). Jaime's sister taught her that policing cultural norms was antithetical to individualism, and that critics of cultural appropriation are trying to strengthen boundaries between groups. While it's important to recognise oppression, a person is only one person and not simply a member or nonmember of a group. When creating our own culture, we are balancing what we create with our heritage cultures as well as those we're interested in [borrowing from] and respectfully mesh together what we learn and what we like.

It is important to cultivate a practise which focuses around a cycle of swadyaya. It is equally important to remember that is the goal of yoga and that it has nothing to do with looking cute in yoga clothes, getting a "yoga body", or how the physical posture looks. Yoga has become a colonised culture of people who use it for the workout, the clothes, the challenging poses that make you look cool, and these people do not pay attention to the important history of yoga and spirituality of the practise. Yoga requires decolonising.

There are steps to decolonising yoga. Firstly, we must inquire within – practise Gandhian swadyaya – self rule and inquiry – and learn the full honest integrity of an authentic yoga practise. Next, we must make sure to be citing cultural references. This is why we study the Gita, and other yogic texts. We must ask ourselves, "for whom is yoga accessible today and how might that be a legacy of past injustices that we have the opportunity to address through our teaching, practise, and our lives?" Our answers must influence our action. We must live, know, share, teach, and practise Sage Patanjali's Eight Limbs. Aside from Asana, the physical practise on the mat, we must be aware of the Yamas which refer to ethical conduct, and niyama which refer to our personal practise, dharana, which means meditation, concentration, and insight, and dhyana, which means being present with whatever arises. Lastly, we must humble and honour journeys – our own and those of others. Ways to humble and honour journeys include listening to their stories, encouraging them to share, honouring our own journey with rituals and rewards.

"By really engaging the full, whole, and multifaceted face of yoga we not only liberate ourselves but we may just overthrow this second colonisation of yoga, freeing ourselves as well as the practitioners of the future to experience the full, liberating, authentic, and true practise of yoga. We allow our own practise to grow and our gifts to really shine."

Detachment

Detachment can be from memory associated with words, and re-associating the words with new, positive connotation. For example, for Jaime, detachment from associating the word "mechanic" with the word and memory, "rapist," and re-associating it with phrases like, "fixed," "good as new," "back on the road," and "helping keep me safe."

From within detachment/separateness, there is still togetherness, oneness, wholeness. To bring the world back together, by means of acts of kindness, one must be able to piece themselves back to wholeness. It takes many acts of kindness to the self in order to begin the process of completing the personal puzzle.

By detaching from feelings surrounding memories and emotions surrounding experiences, one offers themselves a great and courageous act of self care because it allows the most true meaning to be retained from the memories and experiences. By separating the emotions from the experiences and memories, one can hold onto the facts and the lessons. It is valuable to know that though experiences have happened, nobody is defined by how these experiences made them feel. Detachment for Jaime meant to detach from memories but not experiences – i.e. detaching from memories with Dawn and Rosie's group as being able to separate her experiences from the people she didn't want to remember anymore – realising she still had those experiences but that it did not matter with whom they were, because she was still with herself and with the universe. Detachment could be healing.

Through detachment from the ego and the separation of the ego and self, the nature of one's true self becomes more visible. Through detachment from the many aspects of the self, the many facets of the self become more visible. By neatly placing aspects of the self in little boxes, we give ourselves the squares with which to sew our quilt of completeness. Within wholeness, oneness, completeness, togetherness of selves, santosha can be found and cultivated. Santosha will warm us, wrapped in our quilt of whole, true self, and once warm we are able to offer kindness and compassion to others, having quieted our inner storm and made peace with ourselves, our minds no longer clouded by emotion. Relating this yogic thought to the Judaic concept of Tikkun Olam, it becomes a nivritti concept. Through santosha we learn to insert ourselves into the universal puzzle, and discover our role as a universal piece. This role is the path with which we must align, in order to fulfill our duty to our world to piece it back together and repair the damage done by us unto our world.

Jaime's issue [as someone who challenged the norms] was that she felt people at work wanted her to separate herself into tiny boxes, as though her identity was not one whole thing, she felt they expected her to be able to separate her bisexual self, her Wiccan self, and her warrior self from that self of hers which teaches children.

It took Jaime a long time to realise that through separation of selves, the view of the big picture became clearer, as the view of the self shifted to that which is a vast container, from whatever previous self concept was conceived.

Detachment [from emotion] is a nivritti strategy of yoga. This nivritti strategy can be utilised at times where normal emotion can become a distraction or cause problems, such as before or during work. Such skill at stepping out of the moment is required for many jobs involving quick thinking and decision making. It was like placing a spell on oneself to not react to life. The skill in the pause is the pure magic of the spell itself – the moment in which to breathe.

Detachment in Buddhism is a nivritti concept meaning "the art of understanding the impermanence of everything and becoming unattached to it all."

Dharana (concentration)

Dharana refers to the direction of thought and energy on particular subject/intention/mantra – the binding of the mind to one place, object, or idea. It can be thought of as the work it takes to get the mind to the point where it is ready for meditation. Dharana is considered to be less the state of concentration, but more the act of bringing the mind back to the focal point.

Yoga Nidra is a method of travelling through koshas – integrating and relaxing sheaths so intellect and pure consciousness can rest, and works on the three basic koshas. The Koshas are "sheaths" of the body – the first four will fade and be replaced by another body, breath, mind, and intellect, the first four koshas are tainted by trauma, dis-ease, etc.

The Koshas are
1. Anamaya – the physical body
2. Pranayama – the energy/vital body – regulated through asana and pranayama – each asana/pranayama is related to or influences a particular vaya and opens the subtle body. The life force of prana is divided into five functions or "airs"

- Apana – eliminative system, earth, navel to soles of feet, heavy, exhalation, down and up
- Samana – digestive system, water, cool, circular
- Prana - respiratory/cardiovascular systems, mouth to heart, fire, light, inhalation, up and down
- Udana – eating/drinking/speaking, throat, air
- Vyana – limbs, space

3. Manomaya – mental/emotional body – all emotions should not be refused, where we sense emotional vibrations, opposites in emotions, replenished/nourished by deep sleep
4. Vignanamaya – intellect/imagery/wisdom body – memories, ego, self concept (sense of self), believes, right/wrong discrimination, perception, and decision making
anadamaya – bliss body – only layer not on loan which travels with us from life to life – spirit, soul – core of being

Yoga Nidra involves guided breath meditation. Sankalpa are deep intentions to be set at beginning of nidra sessions for the good of the self and simultaneous realisation of truth and for good of world – through setting these we remove samskaras (ingrained habits). The steps of Yoga Nidra are internalisation – sankalpa – rotation of consciousness – breath awareness – manifestation of opposites – creative visualisation – sankalpa and externalisation. Yoga Nidra is referred to as a petal of dharana (release of senses and attachment to them, release of relying on senses to define world and states of being). Healing often appears to progressively proceed physical to mental, and even short term yoga nidra practise has showed increased grey matter volume in brain – especially in the hippocampus, xxx and yyy. In Yoga Nidra we use nyasa which are special mantras/root tones sent via thought into various parts of body. Yoga Nidra asks us to connect to our heartfelt desire, set intentions, find our inner resource (safe haven within body – experience calm, security, well being), scan our body, cultivate an awareness of our breath, welcome our feelings, and helps us to witness our thoughts, experience joy, observe ourselves, and reflect on our practise.

Dhyana (meditation)

Because yoga is a deeply meditative practise, affecting the deeper self, it leaves the energy pathways more easily open. This can lead to one exuding the energy cultivated through their practise, but conversely leaves them more susceptible to absorbing the energy of others. Once aligned with body, mind, and soul purpose, it is easier to tune into other frequencies. This is why shielding oneself from the energy of others is important. It is a skill which allows us to be there for others and be compassionate while not becoming affected by their problems or emotions. A nivritti concept which requires a certain level of dhyana – being present with what occurs. Ritual space blessing is an effective way to shield one's energy field, as well as the use of crystals, singing bowls, burning incense or herbs such as sage, and self energy cleansing. Regularly aligning one's chakras also aids this process of shielding.

Dreams

Before Benji's best friend, Brayan, went off to college, they'd had a dream together to own a bookstore and cafe in Paris. Brayan was Benji's friend who knew his true identity. Brayan and Benji had hooked up plenty of times, and they'd also taken part in orgies together.

Benji was plagued with insomnia, likely a result of his anxiety, bipolar disorder, and PTSD. He was prescribed medication for it and claimed to be unable to sleep without them.

Jaime noticed that many of the people she was friends with had dreams of safe spaces. Rosie and Glitterboii had dreamed with Jaime about having a drag bar in Amsterdam, and Jaime and Sean had dreams of a nightclub. Le Feu wanted to start his own park, Bounty wanted her own library.

One of the marks in the visual symbol for the word Aum/Om represents the dream state. The dream state is a map of our subconscious.

We dream because "dreaming is free" (Blondie).

Identity vs Role Confusion and Bisexuality and Gender Confusion

Identity vs role confusion is a stage of development which mainly affects adolescents, ages thirteen to nineteen. this is the point at which the development of one's self concept (and therefore identity) begins to flourish. What makes up identity? This is different for everyone.

As one begins to figure out how their identity fits into the world, they may experience role confusion as they explore the different roles that they might one day fill. Throughout life one may experience role confusion if an identity has not been firmly established.

Gaydar

Many queer folk claim to have some form of "gaydar," which helps them identify other queers. Jaime theorised that queers were on the same frequency or wavelength and emitted similar energy. It reminded her of the play Am I Blue? In which everyone in the world who was even the slightest bit gay turned some shade of blue for a day. The blue tint was a call to come out so that others would realise that we're everywhere. Like sensing our own species, it seemed that queer folk had chance meetings and were drawn to each other.

Glitterboii had talked to Jaime about how people had theorised that it could be an animal instinct to be queer, due to the absorption of feminine energy in the womb. Bisexuality was normal in other species, like dolphins and giraffes.

Syd used to tell Jaime that he could smell when she was turned on. From biology, Jaime had learned that if someone's body odour smelled good to you, they had the opposite immune system and would create stronger offspring. She also knew about pheromones. Pheromones are in human steroids, excreted through skin, skin glands, and bodily fluids. The Jacobsen's gland (vomeronasal) is the gland which helps us to perceive pheromones. Estraenol is the pheromone in female sweat and secretion.

Androstadienone is the pheromone in male semen and sweat. Jaime wondered if we could all smell those who could smell us. She wondered if we sent out pheromones so that our own kind could find us, seeking the energy of those accepting of our own kind. She wondered if gaydar was our awareness of these pheromones. She did some research and found studies on Towleroad which document times in which gay men and hetero women could detect males while watching ambiguous figures walking forward and being exposed to pheromones masked by cloves. In this same study, hetero males could not detect a male presence, but could detect a female presence, hetero women could not detect a female presence, and lesbian and bisexual women had mixed responses. This study teaches that visual gender perception draws on subconscious chemosensory biological clues. Another study Jaime found was by the National Academy of Sciences in 2005 which determined that the brains of gay men respond similarly to those of straight women when exposed to androstadienone.

Healing Mandalas and Colour Healing

Healing Mandalas

Healing Mandalas include patterns, colours, and designs created to elicit specific effects. Healing Mandalas work by stimulating inner creative forces in a manner peculiar to their design – through integration and transformation – action and interaction within ourselves. They stimulate primal inner sources – sources of healing. Mandalas work best when they are made personally. The creation itself of healing mandalas is intellectually stimulating.

Healing Mandalas can be used as a type of Apotropaic magic, which is intended to turn away harm. A Sigil is a magic design of intention. Many people use protective sigils for home and children, protective sigils on amulets or other jewellery, clothes, healing sigils, and sigils on the body for protection or healing in the form of mandalas, tattoos, and mehndi.

Mehndi Healing Mandalas

Mehndi is a type of body art done with dye from the Henna. Haldi is another type of body art done with plant based dye (Turmeric), and was used alongside Mehndi in Hindu Vedic ritual books as symbolic representations of the outer and inner sun. Many Vedic customs centred around "awakening inner light." The earliest recorded use of Henna was the ancient Egyptians. Though Mehndi is used traditionally at Hindu and Muslim Indian weddings and festivals, other uses are for rituals, as it is mentioned in Vedic texts in rituals to Hindu deities.

We recommend using Henna for Healing Mandalas in less visible places because of how it makes the canvas feel, but also because we are wanting to honour and respecting its traditional cultural place. There is a lot being said currently about Henna and cultural appropriation/misappropriation, begging the question, when and how is it okay to use? Ever? Similarly to how we must question yoga as cultural appropriation because British rule banned Indians from practising it and participate in the decolonising of yoga, we must consider if it is appropriate for us to use such forms of body art. Sherlock's opinion was that policing cultural norms is antithetical to individualism – one person, not simply a member or nonmember of a group, and that critics of cultural appropriate are trying to strengthen boundaries between groups. Making profit off of the other culture is not appropriate. It gets to be appropriative when companies make millions selling yoga gear, and the context of yoga should not be changed and limited to merely a workout. The same goes for Mehndi and Haldi. There must be acknowledgement and connection with cultural and spiritual aspects. It is not appropriative when culture is shared (like when Jaime and Jolie got to be dressed in kimono by their school in Tokyo). Ultimately it comes down to the principle of astya (non stealing) by giving credit where due and having recognition of the fact that the oppressed group was shamed for their expression of culture as well as having recognition that this oppression is still present and has gone on for hundreds of years and the acceptance of the fact that our choice to to appreciate the culture enough to borrow from it does not make us any better than those to whom it belongs.

Colour Therapy

"When feeling low, it may be time to sit down with a gorgeous array of colours on a palette and paint swirls, spirals, blend the rainbow, and feel freely. Any feelings can create a beautiful piece of art that acts as a fresh start." - Kirra Adams

Most colour healing resonates most deeply with the brow chakra, as that is from where one sees. Without the sense of sight, we would not know the beauty and amazement of that which is colour. As there are colours associated with each chakra, colour healing can effectively be directed to resonate with other chakras as well. Several methods of colour healing include visualisation, directing light, breathing colour, creating art, a combination of movement and light, and colour swatches. The Earth mother provides humans with spectacular displays of colour healing, as day turns to night, night turns to day, and seasons change. Each colour has a different meaning for healing, and the following are some examples.

This information comes from the book <u>How to Heal With Color</u>.
White – cleansing, purifying, strengthening
Black – protective, grounding, feminine, magnetic
Red – stimulating, activating, deeper passions, warming
Orange – joy and wisdom
Yellow – enthusiasm for life
Green – calming, balancing, growth

Blue – cooling, relaxing
Indigo – sedative, dynamic healing
Violet – skeletal, stimulating dream activity
Pink – compassion, love, purity
Lemon – vitalising
Purple – purifying
Silver – amplification
Brown – common sense and discrimination

Candle Magick is another method of Colour Therapy. The following information on Candle Magick colour meanings is taken from the books <u>How to Heal with Color</u> and <u>Gay Witchcraft</u>.

White – purity & power, union, all purpose, enlightenment, banishing, protection
Black – protective, grounding, centring, nature, facing shadow, attracting
Red – love, health, attainment of ambitions, passion/sex (life force), power, energy, lust, protection, aggression, warrior spirit
Pink – love and success, clean living, honour, vision of truth and success
Orange- joy and creativity, attracting, memory, mind power, logic, travel, healing
Yellow/gold- fulfillment of desires, understanding/stimulating dream activity, solar energy, health, power, wealth, illumination, revealing truth
Green- growth, movement, abundance, fertility, youthfulness, love, attraction, money, comfort, art, music, food
Blue – perception, quick money*, peace, tranquility, communication, expression, creativity, prosperity, opportunity
Grey/silver – clarity
Brown – neutral, grounding, discernment – St. Anthony the patron saint of lost things
Violet/Purple – spirituality, power, mastery, success, elevation

Purple – intuition, psychic ability, spirituality, awareness, guidance, prosperity

Violet – cleansing, clearing, releasing, spirituality, higher awareness, ritual

Humans Have an Innate Desire to Get High – Why?
From *the Conversation*

Humans have an innate desire to get high, according to an article Jaime had read on the Conversation, whether on drugs or hormones. For centuries, people have experimented with mind altering substances. We have also learned how good it feels to be high from adrenaline, endorphins, or the hormones released after sex.

Perhaps this innate desire is because drugs can provide shortcuts to transcendental religious or spiritual experiences. Religion can help connect people with a larger reality. Drugs mimic states of mind which played an evolutionarily valuable role in making human cooperation possible – like a "hack," enabling transcendent states to be reached quickly. Purists may object to taking drugs because it lacks spiritual discipline.

Psychedelic drugs may play a positive role in improving some people's mental outlook. There have been promising results on the effects of psychedelics on the depressed and terminally ill.

Some people use drugs to seek siddhis, seeing drugs as the means to unlock these powers. Others use drugs to numb pain. For some people the chemicals in our bodies are enough, for others they are not. Drug companies are hyperaware of our innate desire to get high, monitoring our youth eagerly.

"Today's teenager is tomorrow's potential regular customer, and the overwhelming majority of smokers first begin to smoke while still in their teens... the smoking patterns of teenagers are particularly important to Philip Morris" - Philip Morris, internal document (tobacco company, Like We Care)

Inclusive Community

"The circles of women arounds us weave invisible nets of love that carry us when we're weak and sing with us when we are strong" Sark

We must create a community inclusive of people regardless of their age, sex, race, orientation, religion, ability. There were so many inner community struggles (i.e. with the trans and bi communities). The LGBT community is a mirror of the community of humans in general. The need for an inclusive community is representative of the need for the whole human race to become more inclusive of each other. The inner community struggles are representative of the struggles across the human race with each other.

The Last LGBT History Lesson

Some events have already been mentioned, including the September suicides, book club history lessons about Stonewall, the AIDS epidemic and stigma, Matthew Shepard (who was tortured and killed, a hate crime, in 1998), Harvey Milk (the first openly gay politician elected into office, in 1978), and the equal rights movements and women's rights movements. There are others that should be mentioned and many still which should be researched.

Marsha P. Johnson – ACT UP (fight AIDS)
The Stonewall Riots happened on June 28th, 1969 when a raid led to a near week of rioting. June 28tth now tends to be the current pride parade date in New York.

In 1969 bars in New York which openly served booze to queer guests were often raided and denied liquor licenses. It's important to know our history, important to know compassionate role models. Sylvia Rivera and Marsha P. Johnson were very visible in the riots as well as gay liberation marches. They also fed, clothed, and housed homeless queers. They performed such acts of kindness referred to in the concept of Tikkun Olam which are believed to be helping piece back together the world, by creating unity within community and acting through compassion.

We must know our history and develop the respect for older, wiser ones who were paving the way for us, giving us rights, creating and shaping our world (though our world is scary it is not as bad as it was) – creating our culture through our history. The point of Pride, safe spaces, and educational conferences like True Colours is to empower us to become a part of our own history and help pave the way for the next generation.

The Trevor Project Suicide Helpline was formed in 1998. The story of "Trevor" was an intersection of storytelling on stage and screen about a boy's suicide attempt after rejected by peers for coming out. Many people experience some form of rejection when they come out, if they don't experience worse.

Our history teaches us why it's important to know our rights. If people come for us, we can know what laws we are protected by, and who fought to get those laws into life.

The following statistics are an example of why we need to continue to teach our history for inspiration to fight the issues our community is currently facing. GLSEN recommends that "school leaders, education policymakers, and other individuals who are obligated to provide safe learning environments for all students implement comprehensive school anti bullying and harassment policies, support GSAs, provide professional development for school staff on LGBT student issues, and increase student access to LGBT inclusive curricular resources" We are moving toward a future in which all students will have the opportunity to learn and succeed in school regardless of sexual orientation, gender identity, or gender expression.

GLSEN's Safe Space kit guide to being an ally for educators encourages making a safe space visible to students. It is important to make no assumptions, use inclusive language, and respond to bullying and harassment. Teach respect, safety, and equality for all. Use inclusive curricula, and make it engaging.

GLSEN School Experiences of Today's LGBT Youth (2013)

65% of students heard homophobic remarks frequently or often (i.e. "fag," "dyke")
30% of students missed at least one day of school in the past month because they felt unsafe or uncomfortable
85% of students were verbally harassed in the last year
56% of students experienced discrimination at school
18% couldn't bring a same gender date to a school dance
28% were disciplined for PDA not disciplined among hetero students
19% were prevented from wearing clothing deemed "inappropriate" based on their gender
50% of students had a GSA at their school
19% of students were taught positive representations of LGBT people, history, or events (inclusive curriculum)
10% of students' schools had anti-bullying policies that included both sexual orientation and gender identity and expression
96% of students had at least one supportive educator, but only 39% had 11 or more
Results: LGBT students who experienced higher levels of victimisation based on orientation had lower GPAs than students who were less often harassed, LGBT students who experienced higher levels of victimisation based on gender identity were less likely to plan to go to college/trade school than those who experienced lower levels of victimisation, and LGBT students who experienced discrimination at school generally had lower levels of self esteem. In some this also led to feelings of being anti-school.

GLSEN's 2013 State Snapshot of Connecticut found that

87% of students heard gay used in a negative way
78% of students heard homophobic remarks
77% of students heard negative remarks about gender expression
51% of students heard negative remarks about transgender

people

6 in 10 students experienced verbal harassment based on sexual orientation and 4 in 10 students experienced verbal harassment based on the way they expressed their gender
more than 2 in 10 students were physically harassed (pushed or shoved) based on their orientation and 2% of students were physically assaulted (punched, kicked, or injured with a weapon) based on the way they expressed their gender
90% of students experienced relational aggression
49% of students were sexually harassed
50% of students who were harassed or assaulted in school never reported it to school staff, 48% never told a family member about the incident
35% of students who reported incidents said there had been effective intervention by staff
26% of students were taught positive representations of LGBT people, history, and events
39% of students could not access information about LGBT communities on school internet.

The snapshot also found that

8/10 (4/5) of students report verbal harassment, and 4/10 (2/5) report physical harassment
80% of trans students felt unsafe at school because of gender expression
70.8% of gay/lesbian youth were at risk of smoking, and 71.2% of bisexual youth were at risk of smoking
27.5% of gay/lesbian youth were at risk of dating violence, and 23.3% of bisexual youth were at risk of dating violence
25.8% of gay/lesbian youth were at risk of suicide attempts, and 28% of bisexual youth were at risk of suicide attempts.
5% of bisexual youth, 8% of gay/lesbian youth, and 21% of heterosexual youth reported being very happy.

  In her other research, Jaime also discovered that there were 9 million bisexual people, which was 1.8% of the population and 52% of the LGBT community, that 19 million Americans (8.2%) reported engaging in same sex sexual behaviour while 25.6 million Americans (11%) acknowledged some same sex attraction, and that 39% of bisexual females, 33 % of bisexual males, 13% of gay men, and 10 % of lesbians report not disclosing their orientation to their medical provider.

The Medical Marijuana and PTSD Dilemma

Jaime's state offered medical marijuana for people with PTSD. Naturally, people had to jump through hoops to obtain their prescription, but it was possible. Her brain was wracked with questions like "you're young how could you be in crippling pain?" "are you seeing anyone for your insomnia/depression/anxiety/PTSD?" "Do you take anything for it?"

They always ask, "What about that sacrum pain you claim?"

People always asked, but the minute you start to say sexual abuse or marijuana, they didn't want to hear it.

Jaime thought about how she would like to be seeing someone but she can't make a decision on whether or not to go for what she really wanted. When it comes to these kinds of mental and physical problems, one must understand that a counsellor, psychiatrist, psychologist, chiropractor, or meds won't do all the work and that one must participate in active self healing.

Jaime felt intense fear of being turned away for employment as teacher if she became an MMJ patient and unable in current geographical state to get a gun license if she became a MMJ patient. It put Jaime in a difficult spot, because as a teacher, if she had her gun license, she wouldn't be allowed to have a gun at her job if she worked at a school. The only reason she would want a gun is because the rapist who gave her PTSD had a gun, and she wanted to protect herself from other people like that. This put Jaime in a triple pickle. She wanted her medicine and her job. She couldn't find it in herself to believe in medicine made of chemicals she didn't understand, after seeing how Dex was when he took them, even though her sister now was taking some for whatever her problem was that she didn't tell the family about (and her sister was quite successful).

To Jaime, MJ was sometimes as much a part of her daily prescription as yoga was, especially because it helped destroy memories she aimed to stop reliving. Through yoga skills, she actually felt as though she could direct the MJ to the parts of her brain in need of healing. She didn't see it as impairing her ability to teach, and it wasn't something for discussion with her students, much like her sexual orientation and gender expression.

Santosha (contentment)
Jaime had been most struck by the character of contentment when she read <u>the Book of Qualities.</u> The character "stood on her head until all the extra facts fell out" and is further described of having gotten rid of half of her belongings, and become a person who knew from where everything she owned came. Jaime thought that character displayed the yogic qualities.

Santosha could be reached only after one had mastered the concept of Aprigraha. When one was able to be content without objects, they knew true happiness. The bliss body, the body of joy, is the natural state of humans. However, many veils must be pushed away, for there are always many things blocking discernment of personal truths used to reach santosha. Each person's truths of santosha may vary greatly. Santosha is never achieved through material items

Shaucha (purity, honestly, self reflection, ego)
Shaucha is a niyama which involves cleanliness and purity. This includes physical cleanliness of self and space, as well as remaining free from clutter, both externally and internally. Sometimes the purity part of shaucha is referred to as honesty, because this is the point at which one must be honest with themselves about what is cluttering their lives and minds. This is when the ego check comes in, or the reality check, when one must ask themselves, "is this adding value [to my life]?" Purity of thought/speech – lack of negative speech/thought about others.

Yogic thought that all humans/all bodies are impure. Personal thought that achieving "complete permanent purity" is impossible, preference for using yoga more as it applies, less as it is described (as it is so old and life as a Westernised feminist and domesticated human is so different from how life was when the Gita was written). If one can practise every day to be better than the day before it will be worth it. That is how one can use shaucha as daily cleanse. What is your daily shaucha? For some it is showers, laundry, room tidying, dishes, the release of the emotions and senses. The world is in need of shaucha, from normal things like picking up trash, recycling, pollution, to bigger things like cleaning up the views of the masses.

Kriyas are techniques to create energetic cleansing. The following are a few Kriyas.

Nauli, the churning of the belly.
Neti, the cleansing of the nasal passages.
Hrid Dhauti, the scraping of the tongue.
Tratakum, the gazing at a candle flame, which increases concentration, tones and cleanses the eyes.
Kapalabhati, the energising pranayama, the fast pumping of air into the belly.

Swadyaya (self study)

Swadyaya relates to the brow chakra because it requires the gift of sight. In order to fully study oneself, one must be able to see themselves as others do. One must be able to see their strengths and weaknesses clearly, as well as the consequences of their actions. Swadyaya must be repeated time and time again, since we are continuously improving our quality of self.

Tikkun Olam and Oneness/Wholeness

The idea of being whole on own through there are ways to experience the self which require the help of other people (i.e. sex, socialising with friends). Becoming a universal piece of the world through acts of kindness as well as acts of kindness to the self is how Jaime viewed the concept of Tikkun Olam. Healing the self will heal the world. "Slowly integrating pieces –something we picked up here, another we dropped as a child – pieces are important, built who you've become – honour and put in their right place. Expand."

Jaime cared about creating [space for] unity, self healing, acts of kindness to the self – helping to make ourselves a better, more universal piece of the world's big puzzle.

Why Did Jaime Teach?

Why do you choose to work with children? She'd been asked many times. She would answer, "well, because children are so close to the divine. Children are so naturally open and honest. Children naturally seek out the movement they need. Children are so naturally aligned with their life path. They are constantly. Learning without even thinking about it."

But also, childhood is the biggest happiness Jaime could recall. She recognised her inner child as her inner light and yoga helps Jaime to connect with it. She gets to be playful, challenged, experimenting, curious, and relaxed. Being in touch with her inner child helps Jaime to better teach them and also keeps Jaime sane. She believed that if every child learned meditation and self regulation war could potentially be ended.

"Warriors are not what you think of as warriors. The warrior is not someone who fights, because no one has the right to take another life. The warrior, for us, is one who sacrifices himself for the good of others. His task is to take care of the elderly, the defenseless, those who cannot provide for themselves, and above all, the children, the future of humanity." - Sitting Bull

"The best teachers are those who show you where to look, but don't tell you what to see." - Alexandra K. Tremfor

Crown Chakra
Sahasrara
"We are divine."
"Time stands still best in moments that look surprisingly like ordinary life." - Story People by Brian Andreas

The Crown Chakra will show stories of understanding higher purposes, the role to spread love, knowledge, respect, and acceptance, understanding the role to teach. The Crown Chakra involves our connection to the divine. The Crown Chakra represents those moments when we say, "I understand." The mantra for this chakra is "I am the Self. I am here to serve." The Crown Chakra is located in the, and is represented by the colour violet. When healing the Crown Chakra with colour, violet should be used, or if the Crown Chakra is overactive, yellow should be used followed by a small dose of violet. The Crown Chakra embodies the elements of time and space. The Crown Chakra is ruled by the moon. Frankincense helichrysum, lavender, and vetiver are essential oils which affect the Crown Chakra, and one crystal which can be used for the Crown Chakra is Amethyst. One pose which resonates deeply with the Crown Chakra and can be felt in the whole body is sirsasana (headstand).

When someone's Crown Chakra is balanced, they would be wise but grounded. When the Crown Chakra is in excess there is blind obedience, spiritual addiction, and a lack of discrimination. When there is a deficiency in the Crown Chakra there can be dissociation from the body or rigid belief systems.

Sequined Jacket

We met Elliott Wainright at youth group. Somehow, he had been a bit well known on a blogging website. We were all in high school. A group of girls got Elliott to go to youth group back when it met in the attic of a church. It so happened to be someone else's first day, too. That was when they would pass around a sign in sheet. Elliott had signed "Rose to my mom" in parenthesis after his name on the sign in sheet.

Elliott's hair was blue, somewhat, and at a length that was just a bit long for short hair. Elliott was from a different town than either of the two groups of teens who frequented the youth group.

Elliott was one of those lucky people who was naturally very funny. He was also artistically talented. Elliott had always been both talented and passionate. Elliott was one of those funny boys who knew how to speak French, as well. However, Elliott's boyfriend was not too keen on calling him Elliott.

He knew him as Rose and considered him a her. Just like many people in his family did as well.

Elliott agonized sometimes over why he had to be both a boy and a gay one at that. Youth group was good for him, though. He could be himself. He even brought a friend, who was also gay. They went to the same school.

Elliott was liked by boys and girls. Several members of the youth group had a crush on him. Once, they had all gone swimming together and ended up all kissing each other. At the time those types of events felt like typical teenage times.

Some members of the youth group drew farther apart than others, unintentionally. The youth became college students.

Elliott began some surgery, and got a legal name change. He had worked so hard in his youth group days. He had had to tell his family, and break up with his boyfriend. He also had to graduate high school, which is huge in itself.

Some people respected Elliott a lot, he opened doors for them. It changed some people's lives to know him. Elliott was interesting. Pleasant to know.

Elliott struggled too, though. Our hearts went out for him. We couldn't know his struggles.

We loved him for his strength and skills.

He loved us for helping him be himself.

As Rose he was clumsy, awkward. As Elliott he could be brave.

We always recalled him for his bravery. We admired that the most.

Sleepover

"You're so pretty and perfect,"
I sigh into your sheets
and you're so unafraid
of what I openly am
so unafraid to share your bed with me
and you even let me
hold you

your eyes show rocks and streams
your voice sings galaxies
I would like to see the maps
inside your head
tell me places you have been
and who was there with you

tell me stories
just skip the lies
let me taste the midnight summer sky
between your thighs

your skin beneath my fingertips
quivers slightly at my touch
you lean into me
snuggle up and snuggle in

you know you like it
(probably every girl's
least favorite pick-up line)

we stayed up all night talking
making memories and connections
simply synapses firing

and as you lay here
your sweet body against mine
I feel your breathing

I am so close, and I want you so bad

all I have to do
is just reach down
or reach to grab something
soft and wet

insist you wouldn't have to do a thing
because you are so beautiful
you deserve to feel good
you know you like it

I know you like it
but I can't without your permission
well, I could
all I have to do is just reach down

but that's fifteen year old stuff
and I'm too afraid
to lose a new friend
so I'll just hold you and dream
of your sweet strawberries and cream

How Do You Become a Wise One?

Jaime received a letter from a friend one day, after they had received word about Jaime's search for people who could add aspects of diversity that she did not know about to her book and to her system for education and liberation of queer folk. The letter was a piece of prose, anonymously directed at others. Older others would understand.

If you were a seventiess teenage feminist, then you're likely nearing sixty. You're established in your life but not stagnant. You've experienced much. You could, in ways, be considered an expert on some things.

Certainly, in your field you're likely to be considered an expert and be consulted by many. Your opinion is often valued and respected.

All of the experience you've accumulated through your life is of use to those younger than you. They learn by watching you.

At this point in life you likely know people with aids. You likely know people who have transitioned as well. You know people from all walks of life. Your contacts have helped shape you.

You've had to come out before, you've been outed before. You've dealt with many reactions. You know how to handle it. You know how to handle yourself.

On countless occasions, you've shown bravery and courage. You've put yourself out there. You've stood up for what you believed in. You make history.

You got pushed around and stepped on. You got forgotten. You got discriminated against, you got bullied, you got insulted. You decided you wouldn't put up with it anymore. You said, no more. You stood up for future generations.

You made change and your body changed, and as it did you became a wise one, exalted, respected, and treasured.

See your place. Take it proudly.

"Sky Bound (Fallen Angel Stars)"

Do you know why it hurts so much?
Because this is the part
where you become
the goo inside the cocoon

this is the part
where you transform

it's time to earn your wings

[allow yourself to be broken
melt your world
to create a new one]

the fire within
burns electric sound waves
and smoke melts into the air

creating light where there
was none before
as a beacon of light
you are a prism
reflecting each of this
world's holy colours.

Suddenly there are
kaleidoscopic rainbows everywhere
life is fully dipped in paint

laugh when you feel
like you are dying
for you open at the close
and stars form from the crumble [dust]
(let's be loud like love)

"Some People Make Love to the Sky"

Some people make love to the sky
and it can't be explained why
but to give yourself to the earth
is when you feel rebirth

the sun will fill you up
the rain will light up your bones
heart ablaze like fire in a cup
eyes in rainbow tones

to make love to the trees
you must get on your knees
meet yourself on the soft, warm grass
meet your body bare ass

let the rocks rock your body
treat yourself and don't feel naughty
allow the stars to kiss and caress
open the gates of self love and confess

allow yourself the gift of breath
allow yourself to peacefully rest

The Ones I Never Fell For

It's true that Jaime was surrounded by beautiful women at the yoga studio where she was trained to teach. It's true that many of these women were the subject of crushes for many men who attended the studio.

These beautiful women were Jaime's teachers, who became her coworkers. They are the beautiful women from whom she learned, from whom she took her lead. They each provided Jaime with a space to explore her body. They created a space in which her body and mind could become aligned.

Jaime never fell for Christine Christie's big butt because she was her teacher. Jaime never sexualised her in her yoga pants or any asana she learned.

Jaime never fell for her kindred water spirit, Misty. She was tall and thin, but Jaime just wanted to learn from her. She did things Jaime wanted to do, including teach stand up paddleboard yoga.

Jaime never fell for blond and petite Claire, whose classes made her body work hard. She was so down to earth and real with Jaime that she couldn't possibly have become another student with a useless crush on her.

Jaime never fell for the lovely Australian accent that Dakota had. Dakota was full of knowledge and actively sought out more. She helped Jaime continue to cultivate that quality in herself.

Jaime never fell for beautiful, Jewish Rhiannon, and her wonderful restorative classes. She taught Jaime to treat herself with care.

Jaime never had to train herself not to fall for her yoga teachers. It just never happened. She did have to train herself not to check out people taking classes that she was taking and not to check out her students. It is important to let people experience their bodies, even when bodies are vulnerable to the eyes.

"Artists and Colour Schemes"

Just like I can't choose
a favourite gender
as an artist I can't choose
a favourite colour

for you see
they're all quite beautiful
red is sticky summer sunsets
orange is the leaves on the trees lining the parkway

yellow sunny days
green forests and grasses
blue for my precious waves
indigo night skies dotted with stars in masses

purple juicy grapes
and amethyst clusters
silver like the moon
to make us feel all flustered

pink like lips
brown like hair
white like clouds forming ships
black as night that falls everywhere

and girls are make of
the softest snowy mountains
and the deepest valleys
and the excitement climbing

and the purest, freshest
streams that cleanse
your soul
the warmest waters

and girls are made of
that cool breeze

that hits your face
and reminds you you're alive

and girls are made of
all the colours of the rainbow
and the colours of sand
on beaches far away

boys are made of
tall tree trunks
stretching up to the sky
long branches reaching out high

warm fires burning bright
smelling smoke all night
charcoal that gets everywhere
endless campsite air

and boys are made of
CDs and musical instruments
classic cars and roads to anywhere
square marble tiles and rectangle books

lines and shapes of knives
and more bones than skin
and always boys
never men

and girls are sky and stardust
rainbows pure and constellations
boys are planets and suns
so how could I choose just one?

Living Seeing

"You're very bold to wear that here," Jaime's coworker, Meera, said, gesturing to Jaime's rainbow scarf.

"You're bi though, you're able to hide easier, so I don't know why you're being so bold," she continued.

Jaime began to inquire how Meera knew that, before she eve had time to get mad at Meera's comments.

"You've got your pride bracelet. You try to pass it off as some kiddie bracelet but people know those colours." She pointed from the scarf to the bracelet. "Gay pride, bi pride. You know that we work at the young men's CHRISTIAN association, don't you? AND teaching children. I don't know if you really want parents finding out that sort of thing."

Jaime looked Meera up and down, looked at her glasses, her long braid, her long skirt. Then Jaime looked into her eyes and arched an eyebrow.

"Is there something you're hiding, Meera?"

Meera paled and looked around, though she and Jaime were in an empty room. Jaime smirked, recognising what she was facing. She lowered her voice.

"Do you want to go out for food some time? Then we could talk more about what's really bothering you."

Meera looked aghast.

"Some people could get you fired for comments like that," she hissed.

Meera said it as both a warning and an expression that she was truly afraid of it happening. Jaime stuck her tongue behind her teeth and pressed her lips together in a flat line.

Jaime paused for breathing moments. She paused to see that people are like this – both the fearful like Meera and the people who would act against her who Meera was afraid of. Jaime knew she could be bold, and that it was not always wise to be bold. Sometimes she had to check herself. Seeing these things was important. One did not always want to believe that real life could be like that.

But Jaime thought it was important to be unafraid. She hoped she could reach Meera there. Though, thanks to

Meera, she made a temporary decision to tone it down professionally. Meera was in some ways right to play it safe and quiet. Jaime did not disclose to her colleagues at the Christian association or at the Baptist preschool she worked at next that she practised witchcraft. Meera had expressed to her not feeling the freedom at that job to discuss the many deities in her Hindu religion either.

    Jaime had to train herself to see that some people would be okay with things like that while others wouldn't, just like when it came to the gay thing. Living open meant being open to the fact that not everyone would be as open as she was, and that that was okay and she would have to live with it. Living open was living seeing.

Base of the Pyramid

Coracao was the only boy on the cheer squad but it didn't bother him one bit. It was only the school cheer squad for which he was the only boy, he wasn't the only boy on his gym's squad.

Coracao loved tumbling. Moving his body in the ways he was learning felt so freeing. His friends were into cheer first, and he had wanted to be part of the fun.

Coracao knew that boys could be cheerleaders. He knew that the school had had boys on their squad before, even straight boys who cheered with their girlfriends. Nothing held him back from trying out or making the team.

Cheers were all about encouragement. That's where he got his idea. To be a cheerleader, you had to want the best for people. You had to be willing and able to bring out the best in people. You also had to be able to cheer them up.

Cheer was made up of rhythmic words of encouragement set to music with choreographed movement. It was essentially performance art, like drum core, colourguard, and theatre.

Coracao started to wonder, what if he used cheer as protest art. He decided to stage an experiment.

He found the most rainbows and sparkles he could find and donned them. Outside the school he stood with his pom-poms.

"Two, four, six, eight
who do we appreciate?
You, you that's who
you and everything you do!"

Was his first cheer for his peers. It was followed by an acrobatic display and another cheer.

"Hey, hey,
it's okay
it's okay
if you are gay!"

At first, Coracao repeated this display several times. People passed by, no one jeered. Then, a few girls from the squad saw and joined in with their own pom-poms. This was unplanned and filled Coracao with joy. As he gained confidence, he added a third cheer. The girls added their own moves.

"Love, love
that's the word
say it loud and
let's be heard!"

Some passers by clapped along or smiled at the songs.

Coracao was shocked to see it working. He could use cheer as a medium for protest art. Suddenly, his favourite thing could become something that meant something, something that could make a difference somehow. Suddenly he had purpose. From the base of the pyramid he could be support – he could spread love and acceptance. And as a vocal cheerleader he could spread this knowledge. He could teach others from his role there could be more male cheerleading protest artists. He could even form a squad. It was only the tip of the iceberg and the base of the pyramid. Cheerleading had taught Coracao that he had three choices – to give up, give in, or give it his all.

Crown Chakra Connections

Acts of Service
One language of love involves doing things for others that one would not normally do, for the sake of the other person, either because they were asked to or because it is helpful and makes the other's life easier. This language involves giving the other person their time, while recognising the value of their time. This person might prefer giving the service, or receiving acts of service. Many people see great value in being helped by others, and it often helps reinforce feelings of comfort with others because they are consistently making life easier by being helpful.

Alignment
When the crown chakra is properly aligned, people can connect better with the world around them, as well as the world inside of them. When tuned into their own inner workings, people vibrate at a higher frequency. The higher vibration is because people who are tuned into their own inner workings were working on their personal growth and usually had community goals as well.
Aligning with the true self is a lifelong process/journey. Like a phoenix, the self is constantly reborn throughout one's life, adapting as life changes. Or like in Hindu religion, remaining on the wheel of life. The true self is a collectivity of selves, all of the different people one must be. Similar to Krishna's form of facing every way, all humans have the power to fluidly utilise this gift. The true self contains all of the qualities which are unwavering in a person. That which they carry across each of their selves. Each personality a person has carved out for themselves contained similarities – qualities that didn't change with age or go away. Some people also had things they'd always liked or been good at and those were part of their true selves, too.
Jaime's true self was into the beach, camping, surfing, inclined to move around, and was a natural storyteller and writer. Jaime's true self was accepting of

many different types of people and this correlated to her level of bisexuality where she had no preference what someone was if she was interested in or attracted to someone. Her true self aimed for honesty and communication – words. She had battled the ego many times to discover the few qualities she knew about her true self that she knew for certain.

Jaime's true self in relation to her surname Alexander, which meant helper, protector, defender of humankind – why she's a teacher – soul purpose to help future of humans.

Finding the true self means digging through many past selves, as well as considering the kind of self needed or desired to cultivate for the future. These processes involve a cycle of shaucha (self reflection) and swadyaya (self study).

Bloom's Taxonomy of Higher Order Thinking

Creation is the highest level on Bloom's Taxonomy of higher level thinking. Jaime viewed this as including the creation of a service, or the creation which was for a service. Jaime was working towards creating a new world, and creating a higher purpose for herself, creating her vibration, and her sense of meaning. She was creating a purpose and vibration of serving, accepting, and loving. She felt that to teach is to create, because through teaching one could create empowerment. The way to activate the seeds of your creation is by making choices about the results you want to create. When you make a choice, you activate vast human energies and resources which otherwise go untapped. Some may even believe that if creation is highest level of intelligence, then the creation of children is the highest form of creation. The creation of a whole being is something to revel in and something to take an active part in, though we must be aware that we cannot create people to be a certain way just because we want them to be. We must be wary of attempting to mold children into our own ideals. Yet the creation of children is still a marvel and should be respected as such.

Celtic Magick

Jaime grew up with Celtic traditions, and many of her knowledge on Celtic magick came from Llewellyn. Celtic traditions were saved through the Brehon Law including how they sang Veda-like hymns, sacrificed with special plants and occasionally animals or humans, and used sacred fires. British Celts wore swirling blue tattoos or paintings on their bodies. Celts were very clean, they used soap before the Romans. They played lyres and harps, loved song, music, and recitation of legends and epic adventures. Both sexes loved jewellery, and the Celts used artwork, clothing, and jewellery to guard against evil or curses by using apotropaic magick. In the same way, they decorated ordinary objects with spiritual and symbolic designs .Men wore their hair long. The Celts were an energetic people with a zest for life, and tended to be strong psychics in tune with the forces of Nature and the power of the human mind.

The Celts had their own class system which went as follows. Druids, Bards (poets), Ovates (philosophers and prophets), and Druid priests – for which there were special schools available for initiates of either sex and which required twenty years of study. Ovates and Bards were known as Firid. Druids were philosophers, judges, and advisors to tribal leaders. Ovates compiled knowledge of all kinds. Bards praised, ridiculed, and taught through the use of music and poetry. Druids were very powerful and could conquer enemies and cause hardships with words alone. They taught a very special relationship with Nature. The Celts particularly used the colour green to honour the Earth Mother, which is also the colour of the faeries.

Crystal Healing

There were three crystals that Jaime would make readily available to her queer students – amethyst, tangerine quartz, and rose quartz. Jaime had always been drawn to crystals, having found beautiful quartz and pink agate at a young age. She had managed to hold onto them for years without losing them, and felt their energy deeply. She wanted her students to be able to access Amethyst – for it seems that all of us have something to heal from just by being a queer person, Tangerine quartz – because too many of us suffered from sexual traumas and to help us heal from it, working primarily with the sacral chakra, and also stimulating creativity, passion, and sexuality, and Rose quartz – to bring about self love, for so many of us need it, to manifest romantic love, and to fill our hearts as well as those around us with more love than hate

    Jaime was stuck with the question, should stones for protection be made available as well? Should queer kids [have to] protect themselves? Should they learn self defense? Why it's important and why it's messed up, the way she had to be teaching children the times you have to flee from danger versus when you have to stay put in danger (she worried this was instilling fear in the youth)When she was at a crossroads she always chose both – to make protection/self defense available but as a choice (she wouldn't make them learn it).
    Some days required a heavy prescription of crystals, movement, creation, education, and tea. Learning to work with different crystals is like learning to work with different people. They each respond to different things. One could be a crystal child, meaning, becoming like a crystal and reflecting energy out instead of absorbing it.

    Jaime had picked out a crystal for each chakra to make available to her students first.
Red jasper was a protective stone.
Tangerine quartz was a stone resonating with the sacral chakra.
Citrine helped for employment opportunities.
Rose quartz was a love stone.
Blue Topaz opened pathways for communication.
Sugilite connected us with wisdom.
Amethyst helped us heal.

Jaime also wanted to make other crystals available to her students.

Chevron Amethyst for sleep, Lepidolite for reducing stress, depression, insomnia, Moonstone for preventing insomnia and nightmares and easing cramps, Unakite Jasper for patience, persistence, and uplifting energy, Black Obsidian to absorb negativity, Aquamarine for release, and calming energy, Epidote to banish hopelessness, and Turquoise for luck, calming energy, and protection.

There were also crystals for astrological stress. For Aries – Blue Spinel – which restores enthusiasm through setbacks, for Taurus – Blue Lace Agate – which offers clarity when things don't make sense, for Gemini – Chrysocolla – which allows us to move past obstacles, for Leo – Aquamarine – which activates courage when blocked by doubt, for Virgo – Pink Calcite – which supplies energy to prevent emotional repression, for Libra – Charoite – which enables overcoming debilitating fears, for Scorpio – Snowflake Obsidian – which inspires the release of damaging patterns, for Sagittarius – Heliodor – which recharges, for Capricorn – Prasiolite – which encourages expression of hidden emotions, for Aquarius – Chrysoprase – which empowers to move past disappointment, and for Pisces – Fluorite – which provides thriving stability.

Erikson's Generativity vs Stagnation (keep it moving)

Generativity vs stagnation is a stage of development most typically passed through in adulthood, between the ages of forty and sixty-four. However, everyone passes through generativity vs stagnation when making daily choices about whether they are going to take action toward self betterment (i.e. by getting up and going to work every morning). Generativity vs stagnation follows the principle of the mantra "keep it moving," preventing the energy from becoming dead.

Integrity vs Despair (older adulthood, maturity until death)

Integrity vs despair is the last stage of development we pass through before exiting this world, as we come to terms with mortality. On a smaller scale, we are consistently looking for ways to maintain our integrity while avoiding falling into despair about any particular aspect of our lives and the state of the world. John O'Donahue says in his book, <u>Anam Cara</u>, "old age offers the opportunity to integrate and bring together the multiplicity of directions you have travelled."

Some questions to ask oneself while passing through this stage include:
-how would you like to be remembered?
-how has my life been of value?
-how can there continue to be value in my life as I age?
-what is the most meaningful way to experience life at this point in time and space?
-how can your experiences help others?
-what would you like to pass on?
-what have you learned? Was it all worth it?
-what memories have made this life worthwhile?
-what do you have left to do?
-what is the overall quality of life right now?

Quality of Life and Continuous Improvement

Every action now is being done to improve quality of life until death, to make it most comfortable and be able to make the most out of it – making most meaningful version of life. In this way we begin living less out of habit and more out of intent.

"To pray you open your whole self to the sky, to earth, to sun, to moon, to one whole voice that is you, and know there is more than you can't see, can't hear, can't know except in moments steadily growing, and in languages that aren't always sound but other circles of motion" - Joy Harjo

Identity?

What is identity? Identity is made up of many things, including one's gender, sex, orientation, culture/ethnicity/race/nationality, beliefs/values, goals/career path, education, preferences/hobbies, family relations, age, appearance, location/region, mood/attitude/mannerisms/habits/routines, skills/talents, language/dialect/slang use, experiences/conditions/trauma, personality traits, social status, lifestyle, and decisions.

As a child, Jaime was incredibly creative and always had elaborate fantasy play, regardless of where she was playing or what she was using. She had vivid memories of an array of imaginary friends she had created as a child and returned to for many years. She noticed that she had given everyone particular personalities and qualities she felt were representations of herself (you can only create [from] what you know). As an adult, she recognised these imaginary friends that she had created as versions of herself to transform into at different times, as she recognised her collectivity of selves. In many ways, self actualisation/realisation (samadhi) involves a sense of oneness with the fact of the collectivity of selves within a person at any given time, and the ability to harness energy from those selves.

Jaime could recall a few distinctive characters she had created for herself. One was Aimee, the hippie healer. Another was Lynn, the fearless punk rocker. There was also Mikko the telekinetic and
Adrienne, the broody loner who loved the ocean. Jaime felt each of those characters inside of herself on any given day. She sometimes identified more strongly with one over the others. It had always reminded her of the She Daisy song, "Lucky For You, Tonight I'm Just Me," in which the singer described her "multiple personalities" that her ex claimed she had. Jaime also had an identity for her boy self, the self of hers who walked between the borders of gender, with her

androgynous features, and that one she called Ash. Each character was a small piece of her personality. They were somewhat idealised versions of particular qualities in herself. She figured that many people could see their different selves, and her method was just characters because she was born to write. Being a writer was as much of Jaime's identity as being bisexual, a teacher, and a practitioner of yoga was.

Ishvarapranidhana

"One becomes firmly established in practise only after attending to it for a long time, without interruption and with an attitude of devotion." - Yoga Sutra 1.14

Ishvarapranidhana is the niyama which means spiritual devotion.

When someone connects with their body in such a way that they recognise the vessel of their soul as a divine representation of the universe, they began to worship themselves. This includes listening to the body for all that it can do every day, and treating the body with care.

This is when mindfulness comes in, when one becomes more selective about the things they let into their lives. It may begin with becoming more picky about the things they put into their bodies, or with changing their standards about the people with whom their precious time is spent. Time becomes a valuable resource, mindfully spent on meaningful things. *breaking of habits

Ishvapranidhana is being able to look at oneself and know that not only is the universe in the palm of a hand, but it is also within. It is being in touch with the daily blessings of life. Masturbation as devotion to self

Hooping as Ishvarapranidhana

Jaime's coworker Dylen loved music festivals and was eager to learn to hoop. Jaime helped her connect with her body in a whole new way by teaching her how to hoopdance. Dylen took what she learned and made it her own, while seeking more information. Dylen had struggled with her relationship with her body for a long time. After a shower one day, Dylen was drawn to picking up her hoop and practising sky clad. She found that her connection with her hoop was even deeper when she was sky class because she could cultivate greater body awareness. This became a regular ritual after showers for Dylen, and it helped her to become more comfortable with her own naked self after having such a bad relationship with her body for so many years. Hooping sky clad was one thing Dylen used as her method of ishvapranidhana, devotion to her divine vessel.

Asana as Ishvapranidhana

Jaime saw asana as time to honour and worship body, time to treat body to movement. Asana helped form a deeper connection with the vessel for the soul, helping it to reach new limits, achieve new things, and heal itself.

Our Own Divine Lights

Through devotion to the self, we also show our devotion to the divine. We aim to make ourselves our best, and our best selves are those which act out of love. The divine versions of ourselves exists in states of love. When we act out of compassion and show forgiveness, we are being our higher selves. When we devote to ourselves, we must think of ourselves as a loving people and do our best to grow and evolve. We must learn to love everything in our lives, every feeling, thought and action. We devote ourselves to the divine by devoting to ourselves because our aim is to show that within us which is the divine light. Through devotion to the self, we learn how to be whole on our own, and we learn what to do in order to feel whole. Jaime admired that devotion in Le Feu which propelled him to pursue his ambitions, and which helped him to know that he was whole on his own. It had always been a favourite thing of Jaime's about her relationship with Le Feu that they were both so whole on their own, and devoted to the divine lights which would help them better their worlds one day.

Devotion to the self can be an anarcha-feminist concept, for some would prefer us to be dedicated to other things – like material possessions or particular deities. Devoting to ourselves is a radical act. Through yoga we can take back our lives, devoting ourselves spiritually, and live meaningfully.

Organised Religion as Ishvapranidhana

It was understandable that some people used organised religion to express their devotion to the divine. It made worship easy. Prayers and rituals were laid out. Directions could be followed. Community could be found. Organised religion helped people to commit to prayer and rituals at a certain time and frequency, like committing to a workout schedule at a gym or committing to education through classes.

Bisexuality as Ishvapranidhana

Some believe that bisexual people have a natural devotion to bodies as divine because they are typically noticing people more than hetero people do. While reclaiming her sexuality, Jaime turned it into something sacred. Sexuality could depict devotion to freedom of expression of the true self (devotion to the self), and a way to develop an innate understanding of the magick within the body. Jaime had a special relationship with the female body. She worshipped and appreciated it when she made love to one, and also worshipped and appreciated the combination of her female body and genderless soul. She was a shapeshifter, but some people who were bi experienced gender confusion. Nef's recognised Jaime's lack of gender. Sometimes other people did, too. Jaime didn't mind, knowing that one day someone just as devoted to the temples of the bodies would love her for her divine fluidity.

The Ralph Waldo Emerson Trifecta

There is an expression, called the Ralph Waldo Emerson trifecta which is represented by a triangle with god at the top, with self and nature on the sides. God is seen as the connection between the self and nature. God was the self's refined nature. The self was an expression of god, and nature was an expression of god as well. God was all encompassing. The self and nature were also all encompassing (and therefore rays of gods light). This is where we are represented as a container, a diamond multifaceted universal form, when the self was containing the universe. It is common knowledge that we are somehow made from stardust and it is through godlike magic of miracles of the body. By viewing the self as divine we find a new way to cultivate respect and appreciation for the self and the vessel, helping us with seeing the divine more clearly and all around us.

Jean Piaget and the Atman

Jean Piaget believed that children were driven by their own natural, creative wisdom to be the little scientists and explorers that they were. Unbeknownst to him, Piaget was aware of the creative energy of Prakriti, which gives children their Atman. The Atman is the provider of this natural, creative wisdom which children possess.

Maslow's Self Actualisation

There is an intersection of Maslow's Self Actualisation and Samadhi (self realisation). It is through both of these that the development of self concept (idea of who you are) and self esteem occur. Here is the point at which there is a discernment of personal truths and values, and an alignment with one's soul path. Here is where one emits a higher vibration by being their most true self. It is through self actualisation that becoming yourself happens.

Quality Time

One language of love involves the spending of time with people as being incredibly meaningful. To someone whose primary language of love is Quality Time, it does not necessarily matter to them what they are doing with the person that they wanted to spend time with, as long as they were together. The language of Quality Time involves the recognition of time as a valuable resource, and the discernment of those worthy of giving that resource to. The recognition of time as a gift which is never guaranteed allows for the Bhakti approach to be used, by being thankful for each breath one often decides to make the most of each blessed breath.

Tikkun Olam and Putting the Pieces Back Together

Tikkun Olam comes from Judaism and represents acts of kindness performed to help repair of world (found in Mishnah – classical rabbinic teachings) – encourages people to take ownership of the world – participate in repairing the world by participating in tzadakah (justice and righteousness) and g'milut Hasidim (acts of loving kindness).
Some think that we are the pieces of the world which broke apart. By uniting, we would fix the world, putting it back together. Without hate, we could all work towards saving our planet.
Jaime was made aware of the concept of Tikkun Olam through <u>Nick and Norah's Infinite Playlist</u>, and had discussed it with her internet Norah (Slam the Poet), who was Jewish in real life.

Stopping Time

Jaime discovered that there were several ways to stop time in this beautiful world. Sometimes, she felt like they were ways to steal time or borrow time for the self. Her favourite ways were yoga practise, sex, drugs, driving into the sunset (with Sean), dancing, and sleeping. This was a form of spellcasting involving time, resonating with the crown chakra, which helps us to understand the concept of time. Jaime also loved using pranayama to step out of the moment.

    She practised her spell for stopping time. The trees still moved in the wind, she still hear the shells of her blue jellyfish windchimes from Rhode Island that Sean hung beneath her stairs clink and tinkle against one another. But everything else was still.

    She, in fact, was still moving. Her life force was flowing through her body as she breathed herself alive. Her body was moving itself, she was not moving her body. Her mind was still. Focused. Quiet. At peace. Her stomach was settled. Her emotions hung suspended in the slightly sticky summer breeze. Birds sang songs of this summer's day.

    Time had stopped. All that mattered was her breath and her body. Her spell had been successful. The universe filled her with the good magic put out for her intentions.

    Her physical asana practise had evolved greatly. But this, for her, was what the yoga was all about.

    She made a mental note not to forget that the next time she was caught up in challenging physical practise.

"Stopping for a Breath" (Consideration)

    When Smith from Kaboom stops in the middle of his own fantasy, Jaime was reminded of the way she stops in her own. Jaime stopped in her fantasies about women often, getting hung up about whether or not the girl would consent to hooking up with her. This tendency reminded her of the way Charlie from <u>the Perks of Being a Wallflower</u> dreamt of Sam but felt badly about seeing her naked without her permission. In the book, Sam tells Charlie that it's okay he dreamt about it, but not to waste his time thinking about her like that. If it got overwhelming, Charlie would let Sam know when he was thinking of her like that. Charlie also considered what models thought and how they felt about people masturbating to their photos. He didn't want them to feel badly about it. Jaime had read once that we can only dream about people we know, and wondered if perhaps maybe that was why we didn't seem to create people to fantasise about.

Yoga for Recovery

Yoga is an effective practise for those seeking recovery. Be it recovery from depression, anxiety, PTSD, addiction, eating disorders, or illness, yoga can help cultivate the strength for recovery.

In order to recover from anything, one must create a new life in which it is easier to not engage in the thing intended to recover from. In the case of addiction, one must create a life in which it is easier not to use. Such intentional creation often comes in the form of breaking habits.

Each person has different levels of adhikara for each of life's tasks. Where some people will naturally have a propensity to engage in risky behaviour (such as bisexual youth), others will naturally have a propensity to be safer. The road to recovery requires the cultivation of tapas, self discipline.

It is through mindfulness that tapas can be cultivated. By moving mindfully, for example, by intentionally committing to a daily physical practise, the tapas can be cultivated to exploring the self. As the body meets the self in physical practise (on or off the mat) the perfect opportunity arises to connect with the divine self.

"Practise self study to commune with your chosen divinity" - Yoga Sutras 11.44

It is through self exploration that the path to recovery can be found, because the true self knows how best to create an easier life. Once one becomes aligned in their body, mind, and soul, and it is easier to tune into one's own deeper needs.

Many people develop addictive behaviours as coping mechanisms during difficult times. These times may be when people have to cope with the shattering of illusions they had been keeping about their community, world, and self. These times may also have been when any number of horrible things could have gone on with people's families during their formative years, and developing addictive behaviours could easily be learned behaviours. Such addictive behaviours vary from risky behaviour, substance abuse, risky sex, excessive lying or storytelling, stealing, or excessive sleeping, just to name a few. There are plenty of reasons for people to develop addictive behaviours as coping mechanisms.

Healing addictive behaviours is difficult. The addict must be aware of their behaviours and willing to change. Yoga can be used for recovery from addiction, but typical not on its own. Many survivors of addiction who turned to yoga to aid their recovery were also part of programs with professional help specialising in serious recovery.

Gratefulness and Depression

You have to make it out of bed to do the hard stuff in order to be able to do the good stuff. Some days, you have to do all just important, hard, or boring things, and you feel like there is no time for any of the good things. This is where gratefulness comes in. when one feels like there is no time for the good things that make them happy, they must find happiness in daily little things. Depression can get in the way of appreciating the smaller things in life.

Sometimes Jaime found herself concluding that she felt a state of not feeling sad or depressed (overpowering depression with gratefulness meaning the effect of depression is numbed and transformed into a lost feeling) but feeling at a loss for what to do with the happiness cultivated, or feeling lacking the skills to make the most out of it. It begged the question, "ou se trouve?" (where to go?)

Gratitude activates the brain stem region which produces dopamine. Focusing on things to be grateful for increases serotonin production in anterior cingulate cortex. These are the chemicals which make us feel happy or cheerful. Our natural levels of thee chemicals affect our moods.

Why Positive Thinking Isn't the Only Way

A recent trend around positivity culture began breeding people who refused to accept emotions. These people claimed that they were about "good vibes only," but struggled to help their friends through difficult times that produced difficult emotions. It is important to be able to recognise and accept nuanced emotions, reality, and structural issues. Positivity-only culture can become victim blaming quickly, as it begs people to disregard their "negative" emotions.

Many Indigenous beliefs involve sourcing one's goodness from the work they do in their community and sourcing one's happiness in how they care for each other. Failures are sourced in how those things do not get done. When you rely on just yourself to source love, goodness, and happiness, it can be hollow and the accountability is reduced.

Yoga encourages us to accept our emotions, whatever they may be, and to acknowledge the negative within us. Through yoga we can give the negativity a physical way of moving through our bodies and potentially out of them. The point of yoga is not to clear ourselves of negativity, but to be able to be ourselves better, which may involve fully experiencing our more negative emotions.

The following deities are associated with homoeroticism, homosexuality, and gender variance. Further research can be taken from the book <u>Gay Witchcraft</u> by Christopher Penczak.

A List of Deities who will accept you for whoever you are

-Adonis – a fertility god and a lover.

-Apollo (and Hyacinth) – a sun and light god, who took many same-sex lovers.

-Aphrodite (Venus) – a goddess of love on every level.

-Artemis/Diana – a warrior goddess of wild things and protector of women and children.

-Astarte – a Great Mother goddess.

-Asushunamir – companion spirits, who are neither male nor female.

-Athena/Minerva – the wise warrior woman goddess, who could transform into a man.

-Baphomet – a deity of fertility and wealth, pictured as a hermaphrodite.

-Baron Samedi – a god of death and magick who is depicted as transgendered, who sees in both worlds.

-Bona Dea – a "good goddess" of women.

-Bran the Blessed – a battle and resurrection god worshipped by homosexual priests.

-Cernunnos/Herne the Hunter – a god of the wild hunt, who appears at times of crisis.

-Chin – a dwarf deity who introduced homoerotic rituals to the Mayans.

-Damballah – the serpent god of the Voodoo loa, invoked for guidance, who has an androgynous nature and can manifest homoerotically or bisexually. Damballah is also the god of rain and rainbows.

-Dionysus/Bachas – a god of light and ecstasy, who was soft and sensitive, and took many male lovers.

-Ereshkigal – a goddess of the underworld, invoked in Egypt for gay love spells.

-Eros – the patron and protector of homosexual love.

-Erzulie – a goddess of love and beauty who grants those in the creative arts the gift of manifesting beauty.

-Freyja and Freyr – earth gods seen as two sides to the same coin, Freyr being peaceful while Freyja became a warrior goddess. Freyja also specialises in a particular form of shamanic sex magick called Seidr which induces shamanic states through shivering and shaking.

-Ganesha – the remover of obstacles, mixed in sexuality and masculine in gender. Ganesha was also the protector of Parvati's inner chambers which contained the powers of sexuality and kundalini.

-Ganymede -the most famous male lover of Zeus, who pours Ambrosia.

-Gwydion – involved in ritual transgenderism.

-Hecate – the archetypical goddess of the witches, a goddess of love.

-Hermaphrodite – a deity of both genders.

-Hermes/Mercury – a god of travel, who took male and female lovers, and a patron of healers.

-Horus – involved in homoerotic reproduction.

-Hypnos – a sleep god who put a mortal man to sleep forever so that they could enjoy dreams together.

-Indra – a sky god who was both bisexual and transgendered.

-Isis – a Great Mother goddess serviced by gay and transgendered priests who welcomes all.

-Kali Ma – the warrior goddess of Mother Nature.

-Loki – a fire god associated with transgenderism, involved in ritualistic homosexuality, and a god associated with homosexual love.

-Macha – a Celtic triplicity goddess of battle who caused androgynous transformation of men.

-Morgan – the Celtic trinity of war goddesses.

-Odin/Wotan the Wanderer – shapeshifts into a female when it suits him, and involved in homoerotic relationships. Freyja initiated him into Seidr, magick reserved typically for gay or transgendered males.

-Osiris – a fertility god to whom acts of religious sexuality were performed.

-Pan/Faunus – a god of wild things who loves both men and women.

-Quan Yin – a goddess of compassion, who listens to the prayers of the world.

-Sedna – a two-spirit goddess, and a mother goddess of life and death.

-Set – a deity of evil, who was pansexual, and was involved in homosexual reproduction.

-Tezcatlipoca – the Father of Witches whose priests were associated with homosexuality and transgenderism.

-Thoth – a god of communication, child of homosexual union.

-Tlatzoteotl – a goddess who takes the darkness of the world and turns it into gold. A mother and protector of transgendered, lesbian priestesses.

-Xochilpilli – a patron of gay men, gender variance, and male prostitution, who brought homosexuality to the Aztecs. He was a god of flowers, physical pleasure, dancing, and fine food.

-Xochiquetzal – a goddess of creative arts, nonreproductive sex, and protector of lesbians.

-Yemaya – an orisha of oceans, rivers, and water, who shape shifted, and is associated with transgendered and lesbian women, as well as healing, AIDS/HIV, and gay, bisexual, or transgendered men.

-Zeus/Jupiter – a sky and storm god, a granter of prosperity and blessings, who shapeshifted, slept with men and women, and was originally depicted as transgendered since he had the ability to carry a child.

Epilogue

It is time for the ending of all of these stories, and mostly of Jaime's. You may be wondering; how did Jaime achieve her dreams? She cannot take all the credit. She had a support circle of many loving people. It is terribly important to cultivate such a circle so that ambitions can be achieved. It is worth mentioning that without her sister, Jaime would not have achieved her 200 hour certification. However, this story is not about how Jaime achieved her dreams and opened up a yoga studio. This story is about yoga.

Jaime is just a person who was deeply affected by yoga. She was so moved, that she decided to specialise in yoga for depression, anxiety, PTSD, recovery, kids, teens, and LGBT folks. She also wanted to offer yoga for special needs – even if she wasn't doing the teaching. Jaime's purpose was to create a space – a space for learning, growth, empowerment, and creation. She was committed to her passions and intuitively used them to help others.

Confused Girl and Jaime

Jaime was sponsored by a clothing company called Confused Girl in the City. At first, Jaime hadn't been fussed about being sponsored, because she felt like it was not the point of her practise or her pictures. Once she was sponsored by Confused Girl, however, Jaime was loyal to the company and declined other sponsorships. Being backed by a company made Jaime feel like someone believed in her. It also made her feel like she was more credible, like people would be more likely to think that she was a good yoga teacher if she was sponsored by a company.

Jaime realised what it meant for her to have a company tied to her name, and wanted to make sure that she aligned with the values and actions of what she was representing. Confused Girl had stood out to her because they had a line of leggings with designs inspired by healing crystals. Many other items of clothing in the brand displayed empowering phrases, which was another thing that Jaime liked. She liked to wear clothing with messages that represented her values. Confused Girl wanted her to help spread the message of self acceptance and love, empowering other women. The founder believed in accepting yourself when things are tough and you are confused, and embracing yourself. She wanted to support women on their journey of finding their true natures.

Jaime liked the fact that the company participated in yoga seva by giving back. Confused Girl was partnered with the Jodie O'Shea Orphanage in Indonesia, helping to provide food, clothes, and education to children in need. As Jaime worked to develop her studio, Confused Girl helped her support herself by contributing to her income. When the studio opened, Jaime stocked Confused Girl apparel. She also aimed to work with the founder to provide clothing for homeless queer youths.

Community Outreach – Strong Women Inspiring Other Strong Women

Jaime met Rameira Triz at university, and partnered with her for the creation of the studio. She asked Rameira to be a community outreach person, coming to the studio as a resource. She was the team member who told Jaime and the others what kind of programmes and workshops the community needed. She was the team member who figured out what was relevant to the community, and she also gave workshops and talks. Because of her degree in psychology, she was able to be a resource to connect people who came to the studio with counselling programs, mentor programs, and because of her interest in activism, she organised much of what the studio did for the homeless.

Rameira was a Portuguese sex worker who had immigrated at a young age. She became a sex worker to avoid becoming homeless, and ended up getting kicked out of her sixth form school because of her job, and also ended up homeless for some time. She is a liberation focused activist, who devoted most of her spare time to focusing on the community, including issues of sex worker rights, trans rights, migrant rights, and student politics. She believed in people, and that believing in others was the only way that things would get done, having a lot of trust that people are not inherently bad and will help each other in the end.

Rameira was a very open person, because of her Borderline Personality Disorder. She felt that she had to warn people that her life was very intense. She also felt like love was an addiction, and that it was attainable but she hadn't experienced it in a healthy way yet. Jaime had met Rameira because they had been in the LGBT society together, both with fluid sexuality and gender, and both survivors of abuse. They both shared the tendency to be more sexual with women and less romantic with them, and to get along better as friends with boys than girls; and noticing the trend in their friends with similar situations, the girls worked together on unlearning their internalized sexism that prevented them from forming deep connections with other girls.

Rameira had started to educate herself in liberation politics, and joined a group which worked for the rights of sex workers. She noticed a change in her desire to be an academic, and found herself wanting to be able to work as an activist. She noticed that there was a change in her intentions which drove the change in her career aspirations. She wanted the queer community to acknowledge and respect the overlap with the sex worker and migrant communities, and to recognise the privilege of the growing acceptance and support further marginalized communities. She also wanted the community to help remove the capitalist appropriation (and commodification) of the LGBT culture, because she didn't feel like there was any one particular way that the community could or should be represented, and she didn't like the way that people felt like they had to look or act certain ways to belong to the community.

Because Rameira had always felt like she had a sense of community but was always on the outskirts, when Jaime approached her about how she had inspired her to create a position for a community outreach team member, Rameira happily took the position. She was able to pour herself into a cause that she cared about while making money for it. Rameira's position was designed to help Jaime make the studio a better safe space. Rameira and Jaime worked with a team to meet the needs of their community. Rameira provided resources on a variety of topics, from things like self defense, sex worker rights, help for the homeless, and LGBT inclusive safe sex. Rameira's workshops tackled knowledge of the law, statistics, respectful language, the reality of the industry, and were always led by sex workers themselves. She believed that this was what sex worker organisations existed for, and that it is their area of expertise. Much like Annie Sprinkle, Rameira became regarded as a sex expert and sex educator.

  A big part of yoga is yoga seva, or yoga service. Jaime could not in good faith open a studio without it offering services to the community. Jaime was passionate about offering a variety of services including safe sex education, prenatal education and yoga, tolerance trainings for working with sex workers, youth workshops, outside of classroom learning, meditation, linking people with mental health professionals, working with charities, and providing daytime shelter for homeless people (no drugs allowed) who could do odd jobs around the studio to get food from the café as well as providing them with a place to write, draw, plan, set goals, meditate, and connect with people who could help with getting them jobs and homes or nighttime shelter.

Jaime and Happy Hippie

  Jaime discovered the Happy Hippie Foundation one day on Miley Cyrus' Instagram page. Jaime had grown up a fan of Miley, not a super fan, but a fan enough to follow her on Instagram and like her photos. She was delighted to discover that Miley was an activist for LGBT youth.

  Her organisation "rallies young people to fight injustice, provides homeless youth, LGBTQ youth, and other vulnerable youth populations with consistent support services to meet basic immediate needs, and prevention services" (Guidestar). The foundation also helped to treat at risk children with art and animal therapies. Jaime wanted to connect with the organisation to become a resource for them as well as for the organisation to connect her studio with the local and LGBT communities.

Jaime reached out to the Happy Hippie Foundation in order to provide better quality services for the local and LGBT communities. Because Jaime did not exclude the homeless from the local community, she wanted help from the foundation to link her studio with other organisations which would aid the homeless in her community, particularly homeless LGBT youths.

Jaime and Peace by Peace

Jaime knew children's book author Lizzy Rockwell from her hometown. Lizzy had created an intergenerational after school art program in which communal works of art were created for fundraising purposes. This program taught children important life skills of sewing, and they also learned about quilting. It helped bring the community together, linking generations, and linking birth cohorts. The program helped the elderly to connect with the young, and to keep their minds and hands at work.

Jaime saw great beauty in this program, and asked Lizzy to help her set one up that ran in the studio. Its intergenerational nature helped to widen the community which came to the studio, and helped to connect people who may not have had families they could turn to in their times of need. The purpose of the program at Jaime's studio was making quilts for homeless and LGBT youth, as well as sex workers. Many LGBT youth reverted to sex work in times of need and even became homeless because of it. Though some members of the older generation may not have agreed with the lifestyles of the youth they were making quilts for, they still did not believe that those youths deserved to be out in the cold. The program worked on bigger quilting projects to sell to local buildings as fundraising for the community.

Jaime was committed to being able to help LGBT

youth reach a higher quality of life. Being able to provide youth with quilts, clothes from her sponsor, and services and resources provided by the celebrity's foundation were just one way that her studio acted through yoga seva.

How the Case Studies Relate to the Studio

Each case study was a demonstration of a quality represented in a particular chakra, and each person in the studies either used yoga and benefitted from it, or could have benefitted from yoga. The chakras are the rainbow within us all. Jaime's story was representative of the constance of all chakras in daily life. The benefits of yoga are innumerable and this book is only a guide to how to use yoga for healing, and help heal the world through self healing and self care. There is much more to be learned about yoga that cannot be taught through these stories.

Creating a New World with Bloom's Taxonomy of Higher Order Thinking

Blooms created a taxonomy of higher level thinking, the levels of which teachers aimed for all people to reach. The highest level on this pyramid is creation, implying that creation is the highest level of thought we are capable of. Jaime felt we were all meant to be involved in the creation of a new world. We can create a higher purpose for ourselves, we can create a vibration, we can create meaning. Jaime created meaning out of loving, accepting, and serving. She felt that to teach was to create, by creating empowerment. If creation was the highest level of empowerment. If creation was the highest level of intelligence, then the creation of children was the highest form of creation, a feat not for everyone. Jaime wanted to create a centre fostering learning and growth. The Blooms taxonomy of higher level thinking provoked people to use higher order thinking, improve thinking skills, ask and answer analytical questions, and improve and use problem solving skills. The way to activate the seeds of your creation is by making choices about the results you want to create. When you make a choice, you activate vast human energies and resources which otherwise go untapped.

For optimal success, it is important to ask ourselves, how much work do we put into our day? Consider work for our living (money), work on our health, work on our dreams, and consider how to balance the amount of time we want to spend doing work with other things that need to get done (i.e. chores, errands) and things we want to do for fun. What will all of this work create, besides karma?

References and Acknowledgements

With Quotes From

Aadil Palkhivala
Aaron Bjorn
Alexandra K. Tremfor
America Ferrera
Atharva Veda
Avatar the Last Airbender
B.K.S. Iyengar
Brian Andreas
C.G. Jung
Cesare Pavese
Charles M. Blow
Devaya Dharam (instagram @thehoophealer)
Emile Coue
Geeta Iyengar
H. Melt
Harclitis
Hasidic Prayer
How I Met Your Mother
John 4:19
John Kabat-Zinn
Jo Thyssen
Joy Harjo
Julian Arias
Kendall Sturges
Kirra Adams
Kneller's Happy Campers/Wristcutters: A Love Story
Kyle Cease
Lauren Eden
Liane Cordes
Lord Byron
Mahatma Ghandi
Marie-Louise Von Franze
Matthew 18:3
Maya Angelou
Osho
Picasso

Ravi Shankar
Sandra Sabatini
Sark
Sigmund Freud
Sitting Bull
Sonia Choquette
St. Thomas Aquinas
That 70's Show
The Big Bang Theory
The Rocky Horror Picture Show
Walter Benjamin
Yogi Bhajan

Soundtrack

A Better Place, A Better Time by Streetlight Manifesto/Toh Kay (Streetlight Lullabies)
Across the Universe by the Beatles
Androgyny by Garbage
Ashtray Heart by Placebo
Be Ourselves by Borgore
Blow Up by Sammy Adams
Bullet by Hollywood Undead
Dance, Dance, Dance by the Beach Boys
Days of the Old by Every Avenue
Dreaming by Blondie
Every Me, Every You by Placebo
For What It's Worth by Placebo
Here Comes the Sun by the Beatles
Heroes by David Bowie
I Do by Placebo
Losing My Religion by R.E.M.
Love, Sex, Fancy Things by the Floozies
Loud Like Love by Placebo
Lucky For You, Tonight I'm Just Me by SheDaisy
Make It Stop by Rise Against
Meds by Placebo
Moonage Daydream by David Bowie
Nancy Boy by Placebo

Paper Planes by M.I.A.
Promises by Placebo feat. Michael Stipe
Psycho Killer by the Talking Heads
Pumped Up Kicks by Foster the People
Pure Morning by Placebo
Rated R by Belle Vex
Rebel Rebel by David Bowie
Reflection from the Mulan Soundtrack
Rock N Roll Suicide by David Bowie
Stairway to Heaven by Led Zeppelin
Sweet Dreams by Eurythmics
Teenage Angst by Placebo
This Picture by Placebo
Trigger Happy Hands by Placebo
Under Pressure by Queen and David Bowie
Walk on the Wild Side by Lou Reed
When I Get Home, You're So Dead by Mayday Parade
Zen and the Art of Breaking Stuff by the World Inferno Friendship Society
Ziggy Stardust by David Bowie

Acknowledgements

Adam Astor
Amber Nogiec
Aura Talero
Bettina Schindler
Biscuit Bi Magazine
Bring the Hoopla
Bruce Bassock
Caitlyn Lacovara
Confused Girl in the City
Danielle Brown
Derek Perrin
Donna Kuebler
Dr. Brenda Slovin of Slovin Family Chiropractors
Erik Anderson
Erika Goodman
Essential Adornment

Everlides Capozziello
Georgia Leate
Gianina Venegas Abrahams
Giovanna Silvestre
Happy Hippie Foundation
Inner Plane Hoops
Ismini Dres
It Gets Better Campaign
Jason Papailo
Jennifer Campbell Habetz
John Southard
Julian Arias
Liane Nelson
Liv Love Hoops
Lizzy Rockwell
Luke Blaker
Manny Rivera
Meredith Wallace
Mike Robinson
Nicole Perrin
OutSpoken
Peace By Peace
Robert Ortner
Robert Scarpello
Rosalinda Patino
Sareen Anand
Simone Parker
Susan Phillips
Shannon Aleksa
Steph Fellinger
The Loft
The New York Area Bisexual Network
The Therapeutic Light Crew
The Trevor Project
Triangle Community Centre
True Colors Connecticut
UPSU LGBT+ Society
Veronica Pasternak

Thank you to everyone who let me interview them, your help is immeasurable.

Drawing on Theories By

Blooms
Bordieu
Bruner
Elkind
Erikson
Froebel
Gardner
George Herbert Mead
Jean Piaget
Lev Vygotsky
Maslow
Schugurensky

Featuring Artwork By

Aryn Taylor
Charlie Gould (about the author)
Meredith Wallace (cover art)
Robert Scarpello

References

Andrews, T. (2005). *How to Heal with Color*. Woodbury, Minn.: Llewellyn Publications.

Anon, (2018). [online] Available at: http://nbci.nlm.nih.gov/ *

Anzaldua, G. (n.d.). *How to Tame a Wild Tongue*.

Armstrong, J. and Rudúlph, H. (2013). *Sexy Feminism*. Boston: Mariner Books.

Ashtangayoga.info. (2018). *AYI.info - The International Ashtanga Yoga Information Page*. [online] Available at: http://ashtangayoga.info/ .

Astrologyweekly.com. (2018). *Astrology Weekly - astrology articles and information updated weekly*. [online] Available at: http://astrologyweekly.com/

at:http://citeseerx.ist.psu.edu/viewdoc/download?doi=10.1.1.844.7423&rep=rep1&type=pdf
Ayurveda School New York City, (2018). [online] Available at: http://aysnyc.org/

Badinter, E. and Wright, B. (1989). *The Unopposite Sex*. New York: Harper & Row.

Banyanbotanicals.com. (2018). *Ayurveda (Ayurvedic) Products - Buy Organic Herbs Online | Banyan Botanicals*. [online] Available at: http://banyanbotanicals.com/

Berkers, E. (2018). *.: Chakra test, I Ching, Mudras, Acupressure, Exercises, Articles*. [online] Eclectic Energies. Available at: http://eclecticenergies.com/

BiMedia, (n.d.). *Welcome - BiMedia*. [online] Available at: https://www.bimedia.org

BiNet USA, (n.d.). *BiNet USA*. [online] Available at: http://www.binetusa.org/

Birney, B. (2015) *Elements Yoga Teacher Training Manual*

Bisexual Health Awareness Month. (2017). *Bisexual Health Awareness Month.* [online] Available at: http://bihealthmonth.org/

Bksiyengar.com. (2018). *B K S Iyengar - Home.* [online] Available at: http://bksiyengar.com/

Buttenheim, M., Ben-Shahar, T. and McDonough, M. (2016). *Expanding Joy - Let Your Yoga Dance.*

Cabot, L. (2014). *Celebrate the Earth.* Delta.

Campaign, H. (2018). *Advocating for LGBTQ Equality | Human Rights Campaign.* [online] Human Rights Campaign. Available at: http://hrc.org/

Chakra Anatomy. (2018). *Chakra Anatomy.* [online] Available at: http://chakra-anatomy.com/

Chapman, J. (2003). *Yoga for Partners.* Berkeley, CA: Ulysses Press.

Charactercounts.org. (2018). *CHARACTER COUNTS! – Helping millions of young people develop life skills and character.* [online] Available at: http://charactercounts.org/

Chbosky, S. (1999). *The Perks of Being a Wallflower.* New York, N.Y. Pocket Books.

Cheltenham, F. (2010). *Healthy People 2020 Bisexual Fact Sheet.* [ebook] Available at: https://www.dropbox.com/s/ytgpenyfbhgpvj0/HP2020BisexualPeople.pdf?dl=0

Cheltenham, F. (2013). *2013 Bisexual Fact Sheet.* [online] Binetusa.blogspot.co.uk. Available at: http://binetusa.blogspot.co.uk/2013/03/2013-bisexual-fact-sheet.html

Cohn, R. and Levithan, D. (2013). *Nick & Norah's Infinite Playlist.* Johanneshov: MTM.

Cohn, R. and Levithan, D. (2014). *Naomi & Ely's No Kiss List.* London: Electric Monkey.

Cole, M., Lecusay, R. and Rosero, I. (2018). *Commentary: Creating Hybrid After-School Enrichment Activities.* [online]

Learninglandscapes.ca. Available at: http://www.learninglandscapes.ca/index.php/learnland/article/view/Commentary-Creating-Hybrid-After-School-Enrichment-Activities

Comer, K. (2010). *Surfer Girls in the New World Order*. Durham: Duke University Press.

Conner, R., Sparks, D. and Sparks, M. (1998). *Cassell's Encyclopedia of Queer Myth, Symbol, and Spirit*. London: Cassell.

Conway, D. (1995). *Celtic Magic*. St. Paul, Minn.: Llewellyn.

Cunningham, S. (2013). *Magical Herbalism*. [S.I.]: Llewellyn Worldwide, LTD.

CureJoy Yoga, (n.d.). *CureJoy - Expert advice on Cure, Fitness and Beauty*. [online] Available at: https://www.curejoy.com/

CureJoy Yoga, (n.d.). *Curejoy - Home | Facebook*. [online] Available at: https://www.facebook.com/curejoy

CureJoy Yoga, (n.d.). *CureJoy - YouTube*. [online] Available at: https://www.youtube.com/channel/UC2smwyts60kjNqF8TkeKvjw

Decolonizing Yoga. (2018). *How to Decolonize Your Yoga Practise - Decolonizing Yoga*. [online] Available at: http://www.decolonizingyoga.com/decolonize-yoga-practise/

Devi, N. (2010). *The Secret Power of Yoga*. New York: Three Rivers Press.

Eisner, S. (2013). *Bi: Notes for a Bisexual Revolution* Berkeley, CA: Seal Press.

Elephant Journal. (2018). *Elephant Journal: Yoga, Sustainability, Politics, Spirituality.*. [online] Available at: http://elephantjournal.com/

Eraut, M. (1998) *Standards and Vocational Qualifications in Continuing Professional Development (CPD)* QCA discussion paper No. 1 July

Eraut, M. (2004). The Emotional Dimension of Learning. *Learning in Health and Social Care*, 3(1), pp.1-4.

Eraut, M. (2004). The Practise of Reflection. *Learning in Health and Social Care*, 3(2), pp.47-52.

Eraut, M. (2004) Informal learning in the workplace, *Studies in Continuing Education*, pp 26, 247-273

Exhale to Inhale. (2018). *Welcome*. [online] Available at: https://exhaletoinhale.org/

Farhi, D. (2006). *Teaching Yoga*. Berkeley, Calif.: Rodmell.

Farhi, D. and Young, B. (1997). *The Breathing Book*. East Roseville, N.S.W.: Simon & Schuster.

Feminist Fusion (2017) pamphlet

Fenway Health: Health Care Is A Right, Not A Privilege. (2018). *01 – Home*. [online] Available at: http://fenwayhealth.org/

Forney, E. (2013). *Marbles: Mania, Depression, Michelangelo and Me*. Constable & Robinson.

Freymann-Weyr, G. and Romano, C. (2002). *My Heartbeat*. New York, N.Y.: Listening Library.

Gendler, J. (1988). *The Book of Qualities*. New York: Perennial Library.

GLAAD, (n.d.). *GLAAD*. [online] Available at: https://www.glaad.org/

GLSEN. (2018). *State-By-State Research*. [online] Available at: https://www.glsen.org/article/state-state-research

GLSEN School Experiences of Today's LGBT Youth (2013). (2013). [ebook] Available at: https://www.glsen.org/sites/default/files/2013%20National%20School%20Climate%20

Survey%20Full%20Report_0.pdf

Greek-gods.org. (2017). *The Titans, elder gods, first divine rulers - Greek Gods*. [online] Available at: https://www.greek-gods.org/titans.php

Hanh, T. (n.d.). *No Mud, No Lotus*.

Hanscom, A. and Louv, R. (2016). *Balanced and Barefoot*.

Healing Crystals, (n.d.). *Healing Crystals - Crystal Shop & Free Resources*. [online] Available at: http://www.healingcrystals.com/

Healing Crystals For You, (n.d.). *Discover The Healing Power Of Crystals, Pictures & Info On ....* [online] Available at: https://www.healing-crystals-for-you.com/

Healthyplace.org. (2018). *Healthyplace.org*. [online] Available at: http://healthyplace.org/

Hutchins, L. and Kaahumanu, L. (1991). *Bi Any Other Name*. Boston: Alyson Pub.

Judith Hanson Lasater. (2018). *Home*. [online] Available at: http://judithhansonlasater.com/

Klein, J. (2013). *The Bully Society*. New York: New York University Press.

Learning Landscapes. (2012). *Vol 5 No 2 (2012): Informal Learning: Flexible Contexts and Diverse Dimensions LEARNing Landscapes*. [online] Available at: https://plymouth.rl.talis.com/link?url=http%3A%2F%2Fwww.learninglandscapes.ca%2Findex.php%2Flearnland%2Fissue%2Fview%2F30&sig=1b953e89943f515122e0acd3dddb4baf4a65e15835abcb635a7630b314e3a4ce

Learningtogive.org. (2018). *Learning to Give*. [online] Available at: http://learningtogive.org/

Lerner, H., Lerner, H. and Lerner, H. (2003). *The Dance of Anger*. New York: One Spirit.

LGBT Map, (n.d.). *Movement Advancement Project | Home*. [online] Available at: http://lgbtmap.org/

Maltz, W. (2004). *Intimate Kisses*. Novato, Calif.: New World Library.

Map, S., April 5, 2., April 5, 2., April 6, 2., April 6, 2., April 7, 2. and April 7, 2. (2018). *Cafe Astrology .com*. [online] Cafeastrology.com. Available at: http://cafeastrology.com/

Marijuana Doctors. (2018). *Medical Marijuana Doctors & Cards | Marijuana Doctors*. [online] Available at: http://marijuanadoctors.com/

Matthews, T. (2004). *Like We Care*. Baltimore, MD: Bancroft Press.

Milne, A. and Shepard, E. (n.d.). *Winnie-The-Pooh*.

Moody, L. (2018). *Discover Your Love Language - The 5 Love Languages®*. [online] The 5 Love Languages®. Available at: http://www.5lovelanguages.com

Munindo, Shorter, B. and Kittisaro. (2002). *The Gift of Well-Being*. Taipei, Taiwan, R.O.C.: Reprinted and donated for free distribution by the Corporate Body of the Buddha Educational Foundation.

Nakajo, H., Ury, D. and Jones, G. (2008). *Hana-Kimi*. San Francisco, CA: VIZ Media LLC.

National Intimate Partner and Sexual Violence Survey, (2010). [ebook] Available at: https://www.cdc.gov/violenceprevention/pdf/nisvs_report2010-a.pdf

O'Donohue, J. (1998). *Anam Cara*. [Kbh.]: Lindhardt og Ringhof.

One Equal World. (2018). *Home - One Equal World*. [online] Available at: http://www.oneequalworld.com/ .

Open.ac.uk. (2018). *Distance Learning Courses and Adult Education - The Open University*. [online] Available at: http://open.ac.uk/ .

Outdoor-learning.org. (2018). *IOL Home*. [online] Available at: https://www.outdoor-learning.org/

Pagels, E. (1978). Androgyny. *Parabola: Myth and the Quest for Meaning*, (Vol. 3 No. 4).

Parker, S. (2012). *The Laundry Room.* [online] Available at: https://the-virgin-suicide.deviantart.com/art/The-Laundry-Room-282633944

PATAÑJALI, & Shearer, A. (2002). *The Yoga Sutras of Patanjali.* New York, Bell Tower.

PAVES , (n.d.). *Home | PAVES.* [online] Available at: https://paves.ngo/

Penczak, C. (2003). *Gay Witchcraft.* Cork: Red Wheel Weiser.

Prabhavananda, S. (2013). *Bhagavad Gita - The Song of God.* Read Books Ltd.

Ray Long, C. (2018). *Books - Articles - Anatomy - Yoga.* [online] Bandhayoga.com. Available at: http://bandhayoga.com/ .

Rebelle Society. (2018). *Rebelle Society | for the creatively maladjusted.* [online] Available at: http://rebellesociety.com/

Resist, D., Equality, M., Rights, T. and Iconography, G. (2018). *Study Shows Gay And Bi People Respond Positively To Same-Sex Pheromones - Towleroad.* [online] Towleroad. Available at: http://www.towleroad.com/2014/05/study-shows-gay-and-bi-people-respond-positively-to-same-sex-pheromones/

Rogers, A. (2014) *The Classroom and the Everyday: The Importance of Informal Learning for Formal Learning.* Available pp.7-34.(UNESCO, in Rogers, 2014, pp.7-8)

Rogoff, B. (2014). *Learning by observing and pitching in to family and community endeavors: An orientation.* Human Development, 57(2-3), 69-81. doi:http://dx.doi.org.plymouth.idm.oclc.org/10.1159/000356757

Rogoff, B. (2018). *Commentary: Fostering a New Approach to Understanding: Learning Through Intent Community Participation.* [online] Learninglandscapes.ca. Available at: http://www.learninglandscapes.ca/index.php/learnland/article/view/Commentary-Fostering-a%20New-%20Approach-to-Understanding-Learning-Through-Intent-Community-Participation

Rose Rosetree. (2018). *Rose Rosetree - Energy Reading, Energy Healing, Empath Empowerment®, Enlightenment Coaching.* [online] Available at: http://rose-rosetree.com/

Rowling, J. K. (2000). *Harry Potter and the prisoner of Azkaban.* Thorndike, Me.: Thorndike Press.

Sahajayogaportal.org. (2018). *Sahaja Yoga Portal.* [online] Available at: http://sahajayogaportal.org/

Schugurensky, D. (2012) *The forms of informal learning: towards a conceptualisation of the field.* SSHRC Research Network. Online: https://tspace.library.utoronto.ca/bitstream/1807/2733/2/19formsofinformal.pdf

Selva Madre. (2018). *Ayahuasca retreat Iquitos - Perú - Selva Madre.* [online] Available at: http://selvamadre.com/ [Accessed 5 Apr. 2018].

Sije, D. (2010). *Balzac and the Little Chinese Seamstress.* Paw Prints.

Simmons, R. (2003). *Odd Girl Out.* San Diego, Calif.: Harcourt.

Swamij.com. (2018). *Yoga Meditation.* [online] Available at: http://swamij.com/

Swonger, E. (2018). Mandalas *Ed Swonger Fine Art Photography Home Page.* [online] Available at: http://edswonger.com/

Theabsc.com. (2017). *Understanding Sexual Imperialism.* [online] Available at: http://www.theabsc.com/wp-content/uploads/2014/11/Sexual-Imperialism-Infographic.jpg

The BiCast. (2018). *The BiCast.* [online] Available at: http://thebicast.org/

The Chopra Center. (2018). *The Chopra Center.* [online] Available at: http://chopra.com/

The Conversation. (2018). *Why do humans have an innate desire to get high?.* [online] Available at: http://theconversation.com/why-do-humans-have-an-innate-desire-to-get-high-60671

The House of Yoga. (2018). *The House of Yoga.* [online] Available at: http://thehouseofyoga.com/

The National Academies Press, (2011). *The Health of Lesbian, Gay, Bisexual, and Transgender People.* [online] Available at: https://www.nap.edu/read/13128/chapter/1

THE UNIVERSAL ASTROLOGICAL MANDALA. (2018). *THE UNIVERSAL ASTROLOGICAL MANDALA.* [online] Available at: http://charmvirgo.wordpress.com/

Trauma Healed, (n.d.). *Intuitive Compassionate Bodywork ... - traumahealed.com.* [online] Available at: http://traumahealed.com/

UPLIFT. (2018). *UPLIFT - We Are One.* [online] Available at: http://upliftconnect.com/

Valenti, J. (2010). *The Purity Myth.* Berkeley: Seal Press.

Waite, S. (2011). *Children Learning Outside the Classroom.* London: SAGE.

Wickett, K. & Huggins, V. (2011) *Using the Local Community as Part of the Early Years Environmen*t (Chapter 3, 35-49) In: Waite, S., Children Learning Outside the Classroom: from birth to eleven. London: SAGE.

Williams Institue Report, (2011). [ebook] Available at: http://williamsinstitute.law.ucla.edu/wp-content/uploads/Gates-How-Many-People-LGBT-Apr-2011.pdf

Yogainternational.com. (2018). *Study And Download Yoga Online | Yoga International.* [online] Available at: http://yogainternational.com/

Yoga Journal. (2018). *Yoga Journal - Yoga Poses, Classes, Meditation, and Life - On and Off the Mat - Namaste.* [online] Available at: http://yogajournal.com/

Yogananda, (2018). [online] Available at: http://yogananda.co.au/

Yogatrail (2018). *Join the World's Yoga Network!.* [online] Available at: http://yogatrail.com/

Zmark.net, Z. (2018). *Alternative Health, Wellness and Healthy Living Information, Articles and News*. [online] Healthy.net. Available at: http://healthy.net/

Printed in Poland
by Amazon Fulfillment
Poland Sp. z o.o., Wrocław